"Winding through the spy-loving Eisenhower-Kennedy years, Kinzer's book is a Tarantino movie yet to be made: it has the right combination of sick humor, pointless violence, weird tabloid characters, and sheer American waste. It is also frightening to read . . . [and] compelling, not least in the way it illustrates how the law of unintended consequences in covert action can work with an almost delirious vengeance."

—Adam Gopnik, *The New Yorker*

"Absolutely riveting. Stephen Kinzer's *Poisoner in Chief* reads like a spy thriller—but his revelations about the macabre career of the CIA's Sidney Gottlieb are deeply disturbing. Kinzer's work underscores once again the narrative power of biography to unearth our collective history."

—Kai Bird, Pulitzer Prize–winning coauthor of *American Prometheus,* author of *The Good Spy,* and executive director of the Leon Levy Center for Biography

"Stephen Kinzer takes the unusual approach of making Sidney Gottlieb, MK-ULTRA's program manager, the central figure of the story. . . . Reflecting on Gottlieb's culpability, Mr. Kinzer is careful to place his story in historical context. . . . The reader will have to decide how far to venture into this dark thicket." —*The Wall Street Journal*

"Stephen Kinzer has done a great public service with this absorbing and informative portrait of the life and career of Sidney Gottlieb, a CIA scientist who was the Agency's Dr. No in the Cold War—a producer of poison pills, poison darts, and leader of the hunt for the perfect killing machine, à la *The Manchurian Candidate*. It's all in the bone-crunching detail, and Kinzer, a master of American perfidy, has done it again."

—Seymour M. Hersh, author of *Chain of Command: The Road from 9/11 to Abu Ghraib* and *Reporter: A Memoir*

"He's been called Dr. Death, Washington's 'official poisoner,' and a mad scientist. But Sidney Gottlieb never became a household name . . . Now,

pulling together a trove of existing research, newly unearthed documents, and fresh interviews, Kinzer puts the fetid corpus of American Empire back under a microscope. It isn't pretty—but it is instructive."
—*The American Conservative*

"This [book] connects dots between former Nazi torturers, Oregon author Ken Kesey, Boston mobster Whitey Bulger, and an obscure CIA chemist who qualifies as the ultimate James Bond villain. . . . Kinzer's startling reportage on Gottlieb's amok research in secret, international detention cells can't help but evoke more recent memories of Abu Ghraib and the like."
—*The Seattle Times*

"The most powerful and important organs in the invisible government are the nation's bloated and unaccountable intelligence agencies. . . . The best window we have into this shadow world comes with historical accounts of its crimes, including those in Stephen Kinzer's new book, *Poisoner in Chief.*"
—Chris Hedges, *Truthdig*

"It's an awful story, told fast and well." —*San Francisco Review of Books*

"Stephen Kinzer tells the story of Gottlieb, a chemist obsessed with finding a way to control the human brain, no matter how many innocent minds he destroyed in the process."
—*New York Post*

"A stranger-than-fiction account of the CIA's efforts in the 1950s, '60s, and '70s at developing mind control and chemical-based espionage methods, and the chemist, Sidney Gottlieb, who spearheaded the effort . . . The nigh-unbelievable efforts he led are vividly and horrifically re-created in this fascinating history."
—*Publishers Weekly*

POISONER
IN CHIEF

SIDNEY GOTTLIEB AND THE CIA
SEARCH FOR MIND CONTROL

STEPHEN KINZER

ST. MARTIN'S GRIFFIN
NEW YORK

Published in the United States by St. Martin's Griffin, an imprint of St. Martin's Publishing Group

POISONER IN CHIEF. Copyright © 2019, 2020 by Stephen Kinzer. All rights reserved.
Printed in the United States of America. For information, address
St. Martin's Publishing Group, 120 Broadway, New York, NY 10271.

www.stmartins.com

Designed by Kelly S. Too

The Library of Congress has cataloged the Henry Holt edition as follows:

Names: Kinzer, Stephen, author.
Title: Poisoner in chief : Sidney Gottlieb and the CIA search for mind control / Stephen Kinzer.
Description: First edition. | New York : Henry Holt and Company, 2019. | Includes
    bibliographical references and index.
Identifiers: LCCN 2019007076 | ISBN 9781250140432 (hardcover)
Subjects: LCSH: Gottlieb, Sidney, 1918–1999. | Project MKULTRA. | Brainwashing—United
    States—History—20th century. | Hallucinogenic drugs—United States—History—
    20th century. | LSD (Drug)—United States—History—20th century. | United States.
    Central Intelligence Agency—History—20th century.
Classification: LCC JK486.I6 K56 2019 | DDC 327.12730092 [B]—dc23
LC record available at https://lccn.loc.gov/2019007076

ISBN 978-1-250-76262-7 (trade paperback)

Our books may be purchased in bulk for promotional, educational, or business use.
Please contact your local bookseller or the Macmillan Corporate and Premium
Sales Department at 1-800-221-7945, extension 5442, or by email at
MacmillanSpecialMarkets@macmillan.com.

First published in the United States by Henry Holt and Company

First St. Martin's Griffin Edition: 2020

10 9 8 7

LIGARIUS: What's to do?

BRUTUS: A piece of work that will make sick men whole.

LIGARIUS: But are not some whole that we must make sick?

BRUTUS: That must we also.

—Shakespeare, *Julius Caesar*

CONTENTS

POISONER IN CHIEF

1

I Needed More of a Challenge

Years of wandering through distant lands, never knowing who or what lies around the next bend! It is a prospect to stir any adventurous soul. During the second half of the twentieth century, few American souls were as restless as that of Sidney Gottlieb. He spent his career deep inside Washington's secret world. No one knew what he did, but he seemed to have earned a fulfilling retirement.

A more ordinary man might have been happy to spend his later years relaxing, reminiscing, or playing with grandchildren. Gottlieb, however, was a psychic voyager, far from anyone's stereotype of the career civil servant. His home was an eco-lodge in the woods with outdoor toilets and a vegetable garden. He meditated, wrote poetry, and raised goats.

Gottlieb was just fifty-four years old when he retired. His career ended well, with a ceremony at which he was awarded a medal for distinguished service. Soon afterward, he and his wife sold their home and almost everything else they owned. In the autumn of 1973 they set off to seek humanitarian adventure and spiritual fulfillment. Their plan was marvelously vague: board a freighter in San Francisco and go wherever it was going. They had little interest in sightseeing or conventional tourism. The Gottliebs wanted to spend their older years serving the world's neediest people.

Australia was their first stop. After a while there, they booked passage onward. A year of wandering led them to India. They learned of a hospital where victims of leprosy were treated and made their way there to volunteer. Living among the patients, they embraced the work of caring for society's castoffs. Then, on a summer day in 1975, a message from Washington shattered Gottlieb's world. Someone had discovered who he was. The United States Senate wanted to question him.

In two decades at the Central Intelligence Agency, Gottlieb had directed history's most systematic search for techniques of mind control. He was also the CIA's chief poison maker. His work had been shrouded in secrecy so complete as to render him invisible. Now he was being summoned home. He would be expected to account for his deeds, possibly even to appear in public. Never could he have imagined such a twist of fortune.

Soon after Gottlieb arrived in Washington, friends told him he needed a lawyer. One suggested Terry Lenzner, who had worked for the Senate Watergate Committee. Gottlieb called him. After they met, Lenzner wrote: "I was in contact with Dr. Death himself."

For years Gottlieb had overseen medical experiments and "special interrogation" projects in which hundreds of people were tormented and many minds were permanently shattered. No one had ever plunged into this kind of work with more ambition or enthusiasm. Gottlieb justified it all in the name of science and patriotism—until the end, when his conscience finally broke through.

In the years after Gottlieb reluctantly returned to Washington, bits of information about his work began to emerge. He testified at two rounds of Senate hearings. Later he was forced to defend himself against lawsuits filed by people who had come to suspect that they were among his victims. He revealed almost nothing beyond the fact that before leaving the CIA he had destroyed all records of what he did. He was never convicted of a crime. His funeral in 1999 was private.

Enough had become known about Gottlieb to tantalize obituary writers. The *New York Times* published its obituary under the circumspect headline SIDNEY GOTTLIEB, 80, DIES; TOOK LSD TO C.I.A. It called Gottlieb "a kind of genius, striving to explore the frontiers of the human mind for his country while searching for religious and spiritual meaning in his life . . . He served two decades as the senior scientist presiding over some of the CIA's darkest secrets." The *Los Angeles Times* obituary began: "James Bond had Q, the wizard who supplied 007 with dazzling gadgets to deploy against enemy agents. The CIA had Sidney Gottlieb."

Others were sharper. The iconoclastic website *Counterpunch* headlined its obituary PUSHER, ASSASSIN & PIMP: US OFFICIAL POISONER DIES. Another writer concluded that Gottlieb "takes his place among the Jekyll and Hydes of the American 20th century. Whether homesteading in Virginia's verdant hills or safeguarding national security with another experimental torture session, Gottlieb stayed loyal to the positivist credo that rational exploration and productive discipline will lead to good."

In Britain, where obituaries are famously unrestrained, the tone was biting. The *Guardian* called Gottlieb "everything you have dreamed of in a mad scientist in a pulp novel about the CIA—except that he was real." The *Independent* said he was "living vindication for conspiracy theorists that there is nothing, however evil, pointless or even lunatic, that unaccountable intelligence agencies will not get up to in the pursuit of their secret wars." The *Times* was even more vivid:

> When Churchill spoke of a world "made darker by the dark lights of perverted science," he was referring to the revolting experiments conducted on human beings by Nazi doctors in the concentration camps. But his remarks might with equal justice have been applied to the activities of the CIA's Sidney Gottlieb . . . Indeed, what Gottlieb and his CIA henchmen did was only in degree different from the activities which had sent a number of Nazi scientists to the gallows at Nuremberg in 1946 . . . Drugs were not Gottlieb's only weapon against the CIA's enemies. He was also involved in assassination plots which at this distance read like something out of a Jacobean revenge play.

After the ripple of notoriety that followed his death, Gottlieb faded back into obscurity. A few historical studies mention his name. One reports that he was "known to some as the 'dark sorcerer' for his conjuring in the most sinister recesses of the CIA . . . With his club foot, he was perhaps too easy to caricature as a cross between a Bond villain and Dr.

Strangelove, a scientist who always wanted to push further without worrying about the morality of where it all led." In a book called *The World's Worst: A Guide to the Most Disgusting, Hideous, Inept and Dangerous People, Places, and Things on Earth*, Gottlieb is named "the maddest mad scientist." The author gives him grudging credit "for being smart enough to work for an organization that would not only allow him to poison and murder people with such aplomb, but would also protect him from the consequences awaiting any other sociopath."

Gottlieb also turns up briefly in two modern American novels. Barbara Kingsolver's portrait of life in the Congo, *The Poisonwood Bible*, refers to his role in the CIA plot to assassinate Prime Minister Patrice Lumumba. She writes that "a scientist named Dr. Gottlieb was hired to make a poison that would produce such a dreadful disease (the good doctor later testified at the hearings), if it didn't kill Lumumba outright it would leave him so disfigured that he couldn't possibly be a leader of men." A character in Norman Mailer's fevered history of American covert action, *Harlot's Ghost*, discovers a letter from a fictional CIA officer who raves about Gottlieb and calls him "cosmic in scope, interested in everything."

In the 1960s Gottlieb rose to the top of the Technical Services Division, which makes the tools that CIA officers use. Gottlieb ran a bustling gadget shop in Washington and directed the work of several hundred scientists and technicians scattered around the world. They crafted a mind-boggling array of spyware, from a rubber airplane to an escape kit concealed in a rectal suppository. Gottlieb and his team supplied tools of the trade to CIA officers operating in the Soviet Union and dozens of other countries.

"Under Gottlieb's leadership, TSD built worldwide technical capacities critical to virtually all significant U.S. clandestine operations in the last third of the twentieth century," one of his successors wrote. "Yet regardless of Gottlieb's public service and personal charity, his name will always be inextricably linked to the ten-year MK-ULTRA program and the sinister implications of associated words such as drugs, LSD, assassination, and mind control."

NEARLY EVERY DAY for the first twenty years of his life, Sidney Gottlieb passed the side entrance to James Monroe High School in the Bronx. He couldn't avoid it. The hulking school stands directly across the street from the brick row house where he and his family lived. Every time he left home, he saw the stern maxim chiseled into a triangular stone pediment above the side entrance. It is a warning from the British statesman William Pitt: WHERE LAW ENDS, TYRANNY BEGINS.

Many who lived nearby felt that truth deeply. The neighborhood was home to a jumble of immigrants, most of them Jews who had come to America seeking refuge from oppression. Fanny and Louis Gottlieb were typical. They were Orthodox Jews of Hungarian extraction who left central Europe early in the twentieth century. In New York, Louis Gottlieb found work in the garment industry, opened a sweatshop, and made enough money to rent half of a two-family home at 1333 Boynton Avenue. Sidney was the youngest of four children, born on August 3, 1918. He grew up in a vibrant community. The busy main drag, Westchester Avenue, is just two blocks away and was as full of activity then as it is today. Many of Sidney's classmates were like him: smart kids from observant Jewish homes, barely removed from the immigrant experience, who sensed the opportunity America offered and clamored to seize it. Like most of them, he learned Hebrew, had a bar mitzvah, and studied hard.

In two important ways, though, young Sidney stood apart from his friends. First, he was born with deformed feet. According to one relative, his mother screamed when she first saw them. For most of his childhood he was unable to walk. His mother carried him everywhere. The family's sweatshop brought in enough money to pay for three operations. They were at least partly successful. At the age of twelve, the boy walked without braces for the first time. He never needed them again, but the ordeal left him with a lifelong limp.

The other challenge that afflicted Sidney was stuttering. It may have been in part a reaction to schoolmates who, by one account, "viciously harassed" him for his disability. During his high school years, the young man was ostracized, physically scarred, and unable to either walk or speak normally. These handicaps might have led another teenager to withdraw into frustration or self-pity, but Sidney emerged resolute and determined to excel.

After graduating from James Monroe in 1936, Sidney, like many other ambitious sons and daughters of immigrants in New York, enrolled at City College, then known as "the Harvard of the proletariat" for the excellent education it provided free of charge. He studied advanced German and won high grades in math, physics, and chemistry. He also took two courses in public speaking, evidently aimed at helping him overcome his stutter: "Exposition and Rudiments of Speech" and "Declamation and Oration." He took a music course as well—the beginning of a lifelong interest in folk dancing, which he cultivated as a hobby despite, or perhaps because of, the fact that he was born with clubfeet.

City College did not offer courses in agricultural biology, the field Sidney wished to pursue. He decided to transfer to a school where it was taught seriously. The University of Wisconsin had a well-reputed program, and he wrote to inquire. He received a short but cordial reply that ended, "I shall be glad to help you in any way that I can." It was signed by Ira Baldwin, assistant dean of the College of Agriculture. That letter, dated February 24, 1937, marked the beginning of a relationship that would shape secret history.

In order to take specialized courses that would qualify him for admission to the University of Wisconsin, Gottlieb enrolled at Arkansas Polytechnic College, now Arkansas Tech University. The little town of Russellville was nothing like the teeming Bronx streets of his childhood, and his new campus had none of City College's intensity, but he was able to take the courses he wanted: General Botany, Organic Chemistry, Soil Conservation, Elements of Forestry, and Principles of Dairying. He sang in the Glee Club. The yearbook called him "a Yankee who pleases the southerners." According to a campus gossip columnist, he kept company with a fellow student named Lera Van Harmon. The columnist wrote: "Harmon and Gottlieb seem to have a nice affair started. But wait, New York's a fur piece, Harmon." Gottlieb was already reaching beyond the confines of his experience.

"I have been keeping up an A average without too much difficulty," he wrote to Ira Baldwin halfway through the school year, "and am consequently prepared to work so much harder."

Gottlieb's success at Arkansas won him the prize he had sought, admission to the University of Wisconsin. Baldwin welcomed him, became his mentor, and guided him through two successful academic years. He majored in chemistry. Moved by conditions he had seen in New York sweatshops, including the one his father owned, he joined the campus chapter of the Young People's Socialist League. His senior thesis was entitled "Studies on Ascorbic Acid in Cowpeas." In 1940 he graduated magna cum laude. Baldwin gave him a glowing recommendation, mentioning his "slight speech impediment" but praising his intellect and character.

"Mr. Gottlieb is a very high type of Jewish boy," he wrote. "He has easily fit into the situations which he finds here, and is, I think, generally liked and respected by his classmates. He has a brilliant mind, is thoroughly honest and reliable, and is modest and unassuming."

Gottlieb's academic achievement and Baldwin's recommendation combined to secure the young man admission to graduate school at California Institute of Technology. He spent three years there, and on June 11, 1943, he was awarded a doctorate in biochemistry. During those years his life changed in two important ways.

First, he met a woman vastly different from anyone he could have known in the Bronx. Margaret Moore was the daughter of a Presbyterian preacher. She had been born and raised in India, where her father was spreading Christian gospel, but had rebelled against the missionary ethos from an early age. When Gottlieb met her, she was studying preschool education at Broadoaks School in Pasadena, a branch of Whittier College where prospective teachers were schooled in the progressive education theories of Maria Montessori and other innovators. The two had little apparent in common, and might even be seen as polar opposites. Yet they shared a spiritual restlessness. Gottlieb had become estranged from the Judaism he absorbed as a child. Margaret Moore tormented her father with sharp questions about Christianity. Both yearned for an understanding of life beyond what traditional religion offers. In 1942, with World War II raging, they resolved to make their spirit quest together.

"Grad students were not supposed to get married but we did it anyway," Margaret told her parents in a brief note. The wedding was a sign of the couple's disregard for convention: a bare-bones civil ceremony, with no guests or festivities. "Getting married is between two people and not a whole crowd," Margaret wrote. Later she sent an addendum: "Sid's folks want us to have a Jewish wedding, which we are going to do so we will have one fancy wedding anyway. And we most certainly will be married then."

The bride's parents, accustomed to her independent ways, happily accepted the match. "We were very excited to get the cable, Sept. 17th, saying that our Margaret married her Sidney Gottlieb on Sept. 16th in Pasadena," her mother wrote to relatives after hearing the news. "If she has to teach and he to do work for the government, they can undoubtedly get better food by doing it together. How many arrangements have been altered for the duration! And if they have Each Other, they are indeed fortunate in this world full of sorrow."

The other formative event that shaped Gottlieb during his years in California was his rejection by the Selective Service System. He was half-way through graduate school when the Japanese attack on Pearl Harbor brought the United States into World War II. Other students quit school and volunteered for military service, but Gottlieb remained at Caltech until completing his PhD in 1943. He then sought to enlist, having convinced himself that his limp would not disqualify him. When the army turned him down, he was crushed.

"I wanted to do my share in the war effort," he said later. "I felt I had a duty to serve, yet I couldn't convince anyone that I would not be hampered in my performance."

Denied the chance to wear a military uniform, Gottlieb resolved to find another way to serve. In the fall of 1943 he and Margaret moved to Takoma Park, Maryland, a suburb of Washington. He found a job researching the chemical structure of organic soil for the Department of Agriculture. Later he transferred to the Food and Drug Administration, where he developed tests to measure the presence of drugs in the human body. He became prominent enough to be called as an expert witness in several court cases.

"I enjoyed my FDA time, but the work became mostly repetitive and sometimes pretty monotonous," he later recalled. "I needed more of a challenge."

He sought it actively. In 1948 he found a new job at the National Research Council, part of the non-profit National Academies of Sciences, Engineering, and Medicine. There he studied plant diseases and fungicides and was also, as he later recalled, "exposed to some interesting work concerning ergot alkaloids as vasoconstrictors and hallucinogens." Soon afterward he changed jobs again, becoming a research associate at the University of Maryland devoted to studying the metabolism of fungi.

"By this time we had found a very old and primitive cabin near Vienna, Virginia," Margaret wrote years later. "It had no electricity or water or any of that fancy stuff but it sat under three very magnificent oak trees, and when I saw it, I said, 'This will be my home.' Sid, having grown up in New York City, thought I was nuts, but I persuaded him that I knew how to live this way and it was possible, so we borrowed money from all our friends to make a down payment and we moved in our two babies and our few possessions."

A relative who spent four days with the young family during this period wrote a glowing account of their life in a letter to her parents. "Margaret's whole situation is most unusual and interesting—15 acres of pine forest in Virginia with a little log cabin in the midst thereof, about 20 miles from Washington DC," he reported. "Sid is a grand man, full of energy and initiative and brains, and a perfect gentleman and host, with never a dull moment. He has just taken a job with the University of Maryland as a research chemist—his own boss and his own lab with a special assignment to work out a problem with wood for the navy. Penny (4) and Rachel (1) are beautiful and angelic children. They have an interesting group of friends, and the future looks rosy for them. Margaret seemed very natural, and is obviously very happy. She is just as keen on country life as Sid is, so no one needs to feel sorry for her one bit, but only glad."

The Gottliebs had two more children, both boys. "There are so many nice names that we can't use because Sid's folks are Jewish and they would be hurt if we chose something like John or Mary," Margaret wrote to her mother. The boys were named Peter and Stephen. Gottlieb settled comfortably into family life.

"Sid is pitching in more than he ever has before and he's wonderful," Margaret wrote while she was nursing one of her infants. "I feel guilty sleeping when he has to milk the goats."

Despite his satisfying family life, Gottlieb was frustrated. He had no clear path out of his mid-level research on pharmaceuticals and agricultural chemicals. His mentor from the University of Wisconsin, Ira Baldwin, had guided other former students into exciting work during the war, but Gottlieb had been too young. Everything suggested that he was headed for a career as a government scientist. So he was—but he could not have imagined what a phantasmagorical kind of science he would be called to practice.

Dirty Business

White flags hung from many windows as shell-shocked Germans measured the depth of their defeat. Hitler was dead. Unconditional surrender had sealed the collapse of the Third Reich. Munich, like many German cities, lay in ruins. With the guns finally silent, people began venturing out. On a wall near Odeonsplatz someone painted CONCENTRATION CAMPS DACHAU—BUCHENWALD—I AM ASHAMED TO BE GERMAN.

Four United States Army divisions had moved into Munich, but infantrymen were not the only soldiers in town. With them came the Counterintelligence Corps, a semi-clandestine unit whose men wore plain uniforms and identified themselves only as "agent" or "special agent." Their two main tasks were to suppress the black market and find Nazis. Munich had been the birthplace of the Nazi Party, so hunting was good. Agents compiled lists, followed leads, and arrested suspects. A notorious one fell into their hands on May 14, 1945.

It was a splendid day. Among those who stepped out to enjoy the sun, walking silently past bombed-out buildings and piles of rubble, was Dr. Kurt Blome, who had been the Nazis' director of research into biological warfare. Blome was, according to one report, "a well-dressed man, 134 pounds, five foot nine, with dark black hair, hazel eyes, and a pronounced dueling scar on the left side of his face between his nose and his upper lip." He cannot have been surprised when an agent of the Counterintelligence Corps stopped him and flashed a gold-colored badge that said WAR DEPARTMENT MILITARY INTELLIGENCE. The agent asked Blome for identification. Blome produced his passport. The agent checked his list and found Blome's name. Next to it was the code for "Arrest Immediately— First Priority."

Blome was detained and questioned. Interrogators soon concluded that he had much to tell. They sent him to Kransberg Castle, a medieval fortress near Frankfurt that had been turned into a detention center for the highest-ranking suspected war criminals. Other inmates included Albert Speer, Wernher von Braun, Ferdinand Porsche, and directors of the I. G. Farben chemical cartel. In this extraordinary company, Blome's story began to emerge.

As a young student he had joined ultra-nationalist groups and become virulently anti-Semitic. In 1922, after receiving a degree in bacteriology, he spent time in prison for sheltering the assassins of Germany's foreign minister Walter Rathenau, a Jewish socialist. He joined the Nazi Party in 1931. After Hitler seized power two years later, he rose steadily in the Third Reich hierarchy. By the 1940s he was a member of the Reichstag, deputy minister of health, and director of a medical complex at the University of Posen, in what is now Poland. There he tested the effects of germs and viruses on prisoners.

Blome's complex was surrounded by ten-foot walls and guarded by a detachment from the Nazi SS. Inside were a "climate room," a "cold room," incubators, deep freezers, and steam chambers; laboratories devoted to virology, pharmacology, radiology, and bacteriology; a "tumor farm" where malignant viruses were cultivated; and an isolation hospital for scientists who might be accidentally infected with the poisons they handled. Blome developed aerosol delivery systems for nerve gas, to be tested on inmates at the Auschwitz concentration camp; bred infected mosquitoes and lice, to be tested on inmates at the Dachau and Buchenwald camps; and produced gas for use in killing thirty-five thousand prisoners at camps in Poland where patients with tuberculosis were being held. His complex was officially known as the Central Cancer Institute.

Blome fled from Posen as the Red Army approached in January 1945. He was able to destroy some incriminating evidence but did not have time to raze the complex. In a letter to General Walter Schreiber, the Nazi army's chief physician, he said he was "very concerned that the installations for human experiments that were in the institute, and recognizable as such, would be very easily identifiable." For the next several months he worked at another bio-warfare center, also disguised as a cancer research institute, in a pine forest near the German town of Geraberg. It was largely intact, with records and equipment, when Allied troops seized it in April 1945. By that time Blome had moved on to Munich. His capture was only a matter of time.

Interrogators from the Counterintelligence Corps confronted Blome with a letter from Heinrich Himmler, chief of the SS and a principal architect of the Holocaust. In it, Himmler directed Blome to produce toxins that could be used to kill concentration camp inmates who were suffering from tuberculosis. Blome confirmed the letter's authenticity but insisted that Himmler, not he, had directed the Nazi biological warfare program and overseen experiments on prisoners. The interrogators reported this to American intelligence officers who specialized in questioning Nazi scientists.

"In 1943 Blome was studying bacteriological warfare," they wrote. "Officially he was involved in cancer research, which was however only a camouflage. Blome additionally served as deputy health minister of the Reich. Would you like to send investigators?"

From this question grew a far deeper one. Nazi doctors had accumulated a unique store of knowledge. They had learned how long it takes for human beings to die after exposure to various germs and chemicals, and which toxins kill most efficiently. Just as intriguing, they had fed mescaline and other psychoactive drugs to concentration camp inmates in experiments aimed at finding ways to control minds or shatter the human psyche. Much of their data was unique because it could come only from experiments in which human beings were made to suffer or die. That made Blome a valuable target—but a target for what? Justice cried out for his punishment. From a U.S. Army base in Maryland, however, came an audaciously contrary idea: instead of hanging Blome, let's hire him.

TERRIFYING INTELLIGENCE REPORTS from Asia filtered into Washington during 1941. Japanese forces rampaging through China were using germs as weapons—killing thousands of soldiers and civilians by dropping anthrax bomblets, releasing infected insects, and poisoning water supplies with cholera virus. Secretary of War Henry Stimson recognized this tactic as a potential threat to the United States. He summoned nine of the country's leading biologists and asked them to make an urgent study of global research into biological warfare. By the time they completed it, the United States was at war with Japan.

The study's conclusion was alarming. Not only had Japanese scientists begun producing bio-weapons, but their counterparts in Nazi Germany were testing them as well. The effect of these weapons could be devastating.

"The best defense is offense and the threat of offense," the biologists wrote. "Unless the United States is going to ignore this potential weapon, steps should be taken immediately to begin work on the problems of biological warfare."

This moved Stimson to action. "Biological warfare is of course a 'dirty business,' but in light of the committee's report, I think we must be prepared," he wrote to President Franklin Roosevelt. Soon afterward, Roosevelt authorized creation of the first U.S. agency dedicated to studying biological warfare. From its anodyne name—War Research Service—no one could deduce its mission. Anyone curious, though, could have made an educated guess by noting that its director was the renowned chemist George Merck, president of the pharmaceutical company that bears his family name.

Chemical warfare, which caused at least one million casualties during World War I, was already well known, but biological warfare, banned by the Geneva Protocol of 1925, was something new in the modern age. Merck concluded that the United States must join the race. "The value of biological warfare will be a debatable question until it is proven or disproven," he argued in a long memo. "There is but one logical course to pursue, namely, to study the possibilities of such warfare from every angle."

Merck's memo reached American military commanders as they were considering a top-secret request from British prime minister Winston Churchill. Intelligence reports—later proven false—had led British leaders to fear that Hitler was planning a bio-attack on their island. They decided they needed a store of concentrated pathogens to launch in retaliation if such an attack occurred. Britain did not have the facilities, expertise, or budget to develop these toxins. Churchill asked the Americans for help. Roosevelt agreed to look into the possibility of producing bio-weapons for the British, and assigned the job to the army's Chemical Warfare Service. On December 9, 1942, its commanders convened a group of bacteriologists and other specialists at the National Academy of Sciences in Washington. They posed a question that pushed beyond the edge of known scientific engineering: Would it be possible to build a hermetically sealed container in which deadly germs could be produced on an industrial scale?

Patiently, the assembled scientists explained to their military hosts why fabricating toxins on this scale would be prohibitively difficult or impossible. One dissented. Ira Baldwin, the bacteriologist who had been Sidney Gottlieb's mentor at the University of Wisconsin, said he saw no theoretical or technical barrier to the construction of such a chamber.

"Practically all of the people there had been working in pathogenic bacteriology—so-called medical bacteriology—and by and large they were very skeptical," Baldwin later recalled. "Either you couldn't culture in large amounts, or if you did culture it, you couldn't do it with safety. And finally they got around to me . . . And I said, 'The problem is simple. If you can do it with a test tube you can do it with a ten-thousand-gallon tank, with equal safety and perhaps more. And you could preserve the virulence in the ten-thousand-gallon tank. All you have to do is make the same conditions in a ten-thousand-gallon tank that you make in a test tube' . . . So I went home, feeling I had done my bit for the country by venturing an opinion on this subject, and thought no more about it."

Soon after that meeting, General W. C. Kabrich of the Chemical Warfare Service called Baldwin and asked him to return to Washington. He replied that his campus obligations made it difficult for him to travel on short notice.

"We're in hopes that you can arrange to be relieved of your university duties," General Kabrich told him. "We need you here, to do what you said could be done."

Baldwin reported this to the president of the University of Wisconsin. They agreed that he should take a leave of absence to serve the war effort. When he arrived in Washington at the end of 1942, he was told that the army had decided to launch a secret program to develop biological weapons and wanted him to direct it. It was, he realized, "a terrifically big assignment . . . They wanted me to develop a research program, recruit a staff, find a location to build a camp and a laboratory, and then design the pilot plants and the laboratories."

By accepting this job, Baldwin became America's first bio-warrior. He had all the intellectual and academic qualifications to take on such a pioneering role. By personal background, though, he was an unlikely candidate. His grandfather had been a Methodist preacher. He was a part-time pastor himself, held Quaker beliefs, grew up abhorring all forms of violence, and lived austerely. After the United States entered World War II, though, he proved as ready to join its cause as any American.

"To understand the biological warfare program, you do need to understand the climate in which we existed," he told an interviewer years later. "It never occurred to me to say, 'I don't want to do this.' Everybody was doing whatever he was asked to do . . . There is no question that the idea of using biological agents to kill people represented a complete shift of thinking. But it only took me about twenty-four hours to think my way through it. After all, the immorality of war is war itself. You start out with the idea in war of killing people, and that to me is the immoral part of it . . . But I grew up first in medical bacteriology, and you spent your time trying to kill microorganisms to prevent them from causing disease. Now to turn around and think of it as I had to was horrifying to some extent. Yes. No question about it."

Baldwin remained a civilian during the two and a half years he spent establishing and running America's bio-warfare program. His title was created for him: scientific director of the newly formed army Biological Warfare Laboratories, part of the Chemical Warfare Service. The army gave him one of the most sweeping promises it made to any American during World War II: whatever you ask for, we'll provide.

"If I said 'I want that man,'" Baldwin later recalled, "unless the Manhattan Project said they needed him, I got him."

Baldwin's first task was to find a site for his new complex. The obvious choice was Edgewood Arsenal, a thirteen-thousand-acre army base facing Chesapeake Bay in Maryland that had served as headquarters for the Chemical Warfare Service since its founding in 1918. After touring Edgewood, however, Baldwin decided it was too crowded for the bioweapons complex he had been assigned to build. He wanted an entirely new campus.

Baldwin and a couple of Chemical Warfare Service officers set out on a tour of regions outside Washington. They sought a protected area that was reasonably close to the city, remote enough so that experiments could be conducted without attracting notice, and big enough to house dozens of buildings, including large tanks in which deadly germs would be cultivated. First they turned down an offer from the National Institutes of Health in Bethesda, Maryland. Their next idea was to commandeer an island in Chesapeake Bay, but they could not find one that was the right size and also uninhabited. They surveyed and rejected a former shoe factory near Edgewood Arsenal, a weather station in Virginia, and Sugarloaf Mountain in Maryland. Finally, outside the Maryland town of Frederick, they found a former National Guard air base called Detrick (pronounced DEE-trick) Field, named after an army surgeon who had lived nearby and served in World War I.

Airplanes based at Detrick Field had been moved to Europe. What remained were empty barracks, a cavernous hangar, runways, and a control tower. Outside the gate, pastures stretched toward Catoctin Mountain, a majestic Appalachian ridge in which the presidential retreat Shangri-La—now called Camp David—was nestled. Washington is fifty miles away. This thousand-acre base would become the literal nerve center of the U.S. government's search for ways to turn germs into weapons of war and covert action.

The Office of Strategic Services, America's wartime intelligence agency, was using part of Detrick Field as a training base and did not want to give it up but was forced to do so because Ira Baldwin's project had such high priority. On March 9, 1943, the army announced that it had renamed the field Camp Detrick, designated it as headquarters of the army Biological Warfare Laboratories, and reached agreements to purchase several adjacent farms in order to provide extra room and privacy. The first commandant immediately ordered $1.25 million in new construction.

Within three months he had spent $4 million. Everything Baldwin requisitioned was immediately supplied, from custom-made bacteriological equipment to bulk quantities of chemicals to herds of laboratory animals—ultimately more than half a million white mice and tens of thousands of rats, rabbits, guinea pigs, sheep, monkeys, cats, ferrets, and canaries.

Everything about Camp Detrick was shrouded in the deepest secrecy. Military commanders feared that if news of research into germ warfare leaked out, Americans might panic at the prospect of a bio-attack. "I remember one time we had a party and someone said, 'Hey, lots of bacteriologists here, right?'" one veteran of the Chemical Warfare Service recalled years later. "That was quickly shushed up. We were taught at Detrick, 'Don't talk about Detrick.'"

Baldwin began his work by hiring a handful of scientists he knew, including several of his former students from the University of Wisconsin. These first few were quickly followed by dozens and then hundreds more. Ultimately about fifteen hundred came to work at Camp Detrick. All were infused with a sense of mission—even a sense that they might hold the fate of humanity in their hands. "They were passionate about their science," a Camp Detrick historian later asserted. "They were the best in the country. If someone said to you, 'Here is an unlimited budget, here's all the equipment you need, tell me which kind of building you want to work in, we'll build it,' you would jump at the opportunity. And that's just what they did. But the imperative was: we need results very quickly."

By coming to work at Camp Detrick, these scientists joined one of the world's most clandestine fraternities. This required them to accept a new moral order. Upon joining, all were required to sign a vow of secrecy that bound them for life and beyond.

"In the event of my death, I authorize the Commanding Officer at Camp Detrick, Maryland, to make arrangements for and conduct the processing of my remains and to place them in a sealed casket which shall not thereafter be opened," it said. "I authorize post-mortem examination of my remains to be made exclusively by proper army representatives in their discretion."

New arrivals at Camp Detrick, many of them accomplished specialists with advanced degrees, were put through a Special Projects School where they learned "the known technical facts and potentialities of germ warfare." Courses had names like "Production of Agents" and "Food and Water Contamination." The scientists developed such enthusiasm for their new work that they even came up with a school cheer:

> Brucellosis, Psittacosis,
> Pee! You! Bah!
> Antibodies, Antitoxin,
> Rah! Rah! Rah!

Early in 1944, Winston Churchill abruptly changed the bio-weapons order he had sent to President Roosevelt more than a year before. He feared that the Nazis might launch a last-ditch bio-attack on Britain in a desperate attempt to turn the tide of war. Driven by this new sense of urgency, he asked Roosevelt to forget the time-consuming process of developing a new bio-weapon and send him something relatively easy to make: bomblets filled with anthrax spores. He wanted half a million.

Only a few Americans knew of this request. Not all approved. Roosevelt's chief of staff, Admiral William Leahy, wrote to his boss that using anthrax as a weapon "would violate every Christian ethic I have ever heard of, and all of the known laws of war." Global conflict was raging, though, and Britain was under threat. Roosevelt agreed to send Churchill the bomblets he believed he needed.

"Pray tell me when they will be available," Churchill wrote in reply. "We should regard it as a first installment."

Ira Baldwin calculated that tons of anthrax spores would be needed to fill Britain's order. Since the project had such high priority, he was easily able to commandeer a former munitions factory in Vigo, Indiana, and begin converting it into a plant where the United States would produce biological weapons for the first time. Work was underway when, on May 7, 1945, the Nazi army surrendered.

Baldwin returned to the University of Wisconsin soon afterward. He had reason to feel satisfied. Under his leadership, the United States had launched its first bio-weapons program. He had built Camp Detrick into a sprawling research complex complete with a railroad depot, a hospital, a fire station, a cinema, and several recreation halls. Hundreds of scientists, described in one official report as "America's brain trust in their field," were engaged in more than two hundred projects. They produced industrial quantities of anthrax spores, bred mosquitoes infected with yellow fever, and even developed a "pigeon bomb," a bird whose feathers were impregnated with toxic spores. Baldwin also directed work at two field testing stations, one at Dugway Proving Grounds in Utah and another on Horn Island, off the coast of Mississippi. He did what the army hired him to do: bring biological weapons into America's arsenal.

In two and a half years of testing agents for biological warfare, Baldwin and his researchers had learned a fair amount about how to kill large numbers of people with germs. They suspected that Germany and Japan were still far ahead of the United States. Now, with the war over, the key German and Japanese experts were adrift, cast with their priceless knowledge into the post-war chaos. That is why scientists at Camp Detrick were so thrilled when they learned that Kurt Blome had been found and was in Allied custody.

SHOULD EVERYONE WHO helped run the Nazi machine be prosecuted for war crimes, or could some be brought to work for the U.S. government instead? This question came to President Roosevelt in 1944. William Donovan, director of the Office of Strategic Services, asked the president for permission to launch a new recruiting project. Nazi spies were beginning to fall into American hands. Some knew much about the Soviet Union. Donovan wanted authority to grant them immunity from prosecution and "permission for entry into the United States after the war." Even though this project would recruit spies only, not scientists, Roosevelt refused.

"The carrying out of any such guarantees would be difficult, and probably be widely misunderstood both in this country and abroad," he wrote in rejecting Donovan's request. "We may expect that the number of Germans who are anxious to save their skins and property will rapidly increase. Among them may be some who should properly be tried for war crimes, or at least arrested for active participation in Nazi activities. Even with the necessary controls you mention, I am not prepared to authorize the giving of guarantees."

Neither the letter nor the spirit of this directive was ever followed. One of the most senior Nazi intelligence officers, Colonel Reinhard Gehlen, surrendered to American forces in May 1945—a few weeks after Roosevelt's death—and quickly made a deal under which he turned his spy network over to the Office of Strategic Services in exchange for legal protection and a generous stipend. Once it was established that Nazi intelligence officers could be quietly forgiven and brought into America's service, a precedent was set for Nazi scientists. The army established a new covert service, the Joint Intelligence Objectives Agency, for the sole purpose of finding and recruiting scientists who had served the Third Reich. Its officers sought to isolate scientists so they could not return to their wartime work fueling German military power; keep them out of Soviet hands; and, when desirable, arrange new jobs for them in the United States.

At the Kransberg Castle interrogation center, clerks began using paperclips to mark the files of prisoners whose backgrounds presented "the most troublesome cases." From that practice came the code name of the clandestine project by which Nazi scientists were given falsified biographies and brought to work in the United States: Operation Paperclip. President Harry Truman set it in motion on September 3, 1946. His secret order, drawn up by intelligence officers and approved by Undersecretary of State Dean Acheson, authorized the issuance of up to a thousand visas for German and Austrian scientists "in the interest of national security." It specifically forbade cooperation with anyone who had been "a member of the Nazi Party and more than a nominal participant in its activities, or an active supporter of Nazi militarism."

If followed, that restriction would have kept Operation Paperclip small indeed. The operation's main goal was to recruit German rocket scientists, whose job during the war—producing missiles that killed thousands of civilians in London and other European cities—certainly qualified them as active supporters of Nazi militarism. With remarkable alacrity, the Joint Intelligence Objectives Agency cast those concerns aside. Operation Paperclip proceeded as if Truman's stipulation did not exist. Ultimately more than seven hundred scientists, engineers, and other technical specialists who had served the Third Reich came to the United States on Paperclip contracts.

Soon after the war ended, the Chemical Warfare Service was upgraded in importance and renamed the Chemical Corps. Its commanders watched enviously as Nazi spies were brought under American protection and as, soon afterward, the welcome was extended to Nazi rocket scientists. They proposed opening the pipeline wider so they could hire the Nazis they coveted: physicians, chemists, and biologists who could give them results of experiments that had been conducted at concentration camps. The officers running Operation Paperclip found this a fine idea. With their help, three German scientists who had worked on chemical and biological warfare projects arrived at Camp Detrick less than a year after the war ended. All had been members of the Nazi Party. Part of their assignment was to teach Americans about sarin, a gas they had helped develop in Germany that seemed especially promising for battlefield use. In their lectures, the new arrivals used records from their wartime experiments. The records showed that most of their subjects died within two minutes after inhaling their first doses of sarin, and that "age of the subject seemed to make no difference in the lethality of the toxic vapor."

During World War II, Nazi doctors carried out experiments that led to many deaths. Their work gave them, as it had given spies and rocket engineers, experience that some in Washington believed might prove decisive in a future war. For the officers of Operation Paperclip, it was an easy call. Whenever a scientist they coveted turned out to have a blemish on his record, they rewrote his biography. They systematically expunged references to membership in the SS, collaboration with the Gestapo, abuse of slave laborers, and experiments on human subjects. Applicants who had been rated by interrogators as "ardent Nazi" were re-categorized as "not an ardent Nazi." References to their exemplary family lives were added. Once they had been thus "bleached," they became suitable candidates for Paperclip contracts.

"In effect," according to one study of this period, "the scientific teams wore blinders. Dazzled by German technology that was in some cases years ahead of our own, they simply ignored its evil foundation—which sometimes meant stepping over and around piles of dead bodies—and pursued Nazi scientific knowledge like a forbidden fruit."

This practice did not go unchallenged. The State Department assigned several diplomats to Operation Paperclip, and they objected to "bleaching." Consular officers threatened to withhold visas for scientists implicated in war crimes. At home, the Federal Bureau of Investigation announced that it would conduct its own checks of former Nazis seeking entry into the United States. The American Federation of Scientists wrote to President Truman warning him that some applicants were hiding bloody pasts. Newspapers reported that one of the first Paperclip contracts had been offered to the industrial chemist Carl Krauch, co-designer of the I. G. Farben chemical plant at Auschwitz, but that before Krauch could be brought to the United States, he was arrested as a war criminal in West Germany and charged with "the enslavement, ill-treatment, terrorization, torture and murder of numerous persons . . . as well as other crimes such as the production and supply of poison gas for experimental purposes on and the extermination of concentration camp inmates."

Some cheered when prominent Nazis were convicted and punished. Captain Bosquet Wev, the pugnacious forty-two-year-old former submarine commander who ran Operation Paperclip, did not. In a stream of vituperative memos to Washington, Wev accused the State Department of sabotaging his operation, "beating a dead Nazi horse" by harping on "picayune details" such as whether a scientist had been an SS member. He warned that if the United States refused to accept tainted Nazi scientists, many could end up working on war-related projects in Germany or the Soviet Union. That prospect, he concluded, "presents a far greater security threat than any former Nazi affiliations which they may have had, or even any Nazi sympathies which they may still have." The dispute spilled into Congress. Recalcitrant diplomats were pilloried as "sinister figures" and "fellow travelers" whose moralizing endangered American security. Press reports portrayed the conflict as showing, in the words of one television commentator, "how a few minor officials in the State Department have succeeded in blocking a program of high military importance."

Once this bureaucratic conflict became political, the outcome was determined. American fears were rising. The Cold War loomed. Diplomats who wished to confine Operation Paperclip within the limits President Truman had set were no match for the combined power of military and security agencies. Their objections were pushed aside.

Scientists at Camp Detrick were eager to learn what Kurt Blome knew. During extended interrogations in Germany, he slowly lowered his guard— enough to suggest that he was keeping terrible secrets. As a reward, and a sign of respect, he was moved from his cell to an apartment in a lovely chalet. Meanwhile his admirers at Camp Detrick worked to arrange a Paperclip contract that would bring him to Maryland. They almost succeeded.

IN THE MONTHS after Japan surrendered to Allied forces on August 15, 1945, several captured Japanese officers told American interrogators that Japan had maintained a secret germ warfare program. They mentioned rumors that poisons had been tested on human subjects at a base called Unit 731, in the occupied Chinese region of Manchuria. Reports of these interrogations were forwarded to the Biological Warfare Laboratories at Camp Detrick. Scientists there, already excited by the prospect of data from Kurt Blome and other doctors who had served the Nazis, pressed for more. They discovered that the army surgeon who ran Unit 731 was a general named Shiro Ishii, and asked the Counterintelligence Corps to find him, just as it had found Blome in Germany. Their plan was the same: keep him out of Soviet hands, then secure his loyalty by saving him from the gallows.

Two obsessions, the extremes of Japanese nationalism and the extremes of medicine, shaped Shiro Ishii. He came from a family of rich landowners and was an outstanding medical student at Kyoto Imperial University. During the late 1920s he became fascinated by the Geneva Protocol that bans biological warfare. Japan, like the United States, had refused to sign it. This meant, by Ishii's reckoning, that it had every right to develop weapons that others could not—and that those weapons could be decisive in a future war. He saw this as his way to contribute to his country's greater glory.

In 1928, after finishing medical school, Ishii set out on what became a two-year tour of biology laboratories in more than a dozen countries, including the Soviet Union, Germany, France, and the United States. Upon his return to Japan, he joined the army's Surgeons Corps. Soon he was helping to run a chemical laboratory where gas masks were tested. Although he became what one writer called "a swashbuckling womanizer who could afford to frequent Tokyo's upmarket geisha houses," he remained professionally frustrated. He pressed the army minister, his patron, for a remote tract of land where he could carry out experiments on human subjects as a way to master techniques of germ warfare. In 1936, after the Japanese seized northeast China, he got his chance. Army commanders gave him a plot south of Harbin, the largest city in Manchuria. Eight villages were razed to make way for a four-square-mile complex that came to house more than three thousand scientists and other employees. Officially this was the Epidemic Prevention and Water Purification Bureau. To those who worked there, and the few others who knew of its existence, it was Unit 731.

"Our God-given mission as doctors is to challenge all forms of disease-causing micro-organisms, block all paths for their intrusion into the body, annihilate foreign matter resident in our bodies, and devise the best possible treatments," Ishii told his men as they began work. "The research work on which we are now to embark is the complete opposite of those principles."

Japanese soldiers began sweeping up "bandits" and other suspicious people in the local countryside, threw them together with captured Chinese soldiers, anti-Japanese partisans, common criminals, and mental patients, and delivered them in batches to Ishii. Between 1936 and 1942, Ishii received at least three thousand and perhaps as many as twelve thousand of these "logs," as he and his comrades called them. All were destined for excruciating death. Ishii was driven to learn everything possible about how the body responds to different forms of extreme abuse. "Logs" were his subjects in almost inconceivable acts of vivisection.

For the brave of heart and strong of stomach, here are some of the experiments in which the lives of prisoners were taken at Unit 731. They were exposed to poison gas so that their lungs could later be removed and studied; slowly roasted by electricity to determine voltages needed to produce death; hung upside down to study the progress of natural choking; locked into high-pressure chambers until their eyes popped out; spun in centrifuges; infected with anthrax, syphilis, plague, cholera, and other diseases; forcibly impregnated to provide infants for vivisection; bound to stakes to be incinerated by soldiers testing flamethrowers; and slowly frozen to observe the progress of hypothermia. Air was injected into victims' veins to provoke embolisms; animal blood was injected to see what effect it would have. Some were dissected alive, or had limbs amputated so attendants could monitor their slow deaths by bleeding and gangrene. According to a U.S. Army report that was later declassified, groups of men, women, and children were tied to stakes so that "their legs and buttocks were bared and exposed to shrapnel from anthrax bombs exploded yards away," then monitored to see how long they lived—which was never more than a week. Ishii required a constant flow of human organs, meaning a steady need for "logs." They included not just Chinese but Koreans, Mongolians, and, according to some reports, American prisoners of war. After each experiment, Ishii's microbiologists would meticulously remove tissue samples and mount them on slides for study. Technicians used their research to prepare poisoned chocolate and chewing gum, as well as hairpins and fountain pens rigged with toxin-coated needles for use in close-quarters killing. In industrial-scale laboratories they bred plague-infested fleas and manufactured tons of anthrax that were placed in bomb casings and used to kill thousands of Chinese civilians.

American interrogators slowly grasped the nature and extent of the horrors that had been perpetrated at Unit 731, but they could find no proof. In the last days of the war, Ishii had ordered the execution of the last 150 "logs" at Unit 731, told his men that they must "take the secret to the grave," and distributed cyanide capsules for them to use if they were arrested. Then he ordered the complex destroyed with explosives.

Japanese police officers, acting on orders from the Counterintelligence Corps, found Ishii living almost openly in his hometown and arrested him. On January 17, 1946, he was brought to Tokyo. He was installed at his daughter's home on a small street. Over the next four weeks, he sat willingly for interviews with a Camp Detrick scientist. They were informal and at times even genial.

"He literally begged my father for top-secret data on germ weapons,"

Ishii's daughter later recalled. "At the same time, he emphasized that the data must not fall into the hands of the Russians."

Ishii admitted no crimes. He insisted that Unit 731 had not spread plague virus in China and that its experiments with toxins were performed only on laboratory animals. American military scientists suspected that he was lying, because reports from captured veterans of Unit 731 suggested that he had overseen experiments in which thousands of human subjects died. Detailed reports of these experiments would greatly accelerate the Americans' research into biological warfare. They offered Ishii a stark choice: Tell us at least some of what you know, and you will be an asset worth protecting; stay silent, and you risk arrest by the Soviets and a possible death sentence. To this they added the promise for which Ishii had been waiting: the Americans were interested in "technical and scientific information . . . and not war crimes."

"If you will give me documentary immunity for myself, superiors, and subordinates, I can get all the information for you," Ishii replied. "I would like to be hired by the U.S. government as a biological warfare expert."

Both sides had reason to pursue this deal. Ishii knew he faced trial and likely execution if he refused to cooperate. Camp Detrick scientists wanted to learn what he knew and were driven by a sense of urgency that overwhelmed whatever moral qualms they might have felt. At their request, the Supreme Command of Allied Powers, led by General Douglas MacArthur, secretly promulgated a new principle: "The value to the US of Japanese biological weapons data is of such importance to national security as to far outweigh the value accruing from war-crimes prosecution."

The next step was to apply this principle to Ishii and his comrades. General MacArthur had to move quickly because the International Military Tribunal for the Far East was about to open its epochal trial of suspected Japanese war criminals. He signed a secret decree granting amnesty to Ishii and all who had worked with him at Unit 731.

"Statements from Ishii," MacArthur reasoned, "can probably be obtained by informing Japanese involved that information will be retained in intelligence channels, and will not be employed as 'War Crimes' evidence."

Thus did the man responsible for directing the dissection of thousands of living prisoners during wartime, along with those who worked with him, escape punishment. Unlike their German counterparts, however, they were not brought to the United States. Instead the Japanese scientists were installed at laboratories and detention centers in East Asia. There they helped Americans conceive and carry out experiments on human subjects that could not be legally conducted in the United States.

"Chalking that up to simple racism does not adequately account for why Ishii and his colleagues were not shipped to the United States," one academic study has concluded. "America was not prepared politically or structurally for an influx of new Japanese scientists . . . There were too many technical and cultural barriers to overcome."

Once Ishii was guaranteed immunity from war crimes prosecution, he began turning over boxes of documents. They were full of uniquely valuable data about how various toxins affect the human body, how these toxins can be spread, and what dosage levels kill most effectively. Scientists at Camp Detrick were delighted.

Ishii then guided the Americans to temples and mountain retreats where he and his men had hidden fifteen thousand microscope slides as the war was ending. Each slide contained a sliver of tissue from a human kidney, liver, spleen, or other organ that had suffered some sort of deadly shock. Victims had died after being exposed to extremes of temperature, or after being infected with anthrax, botulism, bubonic plague, cholera, dysentery, smallpox, typhoid, tuberculosis, gangrene, or syphilis. Often the victims were still conscious when their organs were removed, because Ishii believed that the best data could be collected at the point of death. The slides were sent to Camp Detrick, where scientists reported that they "greatly supplemented and amplified" American research into biological warfare.

"Information has accrued with respect to human susceptibility," they wrote in one report. "Such information could not be obtained in our own laboratories because of scruples attached to human experimentation . . . It is hoped that individuals who voluntarily contributed this information will be spared embarrassment because of it."

While the Americans protected veterans of Unit 731, the Soviets captured twelve of them and charged them with war crimes. All were convicted and given prison terms ranging from two to twenty-five years. Their trials were not widely publicized. Over the following years, whenever reports about Unit 731 and Ishii's work surfaced in the United States, government spokesmen dismissed them as Communist propaganda. Yet the Soviet sentences were light by post-war standards. Evidence later emerged suggesting that both the Soviet and Chinese governments used the expertise of Unit 731 veterans to advance their own bio-weapons programs.

During the war years, Kurt Blome and Shiro Ishii had known of, admired, and encouraged each other's work. Designs of their medical torture centers were remarkably similar. When the Axis was finally defeated in 1945, it was reasonable to expect that they would share the same fate. So they did—but not the fate they might have feared. Scientists from Camp Detrick had rescued Ishii. Now they had to find a way to rescue Blome.

THE BANG OF the gavel that opened the "Doctors' Trial" at Nuremberg was loud and sharp. One witness wrote that it "resounded throughout the large courtroom." Brief formalities followed. The chief prosecutor, General Telford Taylor, presented his opening argument to a rapt audience.

"All of the defendants herein unlawfully, willingly, and knowingly committed war crimes," Taylor began. All had carried out "medical experiments without the subjects' consent . . . in the course of which experiments the defendants committed murders, brutalities, cruelties, tortures, atrocities, and other inhuman acts." In excruciating detail, Taylor described experiments in which prisoners were killed by freezing, application of mustard gas to wounds, surgical removal of bones or muscle, poison bullets, exposure to extreme air pressures, and infection with malaria, typhus, and tuberculosis. Then he charged the defendants with hundreds of thousands of more murders through "the systematic and secret execution of the aged, insane, incurably ill, deformed children and other persons by gas, lethal injections, and diverse other means." The court reporter whose job it was to record this litany wrote afterward that she "was having a great deal of trouble remaining dispassionate emotionally and trying to keep my composure."

Two well-known perpetrators of Nazi medical crimes were not in

Courtroom 600 at the Nuremberg Palace of Justice on that day, November 21, 1946. Heinrich Himmler had committed suicide in his cell. Josef Mengele, who directed medical experiments at Auschwitz, had disappeared. Nonetheless the remaining twenty-three defendants were a worthy gallery. They ranged from Hitler's personal physician to doctors who supervised extreme experiments or mass killings at Auschwitz, Buchenwald, Dachau, Bergen-Belsen, Treblinka, and other concentration camps. Among them was Kurt Blome.

General MacArthur had rescued Ishii from punishment with a stroke of his pen, but rescuing Blome proved more difficult. He had held highly visible positions. Nazi crimes were well known; Unit 731 could be hidden or glossed over because it had operated in remote Manchuria, but Nazi camps were in the heart of Europe. The system for processing suspected war criminals in Germany was more structured and difficult to manipulate than the one in Japan. Blome's admirers at Camp Detrick could not protect him from indictment. Instead they concentrated on securing his acquittal.

Blome put up a spirited defense. Addressing the court in fluent English, he concentrated on two points. First, he insisted that although there was much circumstantial evidence against him—including the letter from Himmler ordering him to supply toxin for "special treatment" of prisoners—no witnesses could be found to testify that he had actually carried out the atrocities he wrote about, discussed, or was ordered to direct. Second, he produced an article from *Life* magazine describing a U.S. Army study in which prisoners at an Illinois penitentiary were infected with malaria so that its effects could be studied. He argued that these experiments, and others that American doctors had conducted in prisons, were no more unethical than his own.

Blome's testimony was not all that helped his case. The desire of scientists at Camp Detrick to protect him was quietly communicated to U.S. military officers involved in the "Doctors' Trial." Verdicts were handed down on August 27, 1947. Seven of the defendants were sentenced to hang. Nine others received prison terms. Seven were acquitted. Blome was among this last group. Judges said that they suspected he had directed experiments on human beings but could find no clear evidence.

"The deck was clearly stacked," according to one German study of this trial. "Convincing proof of Blome's involvement in [SS Dr. Sigmund] Rasher's experiments at the Dachau concentration camp was not presented. His role in experiments with malaria germs and poison gas could supposedly not be proven. Even as prosecutors asked that he be sentenced, they must have realized that it would not happen."

Forty-two days after Blome was found not guilty, the chief of the army's Chemical Corps received a simple message from the Counterintelligence Corps in Germany: "Available now for interrogation on biological warfare matters is Doctor Kurt Blome." Immediately he dispatched a team of Camp Detrick scientists. Blome welcomed them. He was reluctant to discuss his experiments on human subjects, the topic that most interested them. At one session, though, he mentioned that he had investigated an operation in which Polish resistance fighters killed more than a dozen SS officers by squirting typhoid germs from what appeared to be a fountain pen into their food. That fascinated his interrogators. Blome had studied techniques of poisoning without detection. That seemed just the beginning of what he could teach his new friends. Finally he made an offer: bring me to America, and I will revolutionize your bio-warfare program.

FOR A CORE of Americans who served in the military and in intelligence agencies during World War II, the war never really ended. All that changed was the enemy. The role once played by Nazi Germany and Imperial Japan was assumed by the Soviet Union and, after 1949, "Red China." In the new narrative, monolithic Communism, directed from the Kremlin, was a demonic force that mortally threatened the United States and all humanity. With the stakes so existentially high, no sacrifice in the fight against Communism—of money, morality, or human life—could be considered excessive. This conviction, unspoken but almost universally shared in Washington, came to undergird and justify one of the most bizarre covert projects ever launched by any government.

In 1945, President Truman decided that the United States did not need a clandestine intelligence agency during peacetime, and he abolished the Office of Strategic Services. Two years later he changed his mind and signed the National Security Act, which created the Central Intelligence Agency. That law, written in part by Allen Dulles, a former

OSS officer who was aching to return to the clandestine world, is loosely worded. It authorizes the CIA to carry out "functions and duties related to intelligence affecting national security," and to use "all appropriate methods" in that pursuit.

The CIA's first covert operations were in Europe, where the Cold War was most intense. In 1947 its officers hired Corsican gangsters to break a Communist-led strike at the port of Marseille. The next year it ran a successful campaign to prevent Communists from winning a national election in Italy. It sent spies, saboteurs, and commando squads into the Soviet Union and Eastern Europe. These were bold operations, but similar to others that secret services had been carrying out for generations. Then a sudden shock from Budapest gave the CIA—and scientists at Camp Detrick—a new fear that set them on a new course.

On February 3, 1949, the Roman Catholic prelate of Hungary, Cardinal Jozsef Mindszenty, appeared at a show trial and confessed to extravagant charges of attempting to overthrow the government, directing black market currency schemes, and seeking to steal the royal crown as part of a plot to re-establish the Austro-Hungarian Empire. He was sentenced to life imprisonment. Leaders of Western countries were outraged. President Truman denounced the trial as "infamous." Pope Pius XII called it "a serious outrage which inflicts a deep wound," and excommunicated all Catholics involved. Senior CIA officers reacted differently. They focused on the way Mindszenty had behaved during his trial. He appeared disoriented, spoke in a flat monotone, and confessed to crimes he had evidently not committed. Clearly he had been coerced—but how?

At the CIA, the answer seemed terrifyingly obvious: the Soviets had developed drugs or mind control techniques that could make people say things they did not believe. No evidence of this ever emerged. Mindszenty was coerced with traditional techniques like ill treatment, extended isolation, beatings, and repetitive interrogation. The fear that Communists had discovered some potent new psychoactive tool, however, sent a shock wave through the CIA. It also gave Camp Detrick a new mission.

In the first years after World War II, scientists at Camp Detrick found themselves out of favor. The reason was simple. American military planners had concluded that since the United States now had nuclear weapons, developing biological ones was no longer a priority. Political attention, along with the funding that accompanies it, had shifted decisively to nuclear-related programs. That rendered Camp Detrick almost irrelevant. Work slowed down. Many scientists were redeployed or allowed to return to civilian life. Those who remained were looking for a new mission. The Mindszenty trial gave them one.

Alarmed commanders of the Chemical Corps moved quickly. In the spring of 1949 they created a secret team at Camp Detrick, the Special Operations Division, whose scientists would conduct research into ways that chemicals could be used as weapons of covert action. One of the first scientists to join the new division called it "a little Detrick within Detrick . . . Most of the people didn't know what was going on in SO, and got angry because you wouldn't tell 'em."

The coercive use of drugs was a new field, and Special Operations scientists had to decide how to begin their research. CIA officers in Europe were facing a parallel challenge. They were regularly capturing suspected Soviet agents and were looking for interrogation techniques that would allow them to draw these prisoners away from their identities, induce them to reveal secrets, and perhaps even program them to commit acts against their will. The Mindszenty trial stoked their fear that Soviet scientists had already perfected these techniques. That stirred the CIA to urgent action.

3

Willing and Unwilling Subjects

Disorienting waves of dizziness enveloped Dr. Albert Hofmann during an experiment with ergot enzyme at the Sandoz laboratory in Basel on April 16, 1943. He bicycled home with unusual difficulty, lay down, and closed his eyes. At first he felt pleasantly inebriated. Then his imagination began to race. For the next two hours he careened through what he later called "an uninterrupted stream of fantastic images of extraordinary plasticity and vividness, accompanied by an intense, kaleidoscope-like play of colors."

The ergot enzyme, found naturally in fungus that grows on rye and other grains, has been recognized for centuries as therapeutic, but it can also cause spasms and hallucinations. Hofmann, a research chemist, had been testing a new permutation that he hoped would improve blood circulation. When he awoke the next morning, he suspected that ergot, which during the Middle Ages was associated with stories of witchcraft and possession, had been the cause of his intoxication. Yet the symptoms he had experienced did not match any ever recorded. He decided to conduct an experiment with himself as the subject. Three days after his first experience, he swallowed 250 micrograms of the substance he had been testing, a minute amount. Half an hour later, he wrote in his journal that he felt "no trace of any effect." His next entry is a scrawled note that trails off after the words "difficulty in concentration, visual disturbances, marked desire to laugh." This experience, he wrote afterward, was "much stronger than the first time."

> I had great difficulty in speaking coherently, my field of vision swayed before me, and objects appeared distorted like images in curved mirrors . . . As far as I remember, the following were the most outstanding symptoms: vertigo, visual disturbances; the faces of those around me appeared as grotesque, colored masks; marked motoric unrest, alternating with paralysis; an intermittent heavy feeling in the head, limbs and the entire body, as if they were filled with lead; dry, constricted sensation in the throat; feeling of choking; clear recognition of my condition, in which state I sometimes observed, in the manner of an independent, neutral observer, that I shouted half insanely or babbled incoherent words. Occasionally I felt as if I were out of my body . . . An unending series of colorful, very realistic and fantastic images surged in upon me . . . At about one o'clock I fell asleep and awoke next morning feeling perfectly well.

The chemical Hofmann ingested was the twenty-fifth in a series of lysergic acid diethylamides he had compounded, so he named it LSD-25. During that spring week in 1943 he became the first person ever to use it. Within a generation it would shake the world.

In the months after his first inner voyages—only later would they be called acid trips—Hofmann tested LSD on volunteers drawn from among his colleagues at Sandoz. The results were astonishing. Hofmann reported what he called "the extraordinary activity of LSD on the human psyche," and concluded that it was "by far the most active and most specific hallucinogen."

The medical implications of this discovery were unclear. Hofmann thought LSD might open new avenues for research into the biochemical basis of mental illness. His experiments proceeded sporadically and inconclusively. News of them reached Washington at the end of 1949, when an officer of the Chemical Corps reported to L. Wilson Greene, technical director of the Chemical and Radiological Laboratories at Edgewood Arsenal, that Sandoz chemists had discovered a new drug said to produce vivid hallucinations. Greene was riveted. He collected all the information he could find on the subject, then produced a long report entitled "Psychochemical Warfare: A New Concept of War." It concluded with a strong recommendation that the government begin systematically testing LSD, mescaline, and sixty other mind-altering compounds that might be weaponized for use against enemy populations.

"Their will to resist would be weakened greatly, if not entirely destroyed, by the mass hysteria and panic which would ensue," Greene wrote. "The symptoms which are considered to be of value in strategic and tactical operations include the following: fits or seizures, dizziness, fear, panic, hysteria, hallucinations, migraine, delirium, extreme depression, notions of hopelessness, lack of initiative to do even simple things, suicidal mania."

Greene proposed that America's military scientists be given a new mission. At the outer edge of imagination, he suggested, beyond artillery and tanks, beyond chemicals, beyond germs, beyond even nuclear bombs, might lie an unimagined cosmos of new weaponry: psychoactive drugs. Greene believed they could usher in a new era of humane warfare.

"Throughout recorded history, wars have been characterized by death, human misery, and the destruction of property, each major conflict being more catastrophic than the one preceding it," he wrote in his report. "I am convinced that it is possible, by means of the techniques of psychochemical warfare, to conquer an enemy without wholesale killing of his people and the mass destruction of his property."

This report electrified the few American officials allowed to read it. Among them was the director of central intelligence, Admiral Roscoe Hillenkoetter. Seized by its revelations, he asked President Truman to authorize the drug research Greene proposed—and give the job to the CIA. Truman agreed. Hillenkoetter assigned a handful of CIA officers to begin working with Special Operations Division chemists at Camp Detrick.

Under this "informal agreement," which took shape during 1950, two of the most secret covert teams in Cold War America became partners. Military scientists at Detrick could design and concoct all manner of drug combinations, but had no authority to use them in operations. The CIA, by contrast, is an action agency. Officers in its Technical Services Staff, which produced the tools of espionage, were looking for drugs that could be used to loosen tongues, weaken human resistance, open the mind to outside control, or kill people. Under the "informal agreement," scientists who made psychoactive and convulsive drugs began working with CIA interrogators who applied them to prisoners. This joint program, later code-named MK-NAOMI—the prefix MK was for projects run by the Technical Services Staff—was given an immediate shot of cash.

"Under MK-NAOMI," according to one investigator, "the SOD men developed a whole arsenal of toxic substances for CIA use. If Agency operators needed to kill someone in a few seconds with, say, a suicide pill, SOD provided super-deadly shellfish toxin . . . More useful for assassination, CIA and SOD men decided, was botulinum. With an incubation period of 8 to 12 hours, it allowed the killer to separate himself from the deed . . . When CIA operators merely wanted to be rid of somebody temporarily, SOD stockpiled for them about a dozen diseases and toxins of various strengths."

Besides working in their laboratories at Camp Detrick, scientists assigned to MK-NAOMI carried out field tests to learn how biological agents might work in crowded environments. Some observed bioweapons tests conducted by the British military, including one near the Caribbean island of Antigua in 1949 during which hundreds of animals died. That same year, six members of the Special Operations Division entered the Pentagon pretending to be air quality monitors and sprayed mock bacteria into air ducts. Afterward they calculated that if their attack had been real, at least half of those working in the building would have died.

Since some of these scientists were researching bio-warfare—how to wage it and how to defend against it—they wanted to learn how pathogens could be spread in a concentrated population, and what the effects of such an attack would be. In 1950 they decided to carry out a large-scale outdoor test in which harmless but traceable germs would be released into the air of a large American city. They chose San Francisco, not only because it has a coastline and tall buildings but also because its chronic fog would disguise germ clouds. The U.S. Navy supplied a minesweeper specially equipped with large aerosol hoses. Operation Sea Spray, as it was called, was classified as a military maneuver. Local officials were not notified.

For six days at the end of September, as their minesweeper drifted near San Francisco, scientists from Camp Detrick directed the spraying of a bacterium called *Serratia marcescens* into the coastal mist. They had chosen this substance because it has a red tint, making it easy to trace, and was not known to cause any ill effects. According to samples taken afterward at forty-three sites, the spraying reached all of San Francisco's 800,000 residents and also affected people in Oakland, Berkeley, Sausalito, and five other cities. Over the next couple of weeks, eleven people checked in to a hospital with urinary tract infections and were found to have red drops in their urine. One of them, who was recovering from prostate surgery, died. Doctors were mystified. Several of them later published a journal article reporting this "curious clinical observation," for which they could find no explanation.

Although the *Serratia marcescens* bacterium turned out not to have been as harmless as scientists from Camp Detrick had believed, they deemed their "vulnerability test" a success. It was conducted without detection and, by their reckoning, proved that cities were vulnerable to biological warfare. "It was noted that a successful BW attack on this area can be launched from the sea," they wrote in their report, "and that effective dosages can be produced over relatively large areas."

The CIA played only an observer's role in Operation Sea Spray. Full-scale warfare was not its business. Its officers were more interested in the ways that chemical and biological agents could be used to control the minds of individuals. In 1950, Director of Central Intelligence Roscoe Hillenkoetter took the next step in this search. He decreed creation of a new program that would take the CIA's quest for mind control techniques to its next level.

The program was code-named Bluebird, supposedly after someone at a planning meeting described its goal as finding ways to make prisoners "sing like a bird." One of the first Bluebird memos decreed that experiments be "broad and comprehensive, involving both domestic and overseas activity." Another noted that the best subjects would be prisoners, including "defectors, refugees, POWs [and] others." Experiments would be aimed at, according to a third memo, "investigating the possibility of control of an individual by application of Special Interrogation techniques."

Bluebird began amid great enthusiasm. Barely six months after it was launched, its officers asked permission to expand it, including "the establishment and training of four additional teams besides the two currently in use." These teams, they said, would "conduct experiments and develop techniques to determine the possibilities and practicability of the positive use of [Special Interrogation] on willing and unwilling subjects, for operational purposes. Positive use of SI would be for the purpose of operational control of individuals to perform specific tasks under post-hypnotic suggestion . . . This field, if it is found that the application of SI is possible and practicable, offers unlimited possibilities to operational officers."

Around the time that report was written, a fateful change transformed the CIA. A new director, General Walter Bedell Smith, took over in October 1950. One of his first decisions was to hire the ambitious former OSS spymaster Allen Dulles. Although Dulles was in many ways a limited thinker, he liked to imagine himself on the cutting edge of espionage. During his war years in Switzerland he had met and come to admire the psychoanalyst Carl Jung. By the time he began his long career at the CIA, he had become fascinated with the prospect that science could discover ways to manipulate the human psyche.

After six weeks of work at the CIA as a consultant, Dulles officially joined the Agency on January 2, 1951. His title, deputy director for plans, lightly disguised the fact that his job was to oversee the Agency's covert operations—an enterprise that consumed most of its budget. From the beginning of his CIA career to the end, Dulles enthusiastically promoted mind control projects of every sort. He saw them as an indispensable part of the secret war against Communism that he was charged with waging.

Signs of that escalating war were plain to see. Less than a month after Dulles began full-time work at the CIA, the United States carried out its first nuclear test in the Nevada desert, giving Americans a terrifying look at the mushroom cloud that they had been told could engulf them at any moment. Soon afterward, eleven leaders of the Communist Party of the United States were ordered to prison after the Supreme Court upheld their convictions on charges of seeking to overthrow the government. Adding to those shocks was jarring news that two British intelligence officers, Guy Burgess and Donald Maclean, had disappeared. They had been feeding Western secrets to the Soviet Union for years, and later turned up in Moscow.

These frightening developments intensified the sense of barely controlled panic that shaped the early CIA. Allen Dulles immediately focused on Bluebird. He had been on the job for only a few weeks when he sent a revealing memo to two of the senior officers he had assigned to help direct it, Frank Wisner and Richard Helms.

"In our conversation of 9 February 1951," Dulles wrote, "I outlined to you the possibilities of augmenting the usual interrogation methods by the use of drugs, hypnosis, shock, etc., and emphasized the defensive aspects as well as the offensive opportunities in this field of applied medical science. The enclosed folder, 'Interrogation Techniques,' was prepared by my Medical Division to provide you with a suitable background." Dulles added that this "augmenting" could only be carried out overseas because many of its aspects were "not permitted by the United States government (i.e., anthrax etc.)."

Other memos from this period contain equally revealing passages. One stipulates: "Bluebird teams are to include persons qualified in medicine, psychological interrogation, the use of the electroencephalograph, electric shock and the polygraph." Another directs researchers to investigate ways that a person "can be made to commit acts useful to us under post-hypnotic suggestion," along with ways to "condition our own people so they will not be subject to post-hypnotic suggestion." A third asks: "Can a person under hypnosis be forced to commit murder?"

IN A SLEEPY German town called Oberursel, tucked into rolling hills north of Frankfurt, the Nazis had operated a transit camp for captured British and American pilots. The U.S. Army took it over in 1946 and named it Camp King, after an intelligence officer who had been killed a couple of years before. Since it was already configured with prison cells and interrogation rooms, it became the place where recalcitrant ex-Nazis and other prisoners were sent for "special interrogation." Officially it was said to house the 7707th European Command Intelligence Center. That was not the whole story.

Camp King was home base for the "rough boys," a handful of Counterintelligence Corps officers known for abusing prisoners. Some of their methods were traditional, like immersing victims in freezing water or forcing them to run through gauntlets of soldiers who beat them with baseball bats and other weapons. Others were pharmacological. They injected some victims with Metrazol, which was thought to loosen tongues but also causes violent contortions, and others with cocktails of mescaline, heroin, and amphetamines. Victims' screams sometimes echoed through the base.

"The unit took great pride in their nicknames, the 'rough boys' and the 'kraut gauntlet,' and didn't hold back with any drug or technique," one veteran of the Counterintelligence Corps later recalled. "You name it, they used it."

The "rough boys" at Camp King gave Allen Dulles all the muscle he needed for torture of the traditional sort. Most appealingly, as one CIA officer in Frankfurt put it, "disposal of body would be no problem." Dulles, though, was looking beyond traditional methods of interrogation. He resolved to take advantage of Camp King's assets, but in a way that would allow him to test forms of persuasion more sophisticated than what the "rough boys" doled out.

Senior CIA officers saw Bluebird as a portal that might lead them toward an undiscovered world. At Camp King they had a site where they could test any drug or coercive technique. They had a ready supply of human subjects. If any died, disposing of their bodies would be "no problem." Best of all, since their work would be in American-occupied West Germany, they were beyond the reach of law.

Rather than rely on the thuggish "rough boys," the CIA began sending Bluebird teams to Camp King to carry out interrogations. Then it went a step further. Bluebird work was so secret that even a secure army base was not secure enough. Behind tightly closed doors, a far-reaching plan took shape. The CIA would open its own secret prison where captured enemy agents could be used as subjects in mind control experiments. It would be under the formal control of Camp King but located outside the base perimeter and run by the CIA. To put it another way: a CIA "safe house" under the protection of the U.S. Army.

A few miles from Camp King, in the village of Kronberg, a gabled villa stands at the end of what was once a country lane. Over the heavy wooden doors is chiseled the date it was built: 1906. For a generation it was known as Villa Schuster, after the Jewish family that built and owned it. The family was forced to sell during the Nazi era. In early 1951, Americans from the CIA and the Special Operations Division who were looking for a "black site" drove up the lane and found it.

From the outside, Villa Schuster—also known as Haus Waldhof, after the name of the lane that leads to it—looks almost regal, a calm survivor of history's tempests. It is spacious, with an elegant entryway and sturdy beams. The grand living room has a high ceiling, leaded windows, and an imposing fireplace. On the two upper floors are a dozen bedrooms. The basement is a complex of bricked-in storerooms, easily configured as sealed cells.

With the coming of the Cold War in the late 1940s, a different sort of prisoner began arriving at Camp King. Many were from Eastern Europe, including East Germany. Some were captured Soviet agents. Others claimed to be refugees but had been judged unreliable. The guilty were mixed with the simply unfortunate. All were what the CIA called "expendable," meaning that if they disappeared, no one would inquire too closely. The especially expendable, along with those believed to be guarding especially valuable secrets, were sent to Villa Schuster. In its basement, doctors and scientists conducted the most extreme experiments on human beings that had ever been carried out by officers of the United States government.

"This villa on the edge of Kronberg became the CIA's torture house," a German television documentary concluded decades later.

CIA officers who conducted Bluebird interrogations at Camp King and Villa Schuster counted on guidance from "Doc Fisher," a German physician who had worked at Walter Reed General Hospital in Washington and spoke good English. "Doc Fisher" was General Walter Schreiber, the former surgeon general of the Nazi army. During the war he had approved experiments at the Auschwitz, Ravensbrück, and Dachau concentration camps in which inmates were frozen, injected with mescaline and other drugs, and cut open so the progress of gangrene on their bones could be monitored. According to one American researcher, his experiments "usually resulted in a slow and agonizing death." After the war Schreiber was arrested by the Soviets and imprisoned at the notorious

Lubyanka prison in Moscow. Finally he persuaded his jailers to allow him to accept a professorship in East Berlin. Once there, he slipped across to West Berlin and presented himself to officers of the Counterintelligence Corps. As soon as they confirmed his identity, they sent him to Camp King. There he was welcomed like an admired colleague.

"The former chief physician of the German army, who had been responsible for overseeing many concentration camp experiments, sat for weeks of questioning," according to one report. "But these were not the kind of questions an accused prisoner would be asked about crimes against humanity. They spoke as scientists and colleagues, about their knowledge and experiences."

Within a few months after his arrival, Schreiber rose to become Camp King's staff doctor. Part of his job was to advise members of visiting Bluebird teams in techniques of "special interrogation." One CIA-connected researcher, a Harvard Medical School professor named Henry Beecher, spent a long evening with him at Villa Schuster. In retrospect it seems a chilling scene: sitting in an elegant salon, probably sipping good drinks, almost certainly with a fire blazing, these two mutual admirers, one a former Nazi doctor and the other a Harvard professor who worked with the CIA, talked shop. They were among the world's few true experts on the subject of psychoactive drugs and had much to discuss. Directly below their feet were stone cells where "expendables" were kept for use as subjects in Bluebird experiments. Beecher wrote afterward that he found Schreiber "intelligent and cooperative." He enjoyed their "exchange of ideas."

Teams of Bluebird interrogators flew regularly to West Germany to conduct their experiments. Most often, they did their work at Camp King and the nearby "black site" at Villa Schuster. German researchers would later identify other secret prisons where Americans also carried out extreme experiments. One was in Mannheim, near the baroque palace from which princes once ruled the Palatinate. Reports have placed others in Berlin, Munich, and the outskirts of Stuttgart.

At these secret prisons, Bluebird interrogators worked without any outside supervision. This set a precedent that marked a breakthrough for the CIA. By opening prisons, the Agency established its right not only to detain and imprison people in other countries, but to interrogate them harshly while they were in custody without regard for U.S. law.

So successful was this network of prisons in West Germany that the CIA duplicated it in Japan. There, Bluebird interrogation teams injected captured North Korean soldiers with drugs including sodium amytal, a depressant that can have hypnotic effects, and with three potent stimulants: Benzedrine, which affects the central nervous system; Coramine, which acts on the lungs; and Picrotoxin, a convulsant that can cause seizures and respiratory paralysis. While they were in the weakened state of transition between the effects of depressants and stimulants, CIA experimenters subjected them to hypnosis, electroshock, and debilitating heat. Their goal, according to one report, was "to induce violent cathartic reactions, alternately putting subjects to sleep, then waking them up until they were sufficiently confused to be coerced into reliving an experience from their past." CIA officials in Washington ordered the officers who carried out these experiments to keep their true nature secret even from the American military units with which they were working, and to say only that they were conducting "intensive polygraph work."

As the pace of these experiments intensified, scientists at Camp Detrick renewed their interest in Kurt Blome. Immediately after the war, they had declined his offer to come to the United States, but by the early 1950s his knowledge of poisons and hallucinogens seemed to qualify him as an ideal adviser to the Bluebird project. The CIA found him practicing medicine in Dortmund. On a spring day in 1951, an officer visited his office with a proposition. If he would agree to spill his secrets, the CIA would arrange for an "accelerated Paperclip contract" that would bring him to the United States.

Blome was enjoying his new life, but admitted that he liked the idea of a "return to biological research." Finally, drawn especially by the prospect of working once again with his former Nazi comrade Walter Schreiber, who had accepted a Paperclip contract and was at that moment preparing to board a ship for New York, he decided to accept the CIA's offer. He sold his medical practice, listed his home with a real estate broker, and pulled his children out of school so they could concentrate on learning English.

The timing was bad. Schreiber's arrival in the United States set off a scandal. The newspaper columnist Drew Pearson published excerpts from testimony at Nuremberg that implicated him in war crimes, specifically the assigning of doctors to carry out experiments on concentration camp inmates. Much outcry followed. Schreiber's American sponsors reluctantly decided to cancel his Paperclip contract. Rather than return to West Germany, he chose retirement in Argentina.

This scandal erupted as the chief of U.S. Army intelligence in Berlin, Colonel Garrison Cloverdale, was reviewing Kurt Blome's application for a Paperclip contract. He had rubber-stamped dozens of others, but this time he balked. The extent of Blome's crimes, he decided, disqualified him from entry into the United States. In a memo to General Lucius Clay, the High Commissioner for Germany, he recommended that the "accelerated Paperclip contract" be rejected and that Blome be denied a visa. Clay agreed. Cloverdale sent a curt cable to the Camp Detrick scientists: "Suspend shpmt Dr. Kurt Blome—appears inadmissible in view of HICOG."

CIA officers working on the Bluebird project were furious. "Blome contract signed and approved Commander in Chief," one of them wrote in an angry memo. "Subject completing preparations for shipment late November. Has already turned over private practice Dortmund to another doctor. In view of adverse publicity which might ensue and which may destroy entire program, this theatre recommend[s] subject be shipped."

The CIA's appeal was unsuccessful. Admitting Blome to the United States threatened to focus unwanted attention not only on him, but also on the hundreds of other former Nazis who had been quietly brought to work at American military bases and research laboratories. Yet Bluebird operatives remained determined to tap his uniquely valuable store of knowledge.

Fortunately, the ideal job had just become available. Walter Schreiber had been staff doctor at Camp King, and now that post was open. The CIA offered it to Blome. He would resume the work he pursued during his Nazi years: testing what one memo called "the use of drugs and chemicals in unconventional interrogations." Since he would be based at Camp King rather than in the United States, he could help direct the interrogations as well. Blome accepted. His wife refused to move to Camp King with him, and the couple separated. "Doc Blome" was free to devote all of his time to his new work.

Judges at Nuremberg had condemned Nazi doctors for violating universal principles that must always govern experiments on human beings. In their verdict, they enumerated those principles, which became known as the Nuremberg Code, to justify the punishments they meted out and to set immutable laws for future generations.

No copy of the Nuremberg Code is known to have hung at Camp King or any other place where Bluebird teams experimented on prisoners. If it had, experimenters might have been drawn to its first and most essential principle: "Required is the voluntary, well-informed, understanding consent of the human subject in a full legal capacity." Despite the clarity of that imperative, and despite the seven death sentences that had been pronounced on Nazi scientists who were judged to have violated it, the Nuremberg Code was never incorporated into United States law. It did not legally bind Bluebird researchers, experimenters, or interrogators as they set out to answer deep and ancient questions.

What were those questions? After consulting with their new German and Japanese colleagues, CIA officers came up with a list. Answers to these questions, they asserted in a memo in early 1951, would be "of incredible value to this agency."

- Can accurate information be obtained from willing or unwilling individuals?
- Can Agency personnel (or persons of interest to this agency) be conditioned to prevent any outside power from obtaining information from them by any known means? . . .
- Can we guarantee total amnesia under any and all conditions?
- Can we "alter" a person's personality? How long will it hold?
- Can we devise a system for making unwilling subjects into willing agents? . . .
- How can [drugs] be best concealed in a normal or commonplace item, such as candy, cigarettes, liqueur, wines, coffee, tea, beer, gum, water, common medicines, Coke, toothpaste? . . .

- Can we . . . extract complicated formulas from scientists, engineers, etc., if unwilling? Can we extract details of gun emplacements, landing fields, factories, mines? . . .
- Can we also have them make detailed drawing, sketches, plans?
- Could any of this be done under field conditions and in a very short space of time?

"Bluebird is not fully satisfied with results to date, but believes with continued work and study, remarkable results can be obtained," this memo concluded. "Bluebird's general problem is to get up, conduct and carry out research (practical—not theoretical) in this direction."

Three of the first CIA officers Dulles assigned to oversee Bluebird were part of the Agency's inner core: James Jesus Angleton, chief of the counterintelligence staff; Frank Wisner, soon to become deputy director for plans; and Richard Helms, who twenty years later would rise to the top job, director of central intelligence. All were hyper-active and full of ideas. They realized, however, that they lacked the scientific background to answer the multi-layered questions they were asking.

Allen Dulles and his senior officers agreed that Bluebird needed to "get up." Then they went a step further. They decided that Bluebird needed an infusion of expertise and vision from outside the CIA. Dulles and Helms set out to recruit an imaginative chemist with the drive to pursue forbidden knowledge, a character steely enough to direct experiments that might challenge the conscience of other scientists, and a willingness to ignore legal niceties in the service of national security. This would be the first person the United States government ever hired to find ways to control human minds.

4

The Secret That Was Going to
Unlock the Universe

Waves of damp heat enveloped Washington on the morning of July 13, 1951, when Sidney Gottlieb reported for his first day of work at the CIA. In retrospect, that Friday the thirteenth may be seen as a momentous date in America's secret history. It marked the beginning of Gottlieb's hallucinatory career at the intersection of extreme science and covert action.

"Do you know why they recruited you?" Gottlieb was asked during a deposition decades later.

"They needed someone with my background to organize a group of chemists to pursue the kind of work that the CIA thought they were interested in," he replied.

"Did they describe to you at that time what kind of work you would be doing?"

"Very vaguely. They weren't quite sure. It was a question of a new unit being organized there."

"What was your understanding of what your function would be?"

"My understanding? I really didn't have much of an understanding in my mind. I decided I would give it a try for six months."

Bluebird, the CIA's mind control project, was in full flight by 1951. Teams of its officers were testing "special interrogation" techniques at secret prisons in Germany and Japan. They were studying the effects of various drugs, and of techniques like hypnosis, electroshock, and sensory deprivation. That was not enough, however, to satisfy the CIA's deputy director for plans, Allen Dulles.

Dulles considered Bluebird a project of the utmost importance—even one that could mean the difference between the survival and extinction of the United States. Yet as the program grew, it lost focus. Interrogators worked without coordination. No one was in charge. That set Dulles off on his search for a chemist to oversee all CIA research into mind control.

The obvious place to begin the search was the Chemical Corps. Its commanders had remained in close contact with Ira Baldwin, whom they revered for his pioneering bio-warfare work during World War II. Although Baldwin had returned to the University of Wisconsin, he visited Washington regularly and remained influential as a member of the scientific advisory committee to the Chemical Corps. According to one study, he "continued his work from a new desk, without responsibility for day-to-day operations at Camp Detrick."

Several years earlier, Baldwin had guided one of his prize students, Frank Olson, a budding expert in aerobiology, into a covert government job that brought him to Camp Detrick's inner sanctum, the Special Operations Division. He had also stayed in touch with another former student, a talented biochemist who worked in Washington, felt guilty for having been unable to serve in World War II, and dreamed of finding a special way to prove his patriotism. From Baldwin's orbit emerged the man the CIA was seeking.

The summer of 1951 was a fearful time for Americans. Tension in Berlin reached frightening levels. The Korean War, which at first seemed to offer the prospect of easy victory, had turned into an ugly stalemate, and when the American commander in Korea, General Douglas MacArthur, criticized President Truman's handling of the war, Truman fired him for insubordination, setting off outraged protests and demands for Truman's impeachment. At home, Senator Joseph McCarthy was warning that Communists had infiltrated the State Department.

Most Americans could do little more than worry about the ominous state of the world. Allen Dulles had more options. His career had taught him, rightly or wrongly, that covert action can change the course of history. By the early 1950s he had concluded that mind control could be the decisive weapon of the coming age. Any nation that discovered ways to manipulate the human psyche, he believed, could rule the world. He hired Sidney Gottlieb to lead the CIA's search for that grail.

It was a promising choice. Gottlieb had worked for nearly a decade in government laboratories and was known as an energetic researcher. Like many Americans of his generation, he had been shaped by the trauma of World War II—and because he had been unable to fight, this trauma had left him with a store of pent-up patriotic fervor. His focused energy fit well with the compulsive activism and ethical elasticity that shaped the officers of the early CIA.

Culturally, though, those men were distant from Gottlieb. They were polished products of the American aristocracy. Many knew one another through family webs and prep schools, Ivy League colleges, clubs, investment banks, law firms, and the eternally bonding experience of wartime service in the Office of Strategic Services. The CIA officers who took the greatest interest in mind control projects, Allen Dulles and Richard Helms, were exemplars of that elite. Dulles had risen to his post by way of Princeton and the globally powerful Wall Street law firm Sullivan & Cromwell. His trusted aide Helms was born in Philadelphia and attended prep school in Switzerland. Yet when they set out to hire their master magician of the mind, these patricians chose someone utterly unlike themselves: a thirty-three-year-old Jew from an immigrant family in the Bronx who limped and stuttered.

The gap between them extended to private life. Dulles and Helms were gregarious fixtures on the Georgetown cocktail party circuit, as men of their station were expected to be. Gottlieb was strangely, even startlingly different. He and his family lived in an isolated cabin and grew much of their own food. "It's pretty amazing," one of his former colleagues later mused. "In many ways Sid was at the forefront of the so-called counter-culture before anybody knew there was going to be one."

Gottlieb's unusual style of life was not the end of his oddness. He confessed to the CIA psychologist assigned to screen him, John Gittinger, that he had been a socialist in college. Gittinger assured him that a youthful flirtation with the left would not disqualify him. Their interview then turned to more personal matters. Gottlieb mentioned the search for inner meaning that was already beginning to shape his life. Afterward Gittinger wrote that the young scientist "had a real problem to find a spiritual focus, having gone away from Jewishness."

The director of central intelligence, Walter Bedell Smith, had the final say on Gottlieb's hiring, but as in many matters related to covert operations he deferred to Dulles. When the time came for Dulles to choose the American scientist best qualified to shape his mind control program, he reached far beyond his social and economic class. Yet he could not miss the fact that fate had dealt him and Gottlieb one similar blow.

Dulles had also been born with a clubfoot. His condition was not as serious as Gottlieb's. It had required only one operation, carried out in secret because such handicaps were considered shameful in his family's elevated circle. Yet both men wore prosthetic shoes for most of their lives. Neither ever walked normally. Although they were separated by background and experience, this shared handicap became what one writer called "a strong but never mentioned bond between them." Over the next decade they would stumble together through undiscovered frontiers.

GOTTLIEB'S FIRST ASSIGNMENT at the CIA was to take a three-month course in intelligence tradecraft, with what he later called "some historical backgrounds of intelligence thrown in." After completing it, he set out to educate himself further. He learned all he could about CIA research into chemical techniques of mind control, which he found promising but scattered. Dulles and Helms were impressed. They saw in Gottlieb precisely the combination of zeal and creative imagination that they considered essential if Bluebird was to realize its full potential. Soon after hiring him, they rewarded him with an official title: chief of the newly formed Chemical Division of the Technical Services Staff. The TSS was responsible for developing, testing, and building the tools of espionage. Its Chemical Division was Gottlieb's to shape as he wished.

Dulles gave Gottlieb more than a title that summer. He had already concluded that Bluebird was not wide-ranging or comprehensive enough. Now, in Gottlieb, he had someone able to invigorate it. On August 20, 1951, he directed that Bluebird be expanded, intensified, and centralized. He also gave it a new name: Artichoke. Supposedly he chose that name because artichokes were his favorite vegetable; some later researchers guessed that it actually referred to a colorfully murderous New York gangster known as the Artichoke King. Whatever the source of its name, Artichoke quickly subsumed its predecessor projects and became Gottlieb's power base.

Dulles acted from a position of growing strength. Just three days after launching Artichoke, he was promoted to the second-ranking job at the CIA, deputy director of central intelligence. That assured protection and support for mind control experiments at the highest level of American power.

The first directives sent to Artichoke teams suggest the project's extreme nature. One recommends that interrogations be carried out "in a safe house or safe area," with an adjoining room for "recording devices, transformers, etc." and a bathroom because "occasionally the 'Artichoke' technique produces nausea, vomiting, or other conditions which make bathroom facilities essential." Another says that "Artichoke techniques" may be used at any stage of interrogation, either as "a starting point for the obtaining of information [or] as a last resort when all or nearly all the attempts at obtaining information have failed or when a subject is completely recalcitrant or particularly stubborn."

"Our principal goal," says a third directive, "remains the same as it was in the beginning: the investigation of drug effects on ego control and volitional activities, i.e., can willfully suppressed information be elicited through drugs affecting higher nervous systems? If so, which agents are better for this purpose?" A fourth memo reported that "drugs are already on hand (and new ones are being produced) that can destroy integrity and make indiscreet the most dependable individual."

CIA officers and their partners in the army's Special Operations Division were already testing a variety of drugs on prisoners in Germany and Japan. Beginning in 1951 they also carried out an extended series of experiments at a "black site" inside Fort Clayton, in the Panama Canal Zone. The first subject was a prisoner called Kelly, who in reality was a young Bulgarian politician named Dmitri Dimitrov. He had shared information with the CIA, but his CIA handlers came to suspect that he was considering shifting his loyalty to the French intelligence service. To prevent that, they arranged to have him kidnapped and thrown into a Greek prison—the kind of operation that would later be called "extraordinary rendition." After torturing him for six months, his Greek interrogators concluded that he knew no secrets. They returned him to the CIA, which shipped him to Fort Clayton. In 1952 a CIA officer monitoring his case reported that "because of his confinement in a Greek prison and in a military hospital, Kelly has become very hostile toward the United States, and our intelligence operations in particular." He recommended "an 'Artichoke' approach to Kelly to see if it would be possible to re-orient Kelly toward us." Kelly was held at Fort Clayton for three years. No known documents trace the course of his treatment. Years later, in the United States, he tried to interest *Parade* magazine in his story, but the CIA scuttled the article by telling editors he was "an imposter" who was "disreputable, unreliable, and full of wild stories about the CIA."

The experiments performed on Kelly, like those performed on "expendables" in Germany and Japan, produced no worthwhile results and brought the CIA no closer to any of the discoveries it hoped to make. That did not discourage Dulles. He had convinced himself not only that mind control techniques exist but that Communists had discovered them, and that this posed a mortal threat to the rest of the world. Artichoke was his answer.

FEAR OF ENEMIES spread far beyond the national security establishment in Washington. In the early 1950s, as Americans were being warned that Communists were infiltrating their government, they were also told that those same Communists had found ways of controlling people's minds. Thanks to the work of an imaginative propagandist named Edward Hunter, Americans learned a new word: brainwashing.

Hunter had been a militantly anti-Communist journalist in Europe and Asia during the 1920s and '30s, and during World War II he worked as what he called a "propaganda specialist" for the Office of Strategic Services. Later he joined the CIA's Office of Policy Coordination, home of Operation Mockingbird, through which the Agency shaped coverage of world news in the American press.

On September 20, 1950, Hunter published an article in the *Miami News* headlined "BRAIN-WASHING" TACTICS FORCE CHINESE INTO RANKS OF COMMUNIST PARTY. Citing interviews he had conducted with a graduate of North China People's Revolutionary University, Hunter claimed to have discovered a secret program by which Chinese Communists were controlling their people's minds. The name he gave it, he said, came from the Chinese characters *hsi nao*, literally meaning "wash brain."

Popular imagination seized on the concept. "Brainwashing" was a simple way to explain any aberrant behavior, from anti-Americanism abroad to unorthodox political views at home. Hunter expanded his reporting in a longer article for the *New Leader*, which had close ties to the CIA, and then in a book called *Brain-Washing in Red China*, in which he urged Americans to prepare for "psychological warfare on a scale incalculably more immense than any militarist of the past has ever imagined." He became a minor celebrity, giving interviews and testifying before congressional committees. "The Reds have specialists available on their brainwashing panels," he told the House Committee on Un-American Activities. These specialists, he asserted, were preparing psychic attacks aimed at subjugating "the people and the soil and the resources of the United States" and turning Americans into "subjects of a 'new world order' for the benefit of a mad little knot of despots in the Kremlin."

Few scientists took Hunter's rants seriously, but they fit the tenor of the times. The Soviets had successfully tested their first nuclear weapon. Americans were being told that their country could be attacked at any moment. The threat of "brainwashing" seemed even more horrific because it was so unfathomable.

As the CIA promoted the belief that Communists had mastered "brainwashing" techniques, the Agency fell under the spell of its own propaganda. Allen Dulles and other senior officers were seized by the fear that they were losing a decisive race. That led them not only to justify extreme drug experiments, but to convince themselves that America's national security demanded them.

"There was deep concern over the issue of brainwashing," Richard Helms explained years later. "We felt that it was our responsibility not to lag behind the Russians or the Chinese in this field, and the only way to find out what the risks were was to test things such as LSD and other drugs that could be used to control human behavior."

Much of what the CIA called "Artichoke work" qualifies as medical torture. Dosing unwilling patients with potent drugs, subjecting them to extremes of temperature and sound, strapping them to electroshock machines, and other forms of abuse were not, however, the only things these imaginative scientists did. A CIA memo written soon after Artichoke was launched hints at its breadth.

Specific research should be undertaken to develop new chemicals or drugs, or to improve known elements for use in Artichoke work.

An exhaustive study should be made of various gases and aerosols . . . Gas guns, jets, or sprays, both concealed [and] open, should be studied. In addition, the problem of permanent brain injury and amnesia following lack of oxygen or exposure to other gases should be studied.

The effects of high and low pressures on individuals should be examined.

A considerable amount of research could profitably be expended in the field of sound. This research would include the effect on human beings of various types of vibrations, monotonous sounds, concussion, ultra-high frequency, ultra-sonics, the effect of constantly repeated words, sounds, continuous suggestion, non-rhythmic sounds, whispering, etc.

Bacteria, plant cultures, fungi, poisons of various types . . . are capable of producing illnesses which in turn would produce high fevers, delirium, etc.

The removal of certain basic food elements such as sugar, starch, calcium, vitamins, proteins, etc. from the food of an individual over a certain period of time will produce psychological and physical reactions in an individual. A study should be made to determine whether or not the removal of certain food elements from the diet of prisoners over a given period of time will materially condition them for Artichoke work.

Whether an individual will reveal information as a result of electroshock, or while in an electroshock coma, has not yet been demonstrated . . . Whether electroshock can produce controlled amnesias does not appear to be established.

If an electronically induced sleep could be obtained, and that sleep is used as a means for gaining hypnotic control of an individual, this apparatus might be of extreme value to the Artichoke work.

The Agency under no circumstances would consider [lobotomy and brain surgery] as an operative measure. However, it is felt that the subject could be examined.

Special research should be conducted to determine the effect of long and continuous exposure of individuals to infra-red and ultra-violet light.

There are a great many psychological techniques that could be used in connection with the Artichoke work [including] moving or vibrating rooms; distorted rooms; the deliberate creation on an anxiety condition; the creation of panic, fear, or the exploitation of established phobias, etc.; the effect of heat and cold; the effect of dampness, dryness or saturated or dry air; the general problem of disorientation; [and] completely soundproof areas.

It would be a great advantage if a small, effective hypo-spray device should be designed along the lines of a fountain pen. This, of course, would necessarily have to include some effective chemical or drug that could be used in this connection. This would be a very valuable weapon.

Artichoke interrogators thought of themselves as more sophisticated than the "rough boys" at Camp King, but by clinical standards they were spectacularly unqualified. Few had any training in psychology or knew a foreign language. They staggered blindly through dark territory, not knowing what techniques might work but determined to try whatever they could imagine.

Each Artichoke team included a "research specialist," a "medical officer," and a "security technician." By early 1952 four teams were active, one each in West Germany, France, Japan, and South Korea. Several more were added later. "As a rule," according to one memo, "individuals subjected to Artichoke techniques will be entirely cooperative, passive, and lethargic."

Sometimes an Artichoke team would be dispatched at the request of army or CIA interrogators who faced "particularly stubborn" prisoners. A cable sent to Washington in early 1952, for example, reads: "Request permission give Artichoke to [redacted] while team in France. [Redacted] have failed to break subject though convinced he [redacted]." At other times, Artichoke scientists came up with a new drug or other technique they wished to test, and sent out a call for "expendable" subjects. In mid-1952 they asked the CIA station in South Korea to supply a batch.

Desire send Artichoke team from 18 August to 9 September to test important new technique. Desire minimum 10 subjects. Will brief senior officials
types of subjects desired. Technique does not, *not* require disposal problems
after application.

The challenge of producing chemical compounds for use in "Artichoke work" fell to scientists at Camp Detrick. In 1950 they completed
more than two years of work on an airtight spherical chamber in which
controlled doses of toxins could be administered to animal or human
subjects so their reactions could be studied. Officially it was the One-
Million-Liter Test Sphere, but at Camp Detrick everyone called it the
Eight Ball. Designed in part by Ira Baldwin, it stood more than four stories high and weighed 131 tons, making it the largest aerobiology chamber
ever built. Around its "equator" were five airtight ports leading to chambers into which toxins could be sprayed on subjects strapped inside.
Humidity and temperature levels inside each chamber could be regu-
lated, allowing scientists to test the potency of various toxins under different conditions. This became America's secret laboratory for what one
official report called "aerobiological studies of agents highly pathogenic
to man and animals."

Among the CIA men most active in Artichoke experiments was
Morse Allen, a hard-charging security officer who had been the first director of Bluebird and was searching relentlessly for mind control techniques.
Given free rein by Dulles, Allen enthusiastically promoted some of the
most intense Bluebird and Artichoke projects. He pushed for wider
use of polygraphs, which the CIA, unlike some other intelligence agencies, considered reliable and used extensively. In 1950 he fixated on an
"electro-sleep" machine that was supposed to be able to lull subjects
into a trance. He investigated the possibility that electroshock could be
used to induce amnesia or reduce subjects to a "vegetable level." In other
experiments he tested the effects of radiation, temperature extremes, and
ultrasonic noise. In 1952 he was part of a three-man team that traveled to
Villa Schuster in West Germany to test what one report called "dangerous combinations of drugs such as Benzedrine and Pentathol-Natrium
on Russian captives, under a research protocol specifying that 'disposal
of the body is not a problem.'"

Allen, like some other CIA mind control researchers, was especially fascinated with hypnosis. He found "a famous stage hypnotist" in New York who told him that he often had sex with otherwise unwilling women after placing them in a "hypnotic trance." After taking a four-day course from this evidently talented specialist, Allen returned to Washington to test what he had learned. He used secretaries from CIA offices as his subjects, and several times managed to place them in trances and induce them to do things they might not otherwise consider, like flirting with strangers or revealing office secrets.

"If hypnotic control can be established over any participant in clandestine operations," Allen concluded, "the operator will apparently have an extraordinary degree of influence, a control in order of magnitude beyond anything we have considered feasible."

ARTICHOKE GREW FROM a conviction that became an article of faith at the CIA: there is a way to control the human mind, and if it can be found, the prize will be nothing less than global mastery. At times Sidney Gottlieb and his fellow seekers veered into areas like hypnosis and electroshock, but drugs fascinated them most. They were convinced that somewhere in the uncharted universe of psychopharmacology, the drug of their dreams was waiting to be discovered. It would be something miraculous: a "truth serum" that would loosen recalcitrant tongues, a potion that would open the mind to programming, an amnesiac that would allow the wiping away of memory.

The first drug they hoped would work was the active ingredient in marijuana, tetrahydrocannabinol. Even before the CIA was founded, scientists from the OSS had refined this substance into a potent liquid that had no taste, color, or odor. So confident were they about its potential that they code-named it TD, for "truth drug." For months they tested it on themselves, consuming varying doses mixed into candy, salad dressing, and mashed potatoes. Then they tried smoking it. This research led them to what now seem obvious conclusions: the active ingredient in marijuana brings on "a state of irresponsibility . . . appears to relax all inhibitions . . . and the sense of humor is accentuated to the point where any statement or situation can become extremely funny." That was hardly enough to make it a useful tool in interrogation. Researchers moved on.

Cocaine was the next candidate. The CIA sponsored experiments in which mental patients were given it in various forms, including injection. One early report said cocaine produced elation and talkativeness. Later experiments suggested that it could induce "free and spontaneous speech." After a brief period of excitement, though, this drug was also found too unreliable for use in "special interrogation."

Disappointed with marijuana and cocaine, the researchers turned to heroin. Surviving CIA memos note that heroin was "frequently used by police and intelligence officers," and that it and other addictive substances "can be useful in reverse because of the stresses they produce when they are withdrawn from those who are addicted to their use." At the end of 1950 the U.S. Navy, under a secret project called Chatter, gave the chairman of the Psychology Department at the University of Rochester, G. Richard Wendt, a $300,000 grant to study heroin's effects. Wendt established a mini-institute at which students were paid one dollar per hour to ingest measured doses while he observed their reactions. Heroin, though, proved to be no more of a wonder drug than cocaine. Wendt was forced to conclude that it has "slight value for interrogation."

Could mescaline, which in the early twentieth century became the first psychoactive drug to be synthesized in a laboratory, be the answer? This possibility gripped scientists at Camp Detrick. They spent many hours questioning German scientists about mescaline experiments that had been performed on prisoners at the Dachau concentration camp. Those experiments had mixed results, but Nazi doctors believed mescaline might have unexplored potential. That encouraged some of the physicians who worked with Bluebird. Ultimately, however, they realized that the effects of mescaline—like those of marijuana, cocaine, and heroin—are so unpredictable that it cannot be useful as a mind control agent.

During his first months on the job, Gottlieb read piles of reports on these experiments. They detailed the variety of means that had been tested as possible avenues into the human psyche, including hypnosis, sensory deprivation, electroshock, shifting combinations of stimulants and sedatives, and refined forms of marijuana, mescaline, cocaine, and heroin. As Gottlieb read, he was struck by a question: What happened to LSD?

BEING INSATIABLY CURIOUS, Gottlieb naturally wanted to try LSD himself. At the end of 1951, about six months after he was hired, he asked one of his new associates, Harold Abramson, to guide him through his first "trip." Abramson was a physician who had been an officer in the Chemical Warfare Service during World War II. After the CIA was founded in 1947, he became one of its first medical collaborators. He helped design early mind control experiments. The MK-NAOMI project, under which CIA and Special Operations Division officers collaborated to produce toxins and devices to deliver them, was named after his secretary. He was one of the few scientists in the world who had used and administered LSD. That made him an ideal guide. Gottlieb found that first psychic voyage illuminating.

> I happened to experience an out-of-bodyness, a feeling as though I am in a kind of transparent sausage skin that covers my whole body and it is shimmering, and I have a sense of well-being and euphoria for most of the next hour or two hours, and then it gradually subsides.

After this experience, Gottlieb accelerated the pace of his LSD experiments. His first subjects were volunteers, either CIA colleagues or scientists from the Special Operations Division at Camp Detrick. Some agreed to be dosed at specified moments in controlled environments. Others gave permission to be surprised, so different reactions might be observed. Later, Agency trainees were given LSD without forewarning.

"There was an extensive amount of self-experimentation," Gottlieb later testified. "We felt that a first-hand knowledge of the subjective effects of these drugs [was] important to those of us who were involved in the program."

Using LSD whetted Gottlieb's appetite. So did reports from "mock interrogations" in which CIA employees were given LSD and then induced to violate oaths and promises. In one, a military officer swore never to reveal a secret, revealed it under the influence of LSD, and afterward forgot the entire episode. Gottlieb and his platoon of scientists felt the exhilaration of approaching the heart of an eternal mystery.

"We had thought at first," one of them later recalled, "that this was the secret that was going to unlock the universe."

Just a couple of years earlier, L. Wilson Greene of the Chemical Corps had urged that LSD be made the centerpiece of a crash program to prepare for "psychochemical warfare." His ideas were incorporated into Bluebird and Artichoke, but the focus on LSD had been lost. Researchers were comfortable testing drugs and other techniques with which they were at least vaguely familiar. After Gottlieb resolved to press ahead with LSD research, he contacted Greene, who was still with the Chemical Corps and as enthusiastic as ever about LSD. Both men wanted to harness its power.

Greene saw LSD as a weapon of war, for incapacitating enemy armies or civilian populations. This was radically different from the view of its inventor, Albert Hofmann, who hoped it could be used to treat mental illness. Gottlieb shared neither of those ambitions. The true value of LSD, he believed, would lie in its effect on individual minds. He became convinced that of all known substances, LSD was the one most likely to give initiates a way to control other human beings. That would make it the ultimate covert action weapon.

This was a leap of faith. Even the scientists at Sandoz considered LSD deeply mysterious. Few had studied it. Ten years after it was accidentally invented, Gottlieb came to believe that it could be the key to mind control. He was the first acid visionary.

Gottlieb directed just a handful of scientists at the Chemical Division. The Special Operations Division was only slightly larger. These men formed the inner core on which Gottlieb would rely for the next decade. As part of his effort to mold a coherent team, he took groups of them on weekend retreats at cabins in Maryland and West Virginia. These retreats helped form a bond that allowed Gottlieb to use cutting-edge laboratories at Camp Detrick and Edgewood Arsenal to develop substances that he could use in mind control experiments.

"Needless layers of interplay and approval were eliminated," Gottlieb later explained. "Little or nothing was reduced to writing, except essential reports. The right hand never knew what the left was doing, unless we wanted it otherwise."

Skillfully wielding the bureaucratic power that came from Dulles's support, Gottlieb consolidated his control over Artichoke-related projects. Dulles and Helms gave him authority to launch whatever experiments he could conceive. Not everyone at the CIA appreciated this. CIA officers who had worked on mind control projects before Gottlieb arrived bristled at his new influence. So did military men at the Chemical Corps, who felt his growing presence and resented it.

"There were CIA people who infiltrated the laboratories," a Camp Detrick researcher fumed years later. "They worked on their own, and I suspect very few people knew that."

In 1952 Gottlieb helped organize a conference at Edgewood Arsenal on "psycho-chemicals as a new concept of war." Panelists—all of them CIA or Chemical Corps officers with the highest security clearance—discussed chemical compounds that could induce mass hysteria, and aerosol techniques by which these compounds could be sprayed over large areas. The speaker who attracted the most attention was L. Wilson Greene, whose advocacy of LSD had been secret. Almost no one in the room knew of it, or had even heard of the drug. He astonished them by describing what he called the "incredible discovery" of an ergot enzyme that could cause symptoms ranging from hallucinations to suicidal tendencies, even when used in infinitesimal quantities. Then he read from a report by a volunteer who wrote that under the drug's influence he had seen "flickering, glimmering, glittering, scintillating, rapid and slow blotting of colors, sparks, whirling, traveling small dots, light flashes and sheet lightning."

Greene ventured a few thoughts about ways that LSD might be used in war. "In targeted urban areas, the cloud from multiple bombs or generating devices would blanket the densest portion," he said. "Saboteurs or intelligence operatives could release psycho-chemicals from hand-operated generators . . . Upcoming field projects will focus on long-distance cloud travel and the behavior of aerosols when released over populated areas."

Before finishing, Greene noted the presence of Frank Olson and other aerosol experts. He called their work "essential for the development of these weapons," and urged others to take advantage of their expertise. One scientist asked him if LSD would be made available in research quantities. Not yet, Greene replied, but soon.

This presentation intrigued but did not satisfy Gottlieb. He was pleased to see that Greene still shared his belief in LSD's earth-shaking potential. Still, a crucial difference remained: Greene imagined LSD as a battlefield weapon; Gottlieb wanted to use it to control minds.

"I was fascinated by the ideas Greene was advancing," he said later. "He was convinced that it was possible to actually win a battle or larger engagement without killing anyone or destroying any property. While I found this a novel approach to war, I was somewhat skeptical about it. But I was intrigued by the potential application of psycho-chemicals to much smaller situations and conflicts. There I saw tremendous promise."

Until Gottlieb's arrival at the CIA, most experimentation with mind control drugs was aimed at finding a "truth serum." As various drugs were found, one by one, to be useless as reliable aids to interrogation, and as their possible value in inducing amnesia was also discounted, they were pushed aside. The same might have happened with LSD. Early experiments showed that while some who took it became docile and uninhibited, others had completely different reactions, imagining themselves super-powerful and fiercely refusing to cooperate. Some had paranoid breakdowns. Scientists who did "Artichoke work" with LSD—mainly at Villa Schuster in Germany and other secret prisons—were forced to conclude that it was not a reliable "truth serum" and did not wipe away memory. Gottlieb, however, was convinced that LSD had powers yet to be understood. It affected the brain in wildly powerful ways. Because it is colorless, tasteless, and odorless, it seemed ideally suited to clandestine use—and, as one CIA psychiatrist put it, "the most fascinating thing about it was that such minute quantities had such a terrific effect."

Another factor driving Gottlieb to pursue research into LSD was the creeping fear that Soviet scientists must also be on the trail. No evidence ever emerged to suggest that they were, but it seemed a reasonable suspicion. The discovery of LSD had been reported in Russian journals. CIA analysts speculated that Soviet scientists might be stockpiling ergot enzymes as raw material.

"Although no Soviet data are available on LSD-25," they concluded in one assessment, "it must be assumed that the scientists of the USSR are thoroughly cognizant of the strategic importance of this powerful new drug, and are capable of producing it at any time."

Gottlieb's burgeoning ambition quickly outpaced his resources. He began outsourcing experiments to Camp Detrick. The officers he deployed there were told not to reveal that they worked for the CIA, and to identify themselves only as a "staff support group." Some army scientists guessed the truth and disapproved.

"Do you know what a 'self-contained, off-the-shelf operation' means?" one of them asked years later. "The CIA was running one in my lab. They were testing psycho-chemicals and running experiments in my labs, and weren't telling me."

Gottlieb's drug experiments were not confined to Washington and Maryland. He traveled regularly in order to observe and participate in "special interrogation" sessions at detention centers abroad. On these missions he had the chance to test his potions on human prisoners.

"In 1951 a team of CIA scientists led by Dr. Gottlieb flew to Tokyo," according to one study. "Four Japanese suspected of working for the Russians were secretly brought to a location where the CIA doctors injected them with a variety of depressants and stimulants . . . Under relentless questioning, they confessed to working for the Russians. They were taken out into Tokyo Bay, shot and dumped overboard. The CIA team flew to Seoul in South Korea and repeated the experiment on twenty-five North Korean prisoners-of-war. They were asked to denounce Communism. They refused and were executed . . . In 1952 Dulles brought Dr. Gottlieb and his team to post-war Munich in southern Germany. They set up a base in a safe house . . . Throughout the winter of 1952–3 scores of 'expendables' were brought to the safe house. They were given massive amounts of drugs, some of which Frank Olson had prepared back at Detrick, to see if their minds could be altered. Others were given electro-convulsive shocks. Each experiment failed. The 'expendables' were killed and their bodies burned."

Months of experiments like these left Gottlieb unsatisfied. He decided he needed to formalize his relationship with the Special Operations Division at Camp Detrick. It had become one of the world's most advanced biochemical laboratories—though few knew this, since all of its work was secret. Its facilities, including the custom-built test chamber known as the Eight Ball, were unmatched anywhere. Gottlieb wanted to use these assets to propel Artichoke to new heights.

For more than a year, under the terms of MK-NAOMI, the Special Operations Division had been doing research and production work for the CIA. Gottlieb asked Dulles to negotiate a formal accord that would allow him to deepen this cooperation. Officially it would link the army's Chemical Corps and the CIA, but its real meaning was narrower. It would bind the small, super-secret units within each organization that did "Artichoke work": the Special Operations Division at Camp Detrick, run by an elite band of army scientists with advanced research capacity, and their handful of CIA counterparts who, under Gottlieb, were planning to take Artichoke in wildly new directions.

"Under an agreement reached with the Army in 1952," Senate investigators wrote years later, "the Special Operations Division at Detrick was to assist the CIA in developing, testing, and maintaining biological agents and delivery systems. By this agreement, CIA acquired the knowledge, skill, and facilities of the Army to develop biological weapons suited for CIA use."

This secret accord gave Gottlieb new momentum. He had already observed the effects of various drugs on himself and his colleagues. From there he had gone on to feed drugs in much larger doses, and under far more torturous conditions, to prisoners and other helpless subjects. That was not enough. He wanted to know more.

One of the luxuries that Gottlieb's interrogators enjoyed was the knowledge that if any "expendables" died during their experiments, disposing of their bodies would be "no problem." This was not always a fully efficient process, as an American translator who worked at Camp King discovered while sunning herself there one weekend in mid-1952. "Arrived back in Frankfurt from Paris Sun. morning in time to spend all day at the Oberursel swimming pool acquiring a nice tan," she wrote in a letter home. "They dragged a dead man out of the pool at 10 AM."

BOHEMIAN EXPATRIATES IN Paris have been drawn to Le Select since it opened in 1925. It is one of the city's classic literary cafés, with art deco flourishes and large windows overlooking Montparnasse. Henry Miller, Emma Goldman, Samuel Beckett, Pablo Picasso, Man Ray, and Luis Buñuel were regulars. So was Ernest Hemingway, who wrote in *The Sun*

Also Rises of carefree lovers who hail taxis near the Seine and tell the driver, "Le Select!" Hart Crane once started a fight at the bar. Isadora Duncan flung a saucer during an argument over the Sacco-Vanzetti trial. With this pedigree, Le Select naturally attracted a young American artist who came to Paris in 1951.

Stanley Glickman had shown artistic talent from childhood. During his high school years in New York, he took advanced classes and won prizes. After arriving in Paris, he enrolled at the Académie de la Grande Chaumière, spent the following summer studying fresco painting in Florence, and then returned to take classes from the modernist master Fernand Léger. His studio was near Le Select, but after a while he came to prefer another café, Le Dôme, just across the Boulevard du Montparnasse. One evening in October 1952, he was drinking coffee there when an acquaintance appeared and invited him over to Le Select. Reluctantly he agreed.

At Le Select, the two joined a group of Americans whose conservative dress set them apart from the rest of the crowd. Talk turned to politics and grew heated. Glickman rose to leave, but one of the men insisted on buying him a last drink to show there were no hard feelings. Glickman said he'd have a glass of Chartreuse, an herbal liqueur. Rather than call the waiter, the man walked to the bar, ordered the Chartreuse himself, and carried it back to their table. He walked with a limp, Glickman later recalled.

The next few minutes were the last of Glickman's productive life. After taking a few sips from his drink, he began to feel what he later called "a lengthening of distance and a distortion of perception." Soon he was hallucinating. Others at the table leaned in, fascinated. One told Glickman he could perform miracles. Finally, overwhelmed by panic and fearing that he had been poisoned, he jumped up and fled.

After awakening the next morning, Glickman was overcome by another wave of hallucinations. Visions overwhelmed his mind. He abandoned his studies and began wandering aimlessly through Montparnasse. One day he walked into Le Select, sat down, and collapsed. An ambulance brought him to the American Hospital, which maintained a confidential relationship with the CIA. Records say he was given sedatives, but he later asserted that he was treated with electroshock and possibly given more hallucinogenic drugs. His Canadian girlfriend arrived after a week and signed him out of the hospital. He sent her back to Canada, warning that she would ruin her life if she stayed with him.

For the next ten months, Glickman lived as a recluse in his garret, refusing to eat for fear of poison. Finally his parents learned of his condition and brought him home. He never recovered. For the rest of his life he lived in an apartment in Manhattan's East Village, with dogs as his only companions. For a time he ran a small antiques shop. He never again painted, read books, worked steadily, or had a romantic relationship.

"Even in an area known for street characters," according to one chronicle, "he cut a striking figure with his shock of white hair and a red-and-black silk scarf, knotted like a cravat. But most of the time, he just sat on his step with a cup of coffee."

If Glickman was the subject of an Artichoke experiment, why did Gottlieb choose him rather than someone else? Coincidence is a logical possibility. The "acquaintance" who lured Glickman into Le Select might simply have noticed him sitting in a café across the street and suggested him as a conveniently available victim. Later investigation, however, raised another possibility.

Several months before his apparent poisoning, Glickman had been treated for hepatitis at the American Hospital. Artichoke researchers were interested in learning whether people with hepatitis might be especially vulnerable to LSD. Glickman would have been the ideal subject for a test. A later CIA memo summarizing results of experiments conducted during the early 1950s includes this conclusion: "Subjects in whom even a slight modification of hepatic function is present make a very marked response to LSD."

As GOTTLIEB'S FAR-FLUNG research project was reaching new extremes, politics intervened to guarantee its future. On November 4, 1952, Americans elected Dwight Eisenhower to the presidency. His victory ensured that Gottlieb would be free to do whatever he could imagine.

One of the few senior officials in Washington with whom Eisenhower had worked closely was the director of central intelligence, General Walter Bedell Smith, who had been his chief of staff during World War II. After taking office, he made Smith undersecretary of state. That left the top CIA job open. Eisenhower considered several candidates and finally chose the one who wanted the job most fervently: Allen Dulles.

What another director might have done with Gottlieb's mind control project—whether he might have sought to curtail or end it—cannot be known. With Dulles secure in power, though, Gottlieb had free rein. As if this were not enough good news, Eisenhower selected Dulles's older brother, John Foster Dulles, as secretary of state. That meant the State Department could be relied upon to support whatever Gottlieb did abroad, including giving "black sites" all the diplomatic cover they needed.

Newly encouraged, Gottlieb pressed ahead with the task he had been given: pursue mind control research as far as it could go. He had already brought several doctors into his orbit and was pushing them to carry out tests on psychoactive drugs. One of them, Paul Hoch of New York Psychiatric Institute, agreed to inject mescaline into one of his patients so its effects could be observed. He chose a forty-two-year-old professional tennis player named Harold Blauer, who had come to him seeking treatment for depression following a divorce.

Beginning on December 5, 1952, one of Hoch's assistants injected Blauer with a concentrated mescaline derivative, without any explanation or warning. Over the next month he was injected five more times. He complained that the treatment was giving him hallucinations and asked that it be ended, but Hoch insisted that he proceed. On January 8, 1953, Blauer was given a dose fourteen times greater than previous ones. The protocol notes that he protested when he was injected at 9:53 a.m. Six minutes later he was flailing wildly. At 10:01 his body stiffened. He was pronounced dead at 12:15.

"We didn't know if it was dog piss or what it was we were giving him," one of the medical assistants later confessed.

Gottlieb's first eighteen months of experiments brought him no closer to understanding how hallucinogenic drugs could be used to control minds. On the contrary, they forced him to confront frustrating realities. These drugs were no "truth serum." The visions they produced often hindered interrogations rather than helping them. Nor were they effective amnesiacs; subjects often realized they had been drugged and remembered the experience afterward. It seemed that another class of drugs could now be added to barbiturates, sedatives, cannabis extract, cocaine, and heroin on the list of those that cannot be reliably used to make people talk.

This left Gottlieb to choose between two conclusions: either there is no such thing as a mind control drug or there is indeed such a thing and it is waiting to be discovered. He had been hired to explore, not to give up. That was also his nature. Like his Artichoke comrades, he believed he could find a way to control human minds. Before any of the others, he concluded that it lay within LSD. He recognized it as a highly complex substance, believed it might have decisive value in clandestine work, and was determined to study it further.

Once Allen Dulles was installed as director of central intelligence, Gottlieb's bureaucratic ambition grew. He knew Dulles would support any project he proposed. What would that be? This was a period when Gottlieb was conducting his own "self-experimentation" with LSD, so his imagination was fertile. He reflected on the broadening ambition of CIA mind control projects. This was the moment, he decided, to broaden it further.

Gottlieb conceived the idea of a new project that would subsume Artichoke and give him authority over all CIA research into mind control. With this mandate, he would test every imaginable drug and technique, plus some not yet imagined. He would be free not only to experiment on "expendables" at secret prisons abroad, but also to feed LSD to witting and unwitting Americans. From there he would go on to test, study, and investigate every substance or method that might be used as a tool to control minds. All experiments would be conducted under the umbrella of a single program that he would run.

Richard Helms, now chief of operations for the CIA's Directorate of Plans, shared Gottlieb's enthusiasm. Together they composed a memorandum for Dulles describing what this program would aim to do.

Gottlieb was about to launch the most systematic and widest-ranging mind control project ever undertaken by any government. At the same time, he was assuming his other important role: poisoner in chief. They fit together well. Gottlieb was the CIA's senior chemist. He had directed the application of unknowable quantities and varieties of drugs into living humans. As a result of those experiments, he knew as much as any American about the effects of toxins on the human body. If CIA officers or anyone else in the U.S. government needed poison, he was the logical person to produce it.

On the evening of March 30, 1953, Allen Dulles sat down for dinner at his Georgetown home with one of his senior officers, James Kronthal. The two men had been OSS comrades in Europe and remained close. On this night, Dulles had most unpleasant news. He told Kronthal that CIA security officers—two of whom were eavesdropping at that moment— had discovered his awful secret. He was a pedophile who had been compromised on film and blackmailed into working as a double agent, first for the Nazis and then for the Soviets.

Dulles spoke sadly about the ways personal compulsion can destroy careers. The two men parted around midnight. Security officers accompanied Kronthal home. Later that morning he was found dead in his second-floor bedroom. The CIA security director, Colonel Sheffield Edwards, wrote in his report that "an empty vial had been found by the body, and the presumption was that he had taken poison." Years later, one of that era's CIA security officers, Robert Crowley, surmised what had happened—and who had made the poison.

"Allen probably had a special potion prepared that he gave to Kronthal," Crowley said. "Dr. Sidney Gottlieb and the medical people produced all kinds of poisons that a normal postmortem could not detect."

While that dramatic episode was unfolding, Gottlieb and Helms were working on their memorandum proposing that the CIA launch a newly broadened mind control project. Helms sent it to Dulles on April 3—just four days after Dulles hosted Kronthal's farewell dinner.

A redacted version of this memo has been declassified. In it, Helms reports that an "extremely sensitive" research project "has been actively under way since the middle of 1952 and has gathered considerable momentum in the last few months." He recommends that this project be expanded to include experiments of "such an ultra-sensitive nature that they cannot and should not be handled by means of contracts which would associate

CIA or the Government with the work in question." These experiments "lie entirely within two well-defined fields of endeavor."

(a) to develop a capability in the covert use of biological and chemical materials. This area includes the production of various physiological conditions which could support present or future clandestine operations. Aside from the offensive potential, the development of a comprehensive capability in this field of covert chemical and biological warfare gives us a thorough knowledge of the enemies [sic] theoretical potential, thus enabling us to defend ourselves against a foe who might not be as restrained in the use of these techniques as we are. For example: we intend to investigate the development of a chemical material which causes a reversible non-toxic aberrant mental state, the specific nature of which can be reasonably well predicted for each individual. This material could potentially aid in discrediting individuals, eliciting information, implanting suggestion and other forms of mental control.

(b) [redacted]

On April 10, 1953, as Dulles was considering this proposal, he described it in a revealing speech to a group of his fellow Princeton University alumni gathered in Hot Springs, Virginia. He couched his revelations in an ingenious disguise, claiming to be speaking about a Soviet project rather than an American one. No one in the room could have cracked the code as he was speaking. From the perspective of history, however, it is clear that his words applied precisely to the experiments that CIA officers and Camp Detrick scientists were carrying out at that moment, and that were about to become even more intense.

Dulles began his speech by asking "whether we realize how sinister the battle for men's minds has become." He avoided mentioning the techniques his men were using, but did refer to "endless interrogation by teams of brutal interrogators while the victims are being deprived of sleep." The goal of this and other forms of abuse, he said, was "the perversion of the minds of selected individuals, who are subjected to such treatment that they are deprived of the ability to state their own thoughts . . . Parrot-like, the individuals so conditioned can repeat thoughts which have been implanted in their mind by suggestion from outside. In effect, the brain under these circumstances becomes a phonograph playing a disc put on its spindle by an outside genius, over which he has no control."

> We might call it, in its new form, "brain warfare." The target of this warfare is the minds of men on a collective and on an individual basis. Its aim is to condition the mind so that it no longer reacts on a free will or rational basis, but a response to impulses implanted from outside . . . The human mind is the most delicate of instruments. It is so finely adjusted, so susceptible to the impact of outside influences, that it is proving malleable in the hands of sinister men. The Soviets are now using brain perversion as one of their main weapons in prosecuting the Cold War. Some of these techniques are so subtle and so abhorrent to our way of life that we have recoiled from facing up to them.

Dulles finished his speech with a plaintive lament. "We in the West are somewhat handicapped in brain warfare," he said. "We have no human guinea pigs to try these extraordinary techniques."

The opposite was true. Dulles was claiming moral high ground by saying that he, the CIA, and the government of the United States would never stoop to brutal experiments on unwilling human subjects. Through his Bluebird and Artichoke projects, however, he had been conducting such experiments for two years. Dulles never recoiled from the most extreme implications of "brain warfare." The memo Helms had sent him proposed just the kind of no-holds-barred project he wanted to launch.

"It was fashionable among that group to fancy that they were rather impersonal about dangers, risks, and human life," one of the early CIA men, Ray Cline, said years later. "Helms would think it sentimental and foolish to be against something like this."

Under Gottlieb's direction, with Dulles's encouragement and Helms's bureaucratic protection, Artichoke had become one of the most violently abusive projects ever sponsored by an agency of the United States government. The time had come, Dulles now agreed, to intensify and systematize it. Gottlieb had proven himself. He was ready for a new responsibility, unique in American history. Only a handful of people knew he was assuming it.

On April 13, 1953, Dulles formally approved the research project Helms had proposed ten days before. That made Gottlieb America's mind control czar. He set to work with three assets: a starting budget of $300,000, not subject to financial controls; permission to launch research and conduct experiments at will, "without the signing of the usual contracts or other written agreements"; and a new cryptonym. Tradecraft dictates that cryptonyms should have no meaning, so that if discovered they provide no clue about the project they describe. Nonetheless Dulles could not resist giving this new project a name that reflected what he called its "ultra-sensitive nature." Gottlieb's project would be called MK-ULTRA.

5

Abolishing Consciousness

Making the wrong friend in New York during the early 1950s led some people into psychic shock. They were brought to an apartment at 81 Bedford Street in Greenwich Village and given drinks laced with LSD. As they careened through their hallucinogenic trips, CIA operatives monitored their reactions. These unfortunates were unwitting subjects in one of the first MK-ULTRA experiments.

The man Sidney Gottlieb hired to direct this operation, George Hunter White, stands out even in the dazzling MK-ULTRA cast of obsessed chemists, coldhearted spymasters, grim torturers, hypnotists, electro-shockers, and Nazi doctors. He was a hard-charging narcotics detective who lived large in the twilight world of crime and drugs. When Gottlieb offered him a job running a CIA "safe house" where he would dose unsuspecting visitors with LSD and record the results, he jumped at the chance. He imagined that it would be another wild episode in his long series of undercover exploits. It was that and more.

White stood five feet seven inches, weighed over two hundred pounds, and shaved his head. Writers have described him as "fat and bull-like," a "vastly obese slab of a man" who looked like "an extremely menacing bowling ball." His first wife, who divorced him in 1945, called him "a fat slob." He regularly used illegal drugs, keeping for himself a share of whatever he confiscated. His consumption of alcohol—often a full bottle of gin with dinner—was legendary. His other appetite was sexual fetish, especially sadomasochism and high heels. He bought his second wife a closet full of boots, and patronized prostitutes who bound and whipped him. One of his few emotional bonds was with his pet canary. He loved to hold and stroke it. When the bird died, he was deeply pained. "Poor little bastard just couldn't make it," he wrote in his diary. "I don't know if I'll ever get another bird or pet. It's tough on everyone when they die."

After several years as a crime reporter for the *San Francisco Call Bulletin*, White joined the Federal Bureau of Narcotics. Quickly he became one of its crack agents. He made national headlines in 1937 by busting a Chinese American opium ring, supposedly after being initiated into the gang and agreeing to "death by fire" if he ever betrayed its secrets. The men's magazine *True* lionized him in a stirring article headlined WHEN THE ROOKIE TOOK THE TONG. He cultivated his image and lost no chance to enhance it. Sometimes he invited reporters to accompany him on raids.

Without quitting the narcotics bureau, White joined the Office of Strategic Services when World War II broke out. He was sent for paramilitary training at a secret base in Ontario called Camp X, which he later called a "school of murder and mayhem." After completing the course, he became a trainer himself. Several of his trainees went on to long careers at the CIA, including Richard Helms, Frank Wisner, and James Jesus Angleton. Later he was posted to India, where he supposedly killed a Japanese spy with his own hands. He also helped direct OSS "truth serum" experiments in which prisoners were fed various drugs to test their value as aids to interrogation.

During the post-war years, White found a new kind of notoriety by leading the narcotics bureau's campaign against jazz in New York City. He spied on musicians he suspected of using drugs, entrapped them, arrested them, and arranged for them to lose the cabaret cards they needed to perform in New York. In 1949 he made national headlines by arresting Billie Holiday for possession of opium. She insisted that she had been clean for a year and accused White of planting evidence. A jury acquitted her, but the ordeal and White's relentless pressure helped fuel her decline toward early death.

In 1950, White went to work for Senator Joseph McCarthy's committee investigating supposed Communist influence in the State Department. From there he moved to another committee, chaired by Senator Estes Kefauver, that was investigating organized crime. He proved reckless, leaking allegations that both President Truman and Governor Thomas Dewey of New York were tied to the Mafia. Kefauver fired him after less than a year. He was ready for a new adventure when Gottlieb called.

These two Americans, both masters of covert power, could hardly have been more different. White was an adrenaline-driven libertine with a sadistic streak who was rarely sober and reveled in life at the violent fringes of society. Gottlieb was a scientist who ate yogurt. At this moment, though, they fit together well. Gottlieb was looking for someone with street smarts who knew how to bend and break the law while seeming to enforce it. White knew that and more.

White's circle of dubious acquaintances gave him a rich pool of potential subjects for drug experiments. He was accustomed to treating people roughly. He could be relied upon to keep secrets. Since he was still on the payroll of the narcotics bureau, the CIA could deny any connection to him if something went wrong. These qualities made him an ideal partner.

Gottlieb had already tested LSD on volunteers and unsuspecting victims. He was about to begin distributing it to hospitals and medical schools for controlled experiments. In order to learn more about how ordinary people would react to it, he decided to open a "safe house" inside the United States. The subjects would be a new kind of "expendable." Many of those White brought to his "safe house" at 81 Bedford Street were drug users, petty criminals, and others who could be relied upon not to complain about what had happened to them.

The few people who knew about MK-ULTRA considered it crucial to America's survival. Limiting its scope out of concern for a few lives—or even for a few hundred or more—would have seemed to them not simply absurd but treasonous. The "safe house" in New York epitomized this moral bargain.

Allen Dulles had given Gottlieb an almost laughably daunting assignment: discover a wonder drug to defeat freedom's enemies and save the world. It was a supreme challenge to the scientific imagination. Gottlieb was as ready for it as any American.

In May 1952, soon after hearing of White from a colleague at the Technical Services Staff, Gottlieb invited him to Washington for a chat. They talked about the OSS—both its "truth serum" experiments and its fabled Division 19, the gadget shop where artisans crafted silent pistols, poison dart guns, and other tools of the trade. Then the conversation turned to LSD. Gottlieb was surprised to hear how much White knew about it, reflecting the extent of the narcotics bureau's secret experimentation.

White offered to show Gottlieb how he worked. The two of them drove to New Haven, Connecticut, where White was building a case against a businessman who he suspected was a heroin wholesaler. The trip, Gottlieb recalled later, "really gave us a chance to discuss matters of interest." It exposed him to a new world and left him smitten. White, he said, "was always armed to the teeth with all sort of weapons; he could be gruff and loutish, vulgar even, but then turn urbane to a point of eloquence." The CIA did not normally employ people like him.

"We were Ivy League, white, middle class," one of Gottlieb's colleagues later explained. "We were naïve, totally naïve about this, and he felt pretty expert. He knew the whores, the pimps, the people who brought in the drugs . . . He was a pretty wild man."

White married his vivacious second wife, Albertine, in 1951. She shared many of his interests and joined him in group sex, fetish scenes involving leather boots, and the drugging of their friends and other unwitting subjects. By one account she "turned a blind eye to her husband's deviant behavior" and "thoroughly enjoyed the fast company her husband kept." Decades later, a researcher confronted her with the report of a woman who had a mental breakdown after the Whites apparently fed her LSD at their Greenwich Village apartment. He reported that Albertine "descended into a string of expletives that would have embarrassed a sailor. Her tirade left this writer with the firm impression that she was thoroughly capable of having been White's accomplice in his dirty work."

In 1952 the Whites hosted a Thanksgiving dinner party for the CIA counterintelligence chief, James Jesus Angleton, who a decade earlier had been George's student at the OSS "school for mayhem and murder" in Ontario. The next evening the two men met again, this time to drink gin and tonics laced with LSD. They took a taxi to a Chinese restaurant. After they were served, according to White's diary, they began "laughing about something I can't remember now" and "never got around to eating a bite."

Gottlieb spent these months shuttling back and forth between the United States and "safe houses" abroad. Many of his experiments served his focused interest in LSD. This was also the time when Stanley Glickman was drugged in Paris. Even these far-flung experiments, however, did not bring the results Gottlieb wanted. George Hunter White opened a new world. Soon after they met, Gottlieb asked if White would like to work with him. White was interested. Indiscreetly, he recorded the offer in his diary.

"Gottlieb proposes I be a CIA consultant," White wrote. "I agree."

Before Gottlieb could seal their partnership, he faced an unexpected problem. CIA officers in Washington delayed White's application for security clearance. Part of the problem, as White suspected, was cultural. "A couple of crew-cut, pipe-smoking punks had either known me or heard of me during the OSS days, and had decided I was 'too rough' for their league and promptly blackballed me," he wrote later. The delay also reflected Gottlieb's bureaucratic challenge. He was assuming control of what was arguably the American government's most important covert program. It was natural that others in the CIA would resist. The Office of Scientific Intelligence sought to establish control over some aspects of MK-ULTRA. So did the Office of Security. Morse Allen, who had helped run both the Bluebird and Artichoke projects, was in no mood to withdraw. Allen Dulles faithfully supported Gottlieb in these turf battles, but he could not ignore grumbling from senior officers who had reason to resent this newcomer's growing power. They showed their unhappiness by taking a year to approve White's security clearance.

When approval finally came, Gottlieb traveled to New York to deliver the good news in person. He brought a check to cover start-up costs. White used the first $3,400 as a deposit for his lair at 81 Bedford Street.

"CIA—got final clearance and sign contract as 'consultant'—met Gottlieb," White wrote in his diary on June 8, 1953.

The Bedford Street complex was about to become something unique: a CIA "safe house" in the heart of New York to which unsuspecting citizens would be lured and surreptitiously drugged, with the goal of finding ways to fight Communism. It was comprised of two adjoining apartments. Surveillance equipment allowed observers in one to record what was happening in the other. Gottlieb already had "safe houses" abroad where he could drug people as he wished. Now he had one in New York.

That fall, White began prowling Greenwich Village for people he could befriend and then secretly dose with LSD or other drugs. He invented an alias, Morgan Hall, and a couple of fake life stories. "He posed alternately as a merchant seaman or a bohemian artist, and consorted with a vast array of underworld characters, all of whom were involved in vice, including drugs, prostitution, gambling, and pornography," according to one survey of White's career. "It was under this assumed, bohemian artist persona that White would entrap most of his MK-ULTRA victims."

Some of the people White dosed with LSD were his friends, including one who ran Vixen Press, which specialized in fetish and lesbian pulp. Other victims included young women who had the misfortune to cross his path. His diary suggests how they reacted: "Gloria gets horror . . . Janet sky high." White was sufficiently impressed with the power of LSD to begin calling it Stormy in his diary entries. Nonetheless he continued giving it to anyone he could lure into his den. "I was angry at George for that," the Vixen Press publisher said years later. "It turned out to be a bad thing to do to people, but we didn't realize it at the time."

White's connections protected him from exposure. The victim of one of his experiments staggered into Lenox Hill Hospital afterward, claiming she had been drugged. After a couple of hours, she was told that she was probably mistaken and quietly discharged. Episodes like these were kept quiet because the CIA had, as one account put it, "arranged an accommodation with the medical department of the New York City Police Department to protect White from any hassles."

The opening of the "safe house" on Bedford Street contributed to festering tension between the CIA and FBI. Some CIA officers thought of the FBI as a haven for dumb cops and ham-fisted thugs. FBI agents, returning the favor, considered CIA men amateurish prima donnas and, as one put it, "mostly rich boys, trust fund snobs who thought they were God's answer to all the world's ills." Allen Dulles and the FBI director, J. Edgar Hoover, were fierce bureaucratic rivals. It would have been unlike Hoover to complain about the "safe house," but also unlike him not to have learned of it. The news came in a report from his New York office just three weeks after White paid the deposit.

"A confidential informant of this office advised on July 1st that his former supervisor in the Bureau of Narcotics, George White . . . has become associated with the CIA in an 'ultra-secret' assignment as a consultant," the report said. "White and CIA have rented dual apartments at 81 Bedford Street, New York City. In one of these apartments has been set up a bar and quarters for entertainment, while the other apartment is being used by the CIA for the purpose of taking motion pictures through an x-ray mirror of the activities in the former apartment."

Gottlieb closely supervised this operation. He and White met regularly, in Washington and in New York. Their personal bond grew. White had taken up leatherworking as a hobby, and when Gottlieb celebrated his thirty-sixth birthday on August 3, 1954, White gave him a handcrafted belt as a gift.

Folk dancing had become one of Gottlieb's passions, and he sometimes invited colleagues to try a few steps with him. Not all were willing. White was. Gottlieb taught him to dance a jig, and they delighted friends by showing it off. These partners, one clubfooted and the other obese, danced together as they were launching their covert LSD experiments. White's expense reports for the "safe house" at 81 Bedford Street, meticulously submitted to the Technical Services Staff, bear a clearly legible counter-signature: "Sidney Gottlieb, Chief / Chemical Division TSS."

GOTTLIEB AND HIS CIA comrades were hardly the only Americans who believed during 1953 that the world was facing apocalypse. Many others agreed. MK-ULTRA was conceived and launched as Americans were succumbing to deep fears.

"That period, up until about 1954, was a wild and woolly time at the CIA," one retired CIA officer recalled decades later. "It was the old OSS mentality: 'Go out and do it. Doesn't matter if it's a good or bad idea, go do it. We're at war, so anything is justified. We're smarter than most people, we operate in secret, we have access to intelligence, and we know what the real threats are. No one else does.'"

The espionage saga of Julius and Ethel Rosenberg reached its climax during those months. Their trial and conviction on charges of stealing nuclear secrets for the Soviet Union shook the nation. Early in 1953 they appealed for stays of execution. President Eisenhower refused. So did the Supreme Court. The Rosenbergs were executed on June 19. Their case fed a terrifying sense that enemies had penetrated America's inner sanctums.

At the same time, new dangers were said to be emerging abroad. Americans were told that their country was battling the Soviet Union for survival, and that the battle was not going well. "You can look around the whole circle of the world," John Foster Dulles asserted shortly before taking office as secretary of state in 1953, "and you find one spot after another after another after another where the question is: Are we going to lose this part of the world?" The new Eisenhower administration, guided by the Dulles brothers, saw urgent threats emerging from the defiant "third world." A leftist government had been elected in Guatemala. Rebels in Vietnam were intensifying their campaign against the French colonial regime. Prime Minister Mohammad Mossadegh of Iran had nationalized his country's oil reserves. These challenges to Western power were portrayed in the United States not as symptoms of rising nationalism in the developing world, but as coordinated salvoes in Moscow's war of global conquest.

As the crises in Guatemala, Vietnam, and Iran intensified, an anti-Communist uprising broke out in East Berlin. Workers seized government buildings. When local police refused to intervene, Soviet tanks did the dirty work. Leaders of the uprising were arrested, tried, and executed. Americans were told that this could be their fate if Communism continued its march.

Another episode that shocked the CIA was kept secret. In late 1952, two CIA aviators, John Downey and Richard Fecteau, were captured after being shot down while on a clandestine mission over China. The "Red Chinese" offered to release them if the United States would admit publicly that they had been working for the CIA. Eisenhower refused, and the two aviators languished in prison until President Richard Nixon finally admitted the truth two decades later. At the CIA, minds ran wild as officers imagined the exotic tortures to which Chinese interrogators must be subjecting the two prisoners. They falsely presumed that the

Chinese were doing what they themselves were doing: using prisoners as subjects for grotesque drug and mind control experiments.

These frightening events confirmed the existential dread that led Allen Dulles, Richard Helms, and Sidney Gottlieb to justify the extremes of MK-ULTRA. The narrative of encirclement and imminent danger that Americans were fed was distant from reality, but it seized hearts in Washington and had profound effects. It allowed the CIA to convince itself that it was waging a purely defensive war. In its collective mind-set, nothing it did was aggressive. It justified all of its projects, even those that caused immense pain to individuals and nations, as necessary to block Communism's relentless expansion.

At the time Allen Dulles set MK-ULTRA in motion, he was also preparing several other covert operations that would have earth-shattering effects. He sent the chief of his Tehran station $1 million for use "in any way that would bring about the fall of Mossadegh," and by August his men had deposed the Iranian prime minister in the first CIA coup. Immediately he began planning to duplicate the feat in Guatemala. He also expanded the CIA station in Vietnam and intensified operations aimed at fomenting anti-Soviet uprisings in Eastern Europe. In his mind, these projects all fit together. MK-ULTRA was just as integral a part of Dulles's secret world war as any plot against a foreign government.

Even as mind control experiments reached new extremes, and as their human toll began to rise, none of the CIA officers familiar with MK-ULTRA is known to have raised any objection. The CIA's partners in the Special Operations Division, however, were part of the Chemical Corps and therefore under army command. Senior officers at the Pentagon were intensely interested in LSD and other chemicals that they believed could become weapons of war. They had no more desire to limit or curtail experiments than did their CIA counterparts. Worthwhile results, they told Secretary of Defense Charles Wilson in one memo, "could not be obtained unless human volunteers were utilized." Wilson came from a civilian background—he had run General Motors before taking over the Pentagon—and sought restraint. He wanted assurances that human subjects in drug experiments were truly volunteers who had given informed consent, as required by the Nuremberg Code. In mid-1953 he issued a secret directive requiring that before any military unit conducted an experiment on human beings, both the secretary of defense and the secretary of the relevant service must be informed in writing. This rule was more honored in the breach than the observance. Some military units were told of it only orally. Others never heard of it. During the early 1950s, the secretary of the army received at least six requests to authorize experiments on human volunteers. During that same period, however, the army's Special Operations Division was working with Gottlieb on many other experiments that, under the "Wilson Memorandum," should have been reported. So far as is known, none was.

The Special Operations Division was an invaluable MK-ULTRA partner. Its scientists compounded chemicals that CIA officers administered to prisoners in "special interrogation" sessions at secret prisons around the world. Some of them also worked with the CIA's Technical Services Staff to develop gadgets that field agents could use to carry out drug attacks. Much of the science behind them came from experiments on human subjects.

"SOD developed darts coated with biological agents, and pills containing several different biological agents which could remain potent for weeks or months," Senate investigators later reported. "SOD also developed a special gun for firing darts coated with a chemical which could allow CIA agents to incapacitate a guard dog, enter an installation secretly, and return the dog to consciousness when leaving. SOD scientists were unable to develop a similar incapacitant for humans."

AMERICANS SHOULD HAVE been able to celebrate the release of 7,200 soldiers from Communist prisons after an armistice ended the fighting in Korea in July 1953. Instead they recoiled in shock. Many prisoners, it turned out, had written statements criticizing the United States or praising Communism. Some had confessed to committing war crimes. Twenty-one chose to stay behind in North Korea or China. The Pentagon announced that they were considered deserters and would be executed if found.

Most astonishing of all, several pilots among the released prisoners asserted that they had dropped bio-weapons from their warplanes—contradicting Washington's fierce insistence that it had never deployed such weapons. "The most-used germ bomb was a 500-pounder," one pilot reported. "Each had several compartments to hold different kinds of germs. Insects like fleas and spiders were kept separate from rats and voles." These allegations set off a new burst of denials from Washington. Gottlieb, as chief of the Chemical Division, was commissioned to prepare a "press pack" to refute them. In it, two "acknowledged independent experts," both of whom were Gottlieb's friends, wrote that believing the Americans had used germ warfare in Korea was equivalent to believing that "flying saucers have landed."

How could American soldiers have turned their back on duty and sullied their country's honor? A stunned nation struggled for explanations. *Time* examined the defectors' backgrounds and concluded that poor upbringing or emotional problems explained their behavior. *Newsweek* described them as "shifty-eyed and groveling," and said they had betrayed their country in exchange for better treatment, because they had fallen in love with Asian women, or because of the appeal of "homosexualism." Several commentators warned that they represented the weakening of American masculinity and its replacement by a generation of "pampered kids" and "mama's boys."

Beyond the nation's spiritual decline and the feminization of its men, another theory quickly emerged: "brainwashing." In the three years since the propagandist Edward Hunter had invented the term, it had become the last-resort explanation for everything inexplicable. In the minds of most Americans, nothing was more inexplicable than for any of their strapping young men to decide that living under Communism could be better than living in the United States. "Brainwashing" was the easiest and most obvious explanation. The headline over an article in the *New Republic* crystallized American fears: COMMUNIST BRAINWASHING—ARE WE PREPARED?

The shocking behavior of American prisoners convinced many Americans that "brainwashing" existed and had become part of the Communist arsenal. Another aspect of the prisoners' return, which was not made public, intensified fears within the CIA. "Interrogations of the individuals who had come out of North Korea across the Soviet Union to freedom recently had apparently a 'blank' period or period of disorientation while passing through a special zone in Manchuria," a CIA officer wrote in a memo to the Special Operations Division. "This had occurred to all individuals in the party after they had had their first full meal and first coffee . . . Drugging was indicated."

There was no more evidence of this than there was of "brainwashing." Inside the CIA and other security agencies in Washington, however, these reports were taken as further proof that Communist scientists were ahead of their Western counterparts in the race to discover and deploy psychoactive drugs. They also, for the first time, connected the name Manchuria with mind control—a connection that would soon burst into public consciousness.

In the years after fighting ended in Korea, most of the American defectors trickled home. Several spoke about their captivity. None reported that they had been subjected to any pressure that could be described as "brainwashing." Their decisions to defect were the result of individual combinations of anger at the inequalities of American life, desire for adventure, and traditional forms of coercion. In the conformist America of that era, though, "brainwashing" was a magnificently convenient explanation for every form of human behavior that people did not understand.

The CIA fell hard for this fantasy. "There is ample evidence in the reports of innumerable interrogations that the Communists were utilizing drugs, physical duress, electric shock, and possibly hypnosis against their enemies," the chief of the CIA's medical staff wrote in a memo that reflected the panic of that moment. "With such evidence it is difficult not to keep from becoming rabid about our apparent laxity. We are forced by this mounting evidence to assume a more aggressive role in the development of these techniques."

As SIDNEY GOTTLIEB began spreading money to the researchers he had contracted to study LSD, he encountered a predictable problem: supply. Sandoz held the patent, but it was a Swiss company and beyond CIA control. Intelligence reports suggested that Sandoz was already selling large quantities to the Soviet Union and other Communist countries. These reports were false, but they sent shock waves through the CIA.

"[It] is awfully hard in this day and age to reproduce how frightening all of this was to us at the time," one CIA officer testified decades later. "But we were literally terrified, because this was the one material that we had been able to locate that really had potential fantastic possibilities if used wrongly."

In mid-1953 a CIA officer was dispatched to Basel to solve this problem.

He returned with a report asserting that Sandoz had ten kilograms of LSD on hand, which he correctly called "a fantastically large amount." Dulles approved the expenditure of $240,000 to buy it all—the world's entire supply. The two officers he sent to pick it up, however, quickly discovered that their colleague had confused kilograms with grams. Sandoz had manufactured a total of less than forty grams, of which ten were still in stock.

This confusion led Gottlieb to decide that MK-ULTRA needed a reliable supply of LSD—and a pledge from Sandoz that it would not sell any to the Soviets. Sandoz was happy to cooperate. It did so not out of sympathy for CIA mind control projects, about which it knew nothing, but to rid itself of its "problem child." A CIA officer who was sent to Basel reported that Sandoz was "sorry they had discovered this material, since it had been the source of many headaches and bother." As soon as Gottlieb learned that Sandoz had no desire to protect LSD, he secretly began paying an American pharmaceutical company, Eli Lilly, to try to break its chemical code. The company's scientists went to work immediately.

With a scientist's ordered mind, Gottlieb designed a system for organizing the multi-faceted research that was at the heart of MK-ULTRA. He called each of his contracts a "subproject" and assigned it a number. During 1953 he launched more than a dozen. The "safe house" in New York was Subproject 3. Paying scientists at Eli Lilly to break the chemical code of LSD was Subproject 6. Other early "subprojects" were aimed at studying non-chemical means of mind control, including by what one report called "social psychology, group psychology, psychotherapy, hypnosis, sudden religious conversion, and sleep and sensory deprivation."

From the earliest days of MK-ULTRA, Gottlieb and his fellow scientists were tantalized by the potential of hypnosis. They saw it as holding out the promise of an exquisite refinement in the art of political murder. A hypnotized killer could carry out his crime and then forget who had ordered it—or even that he had committed it.

Americans took hypnosis seriously during the early Cold War. In 1950 a Colgate University psychiatrist, George Estabrooks, asserted in the popular magazine *Argosy* that he had the ability to "hypnotize a man—without his knowledge or consent—into committing treason against the United States." That attracted the CIA's attention. After MK-ULTRA was launched, Estabrooks wrote a memo to the CIA saying he could create a "hypnotic messenger" who would be unable to betray a secret mission because "he has no conscious knowledge of what that mission may be." He also offered to take a group of human subjects and "establish in them through the use of hypnotism, the condition of split personality." The CIA officer who received this memo judged it "very important." Estabrooks went on to become a CIA consultant.

In 1953 Morse Allen, who also believed fervently in the potential of hypnosis, ordered the production of a short film called *The Black Art*, for showing to CIA employees only. It depicts an American intelligence officer drugging and hypnotizing an Asian diplomat. In a trance, the diplomat enters his embassy, removes documents from a safe, and turns them over to his handler. The film ends with a persuasive voice-over: "Could what you have just seen be accomplished without the individual's knowledge? Yes. Against an individual's will? Yes. How? Through the powers of suggestion and hypnosis."

This contradicted what many scientists believed. During World War II the OSS had consulted psychiatrists who studied hypnosis. One of them, Lawrence Kubie, who had worked with George Hunter White on "truth serum" experiments, replied that he was "skeptical that it will accomplish anything." Two others, Karl and William Menninger, who ran a highly regarded psychiatric clinic in Kansas, were even more emphatic. "There is no evidence that supports post-hypnotic acts, especially when the individual's mores and morals produce the slightest conflict within him," they concluded. "A man to whom murder is repugnant and immoral cannot be made to override that personal taboo."

Those conclusions did not tell Gottlieb what he wanted to hear. He was determined to investigate the potential of hypnosis under clinical conditions. One of his first ventures was MK-ULTRA Subproject 5, under which a researcher at the University of Minnesota, Alden Sears, conducted a "carefully planned series" of hypnosis experiments on about one hundred subjects. Discretion was guaranteed since, as Gottlieb wrote in a memo, both Sears and his boss, the chairman of the Psychiatry Department, were "cleared through TOP SECRET and are aware of the real purposes of the project." In the same memo, Gottlieb listed the areas he wanted Subproject 5 to investigate.

- Hypnotically induced anxieties;
- Hypnotically increasing the ability to learn and recall complex written matter;
- Polygraph response under hypnosis;
- Hypnotically increasing ability to observe and recall a complex arrangement of physical objects;
- Relationship of personality to susceptibility to hypnosis;
- Recall of hypnotically acquired information by very specific signals.

Despite his avid interest in hypnosis and other possible paths to mind control, Gottlieb never strayed far from his conviction that the most likely path lay through psychoactive drugs, especially LSD. After launching his first hypnosis "subproject," he conceived the idea of another in which hypnotism, drugs, and sensory deprivation would be tested in combination. As his contractor he enlisted Dr. Louis Jolyon "Jolly" West, chairman of the Psychology Department at the University of Oklahoma. West was researching ways to create "dissociative states" in which the human mind could be pulled from its moorings. In his proposal to Gottlieb, he reported that "experiments involving altered personality function as a result of environmental manipulation (chiefly sensory isolation) have yielded promising leads." Gottlieb urged him to go further. The result was Subproject 43, in which West tested what he called "the actions of a variety of new drugs which alter the state of psychological functioning." At least some of these tests were conducted in a "unique laboratory [with] a special chamber in which all psychologically significant aspects of the environment can be controlled . . . In this setting the various hypnotic, pharmacologic, and sensory-environmental variables will be manipulated in a controlled fashion." The CIA paid $20,800 to build the laboratory and support West's research.

Whether directing experiments with drugs, hypnosis, sensory deprivation, or combinations of all three, Gottlieb was searching for a kind of magic. All of his "subprojects" were aimed at finding potions or techniques that could be used to disorient, confuse, and control people. That led him to MK-ULTRA Subproject 4: bringing magic to the CIA.

6

Any Effort to Tamper with This Project, MK-ULTRA, Is Not Permitted

A birdcage disappears into thin air, along with the bird inside. Wilted flowers burst into bloom. A paper napkin is ripped into pieces, the pieces are scattered, and as they float toward the floor they join back together. Olives are transformed into lumps of sugar. Rarer feats follow: the Cantonese Card Trick, the Curious Handkerchief Trick, the Multiplying Thimble Trick.

John Mulholland mystified and amazed crowds in dozens of countries. Following the death of Harry Houdini, his mentor, Mulholland became America's most celebrated magician. Throngs packed grand auditoriums like Radio City Music Hall to watch him do the impossible. Society grandees hired him to astonish guests at private parties. His circle of friends and admirers included Orson Welles, Jean Harlow, Dorothy Parker, Harold Lloyd, Jimmy Durante, and Eddie Cantor. For more than twenty years he edited the *Sphinx*, a professional journal for conjurers, illusionists, and prestidigitators. His library on these and related subjects contained more than six thousand volumes. After his death, the magician David Copperfield bought it.

Mulholland wrote nearly a dozen books himself, with titles like *The Art of Illusion* and *Quicker Than the Eye*. He performed for the king of Romania, the sultan of Sulu, and Eleanor Roosevelt. When not writing or performing, he devoted himself to unmasking fraudulent spiritualists and psychics, often by dramatically revealing their tricks. His mastery of technique and movement was unsurpassed in the world of magic.

The thousands who paid Mulholland to baffle and delight them were not his only admirers. On April 13, 1953—the day MK-ULTRA was formally set into motion—Sidney Gottlieb was in New York to meet him. Theirs was a wonderfully conceived collaboration. Gottlieb's team knew how to compound poisons and concentrate them into pills, capsules, sprays, powders, and drops. Intrepid CIA officers or their agents could bring one of these poisons into the close proximity of a target. The final challenge remained: training officers to administer the poison.

Mulholland was a master of what he called "the psychology of deception." He was also haunted by the fact that rheumatic fever had disqualified him from military service in World War I. Among his writings are profiles of magicians who used their skills to serve their countries, including Jean-Eugène Robert-Houdin, who helped suppress an uprising in Algeria by persuading tribesmen that French magic was stronger than theirs, and Jasper Maskelyne, who designed large-scale illusions to disguise British troop positions in North Africa during World War II. Mulholland was yearning for a way to do patriotic service. Gottlieb gave it to him.

"John was an American and he loved his country, and the fact that he worked for an intelligence agency run by our government made him very proud," a friend recalled years later. "He said yes because his government asked him to."

During his meeting with Gottlieb, Mulholland agreed to teach CIA officers how to distract victims' attention so drugs could be given to them without anyone's noticing. "Our interest was in sleight-of-hand practices, in the art of surreptitious delivery or removal," Gottlieb said later. "Those that were trained became pretty good at it. In some ways, the training was a welcomed relief from more serious matters."

Gottlieb also asked Mulholland to consider writing a manual in which "sleight-of-hand practices" would be codified for officers unable to attend training sessions in New York or Washington. A few days later, Mulholland wrote that he had "given the subjects we discussed considerable thought" and wanted to proceed.

In this and other reports to Gottlieb, Mulholland used a series of euphemisms. CIA officers were "performers" or "operators," the toxins they were to handle were "material," the victim a "spectator," and the act of poisoning a "procedure" or "trick." His manual would adapt a magician's stage show, devised to fool audiences who paid to be fooled, to the world of covert action, where deception was for darker purposes.

Upon receiving this letter, Gottlieb wrote a memo for his file describing the deal he had struck. Mulholland would produce, "in the form of a concise manual, as much pertinent information as possible in the fields of magic as it applies to covert activities . . . Mr. Mulholland seems well qualified to execute this study. He had been a successful performer of all forms of prestidigitation [and] has further studied the psychology of deception."

One item in Mulholland's personal background might have led to suspicion of "deviancy" and prevented his employment. In 1932 he married a woman he had been courting for eight years, but on the condition that she accept his continuing relationship with another longtime girlfriend. She agreed, explaining afterward that Mulholland "was so much a man, one woman's love could not satisfy him." Few at the CIA were that open-minded. Paul Gaynor, director of the Security Research Staff, wrote a memo warning of Mulholland's "sexual proclivities." Had he not been so uniquely qualified for his proposed job, his unorthodox marital arrangement, which he made no attempt to hide, might have led security officers to block his hiring. Under the circumstances, however, Gottlieb and Allen Dulles—one a quintessential outsider with unusual personal habits of his own, the other a relentless adulterer—chose to overlook it.

On May 5, Mulholland received a neatly typed letter informing him that his book proposal had been accepted. The letterhead said "Chemrophyl Associates," listed a post office box as its address, and was signed by one Sherman Grifford. This was a modest disguise, certainly one that Mulholland could penetrate. The name of the fictitious company was easily decipherable: Chemrophyl Associates. So was Gottlieb's pseudonym, for which he used his own initials.

"The project you outlined in your letter of April 20 has been approved by us, and you are hereby authorized to spend up to $3,000 in the next six months in the execution of this work," he wrote. "Please sign the enclosed receipt and return it to me."

After these formalities were completed, Mulholland was asked to sign a pledge acknowledging that he was entering into a "confidential relationship" and that he would "never divulge, publish, nor reveal either by word, conduct, or by any other means such information or knowledge, as indicated above, unless specifically authorized to do so." He agreed. The pledge was countersigned by Gottlieb's deputy, a chemist named Robert Lashbrook.

Mulholland began canceling appointments and postponing freelance writing assignments. He even gave up his longtime job as editor of the *Sphinx*. That allowed him to concentrate on turning his mastery of magic into a tool for spies.

As his deadline approached, Mulholland submitted a draft of his manual along with a letter to "Sherman Grifford" saying that he wished to refine it further.

"Dear Sherman," he wrote, "This is a memo in regard to extension of the manual on trickery. The manual as it now stands consists of the following five sections: 1. Underlying bases for the successful performance of tricks and the background of the psychological principles by which they operate. 2. Tricks with pills. 3. Tricks with loose solids. 4. Tricks with liquids. 5. Tricks whereby small objects can be obtained secretly . . . The manual requires two further sections . . . I believe that properly to devise the required techniques and devices and to describe them in writing would require 12 working weeks."

Gottlieb replied that these ideas "sound excellent to us." Then he wrote a memo to his titular superior, Willis "Gib" Gibbons, chief of the Technical Services Staff, reporting that "under a previous subproject (Subproject 4), a manual was prepared by Mr. Mulholland dealing with the application of the magician's art to covert activities such as the delivery of various materials to unwilling subjects . . . Subproject 19 will involve the preparation of two additional sections to the manual. These are (1) Modified or different methods and techniques for use if the performer is a woman, and (2) Methods and techniques that can be used where two or more people can work in collaboration."

Over the next year Mulholland produced several drafts of his manual, which he called *Some Operational Applications of the Art of Deception.* "The purpose of this paper is to instruct the reader so he may be able to perform a variety of acts secretly and indetectably," he wrote in the introduction. "In short, here are instructions in deception."

This manual was presumed to be lost or destroyed. A copy unexpectedly surfaced in 2007, making it the only full-length MK-ULTRA document known to have survived intact. It was published with an apt title: *The Official CIA Manual of Trickery and Deception.* As with everything Mulholland wrote for the CIA, it is presented in stage language, so that even if it fell into the wrong hands, it might appear to be a manual for performers, not poisoners.

In his manual, and at training sessions for CIA officers, Mulholland stressed one principle. Contrary to the popular cliché, he insisted, the hand is not quicker than the eye. Mulholland taught that the key to magic tricks is not to move the hand quickly, but to distract attention so the hand can do its work. Once a "performer" understood this principle, he or she could learn to administer poison without detection.

Mulholland's manual explains the use of "misdirection," including ways an agent can flick a pill into a victim's drink while distracting him by lighting his cigarette. It tells how capsules can be hidden in and then ejected from wallets, notebooks, or paper pads; how venom can be concealed in a ring; how toxic powders can be dispensed from the eraser cavity of a lead pencil; how female agents can hide poison in brocade beads and "use the handkerchief as a mask for a liquid container"; and how, thanks to advancing aerosol technology, it had become possible "to spray the liquid on a solid such as bread without either the action or the result being noticed."

Gottlieb had assembled an impressive array of poisons. With this manual, Mulholland gave him ways to deliver them. He turned highly developed techniques of stage magic into tools for covert action.

"The fact that he was asked to contemplate such things is emblematic of a unique moment in American history," wrote John McLaughlin, a former deputy director of the CIA who was himself an amateur magician, in an introduction to *The Official CIA Manual of Trickery and Deception.* "American leaders during the early Cold War felt the nation existentially threatened by an adversary who appeared to have no scruples. Mulholland's writing on delivery of pills, potions, and powders was just one example of research carried out back then in fields as diverse as brainwashing and paranormal psychology. Many such efforts that seem bizarre today are understandable only in the context of those times."

How MUCH LSD can a human being take? Gottlieb wanted to know. Could there be a breaking point, he wondered, a dose so massive that it would shatter the mind and blast away consciousness, leaving a void into which new impulses or even a new personality could be implanted?

Finding the answer would require intense experiments. Soon after launching MK-ULTRA, Gottlieb found a physician to conduct them: Harris Isbell, director of research at the Addiction Research Center in Lexington, Kentucky. Officially this center was a hospital, but it functioned more like a prison. The Bureau of Prisons co-administered it with the Public Health Service. Most inmates were African Americans from the margins of society. They were unlikely to complain if abused. That made them fine subjects for clandestine drug experiments.

Isbell had conducted "truth serum" experiments for the Office of Naval Research and was curious about LSD. In his small world, the CIA's interest in LSD was an open secret. Early in 1953 he wrote to ask if the Agency could supply him with "a reasonably large quantity of the drug [for] a study of the mental and other pharmacological effects produced by the chronic administration of the diethyl-amide of lysergic acid."

That request caught Gottlieb's attention. Isbell combined a fervent interest in psychoactive drugs with a ready supply of prisoners and a willingness to use them as research subjects. That made him an ideal MK-ULTRA contractor. On a July day in 1953, Gottlieb visited him in Lexington. They struck a deal. Gottlieb would provide LSD and whatever funds were necessary. Isbell would design and conduct experiments, provide subjects, and file reports.

Carefully observing bureaucratic protocol, Gottlieb cleared this deal with Isbell's superiors. He later wrote that he informed them, "in a secure manner, of our interest in and support of the research program of Dr. Harris Isbell . . . and of our financial support of it." He gave them no details of the "research program." They asked for none. As soon as Dr.

William Sebrell, director of the National Institutes of Health, understood that this was a CIA project, Gottlieb wrote in his report, he "approved highly of our general aims and indicated that he would afford us full support and protection."

"The deal was pretty simple," one investigator later wrote. "The CIA needed a place to test dangerous and possibly addictive drugs; Isbell had a large number of drug users in no position to complain. From the early 1950s onward, the Agency shipped LSD, with any number of other potentially dangerous narcotics, to Kentucky to be tested on human guinea pigs."

Isbell's MK-ULTRA contracts included Subproject 73, to test whether LSD, mescaline, or other drugs could make users more susceptible to hypnosis; Subproject 91, to "perform pre-clinical pharmacology studies required to develop new psycho-chemicals"; and Subproject 147, to study psychotomimetic drugs, a class that produces delusions and delirium. He went on to write or co-author more than one hundred scientific articles, many of them reporting the results of drug experiments. In these articles he refers to his inmate subjects as volunteers. The degree of their informed consent, however, is highly debatable. They were not told what sort of drug they would be fed or what its effects might be. To attract them, Isbell offered rewards including doses of high-grade heroin to feed the habit he was supposedly helping them break. One of his articles refers to a volunteer who "felt that he would die or would become permanently insane" after being given 180 micrograms of LSD, asked not to be dosed again, and required "considerable persuasion" before agreeing to continue.

"I feel sure you will be interested to learn that we were able to begin our experiments with LSD-25 during the month of July," Isbell wrote to Gottlieb soon after they met. "We obtained five subjects who agreed to take the drug chronically. All of these were negro male patients."

A month later Isbell provided an update. He had steadily increased the dosage of LSD he administered to his subjects, up to 300 micrograms. "The mental effects of LSD-25 were very striking," he told Gottlieb. "[They] included anxiety, a feeling of unreality . . . feelings of electric shocks on the skin, tingling sensations, choking . . . Marked changes in visual perception were reported. These included blurring of vision, abnormal coloration of familiar objects (hands turning purple, green etc.), flickering shadows, dancing dots of light, and spinning circles of color. Frequently, inanimate objects were distorted and changed in size."

This did not add much to what Gottlieb already knew, but he was pleased to have secured a supply of "expendables" for research inside the United States. He visited Lexington several times to observe Isbell's experiments. Sometimes he brought Frank Olson or another of his colleagues. All recognized Isbell as a uniquely valuable collaborator.

Later it turned out that one of Isbell's victims was William Henry Wall, a physician and former state senator from Georgia who had become addicted to the painkiller Demerol after a dental procedure. In 1953 he was arrested on drug charges, convicted, and sentenced to a term at the Addiction Research Center. There he became a subject in Isbell's LSD experiments. They left him mentally crippled. For the rest of his life he suffered from delusions, paranoia, panic attacks, and suicidal impulses. A book that his son later wrote about the case is entitled *From Healing to Hell*.

"What Harris Isbell did to my father was to assault him with a poison that permanently damaged his brain," the book says. "The CIA's ill-conceived covert Cold War scheme to find a mind-control drug for use on hostile leaders had caught my father in its hateful web."

One of Isbell's experiments may have been the most extreme in the history of LSD research. Gottlieb wanted to test the effect of heavy doses over an extended period of time. Isbell selected seven prisoners, isolated them, and began the experiment. "I have 7 patients who have been taking the drug for 42 days," he wrote in one progress report, adding that he was giving most of them "double, triple, and quadruple doses." The experiment continued for seventy-seven days. What can happen to a man's mind as he is locked in a cell and force-fed overdoses of LSD every day for so long? It is a gruesome question to ponder. Gottlieb, however, hoped that he might find a point at which massive LSD doses would finally dissolve the mind.

"It was the worst shit I ever had," recalled one subject in Isbell's LSD experiments, a nineteen-year-old African American drug addict named Eddie Flowers. Flowers suffered through hours of overwhelming hallucinations because he wanted the dose of heroin that Isbell offered as payment: "If you wanted it in the vein, you got it in the vein."

Gottlieb appreciated prison doctors like Harris Isbell. They held almost life-or-death power over helpless men, and as government employees they were open to his overtures. He sent them LSD, which they fed to inmates who volunteered in exchange for favors like more comfortable cells, better prison jobs, or credit for "good time." Afterward they wrote reports describing the inmates' responses.

The most enthusiastic of these doctors, Carl Pfeiffer, chairman of the Department of Pharmacology at Emory University, ran four MK-ULTRA "subprojects." All involved the administration of LSD and other drugs to induce psychotic states in what Gottlieb called "normal and schizophrenic human beings." As subjects, Pfeiffer used inmates at the federal prison in Atlanta and at a juvenile detention center in Bordentown, New Jersey. Under Subprojects 9 and 26, he studied ways that "various depressant drugs" can shake a person's psyche "by either altering his metabolism or producing sedation." His assignment under Subproject 28 was to test "depressants which affect the central nervous system." Most intriguingly, under Subproject 47, he would "screen and evaluate hallucinogenic materials of interest to Technical Services." One of his reports describes "epileptic-type seizures produced by chemicals." Another says that LSD "produced a model psychosis . . . Hallucinations last for three days and are characterized by repeated waves of depersonalization, visual hallucinations, and feelings of unreality." Gottlieb later said Pfeiffer's work had been in "an ultra-sensitive area" that lent itself to "easy misinterpretation and misunderstanding," but was worthwhile in the end.

"We learned a lot from the Atlanta experiments," Gottlieb concluded. "The Agency learned that a person's psyche could be very disturbed by those means."

That conclusion is richly confirmed by the recollections of one of Pfeiffer's subjects, James "Whitey" Bulger, a Boston gangster who was later sentenced to life imprisonment for crimes including eleven murders. Bulger was a street-level thug in his mid-twenties when he was sent to the Atlanta Federal Penitentiary after being convicted of armed robbery and truck hijacking. There he volunteered to participate in what he was told was a drug experiment aimed at finding a cure for schizophrenia. What followed is almost unimaginable: along with nineteen other inmates, he was given LSD nearly every day for fifteen months, without being told what it was. In a notebook that he wrote after being released, he described "nightly nightmares" and "horrible LSD experiences followed by thoughts of suicide and deep depression [that] would push me over the edge." He did not tell medical attendants about hearing voices or the "seeming movement of calendar in cell, etc." for fear that if he did so, "I'd be committed for life and never see the outside again." In one passage he describes Pfeiffer as "a modern day Dr. Mengele." It is a trenchant comparison, since the experiments that Mengele and other Nazi doctors conducted at concentration camps were lineal ancestors of MK-ULTRA "subprojects" like the one into which Bulger was drawn.

"I was in prison for committing a crime and feel they committed a worse crime on me," Bulger wrote. His description of his experience is a rare report on an MK-ULTRA experiment from the subject's perspective.

In 1957, while a prisoner at the Atlanta penitentiary, I was recruited by Dr. Carl Pfeiffer of Emory University to join a medical project that was researching a cure for schizophrenia. For our participation we would receive three days of good time for each month on the project . . . We were injected with massive doses of LSD-25. In minutes the drug would take over, and about eight or nine men—Dr. Pfeiffer and several men in suits who were not doctors—would give us tests to see how we reacted. Eight convicts in a panic and paranoid state. Total loss of appetite. Hallucinating. The room would change shape. Hours of paranoia and feeling violent. We experienced horrible periods of living nightmares and even blood coming out of the walls. Guys turning to skeletons in front of me. I saw a camera change into the head of a dog. I felt like I was going insane.

The men in suits would be in a room and hook me up to machines, asking questions like: Did you ever kill anyone? Would you kill someone? Two men went psychotic. They had all the symptoms of schizophrenia. They had to be pried loose from under their beds, growling, barking and frothing at the mouth. They put them in a strip cell down the hall. I never saw or heard of them again . . . They told us we were helping find a cure for schizophrenia. When it was all over, everyone would feel suicidal and depressed, wrung out emotionally. Time would stand still. I tried to quit, but Dr. Pfeiffer would appeal to me: "Please, you're my best subject, and we are close to finding the cure."

At the same time that Gottlieb was supporting Pfeiffer's experiments, he found several other enthusiastic partners. One of the first was James Hamilton, a well-known Stanford University psychiatrist who had worked with George Hunter White on OSS "truth serum" research during World War II and later advised the Chemical Corps on bio-warfare projects. During the 1950s Hamilton signed three MK-ULTRA contracts. His first assignment, which Gottlieb called Subproject 2, was to study "possible synergistic action of drugs which may be appropriate for use in abolishing consciousness," and also to survey "methods to enable the administration of drugs to patients without their knowledge." In Subproject 124, he was to test whether inhaling carbon dioxide could lead people into a trance-like state. Subproject 140, conducted at St. Francis Hospital in San Francisco under the cover of thyroid research, was to measure the possible psychoactive effects of thyroid-related hormones. By one account Hamilton was "one of the renaissance men of the program, working on everything from psycho-chemicals to kinky sex to carbon dioxide inhalation."

As Hamilton was beginning his work, Gottlieb hired another prominent psychiatrist, Robert Hyde, assistant superintendent of Boston Psychopathic Hospital—now the Massachusetts Mental Health Center—to begin a series of LSD experiments. Hyde had a unique credential: he was the first American to take LSD, having been introduced to it by an Austrian psychiatrist shortly after World War II. Colleagues considered him an "amazing and fearless researcher" who harbored a "pathological obsession with discovering more about medicine." As soon as the CIA began funding LSD research, he applied. Soon, according to one study, "hundreds of students from Harvard, Emerson and MIT were unwittingly assisting the Agency's research into the possibility of mind control." Each was paid $15 to drink "a little vial of a clear, colorless and odorless liquid" that might produce an "altered state." They were not told details about the drug they would be ingesting, and as one study later concluded, "none of those involved in the experiments had the proper training or understanding to guide participants." Several had negative reactions. One hanged herself in a clinic bathroom.

Hyde went on to become one of the most prolific early dispensers of LSD, under the umbrella of four MK-ULTRA "subprojects." Gottlieb's assignments to him were remarkably broad, reflecting their recognition of shared interests. Under Subproject 8, Hyde conducted a "study of the biochemical, neurophysiological, sociological, and clinical psychiatric aspects of LSD." Under Subproject 10 he "tested and evaluated the effect of LSD and alcohol when administered to individuals falling under various personality categories." Subproject 63 was to study "the use of alcohol as a social phenomenon, with particular emphasis on those variables that would prove predictive in the assessment and possible manipulation of human behavior." The surviving description of Subproject 66 is most elastic: "Test a number of techniques for predicting a given individual's reactions to LSD-25, other psycho-chemicals, and alcohol."

No connection that Gottlieb made during his first months running MK-ULTRA proved more important and fruitful than the one he sealed with Harold Abramson, the New York allergist who had shepherded him through his first "self-experimentation" with LSD. Abramson was an LSD pioneer. Using stock he ordered from Sandoz, and later the effectively unlimited supply that Gottlieb and Eli Lilly made available to him, he distributed samples to other doctors and gave it to guests during parties at his Long Island home. One of his friends called these parties "wild and crazy, along with all the sex and what have you." Another reported that "you'd be very, very surprised at who attended some of these events."

In mid-1953 Gottlieb gave Abramson $85,000 in MK-ULTRA money for "the conduct of experiments with LSD and other hallucinogenics . . . along the following lines: (a) Disturbance of Memory; (b) Discrediting by Aberrant Behavior; (c) Alteration of Sex Patterns; (d) Eliciting of Information; (e) Suggestibility; (f) Creations of Dependence." The variety of these assignments matched the breadth of Abramson's interest in LSD. He fed it to Siamese fighting fish and described their reaction in a series of articles. More disturbing, he developed a special curiosity about the impact of mind-altering drugs on children. He closely monitored experiments, including one in which twelve "pre-puberty" boys were fed psilocybin, and another in which fourteen children between the ages of six and eleven, diagnosed as schizophrenic, were given 100 micrograms of LSD each day for six weeks.

"It was done with great secrecy," one doctor who worked with the CIA said years later. "We went through a great deal of hoop-de-do and signed secrecy agreements, which everyone took very seriously."

Gottlieb shaped MK-ULTRA almost entirely alone, and so it reflected his own instincts. His deepest conviction was that the key to mind control lay in drugs—specifically, as one study of the period explains, in LSD.

> Within the agency, Dr. Gottlieb . . . found time to lead the chemists of the Technical Services Staff on a series of increasingly daring experiments with LSD. They spiked each other's coffee and liquor; they spread it on their food. They tripped out in their offices and in safe houses in Washington and beyond, in the Maryland countryside. They were stoned for days at a time.
>
> There were moments of black comedy: a hallucinating scientist suddenly decided he was Fred Astaire and grabbed the nearest secretary, convinced she was Ginger Rogers . . . Dr. Gottlieb regarded such incidents as the usual hiccups in searching for the magic technique he was convinced the Communists were using . . . His sixth sense—that deductive reasoning which made him such a respected figure among his peers—convinced Dr. Gottlieb that there might be no quick answers; the only certain way to arrive at the one which mattered, success, was to continue experimenting. In that summer of 1953, he encouraged his staff to go in search of how to take possession of a man's mind. He was no longer only the Beast to Richard Helms's Beauty, but also became known as Merlin, the great wizard. Watching his colleagues expanding their conception of reality under the influence of LSD, he would sometimes dance a jig; those were among some of his happiest hours at the Agency, equaled only by rising at dawn to milk his goats.

As best he could, Gottlieb integrated his home life with his professional quest. He and Margaret wondered what lies beyond the physical reality that human senses can perceive, and his "self-experimentation" with LSD coincided with their shared pursuit of inner wisdom. Years later Margaret described the heterodox spirituality they developed.

> I am impatient when I hear people equate being "good" or "religious" with being Christian. There are many "goods" and many religions, and a Muslim's way to God is very similar to ours, and so is a Hindu's or a Buddhist's, and I can't see that Christianity is more full of love or less full of fears and superstitions . . . Is there a God? There is certainly a Force or a Source that all mankind (and maybe animals too) feels. It amazes and delights me that peoples who have not known of each other's existence on the earth have come to very similar questions and to similar answers down through the ages since our very beginnings. There is Something that we all sense and are familiar with. Please let us not say, "My way is the only way."

Gottlieb never confided his thoughts to paper as his wife did. His spiritual side, however, became part of his mystique. To reinforce that mystique, and to inspire himself, he hung what he said was a verse from the Koran on the wall above his desk: "When they come, it will be asked of them, Did you reject my words when you had no full knowledge of them? Or what was it that you did?"

A CROWD OF reporters pushed toward George Kennan, one of America's most celebrated diplomats, as he stepped off a plane at Tempelhof Airport in Berlin on September 19, 1952. Kennan was then serving as ambassador to the Soviet Union, always a challenging post but especially so during the early Cold War. He began by offering a few bland observations about U.S.-Soviet relations. Then a reporter asked him about his daily life in Moscow. That set him off.

"Don't you know how foreign diplomats live in Moscow?" he snapped. "I was interned here in Germany for several months during the last war. The treatment we receive in Moscow is just about like the treatment we internees received then, except that in Moscow we are at liberty to go out and walk the streets under guard."

Soviet leaders could not abide what they called "slanderous attacks" comparing their country to Nazi Germany. They declared Kennan persona non grata, putting an end to his posting in Moscow. Many in Washington saw him as a martyr to truth. Some wondered, however, why such a gifted diplomat would have spoken such undiplomatic words.

Kennan told friends in the State Department that he had become intensely frustrated with restrictions the Soviets had placed on him, and "blew my top." Richard Davies, who had been his deputy in Moscow, had another explanation. He reported that Kennan had been "under enormous psychological pressure" because he believed he had failed in his mission to ease the Cold War, that he was looking for an escape, and that he spoke provocatively in Berlin knowing that his words would probably lead the Soviets to expel him.

Inside the CIA, a darker theory emerged. Officers who were looking for techniques of mind control already believed the Soviets were ahead of them. They took the Kennan case as proof. That he had simply spoken impulsively, or had planned his comments for a preconceived purpose, seemed to them implausible. Their fixation on LSD led them to another conclusion.

"Helms thinks they may have dosed George Kennan with the drug," the CIA security chief, Sheffield Edwards, told a colleague afterward. "He's convinced it's the only reason Kennan would have acted the way he did."

Gottlieb, in his drive to imagine every possible use of LSD, had already come up with the idea of surreptitiously dosing unfriendly foreign leaders. If those leaders could be made to behave strangely in public, he reasoned, they might lose popularity or fall from power. Like many other ideas that shaped MK-ULTRA, this one was based on fears of what Communists might be doing. Kennan's case seemed to offer proof that a new kind of psycho-war was beginning.

No evidence ever emerged to support the hypothesis that Kennan was drugged. Nonetheless it seized minds inside the CIA. Allen Dulles was a member of the little-known Psychological Strategy Board, which coordinated American "psychological warfare" campaigns, and after he shared his suspicion that Kennan had been drugged, the board decided to begin monitoring American politicians for "signs of a changed personality," and to detain and test any who behaved suspiciously.

The CIA's first mind control projects, Bluebird and Artichoke, were highly classified, but MK-ULTRA was the most secret of all. The number of people who knew even its general outlines was exceedingly small. They included Gottlieb, his deputy Robert Lashbrook, and the handful of scientists who worked for him at the Chemical Division of the Technical Services Staff; his official supervisor, "Gib" Gibbons, head of the Technical Services Staff; his true boss, Richard Helms, to whom he reported on sensitive matters; the deputy director for plans, Frank Wisner; the chief of the counterintelligence staff, James Jesus Angleton; one outside contractor, the New York LSD maven Harold Abramson; members of the Special Operations Division at Camp Detrick, numbering fewer than a dozen; and Allen Dulles. Dulles knew the fewest details. Helms did not tell him everything because, according to a later Senate investigation, he "felt it necessary to keep details of the project restricted to an absolute minimum number of people." This was obedience to the unspoken rules that shaped CIA culture.

"Knowledge was a danger, ignorance a cherished asset," the novelist Don DeLillo wrote in describing this culture. "In many cases the DCI, the Director of Central Intelligence, was not to know important things. The less he knew, the more decisively he could function. It could impair his ability to tell the truth at an inquiry or a hearing, or in an Oval Office chat with the President, if he knew what they were doing . . . The Joint Chiefs were not to know. The operational horrors were not for their ears. Details were a form of contamination. The Secretaries were to be insulated from knowing. They were happier not knowing, or knowing too late . . . There were pauses and blank looks. Brilliant riddles floated up and down the echelons, to be pondered, solved, ignored."

Just outside the inner MK-ULTRA circle were several CIA officers close enough to the truth to inquire or complain. Among them were Sheffield Edwards, chief of the Office of Security; Marshall Chadwell, chief of the Office of Scientific Intelligence; Morse Allen, who continued to run the Artichoke program even after MK-ULTRA was launched; and Paul Gaynor, a retired brigadier general who had preceded Allen as director of Artichoke and went on to head the CIA's Office of Scientific Intelligence. They sensed Gottlieb's spreading authority and, as one memo from Allen to Gaynor suggests, did not approve.

Sometime during the fall of 1953, Mr. Sidney GOTTLIEB made a tour of the Far East for reasons unknown, but undoubtedly in connection with business of TSS . . . GOTTLIEB gave out samples of psychedelic drugs and ran some tests on various people out there using this drug. It is not definitely certain that it was LSD, nor do we know the details Mr. GOTTLIEB used in describing the chemical, but this appears to be the likely chemical. GOTTLIEB is also reported to have given some of the chemical to some of our staff officers in the [redacted] with the idea that the staff officer would place the chemical in the drinking water to be used by a speaker at a political rally in the [redacted] . . .

It has been reported that chemicals, pills, or ampules having a psychedelic effect have been passed around to some of our people in [redacted], and whether these were handed out by GOTTLIEB or other TSS people is unknown . . . [Redacted], recently returned from Germany, said he heard of staff officers who had been given the chemicals and used them on subjects during interrogations . . . [Redacted] recently received information that the [redacted] have been working for TSS secretly on a project known as MK-ULTRA at the [redacted], apparently testing work on drugs and drugs in combination with hypnosis. Details are lacking . . .

In 1942, OSS was attempting to study drugs which might be useful in the interrogation of prisoners of war. Connected with these experiments was one Major George H. White . . . It appears that White or someone else by the name of White has currently been picked up by TSS and is engaged in doing secret work on drugs at an apartment in New York City which TSS has hired for White . . . We are also informed that any effort to tamper with this project, MK-ULTRA, is not permitted.

As MK-ULTRA spread into ever darker reaches, the men involved in it had to consider the possibility of a leak or other security breach. What might happen if one of the initiates had an attack of conscience or change of heart, was captured by enemy agents, or slipped into alcoholism or some other pathology that might loosen his tongue? This concern brought them back to their long-standing interest in induced amnesia. They originally hoped to use it to wipe away the memory of agents who had been programmed to commit crimes. Now they began to imagine another use: as a way to make CIA officers forget what they had done.

In mid-1953 a retired CIA officer underwent brain surgery in Texas. Since he was to be placed under anesthesia, CIA practice required that his doctors and nurses be vetted in advance. As an added precaution, the CIA sent an officer to be present at the surgery. He returned with bad news. While the patient was in a semi-conscious state, he talked uncontrollably about his former job and "internal problems" at the CIA. He knew nothing about MK-ULTRA, but the example was frightening.

"Some individuals at the Agency had to know tremendous amounts of information," a CIA officer later said in explaining this problem. "If any way could be found to produce amnesia for this type of information, it would be a remarkable thing."

IN THE FALL of 1953 Gottlieb traveled to East Asia to monitor the interrogation of prisoners who had been dosed with LSD—known at the CIA as P-1. When asked years later whether he had been "witness to the actual operation of interrogation with P-1" in Asia during this period, he replied: "The answer is yes." He became impatient when asked if the interrogations were committed on "unwitting subjects."

"There is nothing such as a witting P-1 interrogation," Gottlieb said. "The very nature of that kind of interrogation is unwitting. So when you ask, 'Was there any administration of P-1 in interrogations other than unwitting?' that's kind of an oxymoron."

During breaks from interrogation sessions at which he dosed prisoners with LSD at CIA "safe houses" in Asia, Gottlieb took folk dancing lessons. He pursued this passion seriously. His wife shared it. "Sid got back from Manilla [sic] a week and a half ago, and the novelty of having him home has not worn off yet," Margaret reported in a letter to her mother in early November. "His trip was very successful and, to him, very exciting. He enjoys all of life's experiences to the full, and this one was so new to him and he had so much to see and absorb that he came back just about ready to burst. He spent almost all of his free time learning some native Phillipino [sic] dances and getting the right costumes to do them in. Our hobby is still dancing the dances of all countries and teaching them to others."

In that same letter, along with a weather report and news about a swimming party she was planning for her children, Margaret confided that her husband had told her something startling. He had returned from Asia with doubts about his work. Twenty-eight months after joining the Agency, he told his wife that he might quit.

"Sid is considering a new idea these days," Margaret wrote. "He thinks that he would like to stop his career for a while and get an MD with the emphasis on psychiatry, and then do research in that field with maybe some private practice to keep us in bread and butter. This, of course, would take five or six years, and whether or not we could swing it is doubtful . . . Sid says that most people don't know what they really want to do with their lives until they get to be about our age but by then they are tied down with responsibilities and also kind of in a rut and so they go along the way they have started because they are afraid to stop and start over again. This is a big step to take at this late date and it will take nerve to do it, but I would really like for him to at least try to do it."

Leaving MK-ULTRA would not be as simple as leaving a normal job. Gottlieb and his officers were part of a deeply secret fraternity. They could think of themselves as scientists working to defend their country, but they were also torturers. They believed that the threat of Communism justified all they did. Other Americans, though, might disagree. A leak from MK-ULTRA would expose deep secrets. If anyone who knew those secrets were to be stricken with doubts, or wanted to drop out, the result could devastate the CIA.

For a time this fear was hypothetical. Suddenly it erupted into terrifying reality. As Gottlieb pondered his future, one of the other MK-ULTRA men reached his breaking point.

7

Fell or Jumped

Glass shattered high above Seventh Avenue in Manhattan before dawn on a cold November morning. Seconds later a body hit the sidewalk. Jimmy, the doorman at the Statler Hotel, was momentarily stunned. Then he turned and ran into the hotel lobby.

"We got a jumper!" he shouted. "We got a jumper!"

"Where?" the night manager asked him.

"Out front, on the sidewalk!"

A small crowd had already gathered around the body when the night manager arrived. Others rushed over from Pennsylvania Station, across the street. The victim, clad only in underwear, had landed on his back. Blood was gushing from his eyes, nose, and ears, but he was still alive. For a moment he seemed to try to speak.

"It's okay, buddy, we've called for help," the night manager told him. "Just hold on. You'll be okay."

The night manager knew those words were untrue. He wiped blood from the dying man's face, and was grateful when a priest appeared, carrying a Bible. Two police officers followed close behind.

"Jumper?" one of them asked.

"I guess," the night manager replied. Later he recalled that as an ambulance was arriving, the victim "raised his head slightly, his lips moving. His eyes were wide with desperation. He wanted to tell me something. I leaned down closer to listen, but he took a deep breath and died."

The night manager peered up through the darkness at his hulking hotel. After a few moments, he picked out a curtain flapping through an open window. It turned out to be room 1018A. Two names were on the registration card: Frank Olson and Robert Lashbrook.

Police officers entered room 1018A with guns drawn. They saw no one. The window was open. They pushed open the door to the bathroom and found Lashbrook sitting on the toilet, head in hands. He had been sleeping, he said, when "I heard a noise and then I woke up."

"The man that went out the window, what is his name?" one officer asked.

"Olson," came the reply. "Frank Olson."

"And you say you didn't see Mr. Olson go out the window?"

"No, I didn't."

"You didn't think of going down to check on Mr. Olson?"

"I looked out the window. I saw him lying there. There were people running from the station. What could I have done? I could see that he had help. I thought it best to wait here."

The night manager, who overheard this conversation, was suspicious. "In all my years in the hotel business," he later reflected, "I never encountered a case where someone got up in the middle of the night, ran across a dark room in his underwear, avoiding two beds, and dove through a closed window with the shade and curtains drawn." Leaving the police officers, he returned to the lobby and, on a hunch, asked the telephone operator if any calls had recently been made from room 1018A. Yes, she replied—and she had eavesdropped, not an uncommon practice in an era when hotel phone calls were routed through a switchboard. Someone in the room had called a number on Long Island, which was listed as belonging to Dr. Harold Abramson.

"Well, he's gone," the caller had said. Abramson replied, "Well, that's too bad."

To the first police officers on the scene, this seemed like another of the human tragedies they see too often: a distressed or distraught man had taken his own life. They could not have known that both the dead man and the survivor were scientists who helped direct one of the U.S. government's most highly classified intelligence programs.

Early the next morning, one of Olson's close colleagues drove to Maryland to break the terrible news to the dead man's family. He told Alice Olson and her three children that Frank "fell or jumped" to his death from a hotel window. Naturally they were shocked, but they had no choice other than to accept what they were told. Alice did not object when told that, given the condition of her husband's body, family members should not view it. The funeral was held with a closed casket. There the case might have ended.

Decades later, however, spectacular revelations cast Olson's death in a completely new light. First the CIA admitted that shortly before he died his colleagues had lured him to a retreat and fed him LSD without his knowledge. Then it turned out that Olson had talked about leaving the CIA—and told his wife that he had made "a terrible mistake." Slowly a counternarrative emerged: Olson was disturbed about his work and wanted to quit, leading his comrades to consider him a security risk. All of this led him to room 1018A. His story is one of MK-ULTRA's deepest mysteries.

FRANK OLSON, A child of Swedish immigrants, grew up in a lumber town on Lake Superior. Chemistry was his way out. He was a dedicated though not brilliant student, earned his PhD from the University of Wisconsin in 1941, married a classmate, and took a job at Purdue University's Agricultural Experimentation Station. He had enrolled in the Reserve Officers' Training Corps to help pay his college costs, and soon after the United States entered World War II he was called to active duty as a lieutenant and ordered to report to Fort Hood, in Texas. He was in training there when, on December 26, 1942, he received a fateful call from Ira Baldwin, who had been his thesis adviser at the University of Wisconsin. Baldwin had just been drafted into the war effort and assigned to begin urgent research into biological warfare. He wanted Olson, who had studied aerosol delivery systems at Wisconsin, to join him. At Baldwin's request, the army transferred Olson to Edgewood Arsenal in Maryland.

A few months later, the Chemical Corps took over nearby Camp Detrick and established its secret Biological Warfare Laboratories there. Olson was one of the first scientists assigned to Detrick. Construction was still underway when he moved in.

At Camp Detrick, Olson began working with the handful of colleagues who would accompany him throughout his clandestine career. One was Harold Abramson, who on the morning of Olson's death a decade later would receive the cryptic message "Well, he's gone." Others included ex-Nazis who had been brought to the United States on Operation Paperclip contracts. For a time they worked on aerosol technologies—ways to spray germs or toxins on enemies, and to defend against such attacks. Later Olson met with American intelligence officers who had experimented with "truth drugs" in Europe.

"Just as we speculated about the atom bomb project—you have friends who are physics majors and they all go to Los Alamos—we knew when we came here," Alice Olson said years later. "All the wives said they must be working on germ warfare."

Olson was discharged from the army in 1944 but hardly noticed the change. He remained at Camp Detrick on a civilian contract and continued his research into aerobiology. Several times he visited the secluded Dugway Proving Ground in Utah, which was used for testing "living biological agents, munitions, and aerosol cloud production." He co-authored a 220-page study entitled "Experimental Airborne Infections" that described experiments with "airborne clouds of highly infectious agents." In 1949 he was one of several scientists from Camp Detrick who traveled to the Caribbean island of Antigua for Operation Harness, which tested the vulnerability of animals to toxic clouds. The next year he was part of Operation Sea Spray, in which dust engineered to float like anthrax was released near San Francisco. He regularly traveled to Fort Terry, a secret army base on Plum Island, off the eastern tip of Long Island, which was used to test toxins too deadly to be brought onto the U.S. mainland.

This was the period when senior army and CIA officers were becoming deeply alarmed at what they feared was Soviet progress toward mastering forms of warfare based on microbes. Their alarm led to creation of the Special Operations Division. Rumors about its work spread through offices and laboratories. Olson learned of it over an evening game of cards with a colleague, John Schwab, who unbeknownst to him had been named the division's first chief. Schwab invited him to join. He accepted immediately.

Within a year, Olson had become acting chief of the Special Operations Division. His job description was vague but tantalizing: collect data "of interest to the division, with particular emphasis on the medico-biological aspects," and coordinate his work with "other agencies conducting work of a similar or related nature." That meant the CIA.

Olson's specialty was "the airborne distribution of biological germs," according to one study. "Dr. Olson had developed a range of lethal aerosols in handy-sized containers. They were disguised as shaving cream and insect repellants. They contained, among other agents, staph enteroxin, a crippling food poison; the even more deadly Venezuelan equine encephalomyelitis; and most deadly of all, anthrax . . . Further weapons he was working on [included] a cigarette lighter which gave out an almost instant lethal gas, a lipstick that would kill on contact with skin, and a neat pocket spray for asthma sufferers that induced pneumonia."

By the time Olson stepped down as acting chief of the Special Operations Division in early 1953, complaining that pressures of the job aggravated his ulcers, he had joined the CIA. He stayed with the Special Operations Division, which was officially part of the army but functioned as a CIA research station hidden within a military base. There he came to know the men who would soon be running MK-ULTRA, including Sidney Gottlieb and his deputy Robert Lashbrook.

In his laboratory at Camp Detrick, Olson directed experiments that involved gassing or poisoning laboratory animals. These experiences disturbed him. "He'd come to work in the morning and see piles of dead monkeys," his son Eric later recalled. "That messes with you. He wasn't the right guy for that."

Olson also saw human beings suffer. Although not a torturer himself, he observed and monitored torture sessions in several countries. "In CIA safe-houses in Germany," according to one study, "Olson witnessed horrific brutal interrogations on a regular basis. Detainees who were deemed 'expendable,' suspected spies or 'moles,' security leaks, etc., were literally interrogated to death in experimental methods combining drugs, hypnosis, and torture to attempt to master brainwashing techniques and memory erasing."

As Thanksgiving approached in 1953, Olson received an invitation that would have puzzled anyone unaccustomed to CIA rituals. It was headlined DEEP CREEK RENDEZVOUS. Olson and eight others were invited to gather on Wednesday, November 18, for a retreat at a cabin on Deep Creek Lake in western Maryland. "Cabin will have atmosphere—a little bit of Berkeley and a little of Oakland," the invitation said. There were detailed driving directions from Washington and Frederick, Maryland. At the bottom was a striking notation: "CAMOUFLAGE: Winter meeting of scriptwriters, editors, authors, lecturers, sports magazines. Remove CD [Camp Detrick] decals from cars."

The two-story cabin at Deep Creek Lake is in what was then a forested area, perched on a steep hillside that slopes down toward a landing on the lakefront. According to the rental agency, it "accommodates up to ten persons in four bedrooms, living room, kitchen and bath—large stone fireplace, chestnut paneling, with electric range and refrigerator." On the appointed date, November 18, Olson was waiting at his home in Frederick when Vincent Ruwet, who had replaced him as chief of the Special Operations Division, pulled up outside. They made the sixty-mile drive to Deep Creek Lake together. Other guests filtered in during the afternoon.

This retreat was one in a series that Gottlieb convened every few months. Officially it was a coming together of two groups: four CIA scientists from the Technical Services Staff, which ran MK-ULTRA, and five army scientists from the Special Operations Division of the Chemical Corps. In reality, these men worked so closely together that they comprised a single unit. They were comrades in search of cosmic secrets. It made sense for them to gather, discuss their projects, and exchange ideas in a relaxed environment.

The first twenty-four hours at the Deep Creek Lake retreat were uneventful. On Thursday evening the group gathered for dinner and then settled back for a round of drinks. Robert Lashbrook, Gottlieb's deputy, produced a bottle of Cointreau and poured glasses for the company. Several, including Olson, drank heartily. After twenty minutes, Gottlieb asked if anyone was feeling odd. Several said they were. Gottlieb then told them that their drinks had been spiked with LSD.

The news was not well received. Even in their altered state, the unwitting subjects, now witting, could understand what had been done to them. Olson was especially upset. According to his son Eric, he became "quite agitated, and was having a serious confusion with separating reality from fantasy." Soon, though, he and the others were carried away into a hallucinatory world. Gottlieb later reported that they were "boisterous and laughing . . . unable to continue the meeting or engage in sensible conversations." The next morning they were in only slightly better shape. The meeting broke up. Olson headed back to Frederick. By the time he arrived, he was a changed man.

At dinner with his family that night, Olson seemed distant. He said nothing about his trip, could not focus on his children, and refused to eat—even the apple pie Alice had prepared as a special treat. She tried to draw him out, but he stared vacantly into the air.

"I've made a terrible mistake," he finally blurted.

"What did you do?" she asked. "Did you break security?"

"No."

"Did you falsify data?"

"You know I wouldn't do that. I'll tell you later, after the kids go to sleep."

Later, though, Olson told his wife nothing. His puzzling admission came to haunt the case. What "terrible mistake" had he made? Decades later, after a lifetime of immersion in the story of his father's death, Eric Olson settled on an answer.

I think what happened was that at the Deep Creek meeting, they gave Frank a chance to recant. I don't know whether he said "Fuck you!" but in any case, he wouldn't do it. Then, when he got home, he had second thoughts. He began to realize that this could have really heavy implications for himself and his family. The "terrible mistake" was that he didn't recant. In a broader sense, it was that he really didn't understand the people he was dealing with. He thought his opinions would count for something. But their attitude was, "You might make this shit, but we control the operation and we don't take any crap from scientists." It wasn't until the last minute that he realized what he was up against.

The weekend after the encounter at Deep Creek Lake was difficult for both husband and wife. On Sunday evening, in an effort to escape the gloom, they decided to see a movie. A new film called *Martin Luther* was playing at a nearby cinema. It was eerily appropriate: the story of a man stricken by conscience who decides to risk everything by proclaiming what he believes.

"If I have spoken evil, bear witness against me," Luther tells his inquisitors in the climactic scene. "I cannot and I will not recant. Here I stand. I can do no other. God help me."

That scene jarred both husband and wife. "I think we made a poor choice of movie," Alice told her husband after they returned home.

The next morning, November 23, Olson showed up early at Camp Detrick. His boss, Vincent Ruwet, arrived soon afterward. Neither was in good shape. More than four days had passed since they had been given LSD without their knowledge. Ruwet later called it "the most frightening experience I have ever had or hope to have." His condition on that Monday was, by his own later assessment, "what you might call marginal."

Olson began pouring out his doubts and fears. "He appeared to be agitated, and asked me if I should fire him or he should quit," Ruwet later recalled. "I was taken aback by this and asked him what was wrong. He stated that, in his opinion, he had messed up the experiment and had not done well at meetings." Ruwet tried to calm him. His work was excellent and recognized as such, he assured his friend. Slowly Olson was persuaded that resignation was too extreme a reaction. They parted on a hopeful note.

When Ruwet arrived for work the next day, Olson was again waiting to see him. His symptoms had worsened. Ruwet later testified that Olson was "disoriented," felt "all mixed up," said he had "done something wrong," and had concluded that he was "incompetent to do the type of work he was doing."

By this time MK-ULTRA had been underway for seven months. It was one of the government's deepest secrets, guarded by security that was, as Olson had been told when he joined the Special Operations Division, "tighter than tight." Barely two dozen men knew its true nature. Nine had been at Deep Creek Lake. Several of those had been surreptitiously dosed with LSD. Now one of them seemed out of control. This was no light matter for men who believed that the success or failure of MK-ULTRA might determine the fate of the United States and all humanity.

Olson had spent ten years at Camp Detrick and knew most if not all of the Special Operation Division's secrets. He had repeatedly visited Germany. Slides and home movies he took during those trips place him at the building that housed the CIA station in Frankfurt—and that was less than an hour's drive from the secret prison at Villa Schuster. Olson also brought home pictures from Heidelberg and Berlin, where the U.S. military maintained clandestine interrogation centers. Besides Germany, his passport shows visits to Britain, Norway, Sweden, and Morocco. He was one of several Special Operations Division scientists who were in France on August 16, 1951, when an entire French village, Pont-St.-Esprit, was mysteriously seized by mass hysteria and violent delirium that afflicted more than two hundred residents and caused seven deaths; the cause was later determined to have been poisoning by ergot, the fungus from which LSD was derived. Perhaps most threatening of all, if American forces did indeed use biological weapons during the Korean War—there is circumstantial evidence but no proof—Olson would have known. The prospect that he might reveal any of what he had seen or done was terrifying.

"He was very, very open, and not scared to say what he thought," Olson's friend and colleague Norman Cournoyer later recalled. "He did not give a damn. Frank Olson pulled no punches at any time . . . That's what they were scared of, I am sure. He did speak up any time he wanted to."

Olson's doubts deepened as 1953 unfolded. In the spring he visited the top-secret British Microbiological Research Establishment at Porton Down, southwest of London, where government scientists were studying the effects of sarin and other nerve gases. On May 6 a volunteer subject, a twenty-year-old soldier, was dosed with sarin there, began foaming at the mouth, collapsed into convulsions, and died an hour later. Afterward Olson spoke about his discomfort with a psychiatrist who helped direct the research, William Sargant.

A month later Olson was back in Germany. While he was there, according to records that were later declassified, a suspected Soviet agent code-named Patient #2 was subjected to intense interrogation somewhere near Frankfurt. On that same trip, according to a later reconstruction of his travels, Olson "visited a CIA 'safe house' near Stuttgart [where] he saw men dying, often in agony, from the weapons he had made." After stops in Scandinavia and Paris, he returned to Britain and visited William Sargant for a second time. Immediately after their meeting, Sargant wrote a report saying that Olson was "deeply disturbed over what he had seen in CIA safe houses in Germany" and "displayed symptoms of not wanting to keep secret what he had witnessed." He sent his report to superiors with the understanding that they would forward it to the CIA.

"There was no question of not doing that," Sargant said years later. "We and the Americans were joined at the hip in such matters. There were common interests to protect."

Soon after Olson returned home, he sought out his old friend Cournoyer. "He was troubled," Cournoyer remembered years later. "He said, 'Norm, you would be stunned by the techniques that they used. They made people talk. They brainwashed people. They used all kinds of drugs. They used all kinds of torture. They were using Nazis, they were using prisoners, they were using Russians—and they didn't care whether they got out of that or not.'" In another interview, Cournoyer said that Olson "just got involved in it in a way that—he was unhappy about it. But there was nothing he could do about it. He was CIA, and they took it to the end . . . He said, 'Norm, did you ever see a man die?' I said no. He said, 'Well, I did.' Yes, they did die. Some of the people they interrogated died. So you can imagine the amount of work they did on these people . . . He said that he was going to leave. He told me that. He said, 'I am getting out of that CIA. Period.'"

FIVE DAYS AFTER being dosed with LSD, Olson was still disoriented. His boss at the Special Operations Division, Vincent Ruwet, called Gottlieb to report this. Gottlieb asked him to bring Olson in for a chat. At their meeting, Gottlieb later testified, Olson "seemed to me to be confused in certain areas of his thinking." He made a quick decision: Olson must be taken to New York City and delivered to the physician most intimately tied to MK-ULTRA, Harold Abramson.

Alice Olson was surprised to see her husband home from work at midday. "I've consented to take psychiatric care," he told her as he packed a suitcase. Soon afterward Ruwet arrived. Alice asked if she could accompany her husband on the first leg of his trip. Ruwet agreed. A few minutes later, he and the Olsons set off.

In the car, Olson became uncomfortable. He asked where they were going. Ruwet told him their first stop would be Washington, and from there they would fly to New York, where Olson could be treated. Thanksgiving was just two days away, and Alice asked her husband whether he would be home in time for holiday dinner. He said he would.

At the Hot Shoppes diner on Wisconsin Avenue in Bethesda, the group stopped for lunch. Olson refused to touch his food. When Alice encouraged him to eat, he told her he was afraid that he would be served food tainted with drugs or poison.

The belief that the CIA is poisoning one's food is a classic of the conspiracy-addled mind. In most cases it may be safely filed with the belief that aliens torment earthlings by sending messages through their dental fillings. Olson, however, knew from personal experience that the CIA could indeed poison food. People with whom he worked made the poisons.

When the group arrived in Washington, their car pulled up outside an unmarked CIA building near the Reflecting Pool. Ruwet went inside. Frank and Alice Olson lingered in the car. They held hands in the back seat. Alice asked Frank to repeat his promise to return home for Thanksgiving dinner. He did. Then Ruwet reappeared and motioned for Frank to come with him. The couple said their good-byes.

As Gottlieb had directed, Ruwet and Robert Lashbrook escorted Olson to New York. Aboard their flight, Olson was nervous and talkative. He said he felt "all mixed up." Someone, he kept repeating, was out to get him.

From LaGuardia Airport, the three of them rode by taxi to Abramson's office in a brick town house at 133 East Fifty-Eighth Street. Alice Olson had been told that Abramson was chosen because her husband "had to see a physician who had equal security clearance so he could talk freely." That was partly true. Abramson was not a psychiatrist, but he was an MK-ULTRA initiate. Gottlieb knew that Abramson's first loyalty was to MK-ULTRA—or, as he would have put it, to the security of the United States. That made him an ideal person to probe Olson's inner mind.

Olson told Abramson that ever since the Deep Creek Lake retreat, he had been unable to work well. He could not concentrate and forgot how to spell. At night he could not sleep. Abramson sought to reassure Olson, who seemed to relax afterward. Ruwet and Lashbrook picked him up at six o'clock. Later that evening, Abramson joined them at the Statler Hotel, where they had checked in. He brought a bottle of bourbon and several tablets of Nembutal, a barbiturate that is sometimes used to induce sleep but is not recommended for use with alcohol. The four of them talked until midnight. Before leaving, Abramson advised Olson to take a couple of Nembutal if he had trouble sleeping.

"You know, I feel a lot better," Olson said as the evening ended. "This is what I have been needing."

The next morning, Ruwet took Olson to visit the magician John Mulholland. According to a later report in the *New York Times*, Mulholland "may have tried to hypnotize" Olson, leading Olson to ask Ruwet several times, "What's behind this?" By another account, Olson "became agitated when he thought Mulholland was going to make him disappear like one of the magician's rabbits." A few minutes after arriving, he jumped from his chair and bolted out of the house. Ruwet ran after him.

That night, Ruwet and Lashbrook took Olson on a stroll along Broadway. They bought tickets for a musical called *Me and Juliet*. During the intermission, Olson said he feared being arrested at the end of the show. Ruwet scoffed, and guaranteed "personally" that Olson would be home in time for Thanksgiving dinner the next afternoon. Nonetheless Olson insisted on leaving.

The two men returned to the Statler Hotel, leaving Lashbrook to enjoy the second act of *Me and Juliet*. They went to bed without incident. When Ruwet awoke at 5:30 the next morning, Olson was gone. He roused Lashbrook, who was in a nearby room, and the two of them descended to the hotel's cavernous lobby. There they found Olson, sitting in a chair and looking disheveled. He reported that he had been wandering aimlessly through the city and had thrown away his wallet and identification cards.

That day was Thanksgiving. A week had passed since Olson was given LSD at Deep Creek Lake. He still planned to return to his family for holiday dinner. Accompanied by Lashbrook and Ruwet, he boarded a flight to Washington. An MK-ULTRA colleague was waiting when they landed at National Airport. Ruwet and Olson got into his car for the drive to Frederick. Soon after they set out, Olson's mood changed. He asked that the car be stopped.

"What's wrong?" Ruwet asked.

"I would just like to talk things over."

They pulled into the parking lot of a Howard Johnson's in Bethesda. Olson turned to Ruwet and announced that he felt "ashamed to meet his wife and family" because he was "so mixed up."

"What do you want me to do?" Ruwet asked.

"Just let me go. Let me go off by myself."

"I can't do that."

"Well then, just turn me over to the police. They're looking for me anyway."

After some discussion, Ruwet suggested that Olson might want to return to New York for another session with Abramson. Olson agreed. They drove back to Washington and made their way to Lashbrook's apartment near Dupont Circle. Gottlieb, who had broken off his holiday plans upon hearing of the morning's developments, arrived soon afterward. Later he reported that Olson seemed "very mentally disturbed at this time . . . He talked in a clear manner, but his thoughts were confused. He again talked about his incompetence in his work, the hopelessness of anybody helping him, and the fact that the best thing to do was to abandon him and not bother about him."

Given what Olson knew, and his state of mind, that was impossible. Gottlieb ordered Ruwet to drive to Maryland and tell the Olson family that Frank would not be arriving for Thanksgiving dinner after all. Then he drove Olson and Lashbrook to National Airport and put them on a flight back to New York.

After landing, the two scientists took a taxi to Abramson's weekend home in the Long Island town of Huntington. Abramson spent about an hour with Olson, followed by twenty minutes with Lashbrook. The guests then left, checked into a guesthouse at nearby Cold Spring Harbor, and adjourned for a quiet Thanksgiving dinner.

The next morning, Abramson, Lashbrook, and Olson drove back to Manhattan. During a session at his Fifty-Eighth Street office, Abramson persuaded Olson that he should agree to be hospitalized as a voluntary patient—not committed by legal authority—at a Maryland sanatorium called Chestnut Lodge. With that decided, Olson and Lashbrook left, registered at the Statler Hotel for one last night, and were given room 1018A.

Over dinner in the Statler's dining room, Olson told Lashbrook that he was looking forward to his hospitalization. He mused about books he would read. Lashbrook later said he was "almost the Dr. Olson I knew before the experiment." The two returned to their room. Olson washed his socks in the sink, watched television for a while, and lay down to sleep.

At 2:25 in the morning he went out the window.

POLICE OFFICERS FROM the Fourteenth Precinct appeared at the Statler Hotel moments after Olson hit the sidewalk on Seventh Avenue. The night manager took them to room 1018A, opened the door with a passkey, and stood aside as they entered. The window was smashed out, with only a few shards remaining. Lashbrook looked up from the toilet as the officers entered.

It was all quite straightforward, he told them. He had been awoken by the smash of breaking glass, and Olson was gone. Beyond that he had little to say. The officers considered the possibility of foul play, possibly involving a homosexual affair.

"Would you happen to know where Mr. Olson's wallet is?" one of them asked.

"I think he might have lost it a couple of nights ago," Lashbrook replied.

"You're going to have to come with us to the station house."

At the Fourteenth Precinct station on West Thirtieth Street, Lashbrook was asked to empty his pockets. He was carrying several airline tickets, a receipt for a payment of $115 signed by the magician John Mulholland, and notes with names, addresses, and phone numbers for Vincent Ruwet, Harold Abramson, George Hunter White, and Chestnut Lodge, the Maryland sanatorium where Olson was to be hospitalized.

In his wallet were several security passes, including one issued by the CIA and another granting him access to Edgewood Arsenal. The officers asked him to explain.

Lashbrook said he was a chemist working for the Defense Department, and that Olson had been a bacteriologist working for the army. Olson became mentally unstable. He had brought Olson to New York to be treated by Harold Abramson. Then, driven by inner demons, Olson had leapt through the hotel window. That was all, Lashbrook said—except for one important detail: this matter must be kept quiet for national security reasons.

The detectives left Lashbrook alone while they checked his story. Ruwet and Abramson confirmed it. After a few more questions, the detectives told Lashbrook that he was free to leave but should appear at Bellevue Hospital later that morning to identify Olson's body. He returned to the Statler Hotel. Soon afterward there was a knock on his door. A CIA fix-it man had arrived.

Every secret service needs officers who specialize in cleaning up messes. In the CIA of the 1950s, those officers worked for Sheffield Edwards at the Office of Security. The cover-up he directed in the hours and days after Frank Olson died was a model of brisk efficiency.

Immediately after Olson crashed through the Statler Hotel window, Lashbrook called Gottlieb to report what had happened. Gottlieb, in turn, dialed a secret telephone number that connected him to the duty officer at CIA headquarters. He reported that there had been "an incident in a hotel in New York City involving a death" and that it required "immediate attention." The duty officer called Edwards and told him that "an Agency employee assigned to an eyes-only project at Camp Detrick" had committed suicide in New York.

"The subject's name was Frank Olson," he added.

Edwards gave the duty officer two assignments. First he was to call Lashbrook and tell him to move to another room at the Statler Hotel and "talk to nobody until we get someone there with him." Second, he should immediately summon both Gottlieb and Gottlieb's boss—"Gib" Gibbons, chief of the Technical Services Staff—to Quarters Eye, an unmarked CIA building near the Lincoln Memorial.

Both men were waiting for Edwards when he arrived at 5:40 a.m.

They told him what had happened in New York. Edwards later reported that he "questioned Dr. Gibbons and Dr. Gottlieb at some length on certain matters that had occurred prior to this incident." He knew what he was looking for. Edwards had been a co-creator of Bluebird, which carried out experiments with psychoactive drugs beginning in 1950, before MK-ULTRA was created. Under his questioning, Gottlieb revealed a key fact: Olson's CIA colleagues had given him LSD without his knowledge nine days before his death.

With the calm self-assurance for which he was known at the CIA, Edwards announced how the cover-up would unfold. First, the New York police would be persuaded not to investigate, and to cooperate in misleading the press. Second, a fake career—a "legend"—would be constructed for Lashbrook, who as the sole witness would be questioned by investigators and could under no circumstances be recognized as working for the CIA, much less MK-ULTRA. Third, the Olson family would have to be informed, placated, and kept cooperative. Edwards had men to handle the first two jobs. The third was for Gottlieb: find a trusted man to break the news to the new widow. Gottlieb said he had already done so.

"I spoke with Vincent Ruwet, chief of Detrick's SO Division, at about three AM and asked him to go to Olson's home," Gottlieb said. "He's probably there right now."

Ruwet had the awful job of telling Alice Olson that her husband had just died violently—and also to begin the process of keeping the family quiet. Light snow fell as he drove toward the wood bungalow in Frederick. Alice was overwhelmed by the news. She sobbed uncontrollably and collapsed onto the floor. When she could speak, it was to say, "Tell me what happened."

Ruwet told Alice that her husband had been in a New York hotel room and "fell or jumped" through the window to his death. Her screams awoke her nine-year-old son, Eric. When he appeared in the living room, Ruwet told him, "Your father had an accident. He fell or jumped out a window." That phrase came to haunt him.

"For years after that, I was completely stumped and dumbfounded by trying to resolve that alternative," Eric recalled. "There's a big difference between a fall and a jump, and I couldn't understand how either of them could've occurred."

While Alice was being informed of her husband's death at her home in Maryland, Lashbrook was welcoming the CIA cavalry to his room at the Statler Hotel in New York. It took the form of a single officer. In internal reports he is called "Agent James McC." Later he was identified as James McCord, who would go on to become a footnote to American political history as one of the Watergate burglars. McCord had previously been an FBI agent specializing in counterintelligence. Making police investigations evaporate was one of his specialties.

As soon as Edwards called McCord before dawn on November 28, he swung into action. He took the first morning plane to New York and arrived at the Statler Hotel around eight o'clock. Lashbrook had just returned from his brief detention at the Fourteenth Precinct. McCord spent more than an hour questioning him and then, around 9:30, advised him to go to the morgue at Bellevue Hospital, as the police had requested. There he identified Olson's body. While he was away, McCord minutely searched room 1018A and nearby rooms.

Shortly after noon, Lashbrook returned to the Statler Hotel. McCord was waiting. Over the next few hours, according to McCord's later report, Lashbrook made a series of telephone calls and "appeared completely composed." One call was to Sidney Gottlieb. After hanging up, Lashbrook told McCord that Gottlieb had instructed him to go to Abramson's office at 9:15 p.m., pick up a report, and bring it back to Washington.

That evening, Lashbrook and McCord emerged from the hotel and walked across Seventh Avenue to Penn Station. There they met another officer from the CIA's Office of Security, who had come to relieve McCord. The newly arrived officer, identified in reports as "Agent Walter P. T.," suggested to Lashbrook that they take a taxi to Abramson's office. When they arrived, Lashbrook said he wished to speak to Abramson alone. The agent listened through the proverbial keyhole.

"Upon closing the door, Dr. Abramson and Lashbrook started a discussion about security," he wrote in his report. "Dr. Abramson was heard to remark to Lashbrook that he was 'worried about whether or not the deal was in jeopardy,' and that he thought 'that the operation was dangerous and that the whole deal should be re-analyzed.'"

Lashbrook carried Abramson's report to Washington on the midnight train. CIA security officers in New York took care of the remaining details. The investigating police detective concluded that Olson had died from multiple fractures "subsequent upon a jump or fall." That became the official narrative.

"A bacteriologist from the Army biological warfare research center at Camp Detrick fell or jumped to his death early yesterday from a tenth floor room at the Statler Hotel in New York," Olson's hometown newspaper reported. "He was identified by a companion as Frank Olson, 43, of Route 5 in Frederick . . . Olson and his friend, Robert Vern Lashbrook, a Defense Department consultant, went to New York Tuesday because Olson wanted to see a doctor about a depressed state."

At the funeral, a barely composed Alice Olson greeted mourners as if in a daze. Among them were Olson's closest colleagues. Two whom she did not recognize made special efforts to console her. Afterward she asked a friend who they were.

"That was Bob Lashbrook and his boss," the friend replied. "They both work for the CIA, you know."

Later that week, "Lashbrook and his boss" called Alice to arrange a condolence visit. She agreed to receive them. Lashbrook introduced himself, and then presented his boss: Sidney Gottlieb. Both told Alice that her husband had been a fine man and would be sorely missed.

"I really don't know why Frank did it, but I'd be glad to tell you anything I know about what happened," Lashbrook said. Gottlieb was equally solicitous: "If you ever want to know more about what happened, we'll be happy to meet with you and talk." Alice later reflected on what might have been behind their visit.

"It was probably to check me out and see whether I was handling myself and handling the situation, whether I was hysterical," she said. "And I'm sure they left the house feeling ever so much better because I had been gracious and hospitable to them—so that I must have played right into their hands and made them feel fine."

Despite the successful cover-up, Olson's death was a near-disaster for the CIA. It came close to threatening the very existence of MK-ULTRA. Gottlieb, Helms, and Dulles might have taken this as a moment for reflection. In light of this death, they could have reasoned, further experiments with psychoactive drugs should be stopped, at least on unwitting subjects. Instead they proceeded as if it had never happened.

This reflected their view of how vital MK-ULTRA was. If it could provide the key to victory in a future war, something as minor as a single death would hardly be enough to derail it.

"Conspiracy theories aside, if Frank Olson was murdered, it may have been for the simplest reason," one study concluded more than half a century later. "Following his Deep Creek Lake experiment, Sidney Gottlieb may have found himself with a man who was so ill that it was a threat to his program's secrecy. The death of Frank Olson may have been a means to an end, the end of the threat to MK-ULTRA."

Although no one outside the CIA questioned the official story of Olson's death, inside the Agency it was a stunning event. The CIA's general counsel, Lawrence Houston—who together with Dulles had written the 1947 National Security Act that created the Agency—spent two weeks reviewing what he called "all the information available to the Agency relating to the death of Dr. Frank Olson," and wrote a brief memorandum summarizing his findings. "It is my conclusion that the death of Dr. Olson is the result of circumstances arising out of an experiment undertaken in the course of his official duties for the US Government and that there is, therefore, a direct causal connection between that accident and his death," it said. "I am not happy with what seems to me a very casual attitude on the part of TSS representatives to the way this experiment was conducted, and to their remarks that this is just one of the risks running with scientific experimentation . . . A death occurred which might have been prevented, and the Agency as a whole, particularly the Director, were caught completely by surprise in a most embarrassing manner."

Houston handed this memo to the CIA inspector general, Lyman Kirkpatrick, an OSS veteran who had joined the CIA soon after its creation. Dulles had asked Kirkpatrick to investigate Olson's death, but he gave him a less than fully revealing account of what had happened. Some time ago, Dulles told him, Olson had participated in "an experiment" that might have involved LSD, and this experience might have contributed to his suicide. He wanted a report but impressed Kirkpatrick with the need for discretion. Senator McCarthy and other critics of the CIA would certainly seize on this case if they suspected the truth. Besides, Alice Olson was soon to begin receiving survivor's benefits based on the verdict of death by "classified illness," so any other conclusion would create problems for her.

Kirkpatrick interviewed several CIA officers involved in the case. Gottlieb was not among them. He was asked only to submit a written report, and replied with eight short paragraphs. A few sentences shed light on what he called his "fairly close personal relationship" with Frank Olson. Gottlieb estimated that he had met Olson "thirteen or fourteen" times over the previous two years, at Camp Detrick and at CIA offices. He was not asked whether he and Olson had ever traveled together or what their joint projects had entailed.

At Kirkpatrick's request, Harold Abramson, who had known Olson for years, sought to treat him in the days before his death, and was one of the last people to see him alive, also wrote an account of the episode. Kirkpatrick underlined two passages. In the first, Abramson reports that when he met Olson on November 24, "I attempted to confirm what I had heard, that the experiment had been performed *especially to trap him.*" Later Abramson says that at their meeting the following day, Olson spoke of "his concern with the quality of his work, his guilt on being retired from the Army for an ulcer, and *his release of classified information.*"

Although these phrases evidently intrigued Kirkpatrick, he did not probe further. On December 18 he handed his report to Dulles. It did not fix blame but included a startling recommendation: "There should be immediately established a high-level intra-Agency board which should review all TSS experiments and give approval to any in which human beings are involved." Dulles, who knew far more about MK-ULTRA than Kirkpatrick, could not possibly agree to that. He did, however, agree to sign brief letters admonishing the director of the Technical Services Staff, "Gib" Gibbons; his deputy James Drum; and Gottlieb. "Hand carry to Gibbons, Drum, and Gottlieb," he wrote in handwritten instructions to an aide. "Have them note having read, and return to Kirkpatrick for Eyes Only file. These are not reprimands, and no personnel file notations are being made."

In the first two letters, Dulles said he considered "the unwitting application of LSD in an experiment with which you are familiar to be an indication of bad judgment." The one he sent to Gottlieb was only slightly sharper.

"I have personally reviewed the files from your office concerning the use of a drug on an unwitting group of individuals," he wrote. "In recommending the unwitting application of the drug to your superior, you did not give sufficient emphasis to the necessity for medical collaboration and for proper consideration of the rights of the individual to whom it was being administered. This is to inform you that it is my opinion that you exercised poor judgment in this case."

8

Operation Midnight Climax

Even at the CIA, employees gather for holiday parties. As the end of 1954 approached, some rinsed punch bowls while others worried about the world. The Office of Security had a special fear: that Sidney Gottlieb would spike the punch.

It had been a trying year. Communists in Vietnam had overthrown their French overlords and forced them to flee in defeat. China's alliance with the Soviet Union intensified. Secretary of State John Foster Dulles threatened "massive retaliation" against any aggressor. Senator Joseph McCarthy declared that "twenty years of treason" had brought the United States to the brink of a Communist takeover, and when CBS reporter Edward R. Murrow broadcast a sharp reply, McCarthy called him "the cleverest of the jackal pack which is always at the throat of anyone who tries to expose individual Communists or traitors." Congress passed the Communist Control Act, which defined the Communist Party of the United States as "a clear, present, and continuing danger to the security of the United States," and stripped it of "all rights, privileges, and immunities attendant upon legal bodies." Then it voted to create the Distant Early Warning line, a network of radar stations designed to alert Americans if the Soviets sent nuclear bombers over the Arctic. The CIA had managed to overthrow the Iranian and Guatemalan governments, but those successes seemed less than decisive amid the rush of scary news.

Many CIA officers believed they were all that stood between their country and devastation. They saw threats everywhere. As 1954 ended, they learned of a new one. On December 15 the ever vigilant Office of Security circulated a memo warning that rumors about certain officers using LSD, and testing it on unsuspecting subjects, should be taken seriously. It said that LSD, then largely unknown, could "produce serious insanity for periods of 8 to 18 hours and possibly longer." Given its potency, and the unpredictable enthusiasms of officers who had access to it, the Office of Security said it would "not recommend testing in the Christmas punch bowls usually present at Christmas office parties."

That memo reflected how widely rumors about Gottlieb, and the extremes to which he was pushing his mind control project, had spread through the CIA. After Frank Olson's death, he had abandoned thoughts of leaving the Agency and resolved instead to intensify his commitment. An odd aura came to surround him. He was unique not just in character and background, but because of the nature of his work.

If any troubling thoughts crept into the consciences of MK-ULTRA scientists following Olson's death, they were blown away by news of a breakthrough that came just a few weeks later. "Chemists of the Eli Lilly Company working for [the Technical Services Staff] have in the past few weeks succeeded in breaking the secret formula held by Sandoz for the manufacturing of Lysergic Acid, and have manufactured for the Agency a large quantity of Lysergic Acid, which is available for our experimentation," Gottlieb's deputy Robert Lashbrook wrote to his boss late in 1954. "This work is a closely guarded secret and should not be mentioned generally."

Eli Lilly was now able to produce LSD in what it called "tonnage quantities." The CIA was its main customer. Under what Gottlieb called Subproject 18, it paid Eli Lilly $400,000 for a mass purchase of LSD. This would be the costliest "subcontract" in MK-ULTRA's decade-long existence. Assured of a steady supply, he devoted himself to conceiving research projects that might bring him closer to what he believed must be the drug's inner secret. Ten of his first fifty "subprojects" were directly related to the production and study of LSD.

Any systematic study would require controlled experimentation. In the case of LSD, that meant administering it to human subjects in clinical settings where their reactions could be monitored. Neither Gottlieb nor his partners at Camp Detrick had facilities or professional staff for a research project on this scale. It would have to be subcontracted to established hospitals and medical centers. Most of the doctors and others conducting the experiments, however, could not be allowed to know that they were working for the CIA, much less that the ultimate purpose of their experiments was to give the U.S. government tools for mind control. Maintaining that secrecy required "cutouts"—front groups that would agree to funnel CIA money to selected researchers. Among the first were two philanthropic foundations, the Geschickter Fund for Medical Research and the Josiah P. Macy Foundation. At the behest of the CIA, these foundations announced to hospitals and medical schools that they were interested in sponsoring controlled studies of LSD, which thanks to the Eli Lilly breakthrough they could now supply in bulk. With money suddenly available, there was no lack of takers.

"Almost overnight," one survey of this period concludes, "a whole new market for grants in LSD research sprang into existence."

By the mid-1950s, Gottlieb was subsidizing research conducted by many of America's leading behavioral psychologists and psycho-pharmacologists. Few knew that the CIA was the true source of their funding. Many conducted their CIA-sponsored "subprojects" at highly reputed institutions, among them Massachusetts General Hospital, the Worcester Foundation for Experimental Biology, Ionia State Hospital, and Mount Sinai Hospital; the Universities of Pennsylvania, Minnesota, Denver, Illinois, Oklahoma, Rochester, Texas, and Indiana; other universities, including Harvard, Berkeley, City College of New York, Columbia, MIT, Stanford, Baylor, Emory, George Washington, Cornell, Florida State, Vanderbilt, Johns Hopkins, and Tulane; and medical schools at Wayne State University, Boston University, New York University, and the University of Maryland.

Some of these drug experiments required risking the health of participants, like one at the Walter E. Fernald School in Massachusetts in which mentally handicapped children were fed cereal laced with uranium and radioactive calcium. Others, especially those involving LSD, were non-coercive and even attractive. Soon after Dr. Robert Hyde began giving LSD to student volunteers in Boston, doctors, nurses, and attendants who observed the results began signing up to try it themselves. The same thing happened at other research centers.

These LSD experiments were only part of what engaged Gottlieb in the early days of MK-ULTRA. The range of his ambition and imagination was literally mind-boggling. No intelligence officer in history ever searched so intently for ways to capture and manipulate human consciousness. Early in 1955 he wrote a memo listing the "materials and methods" he either was researching or wished to research.

1. Substances which will promote illogical thinking and impulsiveness to the point where the recipient would be discredited in public.
2. Substances which increase the efficiency of mentation and perception.
3. Materials which will prevent or counteract the intoxicating effect of alcohol.
4. Materials which will promote the intoxicating effect of alcohol.
5. Materials which will produce the signs and symptoms of recognized diseases in a reversible way so that they may be used for malingering, etc.
6. Materials which will render the indication of hypnosis easier or otherwise enhance its usefulness.
7. Substances which will enhance the ability of individuals to withstand privation, torture and coercion during interrogation and so-called "brainwashing."
8. Materials and physical methods which will produce amnesia for events preceding and during their use.
9. Physical methods of producing shock and confusion over extended periods of time and capable of surreptitious use.
10. Substances which produce physical disablement such as paralysis of the legs, acute anemia, etc.
11. Substances which will produce "pure" euphoria with no subsequent let-down.
12. Substances which alter personality structure in such a way that the tendency of the recipient to become dependent upon another person is enhanced.
13. A material which will cause mental confusion of such a type that the individual under its influence will find it difficult to maintain a fabrication under questioning.

14. Substances which will lower the ambition and general working efficiency of men when administered in undetectable amounts.

15. Substances which will promote weakness or distortion of the eyesight or hearing faculties, preferably without permanent effects.

16. A knockout pill which can surreptitiously be administered in drinks, food, cigarettes, as an aerosol, etc., which will be safe to use, provide a maximum of amnesia, and be suitable for use by agent types on an ad hoc basis.

17. A material which can be surreptitiously administered by the above routes and which in very small amounts will make it impossible for a man to perform any physical activity whatever.

Years later, reviewing the projects that occupied Gottlieb and his Technical Services Staff comrades during the 1950s, the *New York Times* called them "a bizarre grope into the world of science fiction."

"CIA investigators let their imaginations run," the *Times* reported. "Was there . . . a knockout drug that could incapacitate an entire building full of people? A pill that would make a drunk man sober? . . . They worked on ways to achieve the 'controlled production' of headaches and earaches, twitches, jerks, and staggers. They wanted to reduce a man to a bewildered, self-doubting mass to 'subvert his principles,' a CIA document said. They wanted to direct him in ways that 'may vary from rationalizing a disloyal act to construction of a new person' . . . They wanted to be able to get away with murder without leaving a trace . . . They were aware that it was considered unethical to experiment on people with drugs without their knowledge, but they decided that 'unwitting' testing was essential if accurate information on LSD and other substances was to be obtained."

Soon after Frank Olson died, Gottlieb departed for another of his periodic tours through East Asia. While he was there, he participated in interrogations during which subjects were dosed with LSD. "We did do LSD-related operations in the Far East in the period 1953 to 1954," he later testified.

In 1955, Gottlieb was drafted into a plot to assassinate Prime Minister Zhou Enlai of China. A plane that was to take Zhou to the Asian-African Congress at Bandung, Indonesia, exploded in mid-air, but he had changed his plans and was on another flight. The next day China's foreign ministry called the bombing "a murder by the special service organizations of the United States." An investigation by the Indonesian authorities concluded that a time bomb had blown up on the plane, triggered by an American-made MK-7 detonator.

The next best option, CIA officers decided, was to poison Zhou while he was in Bandung. Gottlieb had provided the toxin that CIA turncoat James Kronthal used to kill himself two years earlier. He could come up with something suitable for Zhou.

The potion Gottlieb concocted was to be placed in a rice bowl from which Zhou would eat. Forty-eight hours later—after Zhou was back in China—he would take ill and die. Shortly before this attempt was to have been made, news of it reached General Lucian Truscott Jr., who was then a deputy director of the CIA. Truscott feared that the Agency's role in assassinating Zhou would become clear and cause great trouble for the United States. His biographer wrote that he was "outraged [and] confronted Dulles, forcing him to cancel the operation." Gottlieb's deadly drops went unused.

A PLATOON OF U.S. Marines trudging along a mountain path in Korea came under sudden mortar attack one afternoon at the end of 1952. Lieutenant Allen Macy Dulles, son of the director of central intelligence, was hit in the arm and back. Refusing evacuation, he led his men forward until another shell exploded near him. A piece of shrapnel tore into his skull and lodged in his brain. Close to death, he was taken to a hospital in Japan and then to the United States. He suffered permanent neurological damage, and although he went on to live a long life, all of it was spent in institutions or under the care of others.

Like many men of his class and generation, the CIA director had distant relationships with his children. Nonetheless his son's traumatic injury deeply affected him. He took the same interest in alternative treatments that any father would. Desperate for a way to bring his son back to a semblance of normality, he corresponded with specialists at psychiatric clinics in the United States and Europe. By early 1954, the wounded warrior was at Cornell Medical Center in New York City, under the care of a neurologist named Harold Wolff. Soon after treatment began, Dulles summoned Wolff to Washington to discuss the medical case at hand. As their conversation continued, the two men found much in common. Wolff shared Dulles's fascination with the idea of mind control. He had developed a theory, woven from various disciplines, that a combination of drugs and sensory deprivation could wipe the mind clean and then open it to reprogramming. He called this "human ecology." Dulles thought Wolff might be useful to the CIA and sent him to Gottlieb.

Wolff was eager for CIA sponsorship. He wrote several research proposals for Gottlieb. In one, he proposed placing people in isolation chambers until they became "receptive to the suggestions of the psychotherapist," showed "an increased desire to talk and to escape from the procedure," and broke down to the point where doctors could "create psychological reactions within them." In another, he offered to test "special methods" of interrogation, including "threats, coercion, imprisonment, isolation, deprivation, humiliation, torture, 'brainwashing,' 'black psychiatry,' hypnosis, and combinations of these with or without chemical agents." Gottlieb was intrigued—all the more so because Wolff had access to a steady flow of patients and made clear that he was willing to use them as unwitting subjects. He approved every proposal Wolff submitted. The experiments proceeded for several years at Cornell Medical Center, at a cost to the CIA of nearly $140,000. Patients were told that the drugs they were given and the procedures they underwent were essential to their treatment. Wolff's chillingly ambiguous purpose was to study "changes in behavior due to stress brought about by actual loss of cerebral tissues."

Other researchers were conducting equally harsh experiments for Gottlieb, but he and Wolff forged a special partnership. In 1955 they conceived the idea of creating a research foundation that would pose as independent but actually be a conduit through which MK-ULTRA money could be given to physicians, psychologists, chemists, and other scientists. Gottlieb had already used established foundations as conduits, but with his empire of "subprojects" expanding so quickly, he wanted one of his own. It emerged as the Society for the Investigation of Human Ecology, with Wolff as founding president. All of its funds came from the CIA. It made a few small grants to support projects of no apparent intelligence value, but those were intended only to preserve deniability. Every major project it sponsored was Gottlieb's.

Soon after establishing this bogus foundation, Wolff reported that he was using it to fund "experimental investigations designed to develop new techniques of offensive/defensive intelligence . . . Potentially useful secret drugs (and various brain damaging procedures) will be similarly tested." Gottlieb and one of his close colleagues, John Gittinger, the chief CIA psychologist, shaped the foundation's research agenda. Gittinger later said that the experiments it funded were in "the areas of influencing human behavior, interrogation, and brainwashing."

One of the first "subprojects" the society commissioned was an intensive study of one hundred Chinese refugees, who were lured to participate with the promise of "fellowships" but were actually being tested to see if they could be programmed to return home and commit acts of sabotage. After the 1956 anti-Communist uprising in Hungary, the society funded a series of interviews and tests among Hungarian refugees to determine the factors that lead people to rebel against their government. Later it paid for a study of how sexual psychopaths repress secrets, and how they can be made to reveal them. The range of its other projects reflects Gottlieb's unflagging imagination: studies of the Mongoloid skull, the effect of owning a fallout shelter on foreign policy views, and the emotional impact of circumcision on Turkish boys; tests to determine whether interrogators could use "isolation, anxiety, lack of sleep, uncomfortable temperatures, and chronic hunger" to produce "profound disturbances of mood [and] excruciating pain"; and research into trance states and "activation of the human organism by remote electronic means." As MK-ULTRA reached its peak, the Society for the Investigation of Human Ecology became the principal portal through which Gottlieb lured talented scientists into his "subproject" netherworld.

WHEN THE AMERICAN Psychological Association convened for its 1954 convention—at the Statler Hotel in New York, where Frank Olson had spent the last night of his life a year before—one of Gottlieb's officers was circulating through the crowd. He reported back that of the several hundred papers the attending scientists presented, one seemed potentially valuable to MK-ULTRA. That paper, and a talk that the author gave in presenting it, described a series of experiments aimed at testing the "effects of radical isolation upon intellectual function." Student volunteers in these experiments—paid for by the Canadian army and conducted at McGill University in Montreal—were blindfolded, fitted with earplugs, and had their hands and feet bound into foam-rubber mitts. Each was sealed into a small soundproof chamber. Within hours, they became unable to follow trains of thought. Most broke down within a few days. None lasted more than a week. The paper's principal author, Dr. James Hebb, asserted that these experiments provided "direct evidence of a kind of dependence on the environment that has not been previously recognized."

This research attracted attention at the CIA. The Office of Security issued a memo telling interrogators that "total isolation" had proven to be "an operational tool of potential." In 1955 the CIA mind control enthusiast Morse Allen sent a report to Maitland Baldwin, a surgeon at the National Institute of Mental Health, describing an experiment in which an army volunteer had been locked into a small isolation box and, after forty hours, began "crying loudly and sobbing in a most heartrending fashion." Baldwin was thrilled. That experiment, he wrote in reply, suggested that "the isolation technique could break any man, no matter how intelligent or strong-willed."

As CIA scientists looked more deeply into the work Hebb had done at McGill, they discovered that one of his colleagues was pushing his experiments further in the coercive direction that especially interested them. In 1956 this remarkable physician, Ewen Cameron, published a paper in the *American Journal of Psychiatry* describing his "adaptation of Hebb's psychological isolation." He reported experiments in which he enclosed patients in small cells, placed them in a "clinical coma" using hypnosis and drugs, including LSD, and then subjected them to endless repetition of simple recorded phrases. Most intriguingly, he compared his patients' responses to "the breakdown of the individual under continuous interrogation."

Cameron was born in Scotland, lived in upstate New York, and commuted to work at McGill, where he was chairman of the Department of Psychology and director of an affiliated psychiatric hospital, the Allan Memorial Institute. Colleagues considered him a visionary. When Gottlieb recruited him, he was president of both the American Psychological

Association and the Canadian Psychiatric Association. The focus of his research, the peculiar nature of his experiments, and the fact that he worked outside the United States combined to make him an ideal MK-ULTRA contractor.

Many psychiatrists of that era considered "talk therapy" to be the most promising way to disrupt patterns that shape the human mind and human behavior, but Cameron rejected it as too slow and unreliable. In his experiments, he sought to learn whether it was possible to stun mentally disturbed patients out of their afflictions by exposing them to extreme heat, subjecting them to electroshock, and even, in one extended experiment, placing them under intense red light for eight hours a day over a period of months. He called this "re-patterning," and believed it could create "brain pathways" by which he would be able to reshape his patients' minds.

"If we can succeed in inventing means of changing their attitudes and beliefs," Cameron wrote, "we shall find ourselves in possession of measures which, if wisely used, may be employed in freeing ourselves from their attitudes and beliefs."

Most of Cameron's patients suffered not from crippling mental disorders but from relatively minor ones like anxiety, family trouble, or postpartum depression. Once they made the fateful choice to come to the Allan Memorial Institute for help, they became his unwitting subjects. Some went on to suffer far greater physical and psychic pains than those they had come to cure.

Cameron began his "treatments" with extreme sensory deprivation. He gave patients drugs that put them into a semi-comatose state for periods ranging from ten days to three months. This produced what he called "not only a loss of the space-time image but a loss of all feeling . . . In more advanced forms, [the patient] may be unable to walk without support, to feed himself, and he may show double incontinence."

To cleanse unwanted thoughts from a patient's mind, Cameron used a technique he called "psychic driving," in which he administered electroconvulsive shocks that reached thirty to forty times the strength other psychiatrists used. After days of this treatment, the patient was moved to a solitary ward. There he or she was fed LSD and given only minimal amounts of food, water, and oxygen. Cameron fitted patients with helmets equipped with earphones, into which he piped phrases or messages like "My mother hates me," repeated hundreds of thousands of times.

In professional papers and lab reports, Cameron reported that he had succeeded in destroying minds but had not found ways to replace them with new ones. After completing his treatment of one patient, he wrote with evident pride that "the shock treatment turned the then-19-year-old honors student into a woman who sucked her thumb, talked like a baby, demanded to be fed from a bottle, and urinated on the floor." Other patients disappointed him. "Although the patient was prepared by both prolonged sensory isolation (35 days) and by repeated de-patterning," he wrote in one report, "and although she received 101 days of positive driving, no favorable results were obtained."

Gottlieb recognized Cameron as a potentially valuable research collaborator but did not want to make the approach himself. Nor did he send another CIA officer. Instead he dispatched Maitland Baldwin, whose position at the National Institute of Mental Health gave him an aura of professional eminence. In Montreal, Baldwin followed the recruiting script Gottlieb had given him. First he confirmed Gottlieb's impression that Cameron would make a fine MK-ULTRA collaborator. Once assured that he had found the right man, he proposed a deal. He suggested that Cameron apply to the Society for the Investigation of Human Ecology for funds to carry out more intense experiments. Cameron did so. His application was quickly approved, and he set off on what Gottlieb called Subproject 68.

Like many other MK-ULTRA collaborators, Cameron was unaware—at least at the beginning—that he was working for the CIA. Gottlieb kept the Agency double-protected. First, he channeled money through what seemed to be a legitimate foundation. Second, he used Maitland Baldwin as his emissary, making it appear that Subproject 68 was civilian research. Their contract specified what it would entail.

(1) The breaking down of ongoing patterns of the patient's behavior by means of particularly intensive electroshocks (de-patterning).

(2) The intensive repetition (16 hours a day for 6–7 days) of the prearranged verbal signal.

(3) During the period of intensive repetition the patient is kept in partial
     sensory isolation.

(4) Repression of the driving period is carried out by putting the patient,
     after the conclusion of the period, into continuous sleep for 7–10 days.

Over the next several years, the CIA sent Cameron $69,000 to carry
out these and other experiments, aimed at finding ways to wipe away
memory and implant new thoughts into people's brains. During this
period, according to the historian Alfred McCoy, "approximately one
hundred patients admitted to the Allan Institute with moderate emotional problems became unwitting or unwilling subjects in an extreme
form of behavioral experimentation." One day in 1955, the CIA officer
who was Gottlieb's liaison to Cameron wrote in his diary: "Dr. G made
clear my job was to ensure acceptable deniability operates all times in
Montreal."

A review conducted decades later concluded that Cameron's techniques had "no therapeutic validity whatsoever" and were "comparable
to Nazi medical atrocities." While the experiments were underway, however, Gottlieb found them irresistible. As soon as one was completed, he
sent Cameron money to conduct more.

DURING THE YEARS Gottlieb was sponsoring experiments that pushed
human subjects to the limit of endurance and beyond, he maintained a sta-
ble and happy family life. By all appearances he was a loving husband and
good father to his four children. He adapted remarkably well to rural life,
happily milking goats, collecting eggs, and helping to tend the family's
gardens. His life was strikingly bifurcated. By day he directed research
that required the sustained infliction of intense mental and physical
pain. On evenings and weekends, he was not only the model dad but
also strikingly spiritual.

Few Americans of Gottlieb's generation, or any generation, had home
lives so surrealistically different from their work lives. Gottlieb cannot
have failed to see the Jekyll-and-Hyde contradiction. Yet he could rec-
oncile it. He was an individualist who could tell himself that he was
working to protect humanity against an enemy whose goal was to wipe

away all possibility of individualistic life. By living outside the suburban mainstream, cultivating his spirituality, and seeking closeness to nature, he was following a personal path that was strikingly unconventional. At work he was doing the same: rejecting the limits that circumscribed more conventional minds and daring to follow his endlessly fertile imagination.

"A chemist who is not a mystic is not a real chemist," the inventor of LSD, Albert Hofmann, said toward the end of his long life. "He doesn't comprehend it."

A JOB FOR a tough guy became vacant at the beginning of 1955: district supervisor at the Federal Bureau of Narcotics office in San Francisco. The bureau's legendary director Harry Anslinger named his most flamboyant agent, George Hunter White, to fill it. That might have been a loss for MK-ULTRA, since White was then luring unsuspecting victims to his "safe house" in New York and dosing them with LSD or whatever other drug Gottlieb wanted him to test. Gottlieb, however, saw a way to take advantage of the transfer. He would hire White to set up a "safe house" in San Francisco where he could do everything he had done in New York and more. This became MK-ULTRA Subproject 42. White called it Operation Midnight Climax.

This "subproject" had intertwined goals. The first was to feed drugs to unsuspecting civilians and observe their reactions, as had been done in New York. This time, though, sex would be added to the mix. At Gottlieb's direction, White assembled a group of prostitutes whose job would be to bring clients to the "pad" and dose them with LSD while he watched and recorded their reactions.

White plunged into his new assignment. He set up his "pad"—it was never called an apartment or a safe house—at 225 Chestnut Street, on Telegraph Hill. It was laid out in an L-shape and had a lovely view of San Francisco Bay. After renting it, White called a friend who owned an electronics shop and asked him to install surveillance equipment so he could monitor what happened inside. The friend wired four DD4 microphones disguised as wall outlets to two F-301 tape recorders that he installed in a "listening post" next door. A CIA officer who visited after the work was complete reported that the place "was so wired that if you spilled a glass of water, you'd probably electrocute yourself."

The San Francisco "pad" was decorated in a style that might be called bordello chic. Pictures of can-can dancers, along with framed Toulouse-Lautrec prints on black silk mats, decorated the walls. The bedroom featured red curtains and large mirrors. Some drawers were filled with tools of the trade, including sex toys and photos of manacled women in black stockings and studded leather halters. "We had a comprehensive library on Chestnut Street," one agent who worked there later testified, "the most pornographic library I ever saw: dirty movies, pictures, everything. The CIA put it up there because of teaching these whores how to hump and how to—'Turn to page 99 in the book, it'll show you how and what.'"

To accommodate his prostitutes, their clients, and himself, White kept the bar well stocked. Several of his associates said that he often watched the proceedings from next door while drinking from a pitcher of martinis and sitting on a portable toilet. Sure enough, among documents that the CIA later declassified is an expense report he filed on August 3, 1955, that includes this entry: "1 Portable toilet, $25; 24 disposal bags @ $.15 each, $3.60—$28.60."

Gottlieb took an all-or-nothing approach to documentation. So far as is known, he wrote nothing substantial about his years of experiments in secret prisons around the world. Yet in matters of expenses and office details he was meticulous. As the Operation Midnight Climax "pad" was being prepared in San Francisco, he composed a lengthy memo approving the purchase of each item used to furnish it. He listed more than a hundred, including drapes, pillows, lamps, ashtrays, an ice bucket, a box spring with mattress, a wastebasket, and a vacuum cleaner—along with more curious items including an easel and an "unfinished painting," two busts, two statuettes, and a telescope. Gottlieb also sent White a detailed memo setting out, with his usual precision, "the mutual administrative responsibilities of the principal research investigator and the sponsor." It stipulates that White must "maintain funds in a separate bank account, obtain a receipt or invoice wherever possible . . . periodically include a general statement of the use of liquor [and] note taxi expenses by date." The only expenses Gottlieb did not want itemized were payments to prostitutes.

"Due to the highly unorthodox nature of these activities and the considerable risk incurred by these individuals," he wrote, "it is impossible to require that they provide a receipt for these payments or that they indicate the precise manner in which the funds were spent."

Although White had been deeply immersed in the New York demimonde, he was a newcomer to San Francisco. For help he turned to a former military intelligence officer named Ira "Ike" Feldman, who had done bare-knuckle work in Europe and Korea. Feldman had retired to California with the vague idea of running a chicken farm.

"Before long, I get a call, this time from White," he recalled years later. "'We understand you're back in the States,' he says. 'I want you to come in to the Bureau of Narcotics.' This was '54 or '55. White was district supervisor in San Francisco. I went in. I go to Room 144 of the Federal Building, and this is the first time I meet George White. He was a big, powerful man with a completely bald head. Not tall, but big. Fat. He shaved his head and had the most beautiful blue eyes you've ever seen. 'Ike,' he says, 'we want you as an agent.'"

Feldman took the job. For the next several months he did undercover work for the narcotics bureau. He ran a sting operation in which he posed as a pimp and, as he later testified, "had half a dozen girls working for me." In another, he used a drug-addicted prostitute to entrap drug users, paying her with doses of heroin. White was impressed.

"One day, White calls me into his office," he recalled. "'Ike,' he says, 'you've been doing one hell of a job as an undercover man. Now I'm gonna give you another assignment. We want you to test mind-bending drugs . . . If we can find out just how good this stuff works, you'll be doing a great deal for your country.'"

Few former intelligence officers could resist such a patriotic pitch, especially at the height of the Cold War. The next time Gottlieb was in San Francisco, Feldman met with him. Gottlieb began by opening his briefcase, pulling out a small glass vial, and laying it on the table in front of him.

"You know what this is?" he asked Feldman.

"Jeez, I don't know what the hell it is."

"It's LSD. We want you and your contacts—we know you got all the broads in San Francisco and you got all the hookers—and we want you to start putting this in people's drinks."

"What are you, crazy? I mean, I could get arrested or something."

"Don't worry about it."

"What does it do?"

"Well, we got about 50 different things we're going to try. This particular stuff here will drive a guy nuts or a woman nuts. It's out of this world."

"I don't know, Sidney. I'll do intelligence work, but I'm not doing that fucking bullshit."

Gottlieb then pulled out the argument that he knew would resolve Feldman's doubts, just as it had resolved his own. "If we can find out just how good this stuff works, you'll be doing a great deal for your country," he said. "It's a matter of national security. If we can get something that will bend these guys' minds and make them talk, make them go crazy, this will do a lot to save our prisoners and things like that."

That persuaded Feldman to return to his country's covert service. His first assignment was to recruit the prostitutes who would work as unwitting MK-ULTRA contractors. Each time one of them brought a client to 225 Chestnut Street, she would be paid $50 to $100. As a bonus, she would be given a "get-out-of-jail-free card" with White's phone number; the next time she was arrested, she could give the number to the police and White would arrange for her release.

"I would go to various bars, various massage parlors, and these cunts all thought that I was a racketeer," Feldman later told an interviewer. He might, for example, want to see whether a subject working on a covert aviation program would reveal its secrets. "I says, 'Honey, I want you to do a favor for me,' and I says, 'I want you to pick up Joe Blow, take him to the apartment and give him a blow job. And while he's there, I want you to ask him, 'Hey, you know that airplane? How high does it fly?'"

Intelligence agencies have for centuries used female agents to seduce men in order to learn their secrets. Gottlieb wanted to systematize the study of how sex, especially in combination with drugs, could loosen men's tongues. He found remarkably little published work to guide him. Most of the research that Dr. Alfred Kinsey reported in *Sexual Behavior in the Human Male* was too clinical to be of much use. It would be another decade before Masters and Johnson published their groundbreaking study *Human Sexual Response*, and still longer before frank works like *The Happy Hooker* and *The Hite Report on Male Sexuality* would appear. Gottlieb decided that the CIA should conduct its own research into how people behave during and after sex. He was already deeply engaged in drug experiments. Operation Midnight Climax gave those experiments a new overlay.

"We were interested in the combination of certain drugs with sex acts," the CIA psychologist John Gittinger testified years later. "We looked at the various pleasure positions used by prostitutes and others . . . This was well before anything like the Kama Sutra had become widely popular. Some of the women—the professionals—we used were very adept at these practices."

White opened the San Francisco "pad" in late 1955. His street agents were the prostitutes Feldman had recruited. Gottlieb, in the dry prose he favored, called them "certain individuals who covertly administered the material to other people." Usually the "material" was LSD, though from time to time Gottlieb brought some new concoction about whose effect he was curious.

"If we were scared enough of a drug not to try it ourselves," one MK-ULTRA man said later, "we sent it to San Francisco."

No drug scared White, who had used more different sorts than almost any American then alive. He grabbed a share of whatever the CIA sent him. "He always wanted to try everything himself," one of his partners said. "Whatever drugs they sent out, it didn't matter, he wanted to see how they worked on him before he tried them on anyone else."

While his prostitutes and their clients had sex, White would watch through a one-way mirror, sitting on his portable toilet. Sometimes Feldman joined him. Their job was to observe the men's reaction to various kinds of sex, and how they behaved when drugs and sex were combined. Feldman marveled at how freely men spoke when they were under the influence of this combination. He recognized it as an intriguing alternative to the old-fashioned interrogation techniques he had used in his military days.

"If it was a girl, you put her tits in a drawer and slammed the drawer," he explained. "If it was a guy, you took his cock and you hit it with a hammer. And they would talk to you. Now, with these drugs, you could get information without having to abuse people."

White, Feldman, and other agents who worked at the "pad" observed that after sex, a man will often speak to the woman next to him. They began assigning their prostitutes to stay with clients for several hours rather than leaving immediately. When combined with the effects of LSD, they hoped, this staged intimacy would lower a man's inhibitions.

"To find a prostitute who is willing to stay is a hell of a shock to anyone used to prostitutes," one officer reported. "It has a tremendous effect on the guy. It's a boost to his ego if she's telling him he was really neat, and she wants to stay for a few more hours . . . Most of the time, he gets pretty vulnerable. What the hell's he going to talk about? Not the sex, so he starts talking about his business. It's at this time she can lead him gently."

Pleased with what he considered the success of his San Francisco operation, Gottlieb ordered it expanded. At his direction, White opened a second safe house outside city limits, in the Marin County town of Mill Valley, which offered the privacy necessary for experiments that went beyond sex and drugs. Among the compounds he fabricated and brought to White for testing were stink bombs, itching powder, sneezing powder, and diarrhea inducers. All were to be tested on men who had met prostitutes and expected nothing more than quick sex, or on groups that were invited to parties. Gottlieb also supplied devices for White to test, including a drug-laced swizzle stick, an ultra-thin hypodermic needle that could be used to poison a wine bottle through the cork, and glass capsules that would release noxious gases when they were crushed underfoot.

Soon after the Marin County safe house opened, a couple of White's agents spent several days in San Francisco finding men they could invite to a party there. Gottlieb wanted to see if he could dose a roomful of people with LSD sprayed from an aerosol can. He produced the can and delivered it to White. On the appointed day, however, according to one agent's testimony years later, "the weather defeated us." Guests arrived as planned, but the room was so hot that windows had to be kept open. That made the experiment impossible. Reverses like these did not discourage White. He remained immersed in his work and did everything Gottlieb asked, always with his special flair.

"When he wasn't operating a national security whorehouse, White would cruise the streets of San Francisco tracking down drug pushers for the Narcotics Bureau," according to one survey of his career. "Sometimes after a tough day on the beat he invited his narco buddies up to one of the safe houses for a little 'R and R.' Occasionally they unzipped their inhibitions and partied on the premises—much to the chagrin of the neighbors, who began to complain about men with guns in shoulder straps chasing after women in various states of undress. Needless to say, there was always plenty of dope around, and the feds sampled everything from hashish to LSD . . . White had quite a scene going for a while. By day he fought to keep drugs out of circulation, and by night he dispensed them to strangers."

Only by Gottlieb's unusual standards could White have been judged qualified to run Operation Midnight Climax. He knew the ways of the street, but he was not equipped to interpret people's actions while they were unknowingly under the influence of drugs. He had no background in chemistry, medicine, or psychology. A psychiatrist who worked with the CIA, James Hamilton of Stanford University Medical School, occasionally dropped by the Telegraph Hill "pad," but usually no health professional was available in case a victim became ill or uncontrollable. Even the chemists, hypnotists, and electro-shockers Gottlieb had dispatched to conduct experiments at overseas detention centers had some training, and at least a vague idea of what they were looking for. In San Francisco, no one was around except White himself and, occasionally, Feldman or another partner.

Clients of prostitutes were not White's only victims. At the end of 1957, a deputy federal marshal named Wayne Ritchie attended a Christmas party at the Federal Building, where White was based. After taking several drinks, he became disoriented. He raced to his locker, grabbed his two service revolvers, walked to a bar in the Fillmore District, pointed one of his pistols at the bartender, and demanded money. Someone knocked him unconscious from behind. Police officers were standing over him when he awoke.

In court, Ritchie pleaded guilty to armed robbery but could offer no explanation for his momentary madness. A sympathetic judge, citing his sterling record—he was a Marine Corps veteran and had been a guard at Alcatraz—let him off without prison time. He spiraled into depression and never recovered. Only twenty-two years later, when he read Gottlieb's obituary, did he come to suspect that he had been dosed with LSD. He sued the CIA. White had died by then, but his sidekick Ira Feldman admitted in a pre-trial deposition that he had surreptitiously drugged people in and around San Francisco. "I didn't do any follow-up," he said. "It wasn't a very good thing to go and say 'How do you feel today?' You don't give them a tip. You just back away and let them worry, like this nit-wit Ritchie." Ultimately a judge denied Ritchie's claim for compensation, ruling that he had not conclusively proven he was drugged, but called the case "troubling" and added: "If Ritchie's claims are indeed true, he has paid a terrible price in the name of national security."

White was a lawman who made his own law. If he drugged unsuspecting citizens because it was a legal way to make people suffer, he was reprehensible. If he did it because he believed it would contribute to national security, he could be seen as morally strong. Whichever it was, his main qualification was his willingness to do whatever Gottlieb wished.

"White was a son of a bitch, but he was a great cop—he made that fruitcake Hoover look like Nancy Drew," Feldman told an interviewer years later. "The LSD, that was just the tip of the iceberg. Write this down: espionage, assassination, dirty tricks, drug experiments, sexual encounters and the study of prostitutes for clandestine use. That's what I was doing when I worked for George White and the CIA." The interviewer asked Feldman if he had ever met Gottlieb. That set off an extended recollection.

Several times Sidney Gottlieb came out. I met Gottlieb at the pad, and at White's office . . . Sidney was a nice guy. He was a fuckin' nut. They were all nuts. I says, "You're a good Jewish boy from Brooklyn, like me. What are you doing with these crazy cocksuckers?" He had this black bag with him. He says, "This is my bag of dirty tricks." He had all kinds of crap in that bag. We took a drive over to Muir Woods out by Stinson Beach. Sidney says, "Stop the car." He pulls out a dart gun and shoots this big eucalyptus tree with a dart. Then he tells me, "Come back in two days and check this tree." So we go back in two days, the tree was completely dead, not a leaf left on it . . . I went back and I saw White, and he says to me, "What do you think of Sidney?" I said, "I think he's a fuckin' nut." White says, "Well, he may be a nut, but this is the program. This is what we do."

Gottlieb's visits to San Francisco were not for purely business purposes. Operation Midnight Climax gave him ready access to prostitutes. According to Ira Feldman, he took full advantage of this perquisite. "He was cock crazy," Feldman said while free-associating about Gottlieb during a legal deposition near the end of his life. He recalled complaining to George Hunter White: "All he wants me to do is get him laid!"

"Anytime that fuck came to San Francisco—'Get me a girl,'" Feldman said. "He always needed a girl."

Feldman could not help adding, with a measure of pride, that every woman he supplied to Gottlieb serviced him free of charge. "All these girls I ever fixed Sidney up with," he said, "they never took any money from him. It was a favor to me."

As if that were not startling enough, Feldman added that Gottlieb had also carried on an affair with White's freewheeling wife, Albertine. "Gottlieb was humping his wife," he said. "They were very good friends. I'd always pick him up. We'd go there. We'd sit. I don't drink. Before you know it, White passed out in the bedroom. And Sidney was on the couch with the old lady, humping her brains out . . . George knew, but he—I think he loved her very much."

In 1955 Georgetown University Hospital in Washington announced plans to construct a six-story, one-hundred-bed addition called Gorman Annex. Gottlieb took note. He was funding many of his MK-ULTRA "subprojects" through dummy foundations and had to take precautions to ensure that the scientists involved did not learn the true source of their funding. This restricted his freedom of action. He wanted his own research hospital—a medical "safe house" inside the United States where CIA scientists, not outsiders, could conduct experiments. The announcement from Georgetown gave him his chance.

Gottlieb conceived the idea of secretly paying part of the $3 million cost of Gorman Annex in exchange for access to its medical facilities. In a memo to his superiors, he proposed that the CIA contribute $375,000 to the building project—which would be matched by other federal funds since it would be funneled through a "cutout" and appear to be a charitable donation. In exchange, he wrote, "one-sixth of the total space in the new hospital wing will be available to the Chemical Division of TSS, thereby providing laboratories and office space, technical assistance, equipment and experimental animals." He listed four "justifications" for what would become MK-ULTRA Subproject 35: "(A) Agency employees would be able to participate in the work without the university or the hospital authorities being aware of Agency interest. (B) Agency sponsorship of sensitive research projects will be completely deniable. (C) Full professional cover will be provided for up to three bio-chemical employees of the Chemical Division. (D) Human patients and volunteers for experimental use will be available under controlled clinical conditions."

"It is a relatively routine procedure to develop a drug to the point of human testing," Gottlieb concluded. "Ordinarily, the drug houses depend upon the services of private physicians for the final clinical testing. The physicians are willing to assume the responsibility of such tests in order to advance the science of medicine. It is difficult and sometimes impossible for TSS/CD to offer such an inducement with respect to its products. In practice, it has been possible to use outside cleared contractors for the preliminary phases of this work. However, that part which involves human testing at effective dose levels presents security problems which cannot he handled by the ordinary contractor. The proposed facility [redacted] offers a unique opportunity for the secure handling of such clinical testing in addition to the many advantages outlined in the project proposal. The security problems mentioned above are eliminated by the fact that the responsibility for testing will rest completely upon the physician and the hospital . . . Excellent professional cover would be provided for up to three bio-chemical employees of the Chemical Division of the TS. This would allow open attendance at scientific meetings, the advancement of personal standing in the scientific world, and as such, would constitute a major efficiency and morale booster."

Gottlieb's proposal to create a secret CIA laboratory inside an established Washington hospital, to be used for experiments on human subjects, was extraordinary even by MK-ULTRA standards. Richard Helms, his unofficial boss, passed the decision up to Allen Dulles. Even more extraordinary, Dulles, according to the researcher John Marks, "took it to President Eisenhower's special committee to review covert operations. The committee also gave its assent [and] the CIA money was forthcoming." This was, Marks wrote, "the only time in a whole quarter-century of Agency behavior-control activities when the documents show that CIA officials went to the White House for approval of anything."

Little is known about the experiments that CIA scientists conducted at Gorman Annex, although the Agency later confirmed that terminally ill patients were among the subjects. Pressed for details two decades later, Director of Central Intelligence Stansfield Turner replied, "There is no factual evidence of what went on. It is just missing. It is not that it didn't happen."

Almost no one, even in the highest reaches of government, knew of Gottlieb's work or even of his existence. At the CIA, however, a handful of senior officers knew enough to connect him to LSD. Gottlieb took a certain pride in this. He liked to tell a story about the time he was walking down the aisle of a plane carrying a cocktail. To his shock, one passenger asked quietly as he passed by, "Is that LSD you're drinking?" He turned and saw that the inquirer was Allen Dulles.

At the end of 1955, Dulles decided it was time to share broad outlines of the CIA's ultra-secret with someone else. He composed a modestly revealing report and sent it to Secretary of Defense Charles Wilson. Whether he was genuinely seeking to keep a senior colleague informed, or simply wanted to limit his liability in case things went wrong, his report is among the few CIA documents to describe MK-ULTRA while it was still underway.

For the past four years the Central Intelligence Agency has been actively engaged in research on a group of powerful chemicals affecting the human mind called psychochemicals. We have developed extensive professional contacts, experience and a considerable amount of information on many psychochemicals including in particular a material known as LSD. This Agency is continuing its interest in this field, and in the light of its accumulated experience offers its cooperation and assistance to research and development programs which the Department of Defense is considering at this time . . .

Since 1951 this Agency has carried out a program of research which has provided important information on the nature of the abnormal behavior produced by LSD and the way this effect varies with such factors as size of dose, differences in the individual and environment. The behavioral effects of repeated doses given over a long time has been studied. We have established that individuals may develop a tolerance to LSD. A search for possible antidotes is being made. It has been found that LSD produces remarkable mental effects when taken in exceedingly small doses. The foregoing became increasingly interesting when it was recently discovered that LSD could be synthesized in quantity. There are many characteristics of LSD and other psychochemicals which either have not been studied or require further study.

This degree of candor was as far as Dulles is known to have gone, at least on paper. He fully understood that MK-ULTRA could function only in absolute secrecy. The "special interrogation" sessions that its officers were conducting at clandestine prisons abroad, the extreme experiments it was sponsoring in hospitals and prisons, the "national security whorehouse" that was at the center of Operation Midnight Climax, the secret financing of Gorman Annex, and the panoply of Gottlieb's other "subprojects" were among the American government's most highly classified programs. If any of them became public, the result might have been not just public outrage, but the end of MK-ULTRA and possibly even the CIA itself. One potential threat had died with Frank Olson. In the months that followed, a new one emerged. It came from an unexpected quarter: the United States Congress.

9

The Divine Mushroom

When Senator Mike Mansfield of Montana rose to address his colleagues on April 9, 1956, he was courtly as always. Some in Washington, though, were horrified by what he proposed.

"Because of the very nature of the Central Intelligence Agency, I think it is important that a joint congressional committee be established for the purposes of making continued studies of the activities of the Agency," Mansfield told his colleagues. "The CIA should, as a matter of law, keep that committee as fully and as currently informed as possible with respect to its activities. Allen Dulles, Director of CIA, may make no mistakes in assessing intelligence, but he should not be the lone judge."

Mansfield proposed to create a twelve-member congressional committee that would "make continuing studies of the activities of the Central Intelligence Agency"; require the CIA to "keep the joint committee fully and currently informed with respect to its activities"; and, most ominously, give the committee power "to require, by subpoena or otherwise, the attendance of such witnesses and the production of such books, papers, and documents . . . as it deems advisable." This was the gravest threat the CIA had yet faced. Its officers had adjusted to the threat of nuclear annihilation, but Mansfield's proposal seemed a dagger to the heart.

In its eight and a half years of existence, the CIA had operated with no effective supervision, other than that exercised directly—and rarely—by the president. It did not take kindly to the idea of cooperating with a congressional committee, especially one with subpoena power. All understood that such a committee would probably uncover unsavory operations that the CIA was conducting in various parts of the world. In his Senate speech, Mansfield mentioned reports that the Agency had funded neo-Nazis in Germany, organized military raids inside China, sent agents to "start a revolution" in Guatemala, tapped the telephone of President José Figueres of Costa Rica, and illegally detained "a Japanese citizen" for eight months. Each of those reports later turned out to be true.

Neither Mansfield nor anyone else, however, had any idea that the Agency was running a program potentially more explosive than any related to covert action abroad. MK-ULTRA was top secret even within the CIA. Only two officers—Gottlieb and Lashbrook—knew precisely what it was doing. A handful of others had a clear idea. All considered it essential that no one else learn what they knew. The public, they realized, was not ready to grasp the necessity of research into mind control that required the establishment of secret prisons and the infliction of great suffering on many people. The headline over one *Washington Star* article—CIA LEADERS ARE COOL TO WATCHDOG PROPOSAL—was an understatement. Dulles knew that he and the CIA could be seriously damaged if the Agency's deep secrets became known. So did Eisenhower. He told aides that Mansfield's bill would be passed "over my dead body."

In public Eisenhower insisted that he, too, wanted tighter oversight of the CIA. He named an eight-member committee, the President's Board of Consultants on Foreign Intelligence Activities, that he said would monitor the CIA and let him know if anything was amiss. Then one of the Agency's most powerful supporters in Congress, Senator Richard Russell of Georgia, announced that his Armed Services Committee, which was charged with reviewing the CIA budget, would establish a new subcommittee to review the Agency's activities. In a letter to one of his colleagues, he made clear that he did not intend this review to be any more intrusive than what his committee was already doing.

"If there is one agency of the government in which we must take some matters on faith," Russell wrote, "I believe this agency is the CIA."

Another of the CIA's friends, Senator Leverett Saltonstall of Massachusetts, made the same point in a speech opposing Mansfield's proposal. "As a member of the Armed Services and Appropriations committees, I consider I have been informed of the activities of the CIA to the extent that I believe it was wise for me to be informed," he said. "It is not a question of reluctance on the part of the CIA officials to speak to us. Instead, it is a question of our reluctance, if you will, to seek information and knowledge on subjects which I personally, as a member of Congress and as a citizen, would rather not have."

Three days of debate in the Senate did not shake support for Mansfield's proposal, but pressure from the White House and the CIA did. Twelve of the thirty-seven co-sponsors removed their names from the proposal and opposed it. Eisenhower pressed Senate leaders to do whatever necessary to ensure that it did not pass. Senator Russell asserted in a speech that it would be better to abolish the CIA than to subject it to possibly unfriendly oversight.

"I am beginning to feel like David facing Goliath," Mansfield said on the third day of debate, "although I fear the results will not be the same."

He was right. Persuaded that the CIA needed absolute secrecy in order to defend the United States, the Senate rejected Mansfield's proposal by a powerful margin, 59–27. The CIA was safe. So was MK-ULTRA.

ON AN AUTUMN evening in Rome two thousand years ago, Emperor Claudius ate a large meal that included a plate of his favorite mushrooms. Several hours later he fell violently ill. He trembled, vomited, gasped for breath, and died before morning. Twentieth-century scientists confirmed what some Romans suspected: Claudius's wife, Agrippina, who wanted to place her son in power, had mixed poisonous mushrooms with the ones her husband liked to eat. The story of her success tantalized the first crop of CIA officers.

"Let's get into the technology of assassinations," one urged in a memo. "Figure out most effective ways to kill—like Empress Agrippina."

Certain mushrooms have long been known to be poisonous, so it was reasonable to imagine that they or their chemical extracts could be used to kill. Once Gottlieb launched his mind control project, though, mushrooms became even more tantalizing. Ancient tradition held that some varieties can produce hallucinations and distortions of perception. Spanish friars who came to Mexico in the sixteenth century reported that natives used mushrooms in religious rituals. These reports fascinated CIA officers who were looking for paths into the human psyche.

At the end of 1952 Morse Allen learned of a Mexican plant whose seeds, called *piule*, had a hypnotic effect. He dispatched a CIA officer to collect samples of *piule* and any other seed, plant, herb, or fungus that had "high narcotic and toxic value." The officer, who passed himself off as a researcher looking for organic anesthetics, spent several weeks in Mexico. He returned with bags full of samples—and with something else. Several people he met had told him tales of a "magic mushroom." Native shamans and priestesses, they said, used it as a pathway to the divine. They called it "God's flesh."

"Very early accounts of the ceremonies of some tribes of Mexican Indians show that mushrooms are used to produce hallucinations and to create intoxication," Allen wrote after hearing his officer's report. "In addition, this literature shows that witch doctors or 'divinators' used some types of mushrooms to produce confessions or to locate stolen objects or to predict the future . . . [It is] essential that the peculiar qualities of the mushroom be explored."

Gottlieb had the Mexican plant samples analyzed and was told that several did indeed contain possibly psychoactive substances. That led him to look for a chemist he could send to Mexico to find organic toxins—and, if possible, the "magic mushroom." He approached the Detroit-based pharmaceutical firm Parke, Davis and asked if it could recommend a suitable candidate. His offer was tempting: this chemist would remain at Parke, Davis but work for the CIA, which would pay his salary. The company suggested a serious-minded young researcher named James Moore, who as a graduate student had worked on the Manhattan Project. Moore was offered the job and accepted.

"If I had thought I was participating in a scheme run by a small band of mad individuals," Moore said years later, "I would have demurred."

Moore soon realized that he was not the only non-Mexican searching for "God's flesh." A remarkable married couple, Gordon and Valentina Wasson, had preceded him. Gordon Wasson was a successful New York banker who had married a Russian-born pediatrician who was obsessed with mushrooms. On their honeymoon, Valentina shocked him by racing toward patches of mushrooms, kneeling before them in "poses of adoration" and insisting that they were "things of grace infinitely inviting to the perceptive mind." She harvested a basket of them and, to her new husband's horror, ate them for dinner. He told her that he feared being a widower by morning, but she survived without ill effect. That converted him. Together they set out on a lifelong journey into the mushroom world.

In the early 1950s, the Wassons made several trips to southern Mexico in search of the "magic mushroom." Their first two trips were fruitless. Gordon Wasson made a third trip, this time accompanied by a photographer, and in a Oaxacan village they found a young Indian who led them to the home of a Mazatec woman named María Sabina. She was known as a guardian of ancient wisdom who used mushrooms to commune with the infinite. On the night of June 29, 1955, sitting before a rustic altar, she conducted her ritual. She distributed mushrooms to about twenty Indians—and, for the first time in recorded history, to outsiders.

"I am the woman who shepherds the immense," María Sabina chanted as her guests slipped into a different form of consciousness. "Everything has its origin, and I come, going from place to place from the origin."

For the next several hours, as the chants continued, Wasson and his photographer careened into a new world. "We were never more wide awake, and the visions came whether our eyes were open or closed," he wrote afterward. "The effect of the mushrooms is to bring about a fission of the spirit, a split in the person, a kind of schizophrenia, with the rational side continuing to reason and to observe the sensations that the other side is enjoying. The mind is attached by an elastic cord to the vagrant senses."

Wasson could have had no idea that news of his discovery would electrify mind control experimenters in Washington whose ambitions were vastly different from his own.

James Moore heard reports of Wasson's trip and wrote him a letter. He gave no hint that he was working for the CIA. Instead he told a partial truth: he was interested in researching the chemical properties of the "magic mushroom." He correctly guessed that Wasson would be returning to the Mexican town where he had found it, Huautla de Jiménez, and asked to accompany him. To strengthen his case, he mentioned that he knew of a foundation that would help pay for the expedition. A deal was struck. The CIA sent Wasson $2,000, disguised as a grant from the Geschickter Fund for Medical Research. In exchange Wasson agreed to take Moore with him to Mexico. This was MK-ULTRA Subproject 58, aimed at unraveling the secrets of mushrooms.

Wasson, Moore, and two French mycologists made their way to Huautla de Jiménez and found María Sabina. She agreed to repeat the ceremony. Wasson again found it transcendent. The mushrooms, he wrote afterward, gave him "a feeling of ecstasy" and raised him "to a height where you have not been in everyday life, not ever." Moore had the opposite reaction. He did not like the dirt floor, was cold and hungry, had diarrhea, and "itched all over." The ceremony, he wrote in his report, "was all this chanting in the dialect . . . I did feel the hallucinogenic effect, although 'disorientation' would be a better word to describe my reaction."

"He had no empathy for what was going on," Wasson later said. "He was like a landlubber at sea. He got sick to his stomach and hated it all . . . Our relationship deteriorated during the course of the trip."

Despite Moore's discomfort, Gottlieb and his MK-ULTRA comrades considered his trip a great success because he returned with the samples of psychoactive mushrooms they had ordered. CIA officers had already visited a mushroom-producing region of Pennsylvania and told a couple of growers that they might be asking for help producing a rare fungus. Gottlieb cautioned, however, that research into the psychoactive properties of mushrooms must "remain an Agency secret."

Inevitably, word of Wasson's adventure spread beyond his own circle and the circle of MK-ULTRA scientists. *Life* magazine asked him to write about it. The result was a seventeen-page spread, lavishly illustrated, in which Wasson described his experiences. He reported that his "spirit had flown forth and I was suspended in mid-air . . . The thought crossed my mind: could the divine mushrooms be the secret that lay behind the ancient Mysteries?" This article propelled a small horde of curious Americans toward Huautla de Jiménez. María Sabina came to wish she had never shared her people's secret. Wasson regretted that he had pressed her to do so.

Indigenous people in Mesoamerica had for centuries used the "magic mushroom" to bring them closer to invisible spirits. Wasson saw it as an aid to self-discovery, a way to open what the poet William Blake called "the doors of perception." Gottlieb's interest was entirely different. His lifelong search for inner tranquility had led him to believe that the universe embraces forces beyond known science. At the CIA he devoted himself to discovering and harnessing those forces—not as a way to ease pain or expand consciousness, but to serve the interests of one country pursuing one set of political goals at one historical moment. The image of CIA men traipsing through Mexican villages in search of a fungus that would help them defeat Communism seems outlandish in retrospect. Gottlieb, however, saw the "magic mushroom" the same way he saw LSD and every other substance he was investigating. All were potential weapons of covert war.

As Gottlieb consolidated control over his hidden realm, he solidified his position as one of the most powerful unknown Americans. Within the CIA, however, he remained an outsider. One reason was his background. Most officers who led the early CIA were comfortable with the alcoholism and old-boy camaraderie that defined their inbred world. Gottlieb could not penetrate that world and had no wish to do so. When he spoke to officers outside MK-ULTRA, it was often to preach the benefits of goat milk. Instead of joining them after hours, he retreated to his wife, children, and cabin in the Virginia woods.

"Throughout the 1950s and for some time beyond, the Agency was less than a welcoming place for Jews and racial minorities," he recalled years later. "Those who were actually ever hired or involved in operations learned rather quickly to keep their heads down when certain matters were discussed."

The other reason Gottlieb stood apart from the legendary CIA officers of that era—world-shakers like Dulles, Helms, Wisner, and Angleton—was the nature of his work. They did the conventional job of covert action: spying on enemies and trying to weaken or destroy them. Gottlieb worked on a higher plane. If he could discover a way to control the human mind, all other CIA operations, including prized successes like toppling governments in Iran and Guatemala, would fade into insignificance.

By 1957, Gottlieb had spent four intense years directing MK-ULTRA. From the Atlanta Federal Penitentiary to the "safe houses" in New York and San Francisco to the Allan Memorial Institute in Montreal, his "subprojects" were in full swing. His moment as a pioneer, though, had passed. He was approaching his fortieth birthday. A report on his MK-ULTRA work by the CIA inspector general found that "some of the activities are considered professionally unethical and in some cases border on the illegal." Restless as ever, he made an unexpected career choice.

During his years of travel, Gottlieb had met many CIA officers posted at foreign stations. In early 1957 he decided to become one of them. He left his post as chief of the Chemical Division at Technical Services, which he had run since it was created, and began several months of training as a field officer. After completing his course, he moved to Munich, accompanied by his wife and four children. He spoke German, knew the country from visits connected to MK-ULTRA interrogations, and had friends in the CIA network there.

"Gottlieb had wanted to apply his black arts to field work, so he had requested an overseas post as a case officer," according to one history of the CIA. "After being turned down by dozens of base chiefs who wanted no part of him, Munich Base Chief William Hood permitted him to come for a tour. 'He was out in Munich, God bless him, to learn the trade. He came as a case officer, a GS-16 case officer,' [CIA officer John] Sherwood said. Sherwood and Gottlieb became friends, and their families spent a great deal of time together in Munich. Looking back on it, Sherwood said he should have realized that Gottlieb was using innocent human beings in CIA experiments, but 'I thought the guy was a real family man. Hell, we used to go mountain climbing together.'"

The CIA station in Munich was a Cold War command post. From there, officers sent hundreds of partisan fighters on doomed commando missions behind the Iron Curtain and ran a host of other operations against the Soviet Union. Munich was also the base for Radio Free Europe and Radio Liberty, CIA-connected broadcast services that beamed news and anti-Soviet propaganda into Communist countries. Germany's foreign intelligence service, headed by the former Nazi officer Reinhard Gehlen, had its headquarters in the outlying district of Pullach. This concentration of covert resources attracted anti-Soviet exiles. Communist agents stalked them.

On the evening of October 12, 1957, just a few weeks after Gottlieb arrived in Munich, a Ukrainian exile leader, Lev Rebet, collapsed and died on a dark street. Doctors concluded that he had suffered a heart attack. Later a Soviet agent confessed to killing him with a specially designed spray gun that fired poison gas from a crushed cyanide ampule. It was precisely the sort of weapon Gottlieb might have designed.

"When it came to spying, Munich like Hamburg was one of the unsung capitals of Europe," the novelist John le Carré wrote in *The Secret Pilgrim*. "Even Berlin ran a poor second when it came to the size and visibility of Munich's invisible community . . . Now and then frightful scandals broke, usually when one or other of this company of clowns literally forgot which side he was working for, or made a tearful confession in his cups, or shot his mistress or his boyfriend or himself, or popped up drunk on the other side of the Curtain to declare his loyalty to whomever he had not been loyal so far. I never in my life knew such an intelligence bordello."

The CIA has not declassified files that would provide details of Gottlieb's work in Munich. Half a century later, however, the German magazine *Der Spiegel* discovered and published a document showing that in 1958—while Gottlieb was stationed in Munich—German counterintelligence agents informed Chancellor Konrad Adenauer that CIA officers were arresting people in Germany "without the knowledge of German authorities, imprisoning them at times for months, and subjecting them to forms of interrogation forbidden by German law." Adenauer, who closely cooperated with Secretary of State John Foster Dulles, chose to let the matter pass.

"For two years he worked under cover, running foreign agents," according to one survey of Gottlieb's career. "One CIA officer recalls his help in the case of a chemist who had escaped from East Germany. For months the CIA had debriefed the chemist in a safe house. He claimed that he had provided technical support to Communist intelligence services, but CIA headquarters was not convinced that he was who he said he was.

So Gottlieb was asked to interrogate him. Within a single session . . . Gottlieb established that the chemist was telling the truth, and in so doing exposed a system of secret writing that was in use by the other side."

During 1958 Gottlieb made two foreign trips from his base in Munich. One was for pleasure: he took his wife to Paris. He also flew back to Washington for an interval at CIA headquarters. While he was there, he was asked—as experienced officers often were—to address the incoming class of recruits. "He wasn't a very dramatic speaker," one of them recalled years later. "He did not impress me at all."

When he lectured to our group in 1958, he was considered by all of us a strange person, someone who was beyond the pale, doing all sorts of strange things. I thought, "I hope I don't have anything to do with this guy." He was kind of dismissed as an oddball. They flipped off his name and laughed at it. It was kind of, "That crazy guy." He was definitely not a mainstream operations officer. I made a decision of my own never to have anything to do with this guy. He was so far out in the things he was doing that by and large he was considered beyond the pale . . .

You're told that your country wants you to do this super-secret thing. It's not your role to say whether it's a good idea or not. Your job is to develop it. Gottlieb worked his way up in the ranks doing what he was told to do— not by questioning orders, but trying to figure out how to do what was asked . . . We knew there was something going on with LSD experiments. I can't remember ever seeing a document, but it was something that just kind of filtered down.

He was not an operator. He was a scientist, like the people who developed the atomic bomb. If they were told that the bomb was going to be dropped on a civilian population in Japan, at least some would have objected. But many of them thought they were just creating a capacity that might or might not be used. They soldiered on and did their technical work.

He was so low key—a little grey man. An hour after his appearance before you, you'd have trouble recognizing him in a crowd. He was the sort of esoteric scientist so far removed from the practicalities of real life that you had trouble taking him seriously. But you couldn't dismiss him entirely.

Gottlieb worked at the Munich station for two years. In 1959 he returned to a new job at CIA headquarters, created for him: "scientific adviser" to Richard Bissell, the deputy director for plans. Bissell was looking for ways to use chemical and biological agents more effectively in covert operations. Gottlieb's combination of technical expertise and field experience prepared him for the next phase in his career.

As he was settling back into life in the United States, Gottlieb's secret world was jolted by the appearance of a bestselling novel called *The Manchurian Candidate*. It tells the story of a group of American soldiers in Korea who are captured by Communists, brought to a secret base in Manchuria, "brainwashed," and sent back to the United States to commit political murder. In this case fiction lagged behind reality. Gottlieb had found no evidence that post-hypnotic suggestion, induced amnesia, or any other form of "brainwashing" actually exists. Americans, however, had been told that ex-prisoners who praised Communism or confessed to dropping bio-weapons over North Korea and China had been "brainwashed." That made *The Manchurian Candidate* sound terrifyingly real. It grabbed America's Cold War imagination. Gottlieb and his mind control warriors had begun shaping the fictional world that once shaped them.

IN NINETEENTH-CENTURY LONDON, a beautiful young artist's model falls suddenly under the control of a scheming Jew who does not bathe. He seduces her away from her virtuous suitor, wipes away memories of her past life, turns her into a great singer although she could not sing before, and becomes her lover. His weapon is the transfixing power of his eyes.

"There is nothing in your mind, nothing in your heart, nothing in your soul, but Svengali, Svengali, Svengali," he chants as she falls into a trance. Onlookers are amazed.

"These fellows can make you do anything they want," one marvels.

"Aye," replies another. "And then they kill you."

The tale of Svengali was first told in George du Maurier's immensely popular novel *Trilby*, and then in various films including the riveting 1932 version starring John Barrymore. They were part of a wave of stories that introduced the idea of mind control to Americans during the first half of the twentieth century. It proved to be an endlessly appealing trope. So fully did Svengali personify the wicked mind-stealer that his name has entered the English language. Dictionaries define a "svengali" as a person who "manipulates or exerts excessive control over another," "completely dominates another," or "exercises a controlling or mesmeric influence on another, especially for a sinister purpose."

That was what Gottlieb wanted to be and do. He spent years trying to find the secret that allowed Svengali to take over a human mind. Fiction helped shape the belief, within the CIA and in popular culture, that mind control exists and can be mastered.

Two traumatic historical episodes—the testimony of Cardinal Mindszenty during his 1949 trial in Hungary and the behavior of American prisoners in Korea several years later—convinced senior CIA officers that Communists had discovered the key to mind control. They hired Gottlieb to discover that same key. What led them to believe it existed? Part of the answer lies in the cultural conditioning that shaped them. They came of age in an era when mind control was a ubiquitous fantasy. Writers found it irresistible. So did many readers. Fiction led Americans to believe that there must be ways for one human being to capture the mind of another.

The lineage of this fascination may be traced at least as far back as 1845, when Edgar Allan Poe published "The Facts in the Case of M. Valdemar," a story about mesmerism written as if it were the report of a true case. In it, a dying patient is placed into a trance and remains suspended for seven months, alive but without a pulse or heartbeat. The story caused a sensation. Poe finally admitted it was a hoax, but it struck a deep emotional chord. Elizabeth Barrett Browning wrote that Poe had made "horrible improbabilities seem near and familiar."

Ambrose Bierce was also drawn to the idea of mind control. In his 1890 story "The Realm of the Unreal," a magician from Calcutta hypnotizes an entire audience in Baltimore. He claims to have discovered a method by which "a peculiarly susceptible subject may be kept in the realm of the unreal for weeks, months, and even years, dominated by whatever delusions and hallucinations the operator may from time to time suggest." A few years later, Bierce wrote a first-person account, "The

Hypnotist," in which he reported that he had developed "unusual powers" and liked to "amuse myself with hypnotism, mind reading and . . .
the mysterious force or agent known as hypnotic suggestion."

"Whether or not it could be employed by a bad man for an unworthy
purpose," Bierce concluded, "I am unable to say."

The advent of cinema brought mind control fantasies to a mass audience. One of the first great horror films, *The Cabinet of Dr. Caligari,* tells
the story of a diabolical performer who can make normal people commit
murder. Later he is revealed to be the director of the local psychiatric
clinic—a brilliant scientist who uses his knowledge for good or evil, as
he chooses. Caligari has learned, as he writes in his diary at the end of
the film, that a man "can be compelled to perform acts that, in a waking
state, he would never commit."

The first great American film about mind control, *Gaslight,* released
in 1944, won Ingrid Bergman an Academy Award for her portrayal of
a woman whose husband takes control of her mind through what
MK-ULTRA scientists would call sensory deprivation. The husband,
played by Charles Boyer, breaks her will by forbidding her to leave home,
isolating her from visitors, and arranging plots that make her doubt her
sanity. This film also added a word to the lexicon of behavioral psychology, *gaslighting,* to take its place beside *svengali.* "Gaslighting is a form
of persistent manipulation and brainwashing that causes the victim to
doubt her or himself, and ultimately lose her or his own sense of perception, identity, and self-worth," according to one text. "At its worst,
pathological gaslighting constitutes a severe form of mind control and
psychological abuse."

Another popular film released around this time, a Sherlock Holmes
drama called *The Woman in Green,* depicts a different form of mind
control. It presents an elaborate plot devised by Moriarty, the criminal
genius who is Holmes's nemesis. Moriarty kills women, cuts a finger off
each corpse, places the fingers in the pockets of rich gentlemen, con-
vinces them that this proves their guilt, and blackmails them to keep the
secret. How does he make them believe that they are murderers? Holmes
is baffled for a time but suddenly hits upon the explanation: Moriarty
has hypnotized his victims into believing they had committed crimes,
thereby making them willing to pay blackmail. MK-ULTRA was looking

for something different but related: a technique that would make spies, saboteurs, and assassins believe that they were innocent of crimes they had actually committed.

Creatures who act at the command of others appear regularly in science fiction. Blood transfusions and garlic blooms are used to transform victims' personalities in various versions of *Dracula*. The iconic monster in *Frankenstein* is controlled through electrodes implanted in his neck. Other stories depict mind control as a weapon wielded by invading extraterrestrials. "That old bird just opened up my skull," one victim marvels in a 1936 science-fiction novella called *The Brain Stealers of Mars*, "and poured a new set of brains in."

That was what Gottlieb and his MK-ULTRA comrades wanted to learn how to do. Exaggerated fears based on true events led them to believe that the human psyche can be controlled from outside. The stories they imbibed as children and adults made those fears seem real. Lost in the blurry borderland between the fantasy and truth of mind control, they could not bring themselves to recognize the fantasy as a product of creative imagination. What the imagination could conceive, they believed, the clandestine world could make real. MK-ULTRA was an attempt to invent a new reality.

When Macbeth and Banquo meet the three prophetic witches at the opening of Shakespeare's play, they wonder: "Have we eaten on the insane root that takes the reason prisoner?" MK-ULTRA was no more or less than a search for that "insane root"—a drug, potion, or technique that would allow them to imprison reason. Science told them that no such pathway into the human psyche exists. Creative imagination suggested the opposite. Gottlieb and his chemical warriors believed they could transform a persistent legend into reality. Propelled by Cold War terrors, they fell under the spell of imagination.

Public fascination with mind control and "brainwashing" reached a peak during the years MK-ULTRA was active. In the late 1950s, by one count, more than two hundred articles on these subjects appeared in *Time, Life*, and other popular magazines. Many were inspired by the work of the CIA-connected propagandist Edward Hunter. In books and articles, Hunter warned that Communists were preparing a psychic attack that would subject Americans to "unthinking discipline and robot-like enslavement." Other pseudoscientists echoed this warning. Among them was William Sargant, the British psychologist to whom Frank Olson had confided his doubts about extreme experiments; his 1957 book *Battle for the Mind* chronicles his lifelong search for "the most rapid and permanent means of changing a man's beliefs." Writers with more serious credentials, including George Orwell, Aldous Huxley, and Arthur Koestler, had also produced works about aspects of mind control. Science and literature fed on each other to promote a terrifying fantasy.

This fascination gripped a generation of writers in the United States and Britain. Jack Finney's novel *Invasion of the Body Snatchers*, published in 1954, depicts an attack by aliens who seek to take over Earth by replacing human beings with "pod people" who look and act like everyone else but are under hostile control. Two novels published in 1962 take the fantasy of mind control in other directions. The main character in *A Clockwork Orange* is a violent criminal who is taken to the Ministry of the Interior, given drugs, strapped to a chair with his eyes clamped open, and forced to watch films intended to change his behavior. In *The Ipcress File,* British diplomats are kidnapped by Soviet agents and subjected to tortures remarkably similar to the "psychic driving" that Ewen Cameron practiced as part of his MK-ULTRA experiments in Montreal. The file in this novel's title is finally revealed to be based on an acronym. Ipcress stands for Induction of Psycho-Neuroses by Conditioned Reflex with Stress.

All three of these novels were made into highly successful movies, but none of them had anything near the impact of Richard Condon's *The Manchurian Candidate.* Though its literary value is debatable, its timing was perfect. It became one of the bestselling books of 1959. One reviewer called it "a wild, vigorous, curiously readable mélange." It was that and more: the most widely read novel about "brainwashing" ever published in the United States. If anyone doubted the terrible potential of this weapon—or doubted its existence—*The Manchurian Candidate* was the ideal antidote.

The book's plot is simple but gripping. An infantry platoon fighting in Korea is captured and taken to a laboratory where Communist scientists conduct mind control experiments. There the soldiers are made to believe that their sergeant saved their lives during combat. When they return to the United States, their glowing reports earn him a Medal of Honor. What they do not know is that Communists have programmed him to become an assassin. His assignment, embedded so deeply in his psyche that he cannot remember it, is to respond to any order that comes from someone who shows him a Queen of Diamonds playing card. When the order finally comes, it is horrifying: murder a presidential candidate so a pro-Communist dictator can take over the United States.

Americans had been reading stories about "brainwashing" for years before *The Manchurian Candidate* appeared. In serious works like *The Lonely Crowd* and *The Organization Man*, social scientists had suggested that important features of American life, including advertising or psychiatry, were forms of attempted mind control. No one outside the CIA had yet heard of MK-ULTRA, but the belief that hidden conspiracies lie below the surface of national life had already begun to spread. That helps explain what the critic Timothy Melley called "the central place of *The Manchurian Candidate* in the fiction of mind control."

"Postwar conspiracy theory is deeply influenced by the growth of the covert sphere," Melley wrote. "US foreign policy during the Cold War developed around a fundamental contradiction: the public advocacy of democracy versus the deployment of covert strategies and institutions operating outside the purview and control of the democratic public sphere. The incongruity in this strategy—the open secret that US policy relied increasingly on undemocratic, secret means—contributed significantly to suspicion of government, and redirected brainwashing fears toward homegrown targets."

A movie of *The Manchurian Candidate*, starring Angela Lansbury and Frank Sinatra, appeared in 1962 and intensified those fears. The handful of people who were truly immersed in mind control research, though, realized that it had come too late. At the very moment when masses of Americans were finally coming to believe that "brainwashing" was not only real but an imminent threat, Sidney Gottlieb and his MK-ULTRA comrades were reaching the opposite conclusion. "By 1961, 1962, it was at least proven to my satisfaction that 'brainwashing,' so-called—as some kind of esoteric device where drugs or mind-altering kinds of conditions and so forth were used—did not exist," the CIA psychologist John Gittinger said later. "*The Manchurian Candidate*, as a movie, really set us back a long time, because it made something impossible look plausible . . . But by 1962 and 1963, the general idea that we were able to come up with is that 'brainwashing' was largely a process of isolating a human being, keeping him out of contact, putting him under long stress in relationship to interviewing and interrogation—and that they could produce any change that way, without having to resort to any kind of esoteric means."

Fiction anticipated and nourished MK-ULTRA. Stories about "brainwashing," unfettered by science or anything else other than the limits of creative fantasy, caught the American imagination. They ran far beyond anything that CIA scientists were able to discover. Yet the very existence of MK-ULTRA was proof that even many of the wildest fantasies about secret government research into mind control were close to reality. That made the paranoid mind-set seem ever more rational.

10

Health Alteration Committee

Thirteen miles above the Ural Mountains, a blinding orange flash lit up the sky on a spring morning in 1960. A Soviet anti-aircraft missile had found its target. The plane it was aimed at began tumbling wildly. Both wings blew off. Miraculously, the pilot, Francis Gary Powers, managed to eject and open his parachute. Powers was on one of the CIA's most secret missions. He was flying a spy plane, the U-2, that almost no one knew existed. As he floated down, he later wrote, he imagined the "tortures and unknown horrors" that might await him in captivity. Fortunately he had a way out. Around his neck, like a good luck charm, hung a silver dollar he had been given before takeoff. Hidden inside was a pin coated with poison. It was a gift from Sidney Gottlieb and friends.

During the 1950s, as part of MK-ULTRA, Gottlieb had sent agents to search the world for natural poisons. They studied reports of toxic plants and animals, determined where they might be found, consulted with indigenous people, and came home with promising samples. Gottlieb, always fascinated by new chemicals, sent the samples to his partners at what had been Camp Detrick—now renamed Fort Detrick because it had been deemed a permanent installation. Several of them proved to be deadly.

Gottlieb had risen to a new post: chief of research and development for the Technical Services Staff. He had an unmatched knowledge of poisons. That made him the ideal candidate for a delicate mission.

The CIA's deputy director for plans, Richard Bissell, who ran the U-2 project, believed that since his planes would fly at improbably high altitudes, Soviet air defense systems would not be able to shoot them down or even track them by radar. Nonetheless he planned for the possibility that something might go wrong. The existence of the U-2 squadron and the nature of its mission—to photograph Soviet military installations— were among the most highly classified American secrets. If a plane was somehow lost and its pilot fell into enemy hands, much trouble would follow. Bissell asked the Technical Services Staff to provide his pilots with a way to commit suicide if they were captured.

The chemists' first response was to recall for Bissell how the Nazi war criminal Hermann Goering had cheated the hangman at Nuremberg. Goering had slipped a glass ampule filled with liquid potassium cyanide into his mouth, bit down on it, and died within fifteen seconds. That story appealed to Bissell. He ordered six ampules like the one Goering had used. Making them was no great challenge for Gottlieb. He chose the appropriate poison, and a Special Operations Division officer at Fort Detrick made the ampules. One of them was handed to the pilot of the first U-2 mission as he prepared to take off from an American base at Wiesbaden, Germany, on June 20, 1956. President Eisenhower authorized several more flights in the weeks that followed. Each pilot carried one of Gottlieb's ampules.

One of those pilots, Carmine Vito, took off from Wiesbaden at dawn on July 5 and flew into near disaster. His fellow pilots called Vito the Lemon Drop Kid because of his habit of sucking on lemon lozenges. Once he was airborne, he reached for one and popped it into his mouth. He noticed that it felt unusually smooth and had no taste. After spitting it out, he saw to his horror that he had grabbed his cyanide-filled ampule instead of a cough drop. He survived only because he had not bitten it. After returning from his mission, he reported his brush with death. The squadron commander ordered that henceforth the ampules be packed inside small boxes. For the next four years, U-2 pilots tucked those boxes into their flight suits. There were no more near misses.

Because of the extreme sensitivity of U-2 flights over the Soviet Union,

President Eisenhower insisted on approving each one. Bissell and his boss, Allen Dulles, assured the president that the planes were practically invulnerable. Despite this assurance, Eisenhower hesitated to approve a flight scheduled for May 1, 1960. He was due to meet the Soviet leader Nikita Khrushchev at a much-awaited summit in Berlin two weeks later and did not want to risk disrupting it. Finally he was persuaded that the risk was minimal and gave his approval.

By this time, Gottlieb and his partners at Fort Detrick had come up with a new suicide tool. Rather than continuing to supply cyanide ampules for distribution to U-2 "drivers," as the pilots were called, they designed and produced one of the most remarkable devices ever to emerge from a CIA workshop. It was a suicide tool hidden inside a silver dollar. Only one was made, since all agreed that if it ever had to be used, that would mean disaster had struck and the U-2 program would have to be abandoned.

That spring, U-2 flights were taking off from a secret CIA airfield near Peshawar, Pakistan. Each "driver" was given the silver dollar before taking off.

"Inside the dollar was what appeared to be an ordinary straight pin," Francis Gary Powers later wrote. "But this too wasn't what it seemed. Looking at it more closely, we could see the body of the pin to be a sheath not fitting quite tightly against the head. Pulling this off, it became a thin needle, only again not an ordinary needle. Toward the end there were grooves. Inside the grooves was a sticky brown substance."

That substance was a paralytic poison called saxitoxin that can be extracted from infected shellfish. It is related to the algae that cause red tide and other waterborne infections. In a highly concentrated dose, like the one compounded at Fort Detrick, it can kill within seconds.

Powers was flying over what is now the Russian city of Yekaterinburg—coincidentally, the city where a Bolshevik firing squad had executed Czar Nicholas II and the rest of Russia's royal family in 1918—when his plane was rocked by the exploding missile. Soviet military commanders, frustrated by their inability to stop U-2 overflights, had been steadily improving their air defenses in ways the CIA had not detected. The attack that blew Powers out of the air came so suddenly that he did not have time to hit the button that would destroy the plane's fuselage. As he fell, his thoughts turned frantically to the suicide pin he was carrying. Should he use it?

A scene in the 2016 film *Bridge of Spies* depicts the pre-flight briefing that a CIA officer named Williams gave to Powers and his fellow "drivers" inside a hangar at the Peshawar base.

WILLIAMS: It is imperative that these flights remain a secret and this equipment does not fall into enemy hands.

POWERS: And what about us?

WILLIAMS: I don't know if you're kidding, Lieutenant. I'm not. What you know about the plane is as secret as the plane itself. If capture is a foregone conclusion, you go down with your plane. If you think you can ditch and get away—if you're close enough to a border—fine, you know the ejection protocol. But if you ditch [he opens a balled fist to show a silver dollar], you bring the dollar with you. There's a pin inside. [He withdraws the pin.] Scratch your skin anywhere. It's instantaneous. If you think you are about to be captured, you use it. Drivers, you understand me? Spend the dollar.

That dramatic scene was pure invention. In fact, "drivers" were given no clear instructions on how to react if shot down. Powers later testified that the choice of whether to use the suicide pin was left "more or less up to me." He decided not to.

When CIA air controllers lost contact with Powers's plane, they presumed he was dead and that his plane had been vaporized. Hurriedly they concocted a cover story: a research plane studying high-altitude weather patterns over Turkey had run into trouble, the pilot had lost consciousness due to lack of oxygen, and the plane had continued on autopilot, lamentably straying deep into Soviet airspace.

"There was absolutely no—N-O, no—deliberate attempt to violate Soviet airspace, and there never has been," a State Department spokesman told reporters.

The CIA and President Eisenhower presumed the episode would end there. Khrushchev, however, had the last word. In a dramatic speech to the Supreme Soviet a week after the shoot-down, he revealed that large sections of the U-2 had been recovered and that Powers was alive and in custody. Then he held up an enlarged photo of the poison needle.

"To cover up the tracks of the crime, the pilot was told that he must not be taken alive by Soviet authorities," Khrushchev told his comrades. "For this reason he was supplied with a special needle. He was to have pricked himself with the poisoned needle, with a result of instantaneous death. What barbarism!"

In the most humiliating moment of his presidency, Eisenhower was forced to admit that he had authorized his spokesmen to lie about the U-2. His planned summit with Khrushchev collapsed. Powers was put on trial in Moscow. "If the assignments received by Powers had not been of a criminal nature, his masters would not have supplied him with a lethal pin," the prosecutor said in his opening statement. Among witnesses at the trial was a professor of forensic medicine who had been assigned to evaluate the pin. His testimony constitutes the most detailed analysis of one of Gottlieb's tools that has ever been made public.

The following was established during the investigation of the pin. It is a straight ordinary-looking pin made of white metal with a head and a sharpened point. It is 27mm long and 1mm in diameter. The pin is of an intricate structure: there is a bore inside it extending its entire length except for the sharpened point. A needle is inserted in the bore. The needle is extracted when tightly pulling the pin head. On the sharpened point of the needle are deep oblique furrows completely covered with a layer of thick, sticky, brownish mass.

An experimental dog was given a hypodermic prick with the needle extracted from the pin, in the upper third part of the left hind leg. Within one minute after the prick the dog fell on his side, and a sharp slackening of the respiratory movements of the chest was observed, a cyanosis of the tongue and visible mucous membranes was noted. Within 90 seconds after the prick, breathing ceased entirely. Three minutes after the prick, the heart stopped functioning and death set in. The same needle was inserted under the skin of a white mouse. Within 20 seconds after the prick, death set in from respiratory paralysis . . .

Thus, as a result of the investigation it was established that the substance contained on the needle inside the pin, judging from the nature of its effect on animals, could, according to its toxic doses and physical properties, be included in the curare group, the most powerful and quickest-acting of all known poisons.

In fact, Gottlieb had gone well beyond curare, a toxin that is found in tropical plants. Saxitoxin belongs to a class of naturally occurring aquatic poisons that, according to one study, "surpass by many times such known substances as strychnine, curare, a range of fungi toxins, and potassium cyanide." The lethality of Gottlieb's suicide pin and the inability of a leading Russian toxicologist to identify the substance with which he had tainted it were testimony to his talent.

Powers was exchanged for a Russian spy in 1962. He faced a burst of criticism for failing to use his suicide pin, but after emotions cooled he was praised for his service. The CIA awarded him a medal. Allen Dulles said he had "performed his duty in a very dangerous mission and he performed it well."

Gottlieb could not be publicly linked to the episode, but it burnished his reputation within the CIA. He was already the CIA's master chemist. He had, according to one of his colleagues, prepared poison that the compromised CIA officer James Kronthal used to commit suicide in 1953. Two years later he compounded a dose intended to kill Prime Minister Zhou Enlai of China. By crafting the lethal pin that was given to U-2 pilots, he solidified his position as poisoner in chief.

As HE WALKED through the African heat and stepped into an airport taxi, "Joe from Paris" could not avoid reflecting on the war into which he was plunging. The Republic of the Congo, where he had just landed, had won independence from Belgium three months before. It immediately fell into violent chaos. Mutiny in the army set off riots, secession, and government collapse. The United States and the Soviet Union watched with active interest. A Cold War showdown loomed. Joe from Paris arrived carrying America's secret weapon.

The CIA station chief in Leopoldville, the Congolese capital, was expecting him. A couple of days earlier he had received a cable from Washington telling him that a visitor would soon appear. "Will announce himself as Joe from Paris," the cable said. "It is urgent you should see [him] soonest possible after he phones you. He will fully identify himself and explain his assignment to you."

Late on the afternoon of September 26, 1960, the station chief, Larry Devlin, who had a cover job as a consular officer at the American embassy, left work and headed toward his car. A man rose from his chair at a café across the street. "He was a senior officer, a highly respected chemist, whom I had known for some time," Devlin wrote later. Joe from Paris was Sidney Gottlieb. He had flown to the Congo on one of the twentieth century's most extraordinary courier missions. With him he carried a one-of-a-kind kit that he himself had designed. It was poison to kill Prime Minister Patrice Lumumba.

Gottlieb approached Devlin and extended his hand. "I'm Joe from Paris," he said. Devlin invited the visitor into his car. After they were underway, Gottlieb told him, "I've come to give you instructions about a highly sensitive operation."

By the time Gottlieb landed in the Congo, he could look back on almost a full decade at the CIA. He had built MK-ULTRA into the most intense and structured mind control research program in history. Two years in Germany, where he had conducted extreme experiments on "expendables," strengthened his credentials. The research and development job he was given after his return made him one of the chief imaginers, builders, and testers of devices used by American intelligence officers. He assumed it without surrendering control of MK-ULTRA. During this period he was also part of an informal group of CIA chemists that became known as the "health alteration committee." They came together early in 1960 as a response to President Eisenhower's renewed conviction that the best way to deal with some unfriendly foreign leaders was to kill them.

At mid-morning on August 18, 1960, Allen Dulles and Richard Bissell made an unscheduled visit to the White House. They had just received an urgent cable from Larry Devlin in the Congo. "Embassy and station believe Congo experiencing classic Communist effort takeover government," it said. "Anti-West forces rapidly increasing power Congo and therefore may be little time left." This cable seemed to confirm deep fears that Prime Minister Lumumba was about to deliver his spectacularly rich country to the Soviets. After reading it, according to the official note taker, Eisenhower turned to Dulles and said "something to the effect that Lumumba should be eliminated."

"There was stunned silence for about 15 seconds," the note taker wrote, "and the meeting continued."

As soon as Bissell returned to his office, he sent a cable to the Leopoldville station asking officers there to propose ways of carrying out Eisenhower's assassination order. They considered using a sniper with a high-powered rifle—"hunting good here when light is right," one officer helpfully wrote—but ultimately ruled out that option because Lumumba was living in seclusion and no reliable sniper was available. Poison was the logical alternative.

Gottlieb's entire career had prepared him for this assignment. He had founded the CIA's Chemical Division and become the Agency's pre-eminent expert on toxins and ways of delivering them. As director of MK-ULTRA, he had tested drugs on prisoners, drug addicts, hospital patients, suspected spies, ordinary citizens, and even his own colleagues. He had already compounded lethal poisons. For this uniquely qualified chemist, preparing a dose for Lumumba would be simple.

Bissell told Gottlieb that pursuant to an order from "the highest authority," he was to prepare an incapacitating or fatal potion that could be fed to an African leader. He did not name Lumumba. Given that summer's news, though, Gottlieb could hardly have doubted who the intended target was.

"Gottlieb suggested that biological agents were perfect for the task," the science historian Ed Regis wrote in his description of this plot. "They were invisible, untraceable and, if intelligently selected and delivered, not even liable to create a suspicion of foul play. The target would get sick and die exactly as if he'd been attacked by a natural outbreak of an endemic disease. Plenty of lethal or incapacitating germs were out there and available, Gottlieb told Bissell, and they were easily accessible to the CIA. This was entirely acceptable to Bissell."

After receiving his assignment, Gottlieb began considering which "lethal or incapacitating germs" he would use. His first step was to determine which diseases most commonly caused unexpected death in the Congo. They turned out to be anthrax, smallpox, tuberculosis, and three animal-borne plagues. Gottlieb began looking for a match: Which poison would produce a death most like the one those diseases cause? He settled on botulinum, which is sometimes found in improperly canned food. It takes several hours to work but is so potent that a concentrated dose of just two one-billionths of a gram can kill.

Working with partners at Fort Detrick, where he stored his toxins, Gottlieb began assembling his assassination kit. It contained a vial of liquid botulinum; a hypodermic syringe with an ultra-thin needle; a small jar of chlorine that could be mixed with the botulinum to render it ineffective in an emergency; and "accessory materials," including protective gloves and a face mask to be worn while conducting the operation. In mid-September Gottlieb told Bissell that the kit was ready. They agreed that Gottlieb himself should bring it to Leopoldville. He became the only CIA officer known to have carried poison to a foreign country in order to kill that country's leader.

Less than an hour after Gottlieb and Devlin met in front of the American embassy in Leopoldville, they were sitting together in Devlin's living room. There Gottlieb announced that he was carrying tools intended for the assassination of Prime Minister Lumumba.

"Jesus H. Christ!" Devlin exclaimed. "Who authorized this operation?"

"President Eisenhower," Gottlieb replied. "I wasn't there when he approved it, but Dick Bissell said that Eisenhower wanted Lumumba removed."

Both men paused to absorb the weight of the moment. Devlin later recalled lighting a cigarette and staring at his shoes. After a while Gottlieb broke the silence.

"It's your responsibility to carry out the operation, yours alone," he told Devlin. "The details are up to you, but it's got to be clean—nothing that can be traced back to the US government." Then he handed over the poison kit he had made and carried across the Atlantic.

"Take this," he said. "With the stuff that's in there, no one will ever be able to know that Lumumba was assassinated."

Gottlieb coolly explained to Devlin what was in the poison kit and how to use it. One of Devlin's agents, he said, should use the hypodermic needle to inject botulinum into something Lumumba would ingest—as Gottlieb later put it, "anything he could get to his mouth, whether it was food or a toothbrush." Devlin later wrote that the kit also included a pre-poisoned tube of toothpaste. The toxins were designed to kill not immediately, but after a few hours. An autopsy, Gottlieb assured Devlin, would show "normal traces found in people who die of certain diseases."

Rather than return to Washington after delivering his poison kit, Gottlieb remained in Leopoldville. While he waited, Devlin found an agent who was thought to have access to Lumumba and could, as he wrote in a cable to Washington, "act as inside man." Finally, ten days after arriving with his kit, Gottlieb felt confident enough to fly home. He left behind, according to a cable from Devlin, "certain items of continuing usefulness."

The agent Devlin hired to slip Lumumba a tube of poisoned toothpaste, or to poison his food, proved unable to penetrate rings of security. Devlin began exploring other options. He knew that the Belgian security service was just as determined as the CIA to eliminate Lumumba. Its officers worked closely with the Union Minière du Haut-Katanga, the mining conglomerate that was a cornerstone of Belgian political and economic power. On November 29, after Lumumba fled from what he believed was mortal danger in Leopoldville, his enemies found and captured him. For six weeks he languished in a remote jail. On January 17, 1961, a squad of six Congolese and two Belgian officers took him out of the jail, brought him to a jungle clearing, shot him, and dissolved his remains in acid.

What happened to the poison? Devlin later wrote that after Gottlieb handed it to him, "my mind was racing. I realized that I could never assassinate Lumumba. It would have been murder . . . My plan was to stall, to delay as long as possible in the hope that Lumumba would either fade away politically as a potential danger or that the Congolese would succeed in taking him prisoner." To secure the poison, Devlin wrote, he locked it inside his office safe, where it would lose potency. Gottlieb, however, later testified that he had disposed of the poison before leaving Leopoldville, destroying its "viability" and then dumping it into the Congo River.

The CIA achieved its objective in the Congo unexpectedly and elegantly. Eisenhower had ordered the Agency to kill Lumumba, and he had been killed. Although CIA officers worked closely with the Congolese and Belgians who did the deed, they did not participate in or witness the execution. Gottlieb's lethal kit turned out to be unnecessary. Nonetheless he returned to Washington with a new credential. He had not poisoned the leader of a foreign government, but he had shown once again that he knew how.

YES, THE GANGSTER "Handsome Johnny" Roselli told an inquiring CIA man, he had associates in Cuba who could kill Fidel Castro. No, he didn't like the idea of trying to gun Castro down gangland-style, or using a sniper to do the job. The shooter would almost certainly be killed or captured. Roselli said he would prefer something "nice and clean, without getting into any kind of out-and-out ambushing." He and his Mafia partner Sam Giancana offered the CIA a counter-proposal: give us poison that takes time to kill, so our assassin can escape before Castro falls ill and dies. Senior officers at the CIA liked the idea. Sidney Gottlieb had a new assignment.

On May 13, 1960, after hearing a briefing from Allen Dulles, President Eisenhower ordered Castro "sawed off." He did not use what CIA security director Sheffield Edwards later called "bad words," but everyone present understood this as a presidential directive to remove Castro from power by any means including assassination. That gave Richard Bissell and his covert action directorate another murder to plan. Since it would entail making poison and devices by which it could be delivered, Bissell turned to what had been the Technical Services Staff, now renamed the Technical Services Division. Sidney Gottlieb was the man for the job.

At first Gottlieb and his small corps of chemists concentrated on ways to cause Castro's downfall by non-lethal means. They came up with two options. The first grew from Gottlieb's long fascination with LSD. As part of his work directing Operation Midnight Climax, he had planned an experiment, ultimately canceled because of weather conditions, in which an aerosol laced with LSD would be sprayed into a room of unsuspecting partygoers. He had tested such an aerosol at George Hunter White's "pad" in San Francisco. It might now be sprayed in the radio studio from which Castro made live broadcasts that reached millions of Cubans. If

Sidney Gottlieb was born in 1918 to an immigrant family in the Bronx and grew up in this modest brick row house.

At the age of nineteen, Gottlieb left New York to study plant biology at Arkansas Polytechnic College. The yearbook called him "a Yankee who pleases the southerners."

By the time Gottlieb joined the CIA in 1951, it had already opened a "black site" at Villa Schuster, near the German city of Frankfurt. Prisoners were brought to underground cells, given heavy doses of drugs, and subjected to electroshock and other torments. "There were deaths," an investigation concluded years later, "but the number is not known."

Among those who designed drug combinations and "special interrogation" techniques for use on prisoners at Villa Schuster was Kurt Blome, who had directed the Nazis' bio-warfare program. He and Gottlieb searched for ways to wipe away a human mind so a new one could be implanted in its place.

In November 1953 one of Gottlieb's collaborators, Frank Olson, died after plunging from a thirteenth-floor hotel window in New York. Two decades later the CIA admitted that its officers had fed LSD to Olson a few days before his death, driving him to apparent suicide.

In 1975 President Gerald Ford invited the Olson family to the Oval Office and officially apologized. Later, however, Olson's sons became convinced that their father had not committed suicide but was thrown out of the hotel window because he was planning to quit the CIA and reveal deep secrets.

In 1955 the CIA set out to assassinate Prime Minister Zhou Enlai of China while he was visiting Indonesia. Gottlieb made poison to be dropped into Zhou's rice bowl. This plot was aborted at the last moment.

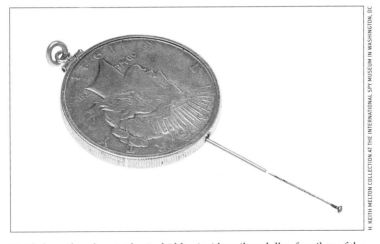

Gottlieb produced a suicide pin, hidden inside a silver dollar, for pilots of the U-2 spy plane to use if they crashed inside the Soviet Union. Francis Gary Powers was carrying this pin when he crashed in 1960 but chose not to use it.

In 1960 Gottlieb made a poison kit for use in assassinating Prime Minister Patrice Lumumba of the Congo (at right in photo). He carried it personally to the CIA station chief there. Lumumba was killed by a Belgian-backed squad before the poison could be used.

MORI DocID: 1451843

14 February 1972

MEMORANDUM FOR THE RECORD:

In November 1962 Mr. ⬚ advised Mr. Lyman Kirkpatrick that he had, at one time, been directed by Mr. Richard Bissell to assume responsibility for a project involving the assassination of Patrice Lumumba, then Premier, Republic of Congo. According to ⬚ poison was to have been the vehicle as he made reference to having been instructed to see Dr. Sidney Gottlieb, in order procure the appropriate vehicle.

A declassified memorandum about the Lumumba assassination plot is one of the few surviving CIA documents that mentions Sidney Gottlieb by name.

Gottlieb compounded various potions intended to kill the Cuban revolutionary leader Fidel Castro. Among them were poison pills, poison cigars, and a wet suit lined with deadly toxin.

Because Gottlieb lived in deep secrecy, no one knew what he looked like. In a re-enactment staged by National Geographic, he was portrayed as balding and avuncular as he poured LSD into Frank Olson's drink.

In Errol Morris's 2017 documentary miniseries *Wormwood*, Tim Blake Nelson (left) played Gottlieb as young and self-confident.

This photo, which the CIA released to the author in 2018, shows for the first time what Gottlieb looked like while he worked for the CIA. It was taken shortly before he retired in 1973.

When Gottlieb testified to a Senate committee about his MK-ULTRA mind control program in 1975, he used the pseudonym "Joseph Scheider," a reference to this nineteenth-century lithograph of a hooded monk. It is Gottlieb as he saw himself: a mysterious guardian of esoteric knowledge, alluring but unsettling, drawing inspiration from a pipe to peer into the human soul.

Photographers were not supposed to take pictures of Gottlieb when he testified in 1975, but some did. He sat with his lawyer, Terry Lenzner, who arranged for him to be granted immunity from prosecution in exchange for his testimony about MK-ULTRA.

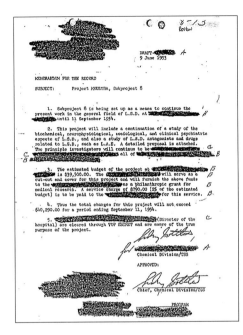

In 1977 Gottlieb was called back to Washington for a second round of testimony about MK-ULTRA. "I feel victimized and appalled," he told senators. "My name is selectively left on released documents where all or most others are deleted."

A Canadian artist, Sarah Anne Johnson, is the granddaughter of Velma Orlikow, whose life was devastated by extreme experiments that Gottlieb sponsored. Among her works is this statue, *Black Out*, which depicts her grandmother in sensory-deprivation restraints. Although Canadian victims of MK-ULTRA experiments received compensation years later, no Americans did. In his last act before leaving the CIA, Gottlieb ordered all MK-ULTRA records destroyed.

Castro became disoriented and incoherent during one of those speeches, he would presumably lose popular support. After some discussion, this idea was discarded as impractical. The CIA never sent aerosolized LSD into Cuba.

Gottlieb's team then came up with an even stranger scheme. They persuaded themselves that part of Castro's appeal, like the strength of Samson, came from his hair—specifically, his beard. If the beard fell away, they thought, so might Castro's power. Finding a chemical that would make a beard fall out was just the kind of challenge Gottlieb enjoyed. He chose a compound based on thallium salts. A bit of brainstorming produced the outlines of a plot. The next time Castro traveled outside Cuba, thallium would be sprinkled into the boots he would leave outside his hotel room to be shined; his beard would then fall out, leaving him open to ridicule and overthrow. Gottlieb's scientists procured thallium and began testing it on animals. Before they could go further, though, they confronted this idea's obvious weaknesses. No one knew when Castro would travel, and even if he stayed at a hotel the CIA could penetrate, his security detail would probably not allow his boots to be handled by unknown outsiders. Besides, the idea that Castro's charisma would disappear with his beard struck some officers as far-fetched. This plot was also aborted.

Destroying Castro without killing him soon came to seem impractical. Gottlieb and his scientists turned their thoughts to assassination. Their first idea was to taint a box of cigars and pass them to operations officers who could find a way to deliver them to Castro. The CIA inspector general who later investigated this plot reported that an Agency officer "did contaminate a full box of fifty cigars with botulinum toxin, a virulent poison that produces a fatal illness some hours after it is ingested. [Redacted] distinctly remembers the flaps-and-seals job he had to do on the box and on each of the cigars, both to get at the cigars and to erase evidence of tampering . . . The cigars were so heavily contaminated that merely putting one in the mouth would do the job; the intended victim would not have to smoke it." The report names Gottlieb as a co-conspirator, although without specifying his role.

"Sidney Gottlieb of TSD claims to remember distinctly a plot involving cigars," it says. "To emphasize the clarity of his memory, he named the officer, then assigned to [the Western Hemisphere Division], who approached him with the scheme. Although there may well have been such a plot, the officer Gottlieb named was then assigned in India and has never worked in WH Division nor had anything to do with Cuba operations. Gottlieb remembers the scheme as being one that was talked about frequently but not widely, and as being concerned with killing, not merely influencing behavior."

The poisoned Cohiba cigars—Castro's preferred brand—were passed to Jacob Esterline, a CIA officer working on the anti-Castro plot. No way was ever found to deliver them. They remained in a CIA safe. Seven years later, one was removed for testing. It had retained 94 percent of its toxicity.

These first bumbling attempts hardly satisfied Bissell. He decided to consult professionals with more experience in murder. That led him to "Handsome Johnny" Roselli, who along with other powerful gangsters had become rich through gambling, prostitution, and drug dealing in Cuba. They were determined to destroy Castro before he could carry out his promise to rid the country of crime and vice. Roselli had a web of contacts in the Havana underworld, which made him an ideal partner for the CIA.

Roselli's suggestion that the assassination be carried out by poison came at an opportune moment. He had never heard of Gottlieb—no one had—but he correctly presumed that the CIA must have someone on its payroll who made poison. Stars were aligning. The CIA had made contact with gangsters who wanted Castro dead. The gangsters wanted poison. Gottlieb could provide it.

Finding ways to kill Castro without using firearms—and, at some points in the plotting, also to kill his brother Raúl and the guerrilla hero Che Guevara—became one of Gottlieb's main preoccupations after his return from the Congo. The challenge tested his peculiarly creative imagination. It rose to the top of his priority list for the same reason it rose to the top for Bissell and Dulles. This assassination had been ordered by the president of the United States.

From Eisenhower, the chain of command was short and direct. He gave his order to Dulles and Bissell. Bissell turned to the redoubtable Sheffield Edwards, who as head of the Office of Security was keeper of the CIA's deepest secrets. Edwards chose an intermediary who could approach Mafia figures without being clearly tied to the CIA: Robert Maheu, a former FBI agent who had become a private detective and worked for the reclusive billionaire Howard Hughes. Maheu became the conduit through which the CIA passed instructions and devices to gangsters who were to assassinate Castro.

Gottlieb's role was to provide the means of killing. Through the partnership agreement known as MK-NAOMI, he had access to scientists at Fort Detrick. Together they conceived a series of ways to assassinate Castro. These included, according to a Senate investigation conducted years later, "poison pills, poison pens, deadly bacterial powders, and other devices which strain the imagination."

Plotting against Castro did not end when Eisenhower left office at the beginning of 1961. His successor, John F. Kennedy, turned out to be equally determined to "eliminate" Castro. The spectacular collapse of the CIA's 1961 invasion of Cuba at the Bay of Pigs intensified his determination. Kennedy and Attorney General Robert Kennedy, his brother, relentlessly pressured the CIA to crush Castro and repeatedly demanded explanations of why it had not been accomplished. Samuel Halpern, who served at the top level of the covert action directorate during this period, asserted that "the Kennedys were on our back constantly . . . they were just absolutely obsessed with getting rid of Castro." Richard Helms felt the pressure directly.

"There was a flat-out effort ordered by the White House, the President, Bobby Kennedy—who was after all his man, his right-hand man in these matters—to unseat the Castro government, to do everything possible to get rid of it by whatever device could be found," Helms later testified. "The Bay of Pigs was a part of this effort, and after the Bay of Pigs failed, there was even a greater push to try to get rid of this Communist influence 90 miles from United States shores . . . The principal driving force was the Attorney General, Robert Kennedy. There isn't any question about this."

For nearly four years, pressure from the White House kept Gottlieb, as well as his CIA superiors, fully focused on killing Castro. The idea of using a sniper to carry out the deed remained active, but it never seemed truly realistic. At one point the Technical Services Division considered crafting what would appear to be a rare seashell, placing a bomb inside, and planting it in an area where Castro liked to scuba dive. This plan was also rejected as impractical. According to a CIA report, "None of the shells that might conceivably be found in the Caribbean area was both spectacular enough to be sure of attracting attention and large enough to hold the needed amount of explosive. The midget submarine that would have had to be used in emplacement of the shell has too short an operating range for such an operation."

What remained was poison. Gottlieb and his colleagues were tasked with making it and imagining how it could be delivered.

One of their ideas was based, like the aborted exploding-seashell plot, on Castro's documented love of scuba diving. President Kennedy had chosen a lawyer named James Donovan (the same man Tom Hanks would play in *Bridge of Spies*) to negotiate the release of Cuban American prisoners who were captured during the failed Bay of Pigs invasion. The CIA came up with the idea of giving Donovan a tainted diving suit to present to Castro. Preparing such a suit was precisely the kind of assignment for which the Technical Services Division had been created.

"TSD bought a diving suit, dusted it inside with a fungus which would produce Madura foot, a chronic skin disease, and contaminated the breathing apparatus with a tubercle bacillus," a CIA officer wrote years later. "The plan was abandoned when the lawyer decided to present Castro with a different diving suit."

These failures brought the CIA, the Technical Services Division, and Gottlieb back to Roselli's original idea: make poison and find a way to feed it to Castro.

According to the official summary of a later interview with Cornelius Roosevelt, who then headed the Technical Services Division, "four possible approaches were considered: (1) something highly toxic, such as shellfish poison to be administered with a pin (which Roosevelt said was what was supplied to Gary Powers); (2) bacterial material in liquid form; (3) bacterial treatment of a cigarette or cigar; and (4) a handkerchief treated with bacteria. The decision, to the best of his recollection, was that bacteria in liquid form was the best means [because] Castro frequently drank tea, coffee, or bouillon, for which liquid poison would be particularly well suited . . . Despite the decision that a poison in liquid form would be most desirable, what was actually prepared and delivered was a solid in the form of small pills about the size of saccharine tablets."

The CIA never fully abandoned the idea of killing Castro with firearms. Evidence suggests that it arranged to smuggle rifles and at least one silencer into Cuba for this purpose. Nonetheless the idea of using poison remained the most appealing option. During 1961 and 1962, intermediaries working for the CIA passed several packets of Gottlieb's botulinum pills—called "L-pills" because they were lethal—to Mafia gangsters for delivery to contacts in Cuba. One batch could not be used because the Cuban official who was to place the pills in Castro's food was transferred to a post in which he no longer had access to the Cuban leader. Pills from another batch were to have been slipped into Castro's food or drink at a restaurant he frequented, but for unknown reasons he stopped visiting that restaurant.

Choosing the poison was not Gottlieb's only contribution to the Castro assassination project. He and his staff also produced two devices for delivering it. The first is described in a CIA report as "a pencil designed as a concealment device for delivering the pills." More elaborate was what the report calls "a ballpoint pen which had a hypodermic needle inside, that when you pushed the lever, the needle came out and poison could be injected into someone." According to another description, the needle was "designed to be so fine that the target (Castro) would not sense its insertion and the agent would have time to escape before the effects were noticed." The date on which a CIA officer in Paris handed this pen to a Cuban CIA "asset" is poignant: November 22, 1963, the same day President Kennedy was assassinated.

Kennedy's successor, Lyndon Johnson, continued to use political and economic means, including sabotage and other forms of covert action, to undermine Cuba's revolutionary government. He also, however, concluded that "we had been operating a goddamn Murder Inc. in the Caribbean," and put an end to assassination plots. One Cuban agent who had received firearms and explosives from the CIA remained in contact with the Agency until 1965, but he never carried out an attack. Talk of murder by chemicals ceased. Making poison to kill foreign leaders would never again be part of Gottlieb's job.

11

We Must Always Remember to Thank the CIA

"Capture green bug for future reference," Ambassador Clare Boothe Luce wrote during one of her LSD adventures. "Do you hear the drum?"

That kind of fractured unreason flashes through the minds of many LSD users. Observing it ultimately led Sidney Gottlieb to conclude that LSD is too unpredictable to be the "truth serum" or mind control drug for which he had so relentlessly searched. Reluctantly he filed it away with heroin, cocaine, electroshock, "psychic driving," and other failed techniques. But it was too late. LSD had escaped from the CIA's control. First it leaked into elite society. Then it spread to students who took it in CIA-sponsored experiments. Finally it exploded into the American counterculture, fueling a movement dedicated to destroying much of what the CIA defended and held dear.

Among the first LSD parties held outside the CIA were those that Dr. Harold Abramson, Gottlieb's favorite physician, threw at his Long Island home on Friday nights. At first he invited only a handful of other doctors. News spread. The guest list widened to include other New York professionals. Invitations were much sought after. "Harold A. Abramson of the Cold Spring Harbor Biological Laboratory has developed a technique of serving dinner to a group of subjects, topping off the meal with a liqueur glass containing 40 micrograms of LSD," *Time* reported in 1955. By the late 1950s, according to the novelist Gore Vidal, LSD had become "all the rage" in New York's high society.

Clare Boothe Luce, a former ambassador to Italy who was married to the publisher of *Time* and *Life* magazines—and who had carried on an extended affair with Allen Dulles—got her LSD from Sidney Cohen, a psychiatrist who had worked at Edgewood Arsenal. The film director Sidney Lumet was another early experimenter. So was the swimmer-turned-actress Esther Williams. The first celebrity to speak publicly about LSD was Cary Grant, the debonair exemplar of 1950s masculinity. He gave a series of interviews to a Hollywood gossip columnist, Joe Hyams, and another to *Look* magazine that became the basis for a glowing pro-file headlined THE CURIOUS STORY BEHIND THE NEW CARY GRANT. After taking LSD more than sixty times, Grant said, he had found a "second youth" and come "close to happiness" for the first time in his life.

"After my series came out, the phone began to ring wildly," Hyams later recalled. "Friends wanted to know where they could get the drug. Psychiatrists called, complaining that their patients were now begging them for LSD . . . In all, I got more than 800 letters."

As LSD leaked into high society, it was also being discovered by groups of young people. Volunteers who took it in experiments at hospitals and clinics, many of them secretly funded as MK-ULTRA "subprojects," raved about their experiences. That led their friends to clamor for LSD just as eagerly as their social betters.

"Researchers were growing lax in controlling the drug," according to one academic study. "They began to share LSD in their homes with friends . . . The drug was spreading into the undergraduate population."

Among the students who took LSD in these early experiments was a budding novelist named Ken Kesey, who was studying creative writing at Stanford. In 1959, after hearing that volunteers were being given mind-altering drugs at the Menlo Park Veterans Administration Hospital, Kesey signed up. The experience thrilled him—so much so that he not only repeated it as often as possible but took a job as a night attendant at the hospital. That gave him access to offices where LSD was kept. He helped himself. Soon he began sharing with friends. His home, according to one study of his career, "turned into a twenty-four-hour psychedelic party as friends and neighbors got high and danced to loud, electric rock music."

At the VA hospital, Kesey gathered material for his novel *One Flew Over the Cuckoo's Nest*, a brilliantly constructed celebration of nonconformity that became one of the first counterculture bestsellers. With the money he earned from royalties, Kesey bought a new home and began throwing "acid tests" at which he served LSD to a wild roster of guests including poets, musicians, and bikers from the Hells Angels gang. Sometimes he mixed it into bowls of punch—just as Gottlieb was said to have done at CIA parties.

Kesey gave LSD a new role in American society. As the 1960s progressed, he was as responsible as anyone for turning it into a symbol of youth culture, free love, hippie rebellion, and opposition to the Vietnam War. His parties, and the troupe of LSD-fueled "merry pranksters" he led on a celebrated trek across the United States aboard a brightly painted bus, helped bring the drug to public consciousness.

The music of the Grateful Dead would also play an essential role in the emerging LSD counterculture. Grateful Dead tours were traveling LSD circuses. Celebrants lost themselves in music and lyrics that sought to enhance their drug experiences. Many of the band's most evocative songs were written by a poet, Robert Hunter, who, like Kesey, credited LSD for his insights—and who, also like Kesey, first tried LSD as a volunteer at a research project covertly financed by the CIA.

Hunter was another of the psychedelic voyagers through whom LSD leaked from MK-ULTRA into the counterculture. "He'd been making some money by taking psychological tests at Stanford, and somehow that gave him the opportunity to earn $140 for four sessions, one per week, taking psychedelic drugs at the VA Hospital under auspices of what would prove to be the CIA," according to one biographer. "He received LSD (lysergic acid diethylamide, commonly called acid) the first week, psilocybin the second, mescaline the third, and a mixture of all three on the fourth." At each session, after the drug took effect, Hunter was brought to see a hypnotist. Later he said the experiments seemed aimed at determining whether these drugs "increased my ability to be hypnotized."

After taking LSD for the first time, Hunter described the experience in a six-page essay. "Sit back picture yourself swooping up a shell of purple with foam crests of crystal drops soft nigh they fall unto the sea of morning creep-very-softly mist," he wrote. It was just a short step from that to "China Cat Sunflower," said to be the first Grateful Dead song Hunter wrote while under the influence of LSD: "A leaf of all colors plays a golden string fiddle to a double-e waterfall over my back."

The radical poet Allen Ginsberg also discovered LSD through Gottlieb. "Psychiatrists who had worked for the US Navy and US intelligence gave Allen Ginsberg his first dose of LSD in 1959, as part of the CIA MK-ULTRA experiments," according to one history of the CIA. According to another, "He volunteered to become an experimental subject at Stanford University, where two psychologists who were secretly working for the CIA to develop mind-control drugs gave him LSD." During his first sessions, Ginsberg listened through headphones to recordings of Wagner's *Tristan und Isolde* and recitations by Gertrude Stein. He went on to become a powerful advocate for the "healthy personal adventure" of psychedelic drug use.

Timothy Leary, the most famous preacher of LSD gospel, came to the drug through a different path, but also one that Gottlieb helped blaze. Leary first became interested in psychedelics when, as a young professor of clinical psychiatry at Harvard, he read Gordon Wasson's 1957 article about "magic mushrooms" in *Life* magazine. Three years later, while vacationing in Mexico, he managed to procure some. "It was above all and without question the deepest religious experience of my life," he later recalled. Leary returned to his post at Harvard, began sponsoring drug experiments, was fired, and then set off on the journey that made him a high priest of LSD. Neither he nor anyone else knew it at the time, but Gottlieb had used MK-ULTRA funds, disguised as a foundation grant, to subsidize Wasson's travel to the Mexican village where he found the mushrooms. Leary's lifelong fascination with LSD, like those of Ken Kesey, Robert Hunter, and Allen Ginsberg, was part of Gottlieb's legacy.

The drug that Gottlieb and his CIA colleagues hoped would allow them to control humanity had the opposite effect. It fueled a generational revolt unlike any in American history. In 1966 LSD was banned in California. The federal government soon followed. President Richard Nixon called Timothy Leary "the most dangerous man in America."

Years later, the Bureau of Narcotics and Dangerous Drugs commissioned a study of how LSD leaked out of government laboratories. It concluded that the drug's "early use was among small groups of intellectuals at large Eastern and West Coast universities. It spread to undergraduate students, then to other campuses. Most often, users have been introduced to the drug by persons of high status. Teachers have influenced students."

That was true as far as it went. John Marks, the researcher who first brought MK-ULTRA to public attention, filled in what was missing. "The authors seem to have correctly analyzed how LSD got around the country," Marks wrote. "They left out only one vital element, which they had no way of knowing: that somebody had to influence the teachers, and that up there at the top of the LSD distribution system could be seen the men of MK-ULTRA."

The subversives who first ripped LSD out of its research cocoon later saw the irony of what they had done. "The United States government was in a way responsible for creating the 'acid tests' and the Grateful Dead, and thereby the whole psychedelic counterculture," Robert Hunter concluded. Allen Ginsberg came to wonder: "Am I, Allen Ginsberg, the product of one of the CIA's lamentable, ill-advised, or triumphantly successful experiments in mind control? Had they, by conscious plan or inadvertent Pandora's Box, let loose the whole LSD fad on the US and the world?"

For years Ken Kesey rejected Ginsberg's insistence that the CIA had been behind the drug research in which they both had participated. Once the existence of MK-ULTRA was revealed in the 1970s, he realized that Ginsberg was right—the research had been conducted for a hidden purpose. "It was being done to make people insane," Kesey said, "to weaken people and try to put them under the control of interrogators."

Several counterculture heroes acknowledged their debt to MK-ULTRA. "The LSD movement was started by the CIA," Timothy Leary asserted when he was at the peak of his fame. "I wouldn't be here now without the foresight of CIA scientists." John Lennon put the same thought more poetically: "We must always remember to thank the CIA and the Army for LSD. That's what people forget. Everything is the opposite of what it is, isn't it, Harry? So get out of the bottle, boy, and relax! They invented LSD to control people, and what they did was give us freedom. Sometimes it works in mysterious ways, its wonders to perform."

UNDER A STAIRCASE in a faded Moscow apartment block, a CIA officer wearing a trench coat bent down into the semi-darkness and reached behind a radiator. He found what he was looking for: a matchbox hanging from a metal hook. Inside were miniature photos of top-secret documents taken by Colonel Oleg Penkovsky, the highest-ranking Soviet intelligence officer ever to become an American spy. Penkovsky had been betraying Soviet secrets for more than a year. Seconds after the officer bent to retrieve his "dead drop" on November 2, 1962, disaster struck. Soviet police agents jumped from the shadows and arrested him. Since he was officially employed by the State Department, he was protected by diplomatic immunity and punished only by expulsion from the Soviet Union. Penkovsky was tried, convicted of treason, and executed.

Some CIA post-mortems on Penkovsky's loss focused on the devices he had been given to use. His camera was a commercially available Minox III, small enough to fit into a fist and equipped to take sharp images but unsuited to covert use because it required two hands. The matchbox he used to "dead drop" his film was serviceable but primitive. His Panasonic radio allowed him only to receive messages, not send any, and the messages could be deciphered only with the help of a code pad. The Technical Services Division looked amateurish, stuck in the past, able to conduct audio surveillance and produce simple items like false documents but not actively looking for ways to use cutting-edge technology in covert operations.

For the CIA, losing Penkovsky came after a series of other humiliations, most notably the U-2 fiasco, the disastrous Bay of Pigs invasion, and the failure to predict construction of the Berlin Wall. As if that were not enough, the Bay of Pigs failure had led President Kennedy to fire Allen Dulles, the only director of central intelligence many officers had ever known. The new director, John McCone, had been chairman of the Atomic Energy Commission and was an outsider to CIA culture.

McCone began by shaking up the team that had been responsible for the CIA's recent failures. Early in 1962 he arranged early retirement for Richard Bissell, the deputy director for plans, who had presided over the Bay of Pigs debacle. To take his place, McCone elevated Richard

Helms—Gottlieb's steadfast patron and protector. A few months later, Helms reshuffled the Technical Services Division, and when the dust settled Gottlieb was its deputy chief. His assignment was to bring it into a new age.

"TSD leadership had mountains to climb," recalled one officer who served there in the 1950s. "One was technology, which was pretty bad."

When Gottlieb joined the CIA in 1951, Technical Services officers numbered in the dozens. By the time he became deputy chief eleven years later, there were several hundred. The division's headquarters was not at the new CIA campus in Langley, Virginia, but in a wonderfully historic complex at 2430 E Street in Washington, near the Lincoln Memorial. It had been the original CIA headquarters, and before that had housed the Office of Strategic Services. The complex was spacious, giving Gottlieb room in the East Building for his Audio Operations staff, in the South Building for Secret Writing, and in the Central Building for Disguise Operations.

Many other Technical Services officers were based at CIA stations overseas. Most often they were called upon to tap a phone line, bug an office, install a hidden camera, or turn a can or brick into a container for hiding microfilm. Gottlieb wanted to offer more. He recognized that technology was becoming steadily more important in covert operations, and he set out to hire engineers, chemists, artists, printers, and all manner of craftsmen. Rather than recruiting from Ivy League universities, he concentrated on technical schools and state colleges. He brought ambitious students to Washington for internships. When he bumped up against a hiring ceiling, he would offer "temporary" contracts that could be indefinitely extended.

"Typically, these technical recruits had shown a childhood penchant for tinkering that eventually turned into engineering and hard-science degrees," one Technical Services officer later wrote. "They were often the first or only member of their family to attend college and many came from rural communities in the Midwest and Southwest. They arrived at the CIA seeking technical opportunities and adventure. It did not take long before these newly minted engineers began delighting in calling operations officers 'liberal arts majors.' For engineers, this less than flattering term summed up both a case officer's educational background and the imprecise, unscientific nature of agent recruiting and handling."

During Gottlieb's years in the top echelon of Technical Services, its officers prided themselves on doing more than simply waiting for gadget orders. They tried to help operations officers imagine new ways to penetrate enemy defenses, uncover secrets, and protect agents. Are Soviet diplomats in a Latin American country discussing sensitive matters under a tree in their embassy compound? No problem: Technical Services developed a tiny microphone and transmitter, encased them inside a projectile, and designed a gun to fire the projectile into the accommodating tree. Does an agent find covert photography of documents too risky? Technical Services invented a "subminiature" camera with a four-millimeter lens that could take up to one hundred pictures despite being small enough to conceal in a pen, watch, or cigarette lighter. Does a spy say he will take risks only if he is given an "L-pill" so he can commit suicide if caught? Technical Services made a pair of eyeglasses with such a pill hidden in one of the temple tips, so that if the agent was trapped and brought in for interrogation, he could pretend to be chewing nervously on his glasses while he was actually biting on the "L-pill."

Whenever counterintelligence officers needed guidance on what drugs to use in an interrogation, Gottlieb was the obvious person to consult. When the Soviet intelligence officer Yuri Nosenko defected to the West in 1962, the CIA counterintelligence chief, James Jesus Angleton, suspected that he was a fake defector sent to disrupt the CIA. Nosenko was held captive at a safe house in Maryland for three years and subjected to almost every torture Gottlieb had ever devised in an effort to force him to confess. He endured seventeen rounds of intense questioning. Electrodes were strapped to his head. For much of his 1,277 days in captivity, he was locked into a small, windowless concrete cell. Later the CIA concluded that he had been a genuine defector and that the way he was treated "went beyond the bounds of propriety or good judgment." At the time, though, Gottlieb and his team were thought to have proven their value once again.

Among the many special interests that Gottlieb pursued at Technical Services was graphology, or handwriting analysis. Some Europeans took graphology seriously, but most Americans dismissed it as unreliable. Gottlieb was an exception. He was always looking for new or little-understood tools that might help him peer into the human mind. In 1958, while he was based in Germany but returning periodically to Washington, he commissioned "a special research study of handwriting analysis" that became MK-ULTRA Subproject 83.

"Graphologists will categorize a number of handwriting samples according to the degree to which these specimens tend to reveal personality dimensions," he wrote. "Other experts in handwriting analysis, including graphologists, handwriting identification experts and experimental psychologists, will examine the above groups of handwriting samples to determine any identifiable characteristics."

This "subproject" perfectly reflected the range of Gottlieb's imagination. His life's work had been the search for exotic knowledge that could be used in the service of covert action. While Subproject 83 was underway, he wrote a memo that set goals for future research into graphology and secured it as part of the CIA tool kit.

> [Redacted] has conducted a detailed study of handwriting analysis . . . More important, however, he has assembled data making it possible to design relevant and meaningful research into the usefulness and applicability of handwriting analyses to intelligence activities . . . In addition, [redacted] will begin to develop technical surveys on other controversial and misunderstood areas. These will include, though not necessarily in the next year: (a) a revision and adaptation of material already developed on deception techniques (magic, sleight of hand, signals etc.); (b) psychic phenomena and extra-sensory perception; (c) subliminal perception; (d) hypnosis; (e) "truth serums"; (f) expressive movements (body type, which facial characteristics etc.).

By the early 1960s, Gottlieb was doing far more than conceiving and overseeing extreme experiments in deep secrecy. He helped run a mini-empire with outposts around the world. That pulled him away from MK-ULTRA. So did his own rising doubts.

Gottlieb conceived MK-ULTRA as a search for ways to control the human mind. For years he pursued that quest to the edge of science and beyond. His imagination was fed by regular LSD use—by his own esti-mate he dosed himself at least two hundred times—and he never hesi-tated to test anything he could imagine. Nonetheless he was in the end a scientist. Years of relentless MK-ULTRA experiments pushed him inex-orably toward an unwelcome conclusion: there is no way to take control of another person's mind.

The first sign that Gottlieb was beginning to give up on MK-ULTRA, so far as is known, came in a memo entitled "Scientific and Technical Problems in Covert Action Operations," which he wrote in 1960. It remains classified, but a later CIA report contains excerpts. One sentence leaps out: "As of 1960 no effective knockout pill, truth serum, aphrodi-siac, or recruitment pill was known to exist." This admission—that years of MK-ULTRA experiments had failed to produce the breakthrough of Gottlieb's dreams—marked the beginning of his acknowledgment that his search had been in vain.

Other MK-ULTRA officers reached the same conclusion. "The pos-sibility of creating a 'Manchurian Candidate' is a total psychological impossibility," said David Rhodes, who spent several years distributing CIA grants as president of the Society for the Investigation of Human Ecology. "But it is intriguing. It is a lot of fun."

Gottlieb continued to direct MK-ULTRA during his first years back from Germany, but it operated on a greatly reduced scale. Many of its "subprojects" ended. Experiments with LSD were curtailed. No more funds were spent for research into electroshock or sensory deprivation. With the use of enough powerful drugs and other extreme measures, Gottlieb had found, it is possible to destroy a human mind. He had dis-covered no way, however, to embed a new personality into the resulting void, or to open the wiped-away mind to control by an outsider.

Even as MK-ULTRA wound down, it remained one of the CIA's most closely guarded secrets. John McCone learned of it after becoming direc-tor in 1961. In an effort to curtail and professionalize it, he created a new directorate for science and technology, and ordered it to take over the "behavioral" work Technical Services had been doing. This pros-pect naturally disturbed Gottlieb and his patron Helms. They managed to persuade McCone that he should protect MK-ULTRA from prying eyes, even those with top-secret clearance. It was not moved into the new directorate. Instead it remained in the covert action directorate, under Helms's friendly supervision.

This bureaucratic victory ensured that the story of MK-ULTRA's past would remain tightly held. The question of its future remained to be resolved. McCone did not share his predecessor's fascination with the idea of mind control. If there were to be any further experiments in this area, he decreed, they should be conducted by the new Science and Technology Directorate, not by Gottlieb and his Technical Services Division.

MK-ULTRA had been Gottlieb's child. He designed it, helped Richard Helms draft the memo to Allen Dulles that brought it into being in 1953, conceived the 149 "subprojects" that pushed its mind control research into hitherto unimagined realms, and monitored the results of extreme experiments at detention centers on four continents. In a decade of work, he had failed to produce a "truth serum," a technique to program the human mind, or a potion to work any kind of psychic magic.

Acting on his growing suspicion of MK-ULTRA, McCone directed the CIA's inspector general, J. S. Earman, to find out what it was and what it did. Earman submitted his report on July 26, 1963. A note at the top says it was prepared "in one copy only, in view of its unusual sensitivity."

"MK-ULTRA activity is concerned with the research and development of chemical, biological, and radiological materials capable of employment in clandestine operations to control human behavior," the report begins. "Over the ten-year life of the program, many additional avenues to the control of human behavior have been designated by TSD management as appropriate to investigation under the MK-ULTRA charter, including radiation, electroshock, various fields of psychology, psychiatry, sociology, and anthropology, graphology, harassment substances, and paramilitary devices and materials."

The report does not name Gottlieb or his deputy Robert Lashbrook, but refers to them: "There are just two individuals in TSD who have full substantive knowledge of the program, and most of that knowledge is unrecorded. Both are highly skilled, highly motivated, and professionally competent individuals . . . The final phase of testing MK-ULTRA materials involves their application to unwitting subjects in normal life settings . . . The MK-ULTRA program director has, in fact, provided close supervision of the testing program and makes periodic visits to the sites." Then, after assessing Gottlieb's "testing program," the inspector general reaches four conclusions.

a—Research in the manipulation of human behavior is considered by many authorities in medicine and related fields to be professionally unethical, therefore the reputations of professional participants in the MK-ULTRA program are on occasion in jeopardy.

b—Some MK-ULTRA activities raise questions of legality implicit in the original charter.

c—A final phase of the testing of MK-ULTRA products places the rights and interests of US citizens in jeopardy.

d—Public disclosure of some aspects of MK-ULTRA activity could induce serious adverse reaction in US public opinion, as well as stimulate offensive and defensive action in this field on the part of foreign intelligence services . . . Weighing possible benefits of such testing against the risks of compromise and of resulting damage to CIA has led the Inspector General to recommend termination of this phase of the MK-ULTRA program.

The report went on to suggest a series of steps to bring MK-ULTRA under tighter control. Its contracts should be audited. Gottlieb should file regular updates describing his work. Project managers should update their "notably incomplete" files. The conclusion is understated but profound: "A redefinition of the scope of MK-ULTRA is now appropriate."

Gottlieb had directed MK-ULTRA with only the loosest supervision. Suddenly he faced the prospect of oversight. Yet sharing the secrets of MK-ULTRA was unthinkable. How should he respond? A more combative bureaucrat might have chosen to resist the inspector general's report, defend the essential value of MK-ULTRA, and insist that it be allowed to continue functioning within its opaque shroud. Instead, in true Buddhist fashion, Gottlieb not only embraced the inspector general's report but suggested that its critique of his work was not deep enough. His response may be read as both an admission of defeat and a protective measure. Instead of redefining the scope of MK-ULTRA, he suggested, let the program fade away entirely.

It has become increasingly obvious over the last several years that the general area had less and less relevance to current clandestine operations. The reasons for this are many and complex, but two of them are perhaps worth mentioning briefly. On the scientific side, it has become very clear that these materials and techniques are too unpredictable in their effect on individual human beings, under specific circumstances, to be operationally useful. Our operations officers, particularly the emerging group of new senior operations officers, have shown a discerning and perhaps commendable distaste for using these materials and techniques. They seem to realize that, in addition to moral and ethical considerations, the extreme sensitivity and security constraints of such operations effectively rule them out.

Over the final months of 1963, MK-ULTRA slowed toward dignified expiration. Remaining "subprojects" ended and were not renewed. Apartments in New York and San Francisco to which victims had been lured for drug experiments were closed. Gottlieb focused on his other work. He was reinventing himself. The drug experimenter and poison maker became a designer of spy tools. When Gottlieb addressed the incoming class of CIA recruits in 1963, he referred only obliquely to MK-ULTRA.

"I remember him saying that the Soviets were doing a lot of research into mind control, and that we needed to keep up with them," one of the recruits later recalled. "As far as anyone knew, that was what he did—that was the justification for his work. It seemed quite reasonable. Nobody thought, 'What a horrible thing.' You didn't get any sense of a mad scientist or someone who was off the rails or anything like that."

For ten years Gottlieb directed systematic, intense, and far-reaching research into mind control. Finally he and his comrades were forced to face their cosmic failure. Their research had shown them that mind control is a myth—that seizing another person's mind and reprogramming it is impossible.

The ride of a lifetime was ending. There would be nothing like MK-ULTRA again. Gottlieb had every reason to believe that he had put his wild adventure behind him.

12

Let This Die with Us

As Sidney Gottlieb rose into the top ranks of the CIA during the 1960s, his family life remained rich. He expanded his Virginia cabin into a split-level house with large windows and modern conveniences. It was set far back from the road, in a forested glen at the end of a long gravel driveway. The grounds were built around a large swimming pool. On some summer weekends, dressed only in shorts, Gottlieb would sit cross-legged near the diving board and meditate.

In his late forties, Gottlieb was trim, fit, and handsome, with penetrating blue eyes. He rose before the sun and enjoyed being outdoors. When weather allowed, he spent hours gardening and working on his property. He liked to swim—whenever he arrived at a hotel, he headed for the pool—and developed an interest in sailing. He played tennis. Hours under the sun gave him a ruddy tan.

Gottlieb's four children—two boys and two girls—were no more or less troublesome than other teenagers. His wife sprinkled her letters to relatives with reports about rowdy sons and sullen daughters. She wanted them to think freely and nourish their spirituality.

"The way we thought about our children's upbringing in spiritual matters was that it was very important," Margaret Gottlieb wrote years later. "But since Sid and I came from such very different but very strong religious backgrounds, we wanted to give them the tradition of each and some knowledge of how all mankind has related to the subconscious, to the need to understand what is out there beyond. We always went to the Passover celebration at Sid's home . . . We spent two years in Germany and by the time we came home, Sid's father was sick and then died, so we didn't go home anymore . . . We feel that it is very important to be connected to age-old tradition, to feel that you are part of a large community—your family, your neighborhood, your school, your town, your church. I wanted my kids to have an acquaintanceship with the Bible, to have the sound of it in their ears. I wanted them to have great music, great poetry, great books, old folk tales, to have heard about folk customs, to know how their ancestors lived, moved and spoke."

The elder son, Peter, was seventeen years old when, in the summer of 1966, he brought home a girlfriend. She was one of his classmates at James Madison High School. Half a century later, she looked back over their romance. She remembered it as "kind of like going steady, puppy love, very innocent." Her recollections provide a uniquely intimate view of the family.

The girlfriend, who in an interview asked to be identified as Elizabeth, was delighted to fall into the Gottlieb orbit.

"I was a smart kid, but I came from a very Catholic background, a big family where everyone was preoccupied with the daily struggles of life," she said. "The Gottlieb family dynamic was so different from what I experienced growing up. They would have discussions about politics and what was happening in the world. They had so many more books— Sidney had a library in a den off the eating area. And they were so much more frank and open with each other than I was used to. I remember a time when one of Peter's sisters yelled, 'Oh shit! I've got my damn period again!' And I thought, 'Well, this is different.'"

Elizabeth recalls Sidney and Margaret emerging one evening in full Bavarian costume. He wore knee-length leather breeches with suspenders, and she wore an embroidered dirndl. They were on their way to an evening at one of their dancing clubs. "This was real folk dance," Elizabeth said, "not square dance."

The summer was a revelation for Elizabeth in several ways. "There was no religious feeling in that household, but I would say that Sidney had mystical leanings," she said. "So did his wife. They would talk about esoteric subjects that never came up at my dinner table at home. I remember feeling kind of entranced by their whole dynamic as a family. It was exotic. They were very unusual people. He meditated, but they weren't wackos or anything like that. There was something I just couldn't put my finger on."

Toward the end of Elizabeth's summer romance, that "something" came suddenly into focus.

One day that summer, we were out at the house swimming. The parents had gone to the store to buy food for dinner and Peter goes, kind of conspiratorially, "Come here. I want to show you something." He takes me into his father's den, his library, and says, "Turn around." He did something—he didn't want me to see what he did—and the wall of books opened up. Behind it was all this stuff. Weapons—I couldn't tell which kind, but guns. There was other stuff back there. It was like a secret compartment. I asked him, "What is *that* for?" He closed it back up quickly and said, "You know, my father has a price on his head." I said, "Why? Is he a criminal?" He said, "No, he works for the CIA." Then he said, "You know, my dad has killed people. He made toothpaste to kill someone." Later on he told me, "Don't tell anyone that you were in there, and don't ever tell anyone you know that my father kills people."

Looking back, Elizabeth concluded that Margaret Gottlieb "had to know" what her husband did for a living. "I also think all the kids knew about the secret compartment," she said. "You just got a sense that there were certain things they knew they had to follow, kind of unspoken protocols. You had to honk your horn when you arrived at the bottom of the driveway. Guests could come over, but only at certain times. There were little rules that had to be followed. This explains what was behind that wall of books. There probably was a worry about security, and someone coming after him."

SILENT CIA OFFICERS watched intently as a veterinarian anesthetized a gray-and-white cat on the operating table of a modern animal hospital.

When the first incision drew blood, one of the spectators—an audio engineer from Gottlieb's Technical Services Division—felt faint and stepped back to sit down. The others followed the vet's every move. He implanted a tiny microphone in the cat's ear canal, connected it with ultra-fine wire to a three-quarter-inch-long transmitter at the base of her skull, and added a packet of micro-batteries as a power source. Then he sewed up his incisions. The cat awoke and, after a recovery period, behaved normally.

"Acoustic Kitty" was conceived as the CIA's answer to a nagging surveillance problem. Bugging devices that its officers placed in foreign embassies often picked up too much background noise. Someone—a case officer or a "tech" from Gottlieb's shop—observed that cat ears, like human ears, contain a cochlea, a natural filter that screens out much of that noise. Why not try to turn a living cat into a surveillance device? Even if it proved unable to filter out background noise, it would allow "audio access" to targets who allowed cats to wander through their offices or conference rooms. This idea led to many months of experimentation and, ultimately, the creation of "Acoustic Kitty" in a CIA-contracted operating theater.

This cat was a miracle of technology. After the operation, she showed no outward scars, walked normally, and could do everything other cats did. The microphone and transmitter implanted within her worked perfectly. Finally her CIA handlers brought her to a park for a test mission. They pointed her in the direction of two men lost in conversation, supposedly with this command: "Listen to those two guys. Don't listen to anything else—not the birds, no cat or dog—just those two guys!" Any cat owner could guess what happened next. The cat took a few steps toward the men and then wandered off in another direction.

"Technically the audio system worked, generating a viable audio signal," according to one report of this experiment. "However, control of the cat's movements, despite earlier training, proved so inconsistent that the operational utility became questionable. Over the next few weeks, Acoustic Kitty was exercised against various operation scenarios, but the results failed to improve."

This aborted project was part of a CIA effort to test the value of animals—birds, bees, dogs, dolphins, and others—for electronic surveillance. No one considered it a failure. The official directive that ended it in 1967 concludes that further attempts to train animals "would not be practical," but adds: "The work done on this problem over the years reflects great credit on the personnel who guided it."

In an earlier era, that would have been a tip of the hat to Gottlieb and his fellow craftsmen-scientists at the Technical Services Division. It still was, but the "Acoustic Kitty" project was not run by Technical Services alone. Officers from the new Directorate of Science and Technology, which steadily expanded into what had been Gottlieb's domain, were also involved. Technical Services was able to remain autonomous—and to protect MK-ULTRA secrets—thanks to the vigilant patronage of Richard Helms. Nonetheless its mandate narrowed. Projects that would in the past have been its responsibility were transferred to the new directorate. Among them were "behavioral" experiments involving induced amnesia, implanted electrodes, and the cultivation of false memory.

With many of Gottlieb's responsibilities assigned to other CIA officers, MK-ULTRA ceased to exist as an active project. In 1964 the cryptonym was officially retired. A new one, MK-SEARCH, was assigned to its successor project, whose purpose was "to develop a capability to manipulate human behavior in a predictable manner through the use of drugs." The work Gottlieb had pioneered would continue, but in a more conventional scientific environment and stripped of its most brutal extremes.

If the demise of MK-ULTRA troubled Gottlieb, his concern was wiped away by the fortuitous results of unexpected turmoil at the top of the CIA. John McCone resigned as director in 1965. The tenure of his successor, Admiral William Raborn, was brief and unhappy. When Raborn resigned in 1966, President Johnson chose Richard Helms to succeed him. Gottlieb's bureaucratic godfather had reached the top. The result was not long in coming: Helms named Gottlieb chief of the Technical Services Division. The chemist whom some colleagues called "that clubfooted Jew" was now master of the CIA tool shop and its network of subsidiaries around the world.

ON FEBRUARY 14, 1970, a fiat from the White House shook Sidney Gottlieb's world. President Nixon, declaring that he feared the outbreak of a global pandemic, ordered government agencies to destroy their stores of bio-weapons and chemical toxins. Army scientists dutifully complied. Gottlieb hesitated. He asked the chief of his Chemical Division, Nathan Gordon, for an inventory of CIA stocks. Gordon reported that the CIA's "health alteration committee" medicine chest at Fort Detrick contained ten biological agents that could cause diseases including smallpox, tuberculosis, equine encephalitis, and anthrax, as well as six organic toxins, among them snake venom and paralytic shellfish poison. Both men were disturbed at the prospect of losing this deadly pharmacopeia. Gordon suggested that it be secretly moved out of Fort Detrick. He even found a research center in Maryland willing to warehouse it for $75,000 a year.

A couple of days later, however, Gordon and Gottlieb met with Richard Helms and Tom Karamessines, the CIA's deputy director for plans, and agreed that the Agency had no realistic option other than to follow the president's order and destroy its stock of poison. It did so—but one batch, the paralytic shellfish poison known as saxitoxin, escaped destruction. This was one of Gottlieb's prize poisons. Fabricating it had required extracting and refining minute amounts of toxin from thousands of Alaskan butter clams. The resulting concentrate was so strong that a single gram could kill five thousand people. Gottlieb had used it to make "L-pills" for agents who thought they might have to kill themselves, and to coat the suicide needle given to pilots of the U-2 spy plane.

Two canisters containing nearly eleven grams of this poison—enough to kill 55,000 people—were in one of Gottlieb's freezers. Before army technicians could remove them, two officers from the Special Operations Division packed them into the trunk of a car and drove them to the navy's Bureau of Medicine and Surgery in Washington, where the CIA maintained a small chemical warehouse. Nathan Gordon later testified that he ordered this operation himself, without consulting Gottlieb. He said he had never seen a directive requiring the destruction of toxins, and in any case believed that the CIA should keep some on hand in case "higher authority" should ever need it. By the time the eleven grams of shellfish poison were discovered and destroyed in 1975, Gottlieb had retired.

The seven years during which Gottlieb ran Technical Services—he was its longest-serving chief—were a period of frenetic global activity for the CIA. Its officers ran operations every day, in almost every country on earth, and required an endless array of tools and devices. Gottlieb's men and women provided them: individually tailored disguises to help officers evade surveillance; cameras hidden inside key chains, tie clips, wristwatches, and cigarette lighters; a thumb-sized single-shot pistol; a pipe that concealed a radio receiver; cars with secret compartments in which agents could be smuggled out of hostile countries; and a compressor that squeezed Soviet currency into tiny packets so large amounts could be passed in small containers.

Gottlieb's "concealment engineers" also crafted a remarkable device intended to entrap Philip Agee, a retired CIA officer who had become a fierce critic of the Agency. In 1971, when Agee was in Paris working on a tell-all book, he met a woman later described as "a blonde, bosomy and wealthy heiress of an American businessman in Venezuela." She encouraged his work, gave him money, lent him her apartment as a work space, and gave him a portable typewriter. Being a trained covert operative, Agee quickly discovered that the typewriter was crammed with tiny electronic devices, including microphones, a transmitter, and fifty miniature batteries. The woman who gave it to him turned out to have been a CIA officer. It was well crafted, an exemplar of Gottlieb's art. Agee found it so ingenious that he featured it on the cover of his book *Inside the Company: CIA Diary*. The lining of the typewriter lid is peeled back to reveal the battery array concealed beneath.

Some of the requests for exotic devices that Gottlieb received from operations officers had a peculiar origin. He ran Technical Services at a time when spy-versus-spy television shows like *Secret Agent*, *The Man from U.N.C.L.E.*, *Get Smart*, *I Spy*, and *Mission: Impossible* were immensely popular. The craze for James Bond movies exploded at the same time. Scriptwriters competed to invent the most outrageously imaginative gadgets for their fictional spies to use. Real spies took notice. Operations officers would become intrigued by a gadget from a TV show or film, and ask whether it could be made to function in real life. These inquiries were so persistent that for a time Technical Services added extra officers to its telephone switchboard on the morning after each episode of *Mission: Impossible* was broadcast. Officers who had been intrigued by some piece of spyware they saw on the show would call to ask: "Could *you* do that?" Gottlieb's crew took each of these orders seriously, and they filled more than a few.

Inevitably, given the era, Gottlieb and his Technical Services Division became deeply involved in the Vietnam War. The CIA station in Saigon was enormous and included a contingent of officers from Technical Services. One of them later estimated that equipment produced by Gottlieb's officers was used in "thirty to forty missions a day in Laos and Vietnam."

Engineers from Technical Services designed a portable "triple-tube rocket launcher" for commandos to use in destroying enemy fuel depots. Another team built a wooden superstructure to be fitted around a high-powered patrol boat so it would look like an innocent junk. Forgers made false documents for Vietnamese agents. Engineers designed sensors to be placed along the Ho Chi Minh trail, where they could be used to guide bomb strikes. They also produced mini-transmitters to be hidden in the stocks of rifles that would be abandoned on battlefields in the hope that enemy troops would recover them and become easier to track. One team invented an advanced compass for use by covert teams operating inside North Vietnam. It looked like a cigarette pack but contained miniaturized maps that were dimly backlit so they could be used in night operations.

"Throughout 1968, Dr. Gottlieb continued to preside over his empire of scientists who still prowled the backwaters of the world seeking new roots and leaves which could be crushed and mixed in the search for lethal ways to kill," according to one study of American intelligence during this period. "In their behavior laboratories, the psychiatrists and psychologists continued experimenting. Once more they had turned to an earlier line of research: implanting electrodes in the brain . . . An Agency team flew to Saigon in July 1968; among them were a neurosurgeon and a neurologist . . . In a closed-off compound at Bien Hoa Hospital, the Agency team set to work. Three Vietcong prisoners had been selected by the local station. How or why they were chosen would remain uncertain. In turn each man was anaesthetized and, after he had hinged back a flap in their skulls, the neurosurgeon implanted tiny electrodes in each brain. When the prisoners regained consciousness, the behaviorists set to work . . . The prisoners were placed in a room and given knives. Pressing the control buttons on their handsets, the behaviorists tried to arouse their subjects to violence. Nothing happened. For a whole week the doctors tried to make the men attack each other. Baffled at their lack of success, the team flew back to Washington. As previously arranged in case of failure, while the physicians were still in the air the prisoners were shot by Green Beret troopers and their bodies burned."

While this experiment was failing in Vietnam, another one in Israel also failed. The Israeli intelligence agency, Mossad, had an intimate connection to the CIA through James Jesus Angleton, the CIA officer who managed their relationship, and the two services often shared intelligence. As head of the CIA's counterintelligence staff, Angleton knew much about MK-ULTRA. Mossad was curious about one of the central MK-ULTRA goals: creating a programmed killer. Mossad officers thought this technique might help them assassinate the Palestinian leader Yasir Arafat. "The Israelis spent three months in 1968 trying to transform a Palestinian prisoner into a programmed killer," according to a study of Mossad's assassination program. "Within five hours of being released to carry out his mission, he had turned himself in to the local police, handed over his pistol and explained that Israeli intelligence had tried to brainwash him into killing Arafat."

Gottlieb's operation reached a peak of activity during the late 1960s. His ability to oversee a worldwide network of officers—informed by his years running MK-ULTRA—secured his reputation as a skilled administrator. He worked hard, happy with five hours of sleep each night. At lunchtime he snacked on food he brought from home, usually raw carrots, cauliflower, or other vegetables, homemade bread, and goat milk. He was known as a compassionate boss who made a point of mixing with his subordinates. "Gottlieb's personal attention to the TSD 'family' became legendary," one of his successors reported. "He had a self-deprecating sense of humor, liked to show off folk-dance steps, and remembered names, spouses' names, birthdays, and hobbies."

"It sounds hokey, but he had a touch with that kind of thing," said a chemist who worked for him. "It came across as, 'The boss knows me.'"

By the early 1970s Gottlieb had secured his place as one of the CIA's veteran leaders. Suspicions that followed him during his MK-ULTRA days seemed to have dissipated. His management style won him many admirers. So did his willingness to bend with the bureaucratic winds. His MK-ULTRA past might have threatened his position, but with Helms in place as director of central intelligence the past was safely secret.

That secrecy began to unravel in the pre-dawn hours of June 17, 1972. A security guard at the Watergate complex in Washington noticed a piece of tape over a door lock at the office of the Democratic National Committee. He called the police. Several intruders were arrested. They turned out to have connections to the White House and the CIA. Gottlieb's Technical Services Division had prepared false identity papers for two of them, Howard Hunt and G. Gordon Liddy, and had provided Hunt with implements of espionage including a speech alteration device, a camera concealed in a tobacco pouch, and a wig-and-glasses disguise. The Watergate break-in led to a series of discoveries that shattered American politics, leading ultimately to President Nixon's resignation. It also set off the chain of events that ended Gottlieb's career.

Eager to contain the political damage of Watergate, Nixon sought help from the CIA. Helms refused to create a cover story that would exculpate the White House. On February 1, 1973, Nixon fired him. Suddenly Gottlieb's protector was gone. He was alone and vulnerable.

As Helms was packing to leave, he summoned Gottlieb for a farewell. Their talk turned to MK-ULTRA, now fading from memory but still alive in files that documented years of experiments and interrogations. They made a fateful decision. No one, they agreed, could ever be allowed to see those files. They would certainly cause outrage if made public—and could also be used as evidence to prosecute Gottlieb and Helms for grave crimes.

"Early in 1973, Dr. Gottlieb, then C/TSD [chief of the Technical Services Division], called [redacted] and me to his office and requested that we review our Branch holdings and assure him that there were no extant records of the drug research program which had been terminated many years before," a CIA psychologist wrote in a memo two years later. "Dr. Gottlieb explained that Mr. Helms, in the process of vacating his chair as DCI, had called him and said, in effect, 'Let's take this with us' or 'Let's let this die with us' . . . There were no relevant investigations taking place at the time, and no relevant caveats on reduction of files. Mr. Helms seemed to be saying, 'It was our bath; let us clean the tub.'"

In one of his last acts as director of central intelligence, Helms ordered all MK-ULTRA records destroyed. The chief of the CIA Records Center in Warrenton, Virginia, was alarmed. He called Gottlieb and asked for confirmation. Gottlieb took the matter seriously enough to drive to the Records Center, present the order in person, and insist that it be carried out forthwith. On January 30, 1973, seven boxes of documents were shredded.

"Over my stated objections, the MK-ULTRA files were destroyed by order of the DCI (Mr. Helms) shortly before his departure from office," the chief of the Records Center wrote in a memo for his file.

Around the same time, Gottlieb directed his secretary to open his office safe, remove files marked "MK-ULTRA" or "Secret Sensitive," and destroy them. She did as she was told. Later she said she had made no record of what she destroyed and "never thought for a moment to question my instructions." With these blows, a historic archive was lost.

Helms's successor, James Schlesinger, arrived determined to make changes. "Schlesinger came on strong," one of his successors wrote in a memoir. "He had developed some strong ideas about what was wrong with [the CIA] and some positive ideas as to how to go about righting those wrongs. So he arrived at Langley, his shirttails flying, determined, with that bulldog, abrasive temperament of his, to implement those ideas and set off a wave of change."

Gottlieb was an obvious target. By CIA standards he was a grizzled veteran, having joined the Agency just four years after it was founded and served for twenty-two years. The program with which he was most closely associated, MK-ULTRA, was no longer well regarded. He had been a Helms protégé, and the Helms era was over. Finally, he was tainted by the fact that his Technical Services Division had collaborated with the Watergate burglars.

Immediately after taking office, Schlesinger changed the name of the Technical Services Division. It became the Office of Technical Services. Gottlieb was still the chief, but he must have anticipated what was coming.

One afternoon in April, Schlesinger telephoned John McMahon, an experienced CIA officer who had worked on the U-2 project. He asked McMahon to be at his office the next morning at 9:30. When McMahon appeared, pleasantries were brief.

"I've got a job for you," Schlesinger told him.

"What's that?" McMahon asked.

"I want you to go down and run OTS."

"I don't know anything about OTS."

"I want you to go down there and run it anyway. Make sure you know what's going on."

With that, Gottlieb was out and McMahon was in. There remained only the question of when to make the change. Schlesinger, not a patient man, brushed off the idea of waiting until the first day of May. Instead he looked at his watch and asked, "How about 10 AM?"

"We drove down to OTS," McMahon recalled years later. "I walked in and said, 'Hi, I'm your new leader.' It was a very awkward occasion."

For Gottlieb it was more than awkward. He might have sought to remain at the CIA in a reduced capacity, but that would have suited neither his wishes nor those of the Agency. A clean break was best for all.

Before departing, Gottlieb was asked to write a memo listing the kinds of help Technical Services was giving to other government agencies that carry out covert operations. It describes one aspect of the work he had been doing for more than a decade.

Department of Defense: Documents, disguise, concealment devices, secret writing, flaps and seals, counter-insurgency and counter-sabotage courses.

Federal Bureau of Investigation: At the request of the FBI we cooperate with the Bureau in a few audio surveillance operations against sensitive foreign targets in the United States.

Bureau of Narcotics and Dangerous Drugs: Beacons, cameras, audio and telephone devices for overseas operations, identity documents, car-trailing devices, SRAC [short-range agent communications], flaps and seals, and training of selected personnel responsible for the use thereof.

Immigration and Naturalization: Analyses of foreign passports and visas, guidance in developing tamper-proof alien registration cards, [redacted].

Department of State: Technical graphics guidance on developing a new

United States passport, analyses of foreign passports, car-armoring and personnel locators (beacons) for ambassadors.

Postal Services: The office of Chief Postal Inspector has had selected personnel attend basic surveillance photographic courses, has been furnished foreign postal information and has been the recipient of letter bomb analyses . . . We also have an arrangement with the Post Office to examine and reinsert a low volume of certain foreign mail entering the United States.

Secret Service: Gate passes, security passes, passes for presidential campaign, emblems for presidential vehicles, [and] a secure ID photo service.

US Agency for International Development: We furnish instructors to a USAID-sponsored Technical Investigation Course (counter-terror) at [redacted].

White House: Stationery, special memoranda, [and] molds of the Great Seal have been furnished.

Police Representing Washington, Arlington, Fairfax and Alexandria: During the period 1968–1969 a series of classes reflecting basic and surveillance photography, basic audio, locks and picks, counter-sabotage and surreptitious entry were given to selected members from the above mentioned cities.

Sidney Gottlieb retired from the CIA on June 30, 1973. Before departing he was awarded one of the Agency's highest honors, the Distinguished Intelligence Medal. CIA officers receive this award "for performance of outstanding services, or for achievement of a distinctly exceptional nature." As protocol dictates, the ceremony was private and Gottlieb had to return the medal after holding it for a few moments. The citation that accompanied it has not been declassified.

13

Some of Our People Were
Out of Control in Those Days

One of the most shocking cables ever sent by a director of central intelligence was delivered to case officers around the world on May 9, 1973. James Schlesinger, who had been running the Agency for barely four months—and who had just fired Gottlieb—wanted to stun the CIA out of ingrained habits. The Watergate scandal had set off public demands for candor and transparency in government. Schlesinger took advantage of that climate to send his shattering cable. Even he could not have imagined all it would produce.

"I am determined that the law shall be respected," Schlesinger wrote. "I am taking several actions to implement this objective. I have ordered all the senior operating officials of this Agency to report to me immediately on any activities now going on, or that have gone on in the past, which might be considered to be outside the legislative charter of this Agency. I hereby direct every person presently employed by CIA to report to me on any such activities of which he has knowledge. I invite all ex-employees to do the same. Anyone who has such information should call my secretary (extension 6363) and say that he wishes to talk to me about 'activities outside the CIA's charter.'"

Two days later, President Nixon announced that he was moving Schlesinger to a new job, secretary of defense. Then, eager to defend himself against charges that he was seeking to use the CIA as a political tool, Nixon named a career officer, William Colby, as its new director. Colby had a reputation as steely and harsh, shaped largely by his years of work in Vietnam, where he directed a campaign code-named Phoenix, aimed at "neutralizing" civilians who were thought to be collaborating with enemy forces. Torture had been part of Phoenix, and Colby himself had confirmed that its agents killed more than twenty thousand Vietnamese. Yet by the time Nixon named him to head the CIA, he was in the midst of a personal voyage. His determination to reveal the CIA's past excesses turned out to be even more fervent than Schlesinger's.

"He was a Roman Catholic, and after his eldest daughter's death from a combination of epilepsy and anorexia nervosa, he seemed to change, becoming more religious and more reflective," according to one intelligence historian. "Colby's colleagues noticed a change in him, and put it down to his daughter's death and the harassment he faced over Phoenix. In retrospect they felt that he had 'got religion,' that he was a 'soldier priest,' and that in his own way he was trying to do the best for the Agency, convinced that if he made a clean breast of the CIA's secrets, they could be put in the past . . . Implicit in his decisions was a recognition that the Agency's secrets were going to come out anyway. So he contrived to involve America's political leadership in the embarrassment of discovery."

Soon after Colby took office, he was handed a thick loose-leaf book that would change the CIA forever. Inside were all the responses that CIA officers had sent to Schlesinger after he ordered them to report illegal acts they had committed or knew about. They filled 693 closely typed pages. Among them were references to "research into behavioral drugs" and "human volunteers." Gottlieb's name appeared once.

"In January 1973, Dr. Sidney Gottlieb, advising that he was acting on instructions from DCI Richard Helms, ordered the destruction of all records associated with drug research and testing," one response said. "On 31 January 1973, seven boxes of progress reports, from 1953 to 1967, were recalled from the archives and destroyed. In addition, twenty-five copies of a booklet entitled 'LSD-25: Some Un-Psychedelic Implications' were destroyed."

After combing through this mass of material, which came to be known as the CIA "family jewels," Colby delivered a summary to the chairmen of the House and Senate Armed Services Committees, which were officially charged with overseeing the CIA. Guided by old habit, they agreed that the "family jewels" should remain secret. For the next year, Washington was increasingly consumed by the Watergate scandal, which led to Nixon's resignation on August 9, 1974, and his replacement by Vice President Gerald Ford. The "family jewels" remained safely tucked away.

Several months later, the investigative reporter Seymour Hersh, who had won a Pulitzer Prize for exposing the My Lai massacre in Vietnam, called Colby and said he had uncovered "a story bigger than My Lai." Hersh had learned about one of the "family jewels," a program called MH-CHAOS—MH was the prefix for projects with worldwide reach—under which the CIA had compiled dossiers on thousands of American journalists and anti-war activists. Colby did not deny the story. On Sunday, December 22, 1974, it ran on the front page of the *New York Times*.

"The Central Intelligence Agency, directly violating its charter, conducted a massive illegal domestic intelligence operation during the Nixon Administration against the anti-war movement and other dissident groups in the United States," Hersh's article began. It did not refer to drug experiments or anything else connected to MK-ULTRA. The wave of investigations it set off, however, would ultimately reach Sidney Gottlieb.

Revelations about MH-CHAOS led members of Congress to propose establishing a special committee to investigate illegal acts by the CIA. President Ford was resolutely opposed, as were senior CIA officers. This was the first time that an outside force had threatened the Agency's secrecy since Mike Mansfield's failed attempts to establish a congressional oversight committee in the 1950s.

The political climate in Washington, so protective of the CIA for so long, had decisively changed. Stories about CIA excesses were spilling into the press. Americans demanded to know more. This made it impossible for President Ford to oppose the idea of an investigation. Instead he tried to pre-empt Congress.

"Unnecessary disclosures would almost certainly result if I let Congress dominate the investigation," Ford wrote in his memoir. "I decided to take the initiative." On January 4, 1975, Ford announced the formation of his own CIA commission. He wanted a bland report that would find some mischief but no great crimes. This, he hoped, would reassure members of Congress and discourage them from conducting their own investigation. He described the United States as "beset by continuing threats to our national security," said that the CIA was "fundamental in providing the safeguards that protect our national interests," and praised its "notable record of many successes." Congress, he suggested, should "consider the findings and recommendations of the commission" and "avoid a proliferation of hearings."

To ensure that his commission produced a forgiving report, Ford chose Vice President Nelson Rockefeller as its chairman. Rockefeller was a quintessential political insider whose ties to the CIA dated back to the 1950s, when he served with Allen Dulles on the Operations Coordinating Board, a secret subcommittee of the National Security Council that was responsible for conceiving and developing covert action projects.

Hours after Ford announced formation of the Rockefeller Commission, he met with Richard Helms, who was then serving as the U.S. ambassador to Iran. Helms knew as much as anyone alive about the history of American covert operations—including MK-ULTRA. "Frankly, we are in a mess," Ford told him, adding that he planned to give the Rockefeller Commission a narrow mandate and to warn its members that exceeding it "would be tragic."

"It would be a shame if the public uproar forced us to go beyond, and to damage the integrity of the CIA," Ford said. "I automatically assume what you did was right unless it's proven otherwise."

That amounted to an assurance that, if at all possible, Helms would be shielded from accountability for the CIA's actions on his watch. He was gratified but still uneasy. If the "family jewels" were made public, the reaction could be uncontrollable.

"A lot of dead cats will come out," Helms warned the president. "I don't know everything which went on in the Agency. Maybe no one does. But I know enough to say that if the dead cats come out, I will participate."

All members of the Rockefeller Commission—officially the President's Commission on CIA Activities Within the United States—were charter members of the political elite who could be relied upon to do whatever possible to protect the CIA. Among them were General Lyman Lemnitzer, a former chairman of the Joint Chiefs of Staff; the labor leader Lane Kirkland, whose AFL-CIO was a main conduit for CIA funding of anti-Communist trade unions abroad; Ronald Reagan, who had just completed two terms as governor of California; and C. Douglas Dillon, a former secretary of the treasury. They worked for five months. Rockefeller steered them away from sensitive matters, but even he could not contain the oddly talkative director of central intelligence William Colby. Rather than claim ignorance or poor memory, Colby gave surprisingly candid answers. In his first session he testified that the CIA had conducted LSD experiments that resulted in deaths. Later he referred to assassination plots. His candor disturbed members of the hear-no-evil commission. Afterward Rockefeller pulled him aside.

"Bill, do you really have to present all this material to us?" Rockefeller asked. "We realize that there are secrets you fellows need to keep, and so nobody here is going to take it amiss if you feel that there are some questions you can't answer quite as fully as you seem to feel you have to."

The Rockefeller Commission's report, issued on June 11, 1975, was as mild as circumstances allowed. It concluded that the CIA had carried out "plainly unlawful" operations, including spying on protest groups, tapping phones, committing burglaries, and opening mail. Stories about assassination plots against foreign leaders had begun to circulate in Washington, but the commission report said that "time did not permit a full investigation."

Although the report did not mention MK-ULTRA by name, it did say that the CIA had run a project "to test potentially dangerous drugs on unsuspecting United States citizens," another that involved giving drugs to prison inmates, and a third in which "unsuspecting volunteers" were given LSD at two secret sites. No further investigation was possible, it concluded, because records of these operations had been destroyed and "all persons directly involved in the early phases of the program were either out of the country and not available for interview or were deceased."

Buried deep inside the report was a paragraph so startling that dry prose could not dilute its power.

On one occasion during the early phases of this program, LSD was administered to an employee of the Department of the Army without his knowledge while he was attending a meeting with CIA personnel working on the drug project. Before receiving the LSD, the subject had participated in discussions where the testing of such substances on unsuspecting subjects was agreed to in principle. However, this individual was not made aware that he had been given LSD until about 20 minutes after it had been administered. He developed serious side effects and was sent to New York with a CIA escort for psychiatric treatment. Several days later, he jumped from a tenth floor window of his room and died as a result.

The next day, articles about the Rockefeller Commission report dominated front pages across the United States and beyond. Most of them focused on new revelations about the MH-CHAOS surveillance program. The *Washington Post* ran four stories. One was headlined SUICIDE REVEALED.

A RINGING TELEPHONE woke Eric Olson at his apartment near Harvard University, where he was pursuing a graduate degree in psychology. His brother-in-law was calling.

"Have you seen today's *Washington Post*?" he asked.

"No, why?" Olson replied.

"There's a story in it that you need to read right away. It's about your father."

"My father? What about my father?"

"Go out and get a copy, then call me back."

Olson dressed, jogged to the Out-of-Town Newsstand in Harvard Square, bought the *Post*, and saw the headline: SUICIDE REVEALED.

"A civilian employee of the Department of the Army unwittingly took LSD as part of a Central Intelligence Agency test, then jumped ten floors to his death less than a week later, according to the Rockefeller Commission report issued yesterday," the story began. That sentence contained two inaccuracies: the victim was a CIA officer, not an army employee, and his "jump" was thirteen floors, since by the numbering system at the Statler Hotel, room 1018A was on the thirteenth floor. Nonetheless Eric Olson had a flash of recognition

"It was amazing," he said years later. "It was truly amazing. An Army scientist—that was the label, an 'Army scientist'—was drugged in 1953 with LSD by the CIA, reacted badly, was taken for medical attention to New York, but unfortunately jumped out the window. Then you go: 'Drugs? LSD? What?' It was this amazing combination of enlightenment and befuddlement at the same time. Both about 'Why are drugs now involved in this?' but also 'Is this my father?' And at the same time: How many scientists were jumping out of windows in New York in 1953?"

This story, with its lurid mix of drugs, death, and the CIA, proved irresistible. For the next several days, reporters barraged the CIA with demands to know more about the scientist who "jumped ten floors to his death" after being dosed with LSD. The Olson family called a press conference. On the day before it was to be held, Eric Olson invited the reporter Seymour Hersh to the family home in Frederick. Hersh was characteristically blunt.

"This must be the most goddamn incurious family in the United States!" he marveled. "How you could have lived with that bullshit story for twenty-two years is beyond me."

At the press conference, held in the family's backyard, Alice Olson read a statement saying that the family had decided to "file a lawsuit against the CIA, perhaps within two weeks, asking several million dollars in damages." She insisted that her husband had "not acted irrational or sick" during the last days of his life, but was "very melancholy" and "said he was going to leave his job."

"Since 1953, we have struggled to understand Frank Olson's death as an inexplicable 'suicide,'" she said. "The true nature of his death was concealed for twenty-two years."

Besides announcing plans to sue the CIA, the Olson family also asked the New York Police Department to open a new investigation. Manhattan district attorney Robert Morgenthau replied immediately, promising that his office would begin "looking into certain aspects" of the case. The New York police commissioner, Michael J. Codd, said he had ordered detectives "to look at the whole matter as to just what may have been the totality of circumstances under which Mr. Olson died."

Several stories about Olson's death quoted Robert Lashbrook, who was with him in room 1018A on the night he died. "I don't really know what I should say and what I shouldn't," Lashbrook told the *Washington Post* in a telephone interview. Then he mentioned that immediately after Olson's death, he had called a "CIA employee" to report what had happened—and that the employee's name was Sidney Gottlieb.

On the same day the *Post* ran that interview, the *New York Times* also published Gottlieb's name. It described him as "chief of the Central Intelligence Agency's testing of LSD" and quoted unnamed Rockefeller Commission investigators as asserting that he had "destroyed the drug program's records in 1973 to hide the details of possibly illegal actions." The *Times* also said that Gottlieb had been "personally involved in a fatal experiment" that led to Frank Olson's death.

The Rockefeller Commission previously reported the destruction of records on the LSD experiments, but did not mention Dr. Gottlieb by name. It also reported a program through the Federal Bureau of Drug Abuse Control in which the CIA had arranged to test LSD on "unsuspecting volunteers" in two programs, one in the West and the other along the East Coast. Staff sources on the Rockefeller commission said this program was also commanded by Dr. Gottlieb . . . [The staff] attempted to interview Dr. Gottlieb and was told by the Agency that he was unavailable. The *New York Times* tried unsuccessfully to reach him.

Those stories pierced Gottlieb's shroud of anonymity for the first time. He was gone but, to his eternal dismay, not forgotten.

Alarm bells went off at the White House after the Olson family announced its plan to sue the CIA. A lawsuit, if allowed to proceed, would give the family, as well as homicide detectives in New York, a tool they could use to force disclosure of deep secrets. President Ford's chief of staff, Donald Rumsfeld, and his deputy Dick Cheney, recognized the danger. Cheney warned Rumsfeld in a memo that a lawsuit might force the CIA "to disclose highly classified national security information." To head off this looming disaster, he recommended that Ford make a public "expression of regret" and "express a willingness to meet personally with Mrs. Olson and her children."

Ford took his aides' advice. He invited Alice Olson and her three adult children to the White House. On July 21, 1975, they met in the Oval Office. It was a unique historical moment: the only time an American president has ever summoned the family of a CIA officer who died violently and apologized on behalf of the United States government.

"With deepest sincerity and conviction, I hereby extend that apology . . . for the uncertainties and anguish experienced by the family over this extended period," Ford said after greeting the Olsons. He said he had directed the CIA to give them whatever documents it had that might shed light on the case. Later they met with William Colby at CIA headquarters at Langley. He apologized for what he called a "terrible thing" that "should never have happened."

"Some of our people were out of control in those days," Colby said. "They went too far. There were problems of supervision and administration."

White House lawyers offered the Olson family $750,000 in exchange for dropping its legal claims. After some hesitation, the family accepted. Congress passed a special bill approving the payment. That would have closed the case if Frank Olson had remained quiet in his grave.

AFTER RETIRING FROM the CIA, Sidney Gottlieb could hardly have taken a normal job. For two decades he had lived under deep cover. He had conceived and directed a mind control program with global reach, overseen extreme interrogations, concocted poisons to kill foreign leaders, and crafted tools of mayhem for spies. What job could follow that?

With help from his old friend Richard Helms, Gottlieb quietly became a consultant to the Drug Enforcement Administration. To get the job, which was designated as "sensitive," he had to complete an extended application. He wrote that he was fifty-five years old, stood six feet tall, weighed 175 pounds, had hazel eyes and gray hair, spoke good German and fair French, and had "top secret plus many special clearances." In one section of the application, he was asked to summarize what he had done in his previous job.

"Responsible for broad program involving research, development and production of equipment and software in a wide range of scientific and engineering fields, and the deployment and application of those assets worldwide," he wrote. "Had total responsibilities for mgmt. of funds, personnel and direction of activities."

Gottlieb spent seven months at the Drug Enforcement Administration, most of it preparing what its director John Bartels called "a management study on research facilities." This interlude, which ended in May 1974, gave him time to reflect on his future. Quiet retirement was implausible. Gottlieb was still youthful and vigorous. By nature he was an explorer, a seeker, a wanderer. Government service had not made him rich, but it left him with a home in Virginia, some savings, and a pension of $1,624 per month. His children were out of high school. Both he and his free-thinking wife, Margaret, thirsted for adventure. Together they set out to imagine a new life. The leap they decided to take was unconventional, to say the least, but utterly consistent with their restless inner spirits.

"Sid retired from government at an early age and we had to decide what to do with the rest of our lives," Margaret Gottlieb wrote years later in an essay for her family. "With the thought that we would free ourselves from all our material things which might stand in the way of making unimpeded choices, we sold everything—house, land, cars, goats and chickens. The children took what they wanted, and we booked ourselves onto a freighter, leaving from San Francisco and heading for Perth, Australia. This trip continued, sometimes on land, sometimes by sea and sometimes by air, for two years. We were in Africa, Australia, and India, and many places in between. We were just following our noses, getting volunteer jobs wherever we were and spending as long as we wanted."

In India, the couple volunteered to work at a hospital in the northern state of Uttar Pradesh where lepers and other severely afflicted patients were treated. Margaret, who had been born and brought up at a mission station in Uttar Pradesh, did not adjust well. Her feelings for India were deeply conflicted. After a few months she fell ill.

"I never wanted to go back to India," she wrote in a letter home. "I have never had any nostalgia for it and have always felt that it was such a hopeless place . . . Then Sid and I went back to India, and I was there working in a mission hospital for three months and I got sick. I just couldn't stand it—the whole thing. I found that in the forty years since I had left, nothing had changed—*nothing* . . . Village life is the same: the dirt, the monkeys, the stray dogs, the filth, the open gutters, the people defecating and peeing wherever they happen to be, the bribery, the total contrariness of everything. Nothing makes sense—to us! All the years that the British and the missionaries had spent had made no difference at all. OK, I accept that and now I know it. So it seems to me that they are a people who have a way—their way, which indeed has been in use and functioning for them a great deal longer than our way has been functioning for us—and they need to be left to do it their way."

While Margaret Gottlieb was convalescing and musing about the effects of imperialism in India, her husband became the subject of unwanted attention back home. They had been on the road for two extraordinary years. Suddenly the past came calling.

Scandals were raining down on the CIA. The Rockefeller Commission's mild report did not satisfy critics. Determined to dig deeper, the Senate formed a Select Committee to Study Governmental Operations with Respect to Intelligence Activities, headed by Senator Frank Church of Idaho. Its investigators found several documents mentioning plots to assassinate foreign leaders. The names of most CIA officers who sent or received these documents were redacted. One name, however, appeared several times: Sidney Gottlieb.

Church Committee investigators asked the CIA for permission to interview this mysterious officer. They were told that he had retired and left the United States. The investigators insisted. Finally, with help from the CIA's legal office, they found him.

Gottlieb was in India when, on a spring day in 1975, he received a most disconcerting message. The Church Committee wanted to talk to him. His world travels were over.

In a secluded glen a few miles from the White House, Gottlieb first met the defender who would secure his future. He had returned from India to find the capital in an investigative frenzy. His besieged former colleagues at the CIA warned him that he might be among the targets, and urged him to hire a lawyer. One suggested a hard-charging Washington insider, Terry Lenzner, who had recently given a talk at Langley about the legal rights of CIA officers.

Soon afterward, Lenzner received a telephone call from a man whose "husky voice had a pronounced stutter." Gottlieb introduced himself. He asked for a meeting and "underscored his desire for discretion." Lenzner suggested Rosedale Park, around the corner from his home.

"I sat waiting on a park bench," Lenzner wrote afterward. "A man with a limp came toward me. He was casually dressed, and his clubfoot dragged behind him. He approached cautiously, casting furtive glances around him—subtly enough that it was clear to me he had been well trained in the art of counter-surveillance. Once he took a seat beside me, he offered his hand. 'I'm Sid Gottlieb.'"

Lenzner replied that he was "glad we could get together," and then Gottlieb began. He said he was outraged that Americans had taken to attacking the CIA, which was "devoted to the defense of this country." As for suggestions that he had acted improperly, they were outrageous and he planned to hold a press conference to say so. Lenzner suggested that this might be unwise, since "all he would accomplish by going public would be to put an even larger target on his back." Gottlieb pondered for a moment. Then he said he might be interested in retaining Lenzner's services—but with a most unusual pre-condition.

"Before we work together," he told Lenzner, "I'm going to need a sample of your handwriting."

"Why is that?"

"I have someone at the Agency who can analyze it and tell me whether I should trust you."

Lenzner could not have known it, but this was an expression of the interest in graphology that Gottlieb had nurtured since his MK-ULTRA days. He wrote out several random sentences. Gottlieb folded the paper, put it in a pocket, said, "I'll get back to you," and walked away. A couple of days later he called.

"You checked out," Gottlieb told him. "No character defects."

Gottlieb's immediate problem was the newly created Church Committee, at whose summons he had returned to the United States. Its investigators wanted to question him about his role in assassination plots. He was willing, but Lenzner cautioned him: "Before you talk to any committee or anyone else, we're going to ask for immunity from prosecution."

"I'm not going to do that," Gottlieb told him. "I'm not going to hide behind the Fifth Amendment."

' "Look, Sid, the goal here is to keep you out of the newspapers and, at a minimum, out of jail," Lenzner replied. "You don't understand how this works. You could very well be the fall guy in this whole investigation."

Lenzner, who had defended the radical priest Philip Berrigan and whose liberal friends were aghast when he agreed to represent Gottlieb, soon won his new client's confidence. The two spent many hours together. Gottlieb could not confess all he had done, but his monologues, as Lenzner later recounted them, offered a flash of insight into his mind and memory.

> Because of his expertise in poisons, Gottlieb told me that he was put in charge of assassination programs for the agency. He managed several attempts to assassinate foreign leaders . . . Surprisingly, much of Sid's work did not focus on US enemies abroad. The CIA also conducted experiments on American citizens. Sid was not at all defensive about the LSD program in general, and indeed thought it was essential to American security . . . Sid said that he had supervised LSD experiments on more than twenty unsuspecting people. He had experimented with LSD on himself too. When we discussed individual cases—subjects or victims of the program, depending on your point of view—he seemed pained. As an academic exercise, Sid could go on confidently about the rightness of his activities. But he wasn't so comfortable talking about individual cases or real people whose lives were affected. Not surprisingly, he wasn't enthusiastic about talking about Olson.

Lenzner outlined what he saw as Gottlieb's legal challenges. The Church Committee was investigating assassination plots in which Gottlieb had been involved. In New York, the district attorney was looking into Frank Olson's death. Gottlieb no longer wielded power at the CIA and had few remaining friends there. Besides, as Lenzner wrote, "with his stutter, club foot and immigrant roots, Sid did not fit into that crowd." He looked like "a ripe, juicy target."

"They could try to pin Olson's death on you," Lenzner warned him.

That sobered Gottlieb. He agreed to present the Church Committee with an ultimatum: no testimony without immunity.

The committee was consumed with preparations for a momentous season of public hearings probing all manner of "unlawful or improper conduct" by the CIA. At the first hearing, William Colby revealed the existence of MK-NAOMI, the partnership between the CIA and the army's Special Operations Division at Fort Detrick. He produced a summary of its work written in 1967, when Gottlieb was running the Technical Services Division. It said MK-NAOMI had two purposes: to "stockpile severely incapacitating and lethal materials for specific use of TSD," and to "maintain in operational readiness special and unique items for the dissemination of chemical and biological materials." Colby testified that despite having spent a quarter century at the CIA, he had not heard of MK-NAOMI until becoming director.

Distracted by a cascade of hearings and lacking the wherewithal to battle Lenzner, whom one associate compared to "General Patton on steroids," the Church Committee granted Gottlieb the immunity he had demanded. On October 7, 1975, he began answering questions from senators and staff investigators. Later he recalled providing "forty-odd hours of testimony before the Senate Select Committee on Intelligence—I do not mean to say that the testimony was odd."

The committee took Gottlieb's testimony behind closed doors, in a secure Capitol Hill hearing room. It also allowed him to shield his identity by using an alias. He chose "Joseph Scheider." It was a delightful choice. Joseph Scheider was a nineteenth-century New York tobacconist whose name became a footnote to folk culture for its association with a haunting lithograph that adorned packages of his popular smoking tobacco. The lithograph shows a hooded monk staring out with penetrating eyes. In one hand he displays a set of playing cards bearing portraits of monarchs, and in the other he holds a long pipe from which smoke is billowing. He looks like the priest of a mystic cult or a master of unseen forces. Below the picture, in bold capital letters, is the legend JOSEPH SCHEIDER. The tobacconist's name became associated with the image of the inscrutable monk. That monk was Gottlieb as he saw himself: a mysterious guardian of esoteric knowledge, alluring but at the same time unsettling, drawing inspiration from a pipe to peer into the human soul.

As Senate rules require, the Church Committee sealed the "Joseph Scheider" testimony for fifty years. Later committee reports, however, quoted several passages.

"Joseph Scheider testified that he had 'two or three conversations' with Richard Bissell in 1960 about the Agency's capacity to assassinate foreign leaders," one report says. "Scheider informed Bissell that the CIA had access to lethal or potentially lethal biological materials that could be used in this manner . . . After the meeting, Scheider reviewed a list of biological materials available at the army's Chemical Corps installation at Fort Detrick, Maryland, which would produce diseases that would 'either kill the individual or incapacitate him so severely that he would be out of action.' Scheider selected one material from the list which was 'supposed to produce a disease that was indigenous to that area and that could be fatal' . . . The [Congo] Station Officer testified that he received 'rubber gloves, a mask, and a syringe' along with lethal biological material from Scheider, who also instructed him on their use."

Committee members also asked Gottlieb about drug experiments. Lenzner took notes. Later he wove them into a revealing account.

"Sid said he was charged with implementing a program code-named MK-ULTRA," he wrote. "Researchers focused on the psychedelic drug LSD as a potentially powerful tool in espionage . . . Under MK-ULTRA, funding was provided for these experiments—mostly on prisoners, mental patients, and others who weren't in positions to object, like the customers who frequented two brothels run by the Agency in San Francisco and New York. The Agency, sometimes working with the military, also conducted experiments abroad, slipping various pills and lozenges into the drinks of strangers and misfits."

Questioning was proceeding methodically when Senator Richard Schweiker of Pennsylvania leaned forward and handed Gottlieb a heavily redacted document. "Doctor Gottlieb," he asked, "can you tell me what this memo is about?"

Gottlieb looked at the memo and recoiled. He had written it in the 1950s for senior CIA officials. Its title was scary: "Health Alteration Committee." Gottlieb's discomfort was clear. The room fell silent. Lenzner covered the microphone with his hand and whispered into his client's ear.

"What's up, Sid?" he asked.

"I need to talk to you about this," Gottlieb whispered back.

Lenzner announced that his client was feeling unwell and asked for a recess. They retreated to a private office. Lenzner shut the door. When he turned to face Gottlieb, he was startled. "He was breathing heavily, his face still drained of color," Lenzner recalled. "He closed his eyes and began what looked like a slow dance, his arms extended. What on earth was this? As if reading my mind, Sid said: 'Tai chi. Helps me relax.'"

Here in a Capitol Hill anteroom, during a break in questioning about his involvement in CIA drug experiments and assassination plots, Gottlieb's eyes slowly closed. His arms swayed in age-old patterns. Past and present were coming together. Lenzner watched for a few moments and then spoke.

"Sid, help me out here," he said. "What's in that memo?"

"That's the one," Gottlieb murmured from his relaxed state. "The one that worked."

Lenzner pressed him. Gottlieb said the memo described a plot against "a Communist official in an Arab country whom the CIA wanted to get rid of." He had made a scarf that the official received as a gift.

"What kind of scarf?" Lenzner asked.

"One infected with tuberculosis," Gottlieb answered. "He died after a couple of weeks."

This was more than Lenzner would allow his client to admit. "Sid and I sat down and devised a careful answer to avoid revealing this new information without committing perjury," he recalled. "When he returned to the hearing room, Sid said that the Agency had sent a handkerchief 'treated with some kind of material for the purpose of harassing that person who received it.' The senators didn't know enough to ask the right follow-up questions, and Sid made it through the hearing relatively unscathed."

Setting a pattern that would define all of his post-retirement testimony, Gottlieb repeatedly pleaded bad memory. As one writer observed, he "claimed to have forgotten virtually everything he had spent the last twenty-five years researching." As the hearing was ending, the committee's chief counsel, Frederick Schwarz, said he had "one final question." It was about Gottlieb's role in the plot against Lumumba, but it also addressed the larger moral conundrum.

"When you were asked to kill Lumumba, or whatever word was used, did you consider declining to do that?" Schwarz asked. "If not, why not?"

"My view of the job at the time, and the responsibilities I had, was in the context of a silent war that was being waged," Gottlieb replied. "Although

I realize that one of my stances could have been . . . as a conscientious objector to this war, that was not my view. I felt that a decision had been made, as we discussed it, at the highest level that this be done, and that as unpleasant a responsibility as it was, it was my responsibility to carry out my part of that."

Gottlieb survived his secret testimony without damage. The New York police investigation into the Frank Olson case proved inconclusive. Then a new threat appeared. The Department of Justice became interested in him. A *Washington Post* article set off its investigation.

"Sources said Dr. Sidney Gottlieb, who headed the CIA's Technical Services Division and was in overall charge of the Agency's drug tests until his retirement in 1973, returned here recently and has retained former Senate Watergate Committee counsel Terry Lenzner as his lawyer," the *Post* reported. "Gottlieb, 57, was responsible for the destruction of 152 files covering virtually all of the CIA's drug testing . . . The destruction of the CIA's drug files and Gottlieb's disappearance before the Rockefeller Commission investigation compounded the CIA's earlier cloak of secrecy surrounding its drug activities and prevented commission investigators from obtaining many specifics about the drug tests, according to a committee source."

The day after this article appeared, copies circulated at FBI field offices in Washington and Alexandria, Virginia. Destruction of government property is a felony. If Gottlieb had destroyed CIA files, he might be subject to prosecution. The FBI opened an investigation. It began with a background check on Gottlieb that turned up no record of criminal violations in Washington or any nearby jurisdiction. Then it hit a wall.

On October 14, 1975, FBI director Clarence Kelley sent a memo to his Alexandria office entitled "Doctor Sidney Gottlieb: Destruction of Government Property." It brought frustrating news. A lawyer from the Department of Justice had called to report that Gottlieb was giving secret testimony to the Church Committee. "It was indicated that Doctor Gottlieb was granted immunity before testifying," the memo said, "and that he testified concerning the destruction of records in this matter."

That effectively ended an FBI investigation that might have led to Gottlieb's indictment. Lenzner's strategy worked: secure immunity for your client, then have him confess to crimes so he cannot be prosecuted for committing them.

The FBI tried one last gambit. Agents approached Lenzner and asked if he would make Gottlieb available for voluntary questioning. He agreed, but said the questioning would have to wait until Gottlieb finished his Senate testimony. Once the testimony was finished, he withdrew his offer. An internal FBI memo dated December 8 says Gottlieb "may have returned to India by now" and suggests bringing the case "to a logical conclusion." Five weeks later, Kelley sent a curt directive to agents in Alexandria.

"The Criminal Division of the Department of Justice has advised that no further investigation should be conducted on this matter in view of Doctor Gottlieb's attorney not making him available for interview," he wrote. "Discontinue further efforts to interview Doctor Gottlieb."

Not satisfied with this victory, Lenzner sought one more. He asked a federal judge, Gerhard Gesell, to issue an order forbidding the Church Committee from publishing Gottlieb's name in its report on CIA assassination plots. Frederick Schwarz, the committee's chief counsel, resisted. "I argued that no, he is sufficiently high and the office of chief scientist is sufficiently high that he fit within where we would use the actual name," Schwarz recalled years later. Gesell agreed. Two days later, Lenzner was back in court with an appeal. That happened to be the same day that the Senate met in closed session to discuss the Church Committee's assassination report—a session Schwarz could not miss. Rather than appear in court to contest Lenzner's appeal, he backed down and agreed to allow Gottlieb to be identified by his pseudonym. The Senate report, issued a few days later, refers only to "Joseph Scheider," identified as a former adviser to Richard Bissell who "holds a degree in bio-organic chemistry."

Newspapers were less restrained. After Lenzner and his law partner made their courtroom appeal to Judge Gesell, the *New York Times* reported: "They declined to identify their client in public court session. However, the two lawyers represent Dr. Sidney Gottlieb, a retired CIA official who directed the Agency's Technical Services Division. Dr. Gottlieb was questioned in a closed session of the Senate committee earlier this fall on his role in CIA plots to kill Fidel Castro, prime minister of

Cuba, and Patrice Lumumba, a leader in the Congo crisis in 1961 . . . He has also been questioned about the death in a CIA drug experimentation program of an army scientist in 1953 as a result of an overdose of LSD. Dr. Gottlieb destroyed numerous records of his operation at the CIA shortly before leaving the Agency in 1973. He has also been questioned about this."

For Gottlieb the autumn of 1975 was most unpleasant. He had been abruptly pulled away from his new life and back into a world he thought he had escaped forever. After a lifetime of the deepest anonymity, his name was appearing in newspapers. Often it was connected to frightening-sounding CIA projects.

Despite this rude shock, Gottlieb could count himself fortunate. He avoided what might have been a more troublesome fate. Protected by immunity, he had been able to confess to possible crimes. That prevented the Department of Justice from prosecuting him. He even managed to keep his name out of the official record—if not the press—and to be remembered as "Joseph Scheider." Once again, for the second time in as many years, he resolved to drop out of sight and spend the rest of his life in simplicity and service. Fate did not cooperate this time either.

14

I Feel Victimized

After the brief burst of publicity that upset his life in 1975, and his attendant brush with the law, Gottlieb retired to northern California. His mother-in-law and one of his daughters lived nearby. He immersed himself in the anonymity to which he was so well accustomed.

In Washington, meanwhile, investigations of the CIA reached a climax. Over a fifteen-month period the Church Committee held 126 public hearings, interviewed 800 witnesses, and reviewed more than 100,000 documents. It focused on spectacular abuses like domestic spying and assassination plots. Senators finished their work without coming close to understanding what MK-ULTRA had been or what Gottlieb had done.

"Intelligence agencies have undermined the constitutional rights of citizens," the Church Committee concluded in its final report, issued in April 1976. "There is no inherent constitutional authority for the President or any intelligence agency to violate the law."

Tucked away in the committee's six-volume final report was a section entitled "Testing and Use of Chemical and Biological Agents by the Intelligence Community." It included a methodical recounting of the Frank Olson story: Olson was conducting "biological research for the CIA," attended a retreat at which a colleague spiked his drink with LSD, suffered "what appeared to be a serious depression," and "leapt to his death" from a New York hotel window. The report also summarized what the committee had discovered about CIA mind control programs.

- The earliest of the CIA's major programs involving the use of chemical and biological agents, Project Bluebird, was . . . investigating the possibilities of control of an individual by application of special interrogation techniques.
- In August 1951 the project was renamed Artichoke . . . Overseas interrogations utilizing a combination of sodium pentothal and hypnosis, after physical and psychiatric examination of the subjects, were also part of Artichoke.
- MK-ULTRA was the principal CIA program involving the research and development of chemical and biological agents . . . LSD was one of the materials tested in the MK-ULTRA project.
- Because MK-ULTRA records were destroyed, it is impossible to reconstruct the operational use of MK-ULTRA materials by the CIA overseas.

For a quarter century, MK-ULTRA had been the cryptonym that dared not speak its name. Even within the CIA few had heard of it. Now it was appearing in public print. The Church Committee's account of MK-ULTRA was superficial and uninformed, though, and none of its conclusions touched Gottlieb in any direct or dangerous way.

In the months after the Church Committee issued its report, public interest in CIA misdeeds began to fade. The murder of the CIA station chief in Athens after anti-CIA campaigners had published his name and address contributed to a backlash against further investigation. A spasm was ending. Gottlieb seemed to be home free.

Senators also believed they were finished with MK-ULTRA. Nearly two years had passed since "Joseph Scheider" testified about it in secret. With documents destroyed and the few people who knew the truth resolved to stay silent, the case had gone cold.

A sudden discovery reopened it. In 1977 the newly installed director of central intelligence, Stansfield Turner, whom President Jimmy Carter had appointed with a mandate to bring transparency to the CIA, received a Freedom of Information Act request for any MK-ULTRA files that might have escaped destruction. He passed it on to an archivist and encouraged him to make a thorough search. The archivist, as Turner later put it, "did a very diligent job of Sherlock Holmesing." In a depot where CIA financial records were stored, he found a collection of MK-ULTRA expense reports. Among them were references to various "subprojects." The Washington-based researcher whose FOIA request had led to the discovery, John Marks, released a batch of the documents at a press conference.

"Central Intelligence Agency documents released yesterday revealed new details of experiments on unsuspecting citizens designed to control their behavior through exotic drugs, electroshock, radiation and other means," the *Washington Post* reported. "More than 1,000 pages of documents obtained from the Agency under the Freedom of Information Act provided the details on the super-secret project, code-named MK-ULTRA."

These newly discovered documents brought MK-ULTRA to public attention for the first time. Members of the Senate Select Committee on Intelligence, which had succeeded the Church Committee, and of the Senate Subcommittee on Health and Scientific Research, summoned the director of central intelligence to a joint hearing to ask him what he had learned about this "super-secret project."

Turner had been running the CIA for five months when, on the steamy morning of August 3, 1977, bathed in television lights, he took his place before the senators. MK-ULTRA, he began, was "an umbrella project under which certain sensitive subprojects were funded." He said that newly discovered documents described several of these "subprojects," including one that aimed to produce "exotic pathogens" and another to test "hypnosis and drugs in combination." They also revealed that MK-ULTRA experiments had been carried out on unwitting subjects in prisons and at "safe houses in San Francisco and New York City." Others had been conducted by researchers at eighty colleges, universities, hospitals, and pharmaceutical companies, many of whom were unaware that they were working for the CIA.

As soon as Turner finished, Senator Edward Kennedy of Massachusetts addressed him sharply.

"Admiral Turner, this is an enormously distressing report," Kennedy said. "I did not get much of a feeling in reviewing your statement here this morning of the kind of abhorrence to this type of past activity, which I think the American people would certainly deplore and which I believe that you do."

Turner was quick to reply. "It is totally abhorrent to me to think of using a human being as a guinea pig and in any way jeopardizing his health, no matter how great the cause," he said. "I am not here to pass judgment on my predecessors, but I can assure you that this is totally beyond the pale of my contemplation of activities that the CIA or any other of our intelligence agencies should undertake."

Having secured Turner's agreement that MK-ULTRA had been "totally beyond the pale," Kennedy turned to the question of personal responsibility. His investigators had learned the name of the CIA officer who ran MK-ULTRA, but this had not helped them.

"The overall agent, Mr. Gottlieb, has indicated a fuzzy memory about the whole area," Kennedy said. "Is it plausible that the director of the program would not understand or know about details of the program? Is it plausible that Dr. Gottlieb would not understand the full range of activities?"

"Let me say it is unlikely," Turner replied. "I don't know Mr. Gottlieb."

"Has anybody in the Agency talked with Mr. Gottlieb to find out about this?"

"Not since this revelation has come out."

"Not since this revelation? Well, why not?"

"He has left our employ, Senator."

"Does that mean that anybody who leaves is, you know, covered for lifetime?"

"No, sir."

Kennedy became agitated. "It is amazing to me," he told Turner. "Every single document that the staff reviews has Mr. Gottlieb's name on it, and you come to tell us that we don't have to worry any more, we have these final facts, and Mr. Gottlieb has not been talked to."

Turner insisted that he had never claimed to have "final facts" about MK-ULTRA. He added that "if the committee has no objection," his officers would try to locate Gottlieb. That left Kennedy partly satisfied.

"I don't see how we can fulfill our responsibility in this area, and the drug testing, without our hearing from Gottlieb," Kennedy said. "One thing is for sure: Gottlieb knows."

As the hearing drew to a close, Senator Daniel Inouye of Hawaii, who was presiding, sought to reassure Kennedy and his other colleagues. "As part of the ongoing investigation, we had intended to call upon many dozens of others," Inouye said. "One of those will be Dr. Gottlieb."

The work Gottlieb had done during his MK-ULTRA years was still deeply secret. Even the fact of his existence was closely held. He had been pulled out of anonymity during the Church Committee inquiry, but his exposure had been brief and obscure. Two years later the director of central intelligence pronounced his name in public—and the name of MK-ULTRA. Senators were tantalized.

"The word went out to the subcommittee staff," the *New York Times* reported. "Find this man Gottlieb."

As SOON AS Gottlieb learned that he was being summoned to Washington for a second round of testimony before congressional inquisitors, he called Terry Lenzner. Lenzner recommended that they dust off the plan that had worked for them before. Three days before Gottlieb was scheduled to testify, Senator Kennedy, who was to preside, abruptly postponed the hearing. Gottlieb had sent him an ultimatum: no testimony without immunity from prosecution.

"Because the drug testing programs involved were carried out between 1950 and 1973, most of what took place is beyond the scope of the five-year statute of limitations for prosecuting federal crimes," the *New York Times* reported. "Terry F. Lenzner, Mr. Gottlieb's lawyer, could not be reached for comment on his reasons for demanding immunity, but one source familiar with Mr. Gottlieb's activities said that the five-year limitation does not apply in some criminal cases where a conspiracy exists."

Kennedy faced a choice. If he accepted Gottlieb's demand for immunity, he might hear valuable testimony. That would also, however, make any future prosecution of Gottlieb difficult or impossible.

While Senate lawyers were weighing their options, investigators found a trove of MK-ULTRA tidbits in an unexpected place. The widow of George Hunter White, who had died two years earlier, had donated his papers to Foothill Junior College, south of San Francisco. Among them was White's diary. Entries provided rich new details about not only Operation Midnight Climax, but also the roles that Gottlieb and Lashbrook had played in directing it.

White's excesses had undone him. In 1963, the year MK-ULTRA drew to a close, doctors diagnosed him with cirrhosis of the liver. He was fifty-seven years old. His once intimidating frame had shrunk to 135 pounds. For a time he served as the fire marshal of Stinson Beach, California, where according to one researcher he "continued to drink and surround himself with adoring deviants until his death in 1975." Toward the end he wrote a letter to Gottlieb, thanking him for the chance to serve the United States while feeding his own appetites. His words are a unique tribute to MK-ULTRA.

"I was a very minor missionary, actually a heretic, but I toiled wholeheartedly in the vineyards because it was fun, fun, fun," White wrote. "Where else could a red-blooded American boy lie, kill, cheat, steal, rape and pillage with the sanction and blessing of the All-Highest? Pretty good stuff, Brudder!"

Senators were already intrigued by the mass of MK-ULTRA documents that the CIA had found in response to John Marks's FOIA request. White's diary added more details. Kennedy decided that the best way to find out more about MK-ULTRA would be to accept Gottlieb's demand that he be immunized against prosecution. Lenzner then pressed for another concession.

"I insisted that the hearing be held in executive session behind closed doors, and that the witness be protected from exposure to the press and the public," he wrote in his memoir. "I told them that Gottlieb had a heart condition and a crowd of spectators would be too much for him. Sid's cardiologist helped us out with a note warning against over-excitement. Most important, I said, for the safety of his family, it was imperative that Gottlieb's name not be leaked nor a picture of him taken."

When Gottlieb appeared before the Church Committee in 1975, senators knew almost nothing about MK-ULTRA. By 1977 they had learned a bit more. Anticipation grew as it became clear that Gottlieb would soon appear and speak. On September 20, to mark "the first public emergence of the distinguished-looking scientist since he left the CIA in 1973," the *New York Times* published a "Man in the News" profile.

"Sidney Gottlieb has been found," the *Times* reported, "and if he does indeed know the details of the drug experiments, which were part of a CIA program called MK-ULTRA that was under his direction, he will have a chance to say so tomorrow when the Kennedy subcommittee convenes to hear him testify."

The *Times* profile described Gottlieb as a biochemist who had spent years running the Technical Services Division, "the 'gadget shop' where wristwatch radios, exploding tie clips and poison darts—the hardware of the trade—are produced." It said that during his years at the CIA, his official biography had listed him as a consultant to the Defense Department. Most intriguingly, it quoted several of Gottlieb's former associates. One remembered that he always followed orders, "never made a decision on his own," and was "not a guy who would make waves with authority." Another said: "Sid's an honest man, but he's a tinkerer. He likes to fiddle with things." The last line was wounding: "One former CIA official went further, saying that in his opinion Dr. Gottlieb, who he described as a scientist who sometimes failed to see the effects of his work in human terms, should never have been permitted to run the division."

Almost every "Man in the News" profile that ran in the *Times* was accompanied by a photograph. Gottlieb's was not. The text explained that no image of him was known to exist.

On the day the profile was published, Gottlieb arrived as scheduled to testify before the Senate Subcommittee on Health and Scientific Research. He slipped into a closed room. Waiting reporters clamored in vain.

"Dr. Sidney Gottlieb, a key but shadowy figure in the Central Intelligence Agency's secret drug testing program, told his story to a Senate subcommittee today, but he managed to elude the lights and microphone and the crush of reporters waiting for him in the Senate hearing room," the *Times* reported. "Dr. Gottlieb asked for privacy on the ground that his health prohibited his testifying before a crowd. He got his wish. Only his voice, occasionally seeming to break with tension or with anger, came out by loudspeaker from the closed chamber next door where he was questioned."

Gottlieb spoke for most of the morning. He began with a few sentences about MK-ULTRA, which he said was a CIA project "of the utmost urgency" that aimed "to investigate whether and how it was possible to modify an individual's behavior by covert means." Then, without admitting to any specific abuse or even mentioning that he had directed MK-ULTRA, he said he was pained by some of what he had done.

> I would like this committee to know that I considered all this work—at the time it was done and in the context of circumstances that were extant in that period—to be extremely unpleasant, extremely difficult, extremely sensitive, but above all to be very urgent and important. I realize that it is difficult to reconstruct those times and that atmosphere today, in this room . . . The feeling that we had was that there was a real possibility that potential enemies, those enemies that were showing specific aggressive intentions at that time, possessed capabilities in this field that we knew nothing about, and the possession of those capabilities—possible possession—combined with our own ignorance about it, seemed to us to pose a threat of the magnitude of national survival.

Gottlieb became reflective at one other point in his testimony: when Senator Kennedy asked him if Frank Olson's death gave him "any cause to rethink the testing program."

"That was a traumatic period as far as I am concerned," Gottlieb replied. "It was a great tragedy . . . It caused me a lot of personal anguish. I considered resigning from the CIA and going into other work, because it affected us that way. Our final conclusion was to go ahead with the work on the basis [that] the best advice we could get medically was that the causal connection between LSD and the actual suicide was not absolute at all."

"The decision was, 'Don't change anything'?" asked Senator John Chafee of Rhode Island.

"Well," Gottlieb replied, "the best I can respond to that, that seems to be the case."

During this hearing, Gottlieb also publicly asserted the conclusion he had reported to his CIA superiors when he ended MK-ULTRA more than a decade earlier: there is no such thing as mind control. Painstaking research, Gottlieb told the subcommittee, had taught him that the effect of drugs on human beings is "very variable, very unpredictable," and that neither drugs nor other tools could be used "in a finely tuned way to alter behavior."

"The conclusion from all the activities," he said, "was that it was very difficult to predictably manipulate human behavior in this way."

Gottlieb had been warned that Kennedy would ask about his destruction of MK-ULTRA files. When the question came, he produced a prepared statement and read it. He said that before leaving the CIA in 1973, he had decided "to clean out and destroy files and papers which we felt were superfluous and not useful, relevant, or meaningful to my successors." His decision to do this, he said, "had absolutely nothing to do with covering up illegal activities." It was for three other reasons.

- He wanted to contribute to "a continuing and important CIA program of files destruction to handle a burgeoning paper problem."
- The files were "of no constructive use to the Agency" and were "capable of being misunderstood by anyone not thoroughly familiar with their background."
- "The prominent scientists, researchers, and physicians who had collaborated with us" should be protected; "I felt that the careers and reputations of those people would be severely damaged—or ruined, for instance—in today's climate of investigations, if their names and CIA connection were made public."

The hearing went well for Gottlieb. No one asked him what kind of experiments he had directed, or whether he had maintained interrogation centers outside the United States, or if any of his subjects had died. He portrayed himself as a victim, not a perpetrator.

"I feel victimized and appalled by the CIA's policy wherein someone or some group selectively pinpoints my name by failing to delete it from documents released under the Freedom of Information Act," he said. "My name is selectively left on released documents where all or most others are deleted."

Kennedy asked Gottlieb about documents suggesting that his superiors knew about and approved everything he did. "There was a policy review of this project at least once a year, and more frequently than that later," he replied. He added that he could "specifically remember briefing the Director of [the] CIA repeatedly on these matters," and named Allen Dulles, John McCone, and Richard Helms.

Gottlieb did not have to mention that while MK-ULTRA was at its peak, Dulles and his brother, Secretary of State John Foster Dulles, were regularly briefing President Eisenhower at the White House. Years later an academic study concluded that "given the number of informal conversations that Eisenhower had with the Dulles brothers, he almost certainly knew about some of the details of MK-ULTRA . . . His willingness to choose the CIA for semi-lawless deeds suggests that he at least set the tone." The senators, however, were content with Gottlieb's testimony that he had briefed his CIA superiors about MK-ULTRA, and did not ask about Eisenhower.

Gottlieb gave the senators little help. Whenever one of them approached a delicate matter, his memory failed. He answered questions with classic evasion: "I cannot remember . . . I do not have that in my head . . . My remembrance is not that clear . . . I have no specific knowledge of that . . . I am a little hazy."

Even Gottlieb's fuller answers were strikingly devoid of substance. When he was asked about experiments with poisonous mushrooms, for example, he replied with meaningless verbiage. "To answer the question precisely," he said, "I did hear about the mushroom discussion, and my best remembrance of that—and I want to underline this to answer it most accurately—would have to relate it to a particular project from where it was done. But my general remembrance of it: that was a project that was discussing some of the very basic aspects of relating a chemical and a structure to an activity."

As the next day's *Washington Star* reported, Gottlieb showed "remarkable skill in answering questions . . . with words so vague that the senators found themselves with very little substance when Gottlieb was finished." He did, however, offer a bit of historical context that he hoped might help his inquisitors to understand what he had done.

"There was tangible evidence that both the Soviets and the Red Chinese might be using techniques of altering human behavior which were not understood by the United States and which would have implications of national survival," he said. Asked about his use of unwitting subjects in drug experiments, he replied: "There was no advance knowledge or protection of the individuals concerned. Harsh as it may seem in retrospect, it was felt that in an issue where national survival might be concerned, such a procedure and such a risk was a reasonable one to take."

Testimony was not all that Gottlieb left behind on that day. News photographers managed to take his picture. Lenzner had arranged for this not to happen, but the photographers outmaneuvered him. When they entered the chamber where Gottlieb had testified, he did not protest. Photos of him appeared on many front pages the next day, including that of the *New York Times*. They showed him balding but fit, with short hair, pronounced features, and intense eyes, wearing a dark suit and a tie with a bold zigzag pattern.

Although Gottlieb failed to protect the secret of his appearance, he protected all of his others. From his perspective, the 1977 hearing, like the one at which he had appeared under a pseudonym two years before, was successful. No investigator or senator came close to the heart of his mystery. Many of them considered MK-ULTRA to have been a crazy little project that paled in significance beside such transgressions as assassination plots and domestic spying. This allowed Gottlieb and the CIA to keep secrets that might have been the most explosive of all.

"They steered us away," a Church Committee lawyer, Burton Wides, concluded years later. "It makes a lot of sense that Frank Olson was one reason. My educated guess is that he was having qualms, they were afraid he might talk, and for that reason he was pushed out the window."

One prominent member of the Church Committee, Senator Gary Hart, came to a different conclusion. "My guess is that the program did not receive more extended and detailed attention because of three factors," he surmised. "First, time and staff resources; two, a sense on the part of moderate/conservative elements of the committee that it was a sideshow that got off the rails; and three, the necessity of maintaining bipartisanship throughout the two years and beyond by not sensationalizing the most extreme, even bizarre, behavior and thus, in the minds of the Republican side, undermining the credibility of the Agency during the Cold War. For the more conservative members, this was an embarrassing side show—boys will be boys—that was a price of confronting the Communists . . . There very probably would have been a long-range price to pay for a full-scale, sensational focus on MK-ULTRA."

Three other former MK-ULTRA officers testified before Kennedy's subcommittee after Gottlieb was finished. All were equally forgetful and obscure. Robert Lashbrook admitted that he had been Gottlieb's deputy but insisted that "the details of actually what was being done—that I was not aware of." The psychologist John Gittinger, who according to George Hunter White's diary regularly visited the Operation Midnight Climax "safe house" in San Francisco, claimed to have had "not the slightest idea" of what went on inside. In her syndicated column the next day, the sharp-tongued Mary McGrory called them "a rich variety of twits retired from the Company."

"The man who was their chief did much to explain their special cast of mindlessness," McGrory wrote. "Dr. Sidney Gottlieb, who was heard but not seen—his health is not equal to the ordeal of television coverage—sat in a back room and his testimony was piped into the hearing room. He was clearly the most muddled of them all. He had insisted on immunity for his covert appearance, but why is a mystery. He remembered next to nothing."

15

If Gottlieb Is Found Guilty,
It Would Be a Real First

"Damn!" Secretary of Defense Harold Brown shouted at an aide one summer morning in 1979. "There may be a book coming out any day on these programs!"

Brown knew what he and his colleagues in Washington were about to face. The researcher John Marks, who filed the Freedom of Information Act request that led to the release of surviving MK-ULTRA documents, had received more than sixteen thousand pages. For nearly two years, he and four assistants combed through and cataloged them. By the time he was ready to publish his findings, he knew more about MK-ULTRA than anyone other than those who had run it.

Marks was a bearded, thirty-four-year-old Cornell graduate who had volunteered to be a State Department officer in Vietnam in order to avoid the military draft. After eighteen months there, he returned home and went to work for the legendary Ray Cline, a veteran CIA officer who had become chief of the State Department's Office of Intelligence and Research. Later, after quitting the State Department, Marks met a renegade CIA officer, Victor Marchetti. In 1974 the two of them published a book, *The CIA and the Cult of Intelligence*, that revealed much about how the Agency worked. Marks maintained his interest in hidden CIA operations. After reading the Rockefeller Commission report in 1975, he wondered if all

MK-ULTRA documents had really been destroyed. That hunch led him to file the search request that ultimately turned up his trove.

The book that emerged from Marks's research was called *The Search for the "Manchurian Candidate": The CIA and Mind Control*. It was the first comprehensive examination of MK-ULTRA. The intelligence historian Thomas Powers wrote in an introduction that it "expresses two dominant attitudes—fascination with the discoveries of psychological researchers, and anger with their misuse by the CIA for purposes that were narrow and morally careless." He also mused about Gottlieb.

> Sidney Gottlieb (alias "Victor [*sic*] Scheider") secured his place in history by his efforts to provide toxins for political murder, but in that effort he played only a pharmacist's role. More sinister was his sponsorship of research to find a way to make assassination routine, by turning ordinary men into automatons who would kill on command.
>
> Facing up to the fact of the attempt has been agony enough; the heart quails to think of the catastrophe of success. What if Gottlieb and his researchers had succeeded in their wildest dreams, and no secret, nor the life of any "enemy," had been safe from the CIA? The Agency's masters have been prey to lethal daydreams about many opponents for the last forty years—Castro, Ho Chi Minh, Sukarno, Lumumba, Qadaffi, De Gaulle, Nasser, Chou En Lai, Khomeini. How could the United States have resisted the temptation to "remove" these inconvenient figures, if it could only have been done in confident secrecy? Owning agents body and soul, attractive in theory, would have given us much to regret, to deny, and to hide. But Providence is kind, and blessed us with failure.

The Search for the "Manchurian Candidate" clearly identifies Gottlieb as the director of MK-ULTRA. It includes dozens of references to his life and work. The appearance of this book in 1979 ensured that he would not be forgotten.

"Only 33 years old when he took over the Chemical Division, Gottlieb had managed to overcome a pronounced stammer and a club foot to rise through Agency ranks," Marks wrote. "Greatly respected by his former colleagues, Gottlieb, who refused to be interviewed for this book, is described as a humanist, a man of intellectual humility and strength, willing to carry out, as one ex-associate put it, 'the tough things that had to be done.'"

As Marks was publishing his book, a two-man "Victims Task Force" was at work inside the CIA. Director of Central Intelligence Stansfield Turner had created it after receiving what one internal memo called a "surge of letters" from people who had heard descriptions of MK-ULTRA experiments and suspected that they or their loved ones had been victims. The task force could not satisfy them. Each received a simple answer: "Unfortunately, the files available to date do not contain the names of any test subjects." Turner reported to Attorney General Griffin Bell that "fragmentary records and amnesic recollections" made the task of identifying MK-ULTRA victims "well-nigh impossible."

Although the Victims Task Force did not find lists of victims' names, one of its members, a CIA officer named Frank Laubinger, extracted a bit of new testimony from Gottlieb. As his task force was ending its work in 1979, Laubinger sent Gottlieb a letter asking eight questions about MK-ULTRA. They were broadly framed and hardly threatening. Ten days after receiving them, Gottlieb answered by telephone. Laubinger took notes.

"Unwitting testing was performed to explore the full range of the operational use of LSD," he wrote. "Both interrogation and provoking erratic behavior were of interest . . . [Gottlieb] remembers no breakdown of tests and no accurate count of tests. As he recalls, the number was probably about 40. He recalls nothing which would identify any specific tests or test sites."

Publication of John Marks's book interrupted Gottlieb as he was settling into what he hoped would be a new life. "I didn't read that book, and I make it a practice not to read books like that," he later testified. "I did see some galley proofs about that book that Mr. Marks sent me. I felt it was so inaccurate and outrageous that I sent it right back. He wanted me to make whatever corrections I felt were called for. I made no corrections, and I told him in a letter I sent him that rather than make corrections in the book, in order to make the book more accurate I would have to rewrite it, and I did not want to do that."

Around the time this unwelcome book appeared, Gottlieb made a decision that took him further away from his former life. At the age of sixty, he enrolled to study for a master's degree in speech therapy at San

José State University. Having stuttered for his entire life, he wanted to spend his later years helping children who faced the same challenge. Service would be part of a continually active life.

"Sid is going to school in San Jose two days a week and getting all A's," Margaret wrote in a letter to relatives. "He is going to start sailing lessons today, and gracious knows what that will lead to. We go to various kinds of dances four or five times a week and, to top it off, we got a 5' by 9' rug which we are hooking together but he is doing most of . . . We go wine tasting in the Santa Clara Valley. We have been hiking with the Sierra Club once or twice, we have been down to Monterey and Carmel a couple of times, we drove up to the Napa Valley, and we have friends from our college days in San Francisco whom we visit once in a while."

Gottlieb maintained this gentle pace for two years. In 1980, after receiving his degree in speech therapy, he and Margaret decided to return to Virginia, where they had spent most of their married life. Their new home was a five-thousand-square-foot eco-home in the shadow of the Blue Ridge Mountains, near the end of a long, winding gravel path called Turkey Ridge Road.

"The entire place was powered by the sun, and there were large doorways for wheelchairs," one of Gottlieb's CIA colleagues recalled years later. "Gottlieb was fascinated by the concept of building a place to die. He spent a lot of time with mechanical and physical puzzles. There was lots of area for arts projects. The homestead was essentially a duplex where there were two identical homes, one for the Gottlieb couple and one for a younger couple who would take more and more responsibility for the older couple as they neared their death. There was a common room where the couples would dine together. But the concept didn't work out in practice. Even though Gottlieb gave the younger couple a deed to part of the house, they did not get along."

Gottlieb called his new estate Blackwater Homestead, after a stream that ran through it. He and his wife, along with a younger couple with whom they lived, raised goats and chickens. They grew vegetables, fruit, and herbs. Gottlieb built a sundial. The figurine of an Oriental warrior guarded it all. Blackwater Homestead, by one account, "became a kind of spiritual retreat and the focal point of a growing community who found in Gottlieb a charismatic soul mate."

Gottlieb enjoyed the pleasures and demands of life on the land. He spent early mornings meditating while kneeling on pillows and burning incense. Then he would ride his bicycle into town to buy newspapers and collect his mail. He drove a used car and wore sandals. One of his friends described him as "an old hippie."

"The transformation was complete," according to a profile that the *Washington Post* published years later. "It was as if Gottlieb had lost his former self, walking backward, sweeping his trail clean with a branch. In his first life, he had explored how to control the minds of others. In his second, he had gained sway over his own recollections, granting himself immunity and a fresh start . . . Most people in Rappahannock County had no idea Gottlieb had ever worked for the CIA. His virtue was unquestioned, his counsel sought after, his company prized."

Rather than retreat into his memories, Gottlieb embraced community life. He joined the planning board and the arts council, acted in Christmas plays, and helped organize town festivals. Margaret was just as active.

"Since suburbia had taken over our former haunts and since our oldest and dearest friends still lived in and around that same area, we found a place within driving distance but out in the country, and I hope far enough out so that suburbia won't catch up to us again before we die," she wrote in a letter to relatives. "I have never been comfortable living in a city, so our quite isolated country home fills me with peace and quiet. We are in a very rich and close community with all kinds of things to do. I teach with the Literacy Volunteers people who have not finished high school, or non-readers. I go to the county jail once a week for this, and I work in the elementary school too. Sid spent three years in a local middle and high school being a speech pathologist. He also works with the hospice, and in our spare time we raise a good deal of the food we eat."

In 1982 Gottlieb's older brother David died, giving him a chance to muse about paths not taken. David Gottlieb had been riveted by a childhood visit to the Boyce Thompson Institute for Plant Research in Yonkers, New York, and built a lab in the family's basement to study plant biology. His interest was decisive in attracting Sidney to the field. He attended City College, as Sidney did, and went on to join the faculty of the University of Illinois. Over the course of an illustrious career, he cofounded the university's Department of Plant Pathology, discovered new antibiotics, lectured around the world, served on the editorial boards of professional journals, and mentored budding agricultural biologists.

"I have accumulated a number of honors from my professional colleagues that have brought me a pleasurable sense of being valued," David Gottlieb said at one ceremony. "Although I have enjoyed receiving these honors, I have often wondered why I have not been more moved by them. Perhaps it was because I see life as imperfect and destined to remain so."

Despite the loss of his brother, Sidney Gottlieb was entering what could have been the rewarding autumn of his life. He was living close to nature. His friends admired his civic passion. He could claim the quiet satisfaction of one who devotes himself to the good of others. The past, however, always hung over him. In 1984 the CIA, facing a steady stream of inquiries, issued a public "Statement on MK-ULTRA" that did not mention his name but referred to "questionable" research experiments. "In 1983, after questions were raised within the Agency by the Inspector General about the propriety of these subprojects, they were discontinued," the statement said. "Safeguards were subsequently promulgated through Presidential Executive Orders which have been strictly followed."

Years later, a television reporter ambushed Gottlieb near his home, pushed a microphone into his face, and asked if he had any regrets about MK-ULTRA.

"I just don't want to talk about it," a haggard-looking Gottlieb said as he turned away from the camera. "It's a right that you have and that I have. I've gone on to other parts of my life. That's in my past and it's going to stay there."

AT FRANK OLSON's funeral, Gottlieb had told grieving relatives that if they ever had questions about "what happened," he would be happy to answer them. More than three decades later, at the end of 1984, they decided to accept his offer, and called to arrange an appointment. He told them they were welcome. When Alice, Eric, and Nils Olson appeared at his door, his first reaction was relief.

"I'm so happy you don't have a weapon," Gottlieb said. "I had a dream last night that you all arrived at this door and shot me."

Eric was taken aback. "We didn't come here to harm you or anyone, we only want to talk to you and ask you a few questions about my father," he said. Later he came to marvel at what he saw as Gottlieb's manipulative power. "Before we even got through the door, we were apologizing to him and reassuring him," he said. "It was a brilliant and sophisticated way of turning the whole thing around."

Inside, the encounter began with small talk. Margaret Gottlieb and Alice Olson discovered that their fathers had both done mission work in Asia, and spoke briefly about their experiences. Then Margaret withdrew. Gottlieb invited his guests into the living room. He began by telling them what had happened at Deep Creek Lake on November 19, 1953. Frank Olson and others were given LSD, he said, as part of an experiment to see "what would happen if a scientist were taken prisoner and drugged—would he divulge secret research and information?" Then he began musing about Olson.

"Your father and I were very much alike," he told Eric. "We both got into this because of patriotic feeling. But we both went a little too far, and we did things that we probably should not have done."

That was as close to a confession as Gottlieb ever came. He would not say what aspects of MK-ULTRA went "a little too far," or what he and Olson did that they "probably should not have done." Nor would he entertain questions about inconsistencies in the story of Olson's death. When Eric pressed him, he reacted sharply.

"There was a tautness to him," Eric recalled. "He was kind of hyperalert and extremely intelligent. You could feel that right away. I was dealing with a world-class intelligence—and a world-class shrewdness. You felt like you were playing cat-and-mouse and he was way ahead of you. He had a way of decentering you . . . He had a charm that was extraordinary. You could almost fall in love with the guy. The thrust of what he did in the whole session was to say, 'That guy Gottlieb back there did some things that I'm ashamed of, but I am not him. I moved on. I left the Agency, I went to India, and I am teaching children with learning disabilities, and I am consciousness-raising. I am not that guy.'"

"You say that you've been through a change of consciousness, and that now you're a new Gottlieb," Eric told him. "But can't you answer? What about the old Gottlieb? What if we arrange a reunion and rethink the whole thing and where we are in our lives?"

"Look, if you don't believe me, there's no reason for you to be here,"

Gottlieb told his visitors. "There is no reason for me to tell you anything. I agreed to meet with you to tell you what I know."

As the family was rising to leave, Gottlieb pulled Eric aside. "You are obviously very troubled by your father's suicide," he said. "Have you ever considered getting into a therapy group for people whose parents have committed suicide?"

Eric did not follow that suggestion, but it left a deep impression on him. For years he had been confused and depressed by the story of his father's death. Only after meeting Gottlieb, however, did he resolve to bring his search for truth to the center of his life.

"I didn't have the confidence then in my skepticism to ignore his ploys, but when he made that therapy group suggestion—that was the moment when he overplayed his hand," he said. "At that moment I understood how much Gottlieb had a stake in defusing me. And it was also at that moment that the determination to show that he had played a role in murdering my father was born."

Eric Olson waited another decade—until after his mother died—before taking his next step: arranging to exhume his father's body. Several reporters stood near him as a backhoe clawed through the earth at Linden Hills Cemetery in Frederick, Maryland, on June 2, 1994.

"I don't know if we're going to find out what happened to my father," he told them, "but I want to feel we did what we could do to find out."

A forensic pathologist, James Starrs of George Washington University Law School, spent a month studying Olson's body. When he was finished, he called a news conference. His tests for toxins in the body, he reported, had turned up nothing. The wound pattern, however, was curious. Starrs had found no glass shards on the victim's head or neck, as might be expected if he had dived through a window. Most intriguingly, although Olson had reportedly landed on his back, the skull above his left eye was disfigured.

"I would venture to say that this hematoma is singular evidence of the possibility that Dr. Olson was struck a stunning blow to the head by some person or instrument prior to his exiting through the window of room 1018A," Starrs concluded. Later he was more emphatic: "I think Frank Olson was intentionally, deliberately, with malice aforethought, thrown out of that window."

Besides conducting the autopsy, Starrs interviewed people connected to the case. One was Gottlieb. The two men met on a Sunday morning at Gottlieb's home in Virginia. Starrs later wrote that it was "the most perplexing of all the interviews I conducted." Gottlieb's account of what he had done in the period before and after Olson's death was "at least unsatisfactory and at most incredible . . . My overall assessment of this interview was not at all favorable to Dr. Gottlieb or to his lack of complicity in Olson's death."

> Probably the most unsettling, even unnerving moment in my conversation with Dr. Gottlieb occurred toward its close when he spontaneously sought to enlighten me on a matter of which I might not take due notice, so he thought. He pointedly explained that in 1953 the Russian menace was quite palpable . . . Listening awe-struck to him as I gazed at a picture of South African Bishop Tutu on the wall, I was emboldened to ask how he could so recklessly and cavalierly have jeopardized the lives of so many of his own men by the Deep Creek Lodge experiment with LSD. "Professor," he said without mincing a word, "you just do not understand. I had the security of this country in my hands." He did not say more, nor need he have done so. Nor did I, dumb-founded, offer a rejoinder. The means-end message was pellucidly clear. Risking the lives of the unwitting victims of the Deep Creek experiment was simply the necessary means to a greater good, the protection of the national security.

Because Olson's survivors had signed away their right to legal relief when they accepted their $750,000 compensation payment in 1975, they could not sue the CIA. Eric Olson worked closely, however, with prosecutors in New York who were investigating his father's death. In 1999 they persuaded the city's medical examiner to change the classification of Frank Olson's death from suicide to what detectives call CUPPI—"Cause Unknown Pending Police Investigation." Despite their efforts, District Attorney Morgenthau ultimately concluded that he did not have enough evidence to seek criminal indictments in the Olson case, and never presented it to a grand jury.

That hardly allayed the family's suspicions. New tidbits kept emerging, none decisive but each one adding to the weight of circumstantial evidence. One of the most startling was an eight-page CIA manual called "A Study of Assassination," written in 1953—the year Olson died—and declassified in 1997. It is unsigned, but a CIA officer who worked with MK-ULTRA later identified Gottlieb as the author. Some of its advice on ways to kill eerily fits the Olson case.

"The contrived accident is the most effective technique," the manual advises. "When successfully executed, it causes little excitement and is only casually investigated. The most efficient accident, in simple assassination, is a fall of 75 feet or more onto a hard surface . . . It will usually be necessary to stun or drug the subject before dropping him. Care is required to insure that no wound or condition not attributable to the fall is discernible after death . . . A rock or heavy stick will do, and nothing resembling a weapon need be procured, carried, or subsequently disposed of. Blows should be directed to the temple."

Although that and other discoveries sharpened Eric Olson's already powerful suspicion that foul play lay behind his father's death, he could not prove it. Recognizing that painful fact, he and his brother decided that it was finally time to reinter their father's body. On August 8, 2002, the day before the reburial, he called reporters to his home and announced that he had reached a new conclusion about what had happened to his father.

"The death of Frank Olson on November 28, 1953, was a murder, not a suicide," he declared. "This is not an LSD drug-experiment story, as it was represented in 1975. This is a biological warfare story. Frank Olson did not die because he was an experimental guinea pig who experienced a 'bad trip.' He died because of concern that he would divulge information concerning a highly classified CIA interrogation program called 'Artichoke' in the early 1950s, and concerning the use of biological weapons by the United States in the Korean War."

If Gottlieb has been remembered at all, it is as a supporting player in the Frank Olson drama. Actors portray him in two televised documentaries about the case. Since the producers had no photos of him during his CIA days, they had to imagine what he looked like. In the first, called *CIA Secret Experiments* and produced by National Geographic in 2008, Gottlieb appears dapper and white-haired as he pours LSD into Olson's fateful bottle of Cointreau—inaccurate both because he was just thirty-five years old at the time and because, according to witnesses, it was Lashbrook, not Gottlieb, who spiked the drinks that night.

Gottlieb also makes extended appearances in Errol Morris's four-hour film about the Olson case, *Wormwood*, which was released in 2017. The actor who plays him, Tim Blake Nelson, is young and exudes assertive self-confidence. *Wormwood* is built around interviews in which Eric Olson recounts the story of his father's death and his lifelong search for answers. It suggests that the death could have been a murder, and that Gottlieb could have been involved.

In 2017 Stephen Saracco, a retired New York assistant district attorney who had investigated the Olson case and remained interested in it, made his first visit to the hotel room where Olson spent his final night. A video crew filmed him as he opened the door to room 1018A and stepped inside. Some furnishings had been replaced, but the room's dimensions and layout were the same as in 1953.

"Being here now, looking at it live, just raises the question of how he could have done it," Saracco said as he looked around the room. By his reckoning, Olson would have had to reach an extraordinary speed in a small room, dive over a thirty-one-inch-high radiator that stands in front of the window, and smash through the plate glass while ducking to avoid a window divider that is just twenty-nine inches above the radiator. Saracco wondered why, if Olson was intent on killing himself, he would try "that kind of Superman move" rather than simply opening the window and sliding out.

"If this would have been a suicide, it would have been very difficult to accomplish," Saracco concluded. "There was motive to kill him. He knew the deepest, darkest secrets of the Cold War. Would the American government kill an American citizen who was a scientist, who was working for the CIA and the Army, if they thought he was a security risk? There are people who say, 'Definitely.'"

FRANK OLSON WAS not the only one of Gottlieb's victims who returned to haunt him. Once the truth about MK-ULTRA began leaking out, he became the subject of several lawsuits. He was forced to sit for days of harsh questioning. Before him lay a Shakespearean reckoning: Foul deeds will rise, though all the earth o'erwhelm them to men's eyes.

The first hint that Gottlieb would face trouble in court came in the early 1980s, when three former inmates at the Atlanta Federal Penitentiary filed a lawsuit against the CIA and its director William Casey. They asserted that in the two decades since Dr. Carl Pfeiffer used them as subjects in his drug experiments, they had been plagued by hallucinations, flashbacks, paranoia, and other psychic disturbances; charged that the government had been negligent in allowing these experiments to proceed; and asked for damages under the Federal Claims Tort Act. Although Gottlieb was not a named defendant, he would almost certainly have been called to testify if the case had gone to trial. It never did. On April 29, 1983, a federal judge dismissed the former inmates' suit on the grounds that the statute of limitations for the crimes they alleged had expired.

Gottlieb could not celebrate that ruling. Ten days before it was handed down, he had undergone grueling cross-examination in another case. This time the plaintiffs were relatives of Velma Orlikow, a Canadian woman who had been among Dr. Ewen Cameron's victims at the Allan Memorial Institute in Montreal. Orlikow had come to the institute for treatment of post-partum depression in 1957 and was plunged into a nightmare from which she never recovered. Years later her husband, David, a member of the Canadian parliament, sued the CIA. He charged that, at the Agency's direction, Cameron had subjected his wife to "horrific" treatment that left her functioning "at about 20 percent of capacity," unable to read, use a fork and knife, or recognize relatives.

To prosecute their case, the Orlikow family hired Joseph Rauh, one of America's most combative civil rights lawyers. Rauh won an order compelling Gottlieb to submit to pre-trial questioning. During the spring of 1983, he endured three day-long sessions at the Boxwood House Motel in Culpeper, Virginia.

Gottlieb's memory proved improbably blank. When Rauh asked him what division of the CIA he joined when he was hired in 1951, he replied, "I really can't remember that level of detail." Did he conduct research into the effects of electric shock? "I don't remember." What did he tell CIA investigators who questioned him after Frank Olson's death? "I may be having a mental block." Did CIA officers coach him before his congressional testimony in the 1970s? "My memory is hazy about that." Most remarkably: What was his relationship to Richard Helms, the officer with whom he had conceived MK-ULTRA and who for twenty years was his chief patron and protector?

"I don't remember what Mr. Helms's job was," Gottlieb testified. "I really don't remember what his role was."

Rauh was openly scornful. "What Dr. Gottlieb has done is to show a reckless disregard for human life," he said at one point. Gottlieb's lawyer—during these depositions he was represented by CIA attorneys, not Terry Lenzner—jumped to protest.

"You are badgering the witness!" he complained. "You are doing nothing but abusing this man."

In this day-long interrogation and the two others that followed, Gottlieb offered a few intriguing insights. Asked the purpose of MK-ULTRA, he answered with a single reasonably accurate sentence: "MK-ULTRA was a project to investigate the intelligence potential, defensively and then later offensively, of the use of various techniques of behavior control in intelligence operations." He admitted that he had felt "somewhat abused" and "quite angry" when the CIA declassified MK-ULTRA documents with other names redacted but his clearly legible. Pressed about the Olson case, he became indignant.

"I was very upset that a human being had been killed," he told Rauh. "I didn't mean for that to happen. It was a total accident. You are one of the few people to say there was anything purposeful in it."

Gottlieb admitted that some CIA officers had been "disinclined" to use techniques he developed because "they found the idea distasteful and strange. They had moral objections." Asked if he felt responsible for the torments Ewen Cameron had inflicted during his MK-ULTRA work, he replied, "I find it very difficult to answer that question."

"Did you ever consider you should adopt something analogous to the Nuremberg Code?" Rauh asked him.

"We did not," he replied.

The Orlikow case dragged on for five years and was finally settled out of court in 1988. The CIA agreed to pay the Orlikow family, and the families of each of eight other Canadians who suffered at Ewen Cameron's hands, a total of $750,000 in compensation. It did not admit guilt or responsibility.

That was hardly the end of Gottlieb's legal trouble. He faced another lawsuit, filed on behalf of Stanley Glickman, the young artist whose life had collapsed after he met an American with a clubfoot at a Paris café in 1952. Glickman was living in New York when revelations about MK-ULTRA burst into the news. Suddenly, for the first time in the quarter century since he drank that fateful Chartreuse, he understood what might have happened to him.

Urged on by his sister, Glickman began writing letters to the Department of Justice and others he imagined might help. No one did. In 1981 he filed a lawsuit under the Federal Tort Claims Act, charging the CIA with invading his privacy and intentionally harming him. He named two officers as defendants: Gottlieb and Richard Helms.

Lawyers for the CIA managed to delay this suit for years. It might have faded away when Glickman died of heart failure in 1992. His sister, however, refused to let it drop. A judge finally ordered Gottlieb to submit to questioning. On the morning of September 19, 1995, he arrived at the United States District Court in Washington for the first of what would be four full days of intense examination.

Gottlieb once again insisted that he had forgotten most of his past. When he was asked about Bluebird, the first CIA "special interrogation" project, which was at a peak when he joined the Agency, he replied: "The word Bluebird totally confuses me, I can't help you with that." His response to a question about his MK-ULTRA deputy Robert Lashbrook was equally implausible.

"Was he your deputy?" Gottlieb was asked.

"I really don't have a clear memory of who my deputy was," he replied.

On the matter at hand—his alleged drugging of Stanley Glickman at Café Select in Paris—Gottlieb was more precise. He said he had never set foot in Paris before 1958, and therefore could not have been involved in poisoning anyone there six years earlier.

"It never happened," he insisted. "I've given four days of the limited amount of time I have left on a question that is absolutely—absolutely never happened, and it's incredible to me."

That denial did not dissuade Glickman's lawyers. They continued to press their case, and finally won a decisive victory. In 1998 a federal appeals court ruled that since Richard Helms was not alleged to have been directly involved in the drugging, he could not be prosecuted—but that the case against Gottlieb could proceed.

"Assuming that a jury would find that Gottlieb had an obligation to preserve the MK-ULTRA documents that he ordered to be destroyed, the jury would be entitled to draw an adverse inference against Gottlieb," the court's opinion read. "The possibility that a jury would choose to draw such an inference, along with plaintiff's other circumstantial evidence that he was drugged by the CIA—specifically, by Gottlieb—is enough to entitle the plaintiff to a jury trial."

Something almost unthinkable lay ahead. For the first time in Gottlieb's life, it appeared that he would be prosecuted. He would have to testify about MK-ULTRA in public, under oath, and as a defendant.

"If Gottlieb is found guilty, it would be a real first," wrote one reporter who was covering the case. "The Agency has protected its own very well—not only Gottlieb, but others who were part of MK-ULTRA. The trial is scheduled to begin Jan. 3."

GOTTLIEB WON A postponement of his trial for drugging Stanley Glickman. In the first weeks of 1999, as he waited for the trial to begin, detectives in New York began a new push to reopen the Frank Olson investigation. No peace lay ahead. Around this time Gottlieb met one of his old college friends. He remembered that he had once ridiculed this friend's admiration for Matthew Arnold's wistful poem "Dover Beach." He said he had not only changed his view of the poem but had committed it to memory.

> . . . the world, which seems
> To lie before us like a land of dreams,
> So various, so beautiful, so new,
> Hath really neither joy, nor love, nor light,
> Nor certitude, nor peace, nor help from pain;
> And we are here as on a darkling plain
> Swept with confused alarms of struggle and flight,
> Where ignorant armies clash by night.

Even as Sidney and Margaret aged, they remained active in the community around them. "Money is tight these days," Margaret wrote to her family. "Sid is working two days a week in the Culpeper schools doing speech pathology and loving his contact with the kids. Right at this moment he is with a Hospice client, trying to be of help as he passes from this life . . . I volunteer with the adult reading program and I also go to the elementary school and the jail. It's a variety. Other than that we are waiting winter out and we are eager to have it be time to dig up the garden."

The journalist Seymour Hersh, who never stopped trying to uncover secrets, visited Gottlieb during this period. "It was very strange," he later recalled. "Gottlieb was living as if he was in an ashram in India. The place had no electricity and no running water. There was a peat moss toilet outside. He was trying to absolve himself, to expiate. If he'd been Catholic, he would have gone to a monastery. He was a destroyed man, riddled with guilt."

Others who knew Gottlieb in his final years came to similar conclusions. "A lot of Sid's later life was spent atoning, whether he needed to or not, for how he had been exposed publicly as some sort of evil scientist," said a teacher at the Child Care and Learning Center, a preschool where Gottlieb volunteered. A rabbi with whom he became friendly, Carla Theodore, who shared his adventurous spirit—she had been a union organizer in the South before becoming a rabbi—said that Gottlieb had told her that his own children refused to speak to him, and had added: "I too have done things I really regret, but I am learning to keep it to myself."

"I felt that he was on a path of expiation, whether consciously or unconsciously," Rabbi Theodore remembered. "There were enough cries of horror from near and far. It was an extremely big fact of his past. Somehow he was living around it. It was there like a pink elephant. I once asked him if I could talk to him about it, and he said, 'Yes, not many people asked.' But the thing was, his answers were so defended that I gave up after a few minutes. It was a barrier. I wasn't going to get the truth. He was a delightful person to interact with, but at the same time I feel he grieved and suffered, and that that was always there. Maybe, in retrospect, he was as puzzled by what he had done as we were who heard about it."

Gottlieb died on March 7, 1999, at his home in Virginia. He was eighty years old. Margaret did not announce the cause of death.

Obituaries published over the next few days recounted all that was known about Gottlieb's work with MK-ULTRA. In one of them, the CIA psychologist John Gittinger called Gottlieb "one of the most brilliant men I've ever known" and said he was "willing to try anything to discover something."

"We were in a World War II mode," Gittinger said. "During that time of the Cold War, the attitude we had and the Agency had was, we were still fighting a war. And when you are fighting a war, you do things you might not ordinarily do."

The CIA officer who had been Gottlieb's boss during his two years in Munich, William Hood, was equally forgiving. "I do think he was entirely out of line with some of the stuff they were doing," Hood said. But he added: "It's the kind of thing I don't think anyone could understand unless they had been involved in it. Intelligence services should not be confused with the Boy Scouts."

John Marks, whose book *The Search for the "Manchurian Candidate"* brought MK-ULTRA to broad public attention for the first time, struck a similar note.

"He was unquestionably a patriot, a man of great ingenuity," Marks told one obituary writer. "Gottlieb never did what he did for inhumane reasons. He thought he was doing exactly what was needed. And in the context of the time, who could argue? But with his experiments on unwitting subjects, he clearly violated the Nuremberg standards—the standards under which, after World War II, we executed Nazi doctors for crimes against humanity."

Every one of Gottlieb's obituaries grappled with the apparent contradiction between his evidently compassionate nature and the harsh work he did for the CIA. Most tried to find a unifying thread to his life. "Given his altruistic hobbies," one concluded, "some may not know quite what to make of the bizarre biochemist who waged America's Cold War battles in the cerebellums of the unsuspecting. But it was his patriotic faith in the rewards of experimentation and progress that somehow reconciles the communalistic homesteader with the psychedelic Mengele he was in earlier days."

Soon after Gottlieb died, Eric Olson visited Sidney Bender, the New York lawyer who had pursued the Glickman case. They drank a toast to the death of a man they considered a monster. Both had arrived at the same conclusion: Gottlieb died by suicide.

"Besides the case I was pursing, the New York District Attorney's office was investigating Gottlieb for the possible murder of Frank Olson," Bender reasoned. "That was a very serious concern of his. If he was found guilty, what would that mean to the whole CIA? He was the instrument through which it could all be poisoned. Any jury trial would expose the CIA and what he had done, which was criminal in nature. Gottlieb was a guy who always had to be in control, and at the end he decided that he wanted to control his own fate. His death was a way of protecting the CIA, so it wouldn't be tainted by a civil or criminal case. He had been successful in fooling Congress, but the whole thing could have been opened up if there was either a trial in my case—which was about to start—or a murder indictment in the Olson matter. Under no circumstances would he take full responsibility for what he had done. The alternative was to fall on his sword."

The Washington lawyer who defended Gottlieb during his last years of legal entanglements, Tom Wilson, would not go that far. He did, however, say that the prospect of being tried for drugging Stanley Glickman had "greatly dispirited" his client. "He was concerned that he might never find any sense of peace of mind in this life," Wilson told an interviewer, "and just didn't have enough fight left." Another of Gottlieb's friends recalled that he "gradually became depressed, and it's hard to say how much was due to his heart ailment and how much was due to the endless lawsuits. He was not the same man the last few years of his life."

Gottlieb's body was cremated. Margaret asked the funeral home not to disclose what became of the ashes. On a cloudy Saturday afternoon several weeks later, about a hundred people gathered in the gymnasium of Rappahannock High School to remember him. "Gottlieb's two worlds came together," one reporter wrote afterward. "Most who spoke were neighbors and friends from his second life, but there were also white-haired men from Langley who did not speak publicly but mingled afterward."

Friends from Gottlieb's "second life" shared their memories. One praised poems that Gottlieb had composed in his later years. Another recalled the wisdom he brought to their Zen Buddhist study group. A young man in a parka asked the grieving widow if he could say a few words. She did not recognize him, but she nodded in assent. He stepped to the microphone.

"Anyone who knew Sid knew he was haunted by something," he said. Then he asked mourners to join him in reciting the Lord's Prayer in the hope that it would "get rid of this something, so Margaret and the family can live in peace."

With Gottlieb gone, the already sluggish pace of investigations into MK-ULTRA slowed even further. The few other CIA veterans who knew its secrets remained silent until death. A final chapter in the long cover-up could now unfold. It might be entitled, "Everything Was Sidney's Fault."

Gottlieb had long understood that his former colleagues wanted to absolve themselves and the CIA of responsibility for the excesses of MK-ULTRA. All swore to investigators that they knew little or nothing about MK-ULTRA. None hid more than Helms, who had the most to tell but said the least. He feigned ignorance of all but the broadest outlines of MK-ULTRA.

"Helms was a liar, but a charming and skillful liar," recalled the Church Committee's chief counsel, Frederick Schwarz. "He lied about everything that was important."

Portraying Gottlieb as having been unsupervised and out of control was a sensible strategy. It obscured the fact that senior CIA officers like Dulles and Helms approved and encouraged his work. Just as important, it deflected attention away from the institutional responsibility of the CIA, the White House, and Congress.

"Those who had talked to Gottlieb in the past few years," one obituary reported, "say the chemist believed that the Agency was trying to make him the fall guy for the entire program."

16

You Never Can Know What He Was

A seven-thousand-pound bull elephant named Tusko was the most substantial victim of a Gottlieb-inspired LSD experiment. The assailant was "Jolly" West, the portly, bearded psychiatrist who, under MK-ULTRA Subproject 43, had conducted experiments on "suggestibility" and ways to induce "dissociative states." On an August morning in 1962, after making arrangements with the director of Lincoln Park Zoo in Oklahoma City, West shot a dart containing 300,000 micrograms of LSD into Tusko's flank. Five minutes later, according to West's report, the elephant "trumpeted, collapsed, fell heavily onto his right side, defecated and went into status epilepticus." West administered a cocktail of other drugs, but to no avail. Tusko died an hour and forty minutes after being drugged.

Although LSD did not turn out to be good for elephants, West continued to believe that it could be used to reshape the human psyche. He was among several of Gottlieb's scientific collaborators who continued the work he had set in motion even after MK-ULTRA was shut down. They could not accept his conclusion that mind control does not exist.

For several years West ran a clinic in the Haight-Ashbury section of San Francisco, where he gave LSD to volunteers and monitored their reactions. In 1969 he became chairman of the Psychiatry Department at the University of California, Los Angeles, and director of the university's Neuropsychiatric Institute. While holding those posts, he set off an intense controversy by proposing to create a "securely fenced" facility at an abandoned missile site in the Santa Monica Mountains that would become "the world's first and only center for the study of interpersonal violence." Governor Ronald Reagan supported it, but it was blocked after what West called "an outcry against it based on arguments that to study violence was essentially to experiment on underprivileged people, doing brain operations, putting electrodes in their heads, or making guinea pigs out of them." Nonetheless West went on to a successful career studying techniques of behavior modification. Between 1974 and his retirement in 1989, he received more than $5 million in grants from the National Institute of Mental Health, which the CIA has sometimes used as a conduit.

Another of Gottlieb's favorite researchers, Carl Pfeiffer, who ran no fewer than four MK-ULTRA "subprojects," also maintained a lifelong interest in psychoactive drugs. During the 1960s Pfeiffer served on a Food and Drug Administration committee that allocated LSD to researchers. He became prominent for his research into schizophrenia. In 1971 he destroyed records of the LSD experiments he had conducted on prisoners at the Atlanta Federal Penitentiary. If he thought that would wash away all evidence, he was mistaken.

Buried in the 1975 Rockefeller Commission report, but headlined in the *Atlanta Constitution*, was the revelation that Pfeiffer's prison experiments with LSD during the 1950s were not aimed at finding a cure for schizophrenia, as he had told his prisoner subjects, but were part of a covert CIA program. This news reached one of Pfeiffer's victims, the Boston gangster James "Whitey" Bulger. When John Marks's book *The Search for the "Manchurian Candidate"* appeared in 1979, Bulger read it and, according to one biographer, "was enraged to learn how the covert program had destroyed many lives." Once he realized that Pfeiffer had tormented him in the interests of the CIA, not science, he decided to take revenge. He told a member of his gang that he planned to find Pfeiffer and kill him.

"I sleep with the lights on 24 hours a day because I have psychological problems (horrible nightmares) due to my being on a medical project called MK-ULTRA," Bulger wrote. "Until 1979 I thought I was insane."

Pfeiffer never learned that Bulger had spoken about killing him, and he died a natural death. Bulger disappeared after being tipped off that the FBI was about to arrest him for his other crimes, and he was captured in 2011. Two years later he was sentenced to consecutive life terms for crimes including eleven murders. At the trial, no one mentioned LSD, MK-ULTRA, or the CIA. One Boston lawyer with experience representing gangsters, Anthony Cardinale, later asserted that if he had defended Bulger, he would have concentrated on that theme and "would have got him off."

"It's a simple defense," Cardinale told an interviewer. "Nearly two years of LSD testing fried his brain. You bring in expert witnesses, psychiatrists, and others who detail the history of how people who took part in this secret CIA program committed suicide or became institutionalized. I'd have had Bulger sit there doodling and drooling. He's a victim, driven insane by his own government . . . He delusionally believes there's no difference between right and wrong, that he can kill . . . I'm telling you, I could have had a jury feeling sorry for Whitey Bulger. 'He's a victim, ladies and gentlemen, and they—the government—are the reason he did all this. He truly believed he could get away with it. He did not know the difference between right and wrong. They put all this in his head. They damaged and manipulated him to the point they turned him into a psychotic killer.'"

The only American doctor who conducted MK-ULTRA prison experiments as relentlessly intense as Pfeiffer's, Harris Isbell of the Addiction Research Center in Lexington, Kentucky, went on to an equally stellar career. In 1962 Attorney General Robert Kennedy presented him with the U.S. Public Health Service Meritorious Service Award and praised him as "an outstanding investigator." Soon afterward he left the addiction center to become a professor of medicine and pharmacology at the University of Kentucky.

After the MK-ULTRA program was discovered, the nature of Isbell's experiments on prisoners became clear. In 1975 he was called to testify at a hearing conducted by subcommittees of the Senate Judiciary Committee and the Senate Committee on Labor and Public Welfare, which were investigating "human-use experimentation programs of the Department of Defense and Central Intelligence Agency." Senators were curious but not outraged. When one asked Isbell if he had given heroin to his heroin-addicted subjects as payment for their participation in experiments, he replied, "It was the custom in those days."

"It was a different time," Isbell said. "The ethical codes were not so highly developed, and there was a great need to know in order to protect the public in assessing the potential use of narcotics . . . So it was very necessary, and I personally think we did a very excellent job."

Sidney Gottlieb's favorite MK-ULTRA physician, the New York allergist Harold Abramson, also escaped censure for his work. Abramson was one of the few Americans who shared Gottlieb's fascination with LSD during the 1950s, and the only one—outside the CIA and the Special Operations Division at Fort Detrick—who knew the true story of MK-ULTRA. His fascination, unlike Gottlieb's, never waned. During the 1960s and '70s he organized several international conferences on LSD. In 1967 he published a book called *The Use of LSD in Psychotherapy and Alcoholism*. He also worked in the fields for which he was trained—he had never studied psychiatry or pharmacology—and co-founded the *Journal of Asthma*. Shortly before his death in 1980, he was tainted by the revelation that he had treated Frank Olson during his final days. Nonetheless he died with his reputation intact.

"Anyone closely associated with Harold and his life's work," said an obituary in the *Journal of Asthma*, "can recognize that the passing of this pioneer clinical scientist, humanist, medical educator, profound psychoanalyst and man of letters marks the final stage of an era of intellectual ferment and multidisciplinary probing into the mysteries of human existence, aspirations, and suffering."

The physician who conducted what were arguably the most horrific of all MK-ULTRA experiments, Ewen Cameron, died in 1967. According to the *Toronto Star*, "he was found dead under mysterious circumstances after falling off a cliff." Cameron remained a celebrated figure until the end—but that was before any outsider had heard of MK-ULTRA. Once its existence and nature were revealed, victims of his "psychic driving" experiments began coming forward. Two appeared in a searing Canadian television documentary broadcast in 1980. Others spoke out. Their accounts led to a stream of newspaper articles with headlines like HOW THE CIA'S MIND-CONTROL EXPERIMENTS DESTROYED MY HEALTHY,

HIGH-FUNCTIONING FATHER'S BRILLIANT MIND and "SHE WENT THERE HOPING TO GET BETTER"—FAMILY REMEMBERS WINNIPEG WOMAN PUT THROUGH CIA-FUNDED BRAINWASHING. Faced with public outrage and a series of lawsuits, the Canadian government announced an "Allan Memorial Institute Depatterned Persons Assistance Plan" that ultimately provided $100,000 compensation payments to seventy-seven of Cameron's former patients. In 2004 a Canadian judge ruled that an additional 250 victims were eligible.

"To the patients of Dr. Ewen Cameron, our university was the site of months of seemingly unending torture disguised as medical experimentation," the *McGill Daily* concluded in a long report published in 2012. "A respected educational and research institution had hosted some truly macabre events and shaped the course of torture methods for many years to come."

Gottlieb's two most important CIA comrades died within weeks of each other in the autumn of 2002. His right-hand man at MK-ULTRA, Robert Lashbrook, was eighty-four when he succumbed to lung disease at Ojai Valley Community Hospital in California. A brief note in the local newspaper said only that he served in the military during World War II and "had been a chemistry professor." There was no memorial service.

Far more attention was paid when Richard Helms, who spent a quarter century at the CIA and rose to become its director, died at his home in Washington. He was eighty-nine. The *New York Times* obituary said he had "defiantly guarded some of the darkest secrets of the Cold War." It quoted his justification for lying to a congressional committee about his role in overthrowing the government of Chile in 1973: "I had sworn my oath to protect certain secrets."

Like other CIA officers touched by scandal during the 1970s, Helms had to choose which of two promises to keep. Before testifying to Congress he swore to tell "the truth, the whole truth, and nothing but the truth." Yet like all CIA officers, he had signed a secrecy agreement promising "that I will never divulge, publish or reveal either by word, conduct, or by any other means, any classified intelligence or knowledge." He made the same choice Gottlieb and Lashbrook made: keep secrets and lie under oath. They saw it as the patriotic alternative. It also happened to be the one most likely to protect them from opprobrium and prosecution.

Helms was infuriated by the decision of his successor, William Colby, to speak frankly about MK-ULTRA and other covert CIA projects. "I must say Colby has done a startlingly good job of making a total mess," he told an interviewer after retiring. "He must look to sophisticated Washington as the biggest jerk on the block. It is all terribly sad, and he had brought it all on himself by his mumblings, and other matters about which he should have kept his mouth shut." The best Helms could say about his old colleague was, "I don't believe Colby was a KGB agent." Anger at Colby was so intense that after he died while canoeing in 1996, several people including the author of his biography came to believe that CIA officers had killed him as punishment for his candor or to prevent him from saying more.

Helms completed a 496-page memoir shortly before his death, but it does not mention MK-ULTRA. When an interviewer asked him about this omission, he replied: "I see no way to handle it in the amount of space I have available." Later he mused on his old friend's fate.

"Ah, poor Sid Gottlieb," Helms said. "He has been heavily persecuted, but to bail him out of the troubles he's in would take more than just a few minutes, and I'm not sure I'd be much of a contributor to it. The nation just saw something they didn't like and blasted it, and he took the blame for it."

Revelations about MK-ULTRA helped fuel public anger at the CIA. "In retrospect, it is clear that Gottlieb's work lit a fuse to a time bomb that was to explode in the 1970s, destroying a good deal of the Agency's image as a proper defender of American values in the public mind," the intelligence historian John Ranelagh concluded. "Projects designed to develop methods and devices that could kill or control people at long distances and that, during nearly two decades, involved hundreds of people, some outside the Agency on contract, sooner or later were bound to leak."

The explosion of this "time bomb" in the mid-1970s led to the creation of the Senate Select Committee on Intelligence, charged with conducting "vigilant legislative oversight over the intelligence activities of the United States," and the House Permanent Select Committee on Intelligence, with a similar mandate. Then, in 1978, Congress passed the Foreign Intelligence

Surveillance Act, which regulates wiretapping and other forms of surveillance. The era's last major reform was the Intelligence Oversight Act of 1980, requiring the CIA and other intelligence agencies to keep Congress "fully and currently informed" about their activities. These steps provided the legal basis for monitoring clandestine activities. Congress, however, proved reluctant to delve deeply. Many members continued to believe that closely watching the CIA or firmly restricting its activities would threaten national security. That view became even more appealing after the terror attacks of September 11, 2001. Congressional oversight of intelligence agencies has not led to deep changes in the way those agencies operate.

"My sense is that the new oversight procedures adopted in 1975, and strengthened over the next 20 years, have improved the balance between liberty and security in the United States," wrote Loch Johnson, who worked for the Church Committee. "I would hasten to add in a second breath that the quality and consistency of intelligence accountability falls far short of the aspirations advanced by reformers at the time of the Church Committee inquiry."

Gottlieb and the few other CIA officers who knew the full MK-ULTRA story guarded their secrets until death. Their passing, coupled with the destruction of MK-ULTRA records, ensured that much of what he did will remain unknown. So did his wife's discretion.

Years after Gottlieb retired from the CIA, a lawyer taking his testimony in one of the civil suits he faced asked whether he ever discussed MK-ULTRA with anyone outside the Agency. "I talked to my wife quite a bit about it," he replied. Margaret never revealed what he told her. A reporter called her two years after her husband died, but she refused to meet him.

"You never get it right," she said. "You never can know what he was. I would just as soon it was never talked about again."

On November 2, 2011, after more than twelve years as a widow, Margaret Gottlieb died in Virginia at the age of ninety-two. "She was an enthusiastic folk dancer and taught dancing to community groups for many years with Sidney Gottlieb," the *Rappahannock News* reported. "Margaret Gottlieb is lovingly remembered for the great sense of adventure she shared with her husband."

The Gottliebs' four children went on to lead creative and apparently fulfilling lives. Rachel lived in Zambia with her husband, a scholar, and then ran a pre-school in California. Penny became an elementary school teacher. Peter wrote a book about African American history—dedicated "To my parents, Sidney and Margaret Gottlieb"—and served as the state archivist of Wisconsin. Stephen, the youngest, was a guitarist and music teacher.

In 2013, Peter and Penny, along with one of Penny's children, joined a group of volunteers who spent a week building homes for poor families in El Salvador. Their trip reflected the humanism that evidently animated all four siblings. About their father, however, they would not speak. After he died, their mother asked them to promise that they would never discuss him in public. They kept their word.

"The family decided some time ago that they would not talk about this with anyone in your position," one relative told a writer in 2018. "If it were up to me, I'd be willing to talk to you, but that would be breaking an agreement that they made with their mother years ago, so I prefer not to."

Sidney Gottlieb's wife lived longer than any of his other close contemporaries. Once all were gone—and once it became clear that his children would not add to the record of his life—he entered the realm of history. So did the places where he had worked.

The original CIA headquarters at 2430 E Street in Washington, which became Sidney Gottlieb's domain after the CIA moved to Langley, was threatened with demolition in 2014. Intelligence officers who had worked there mobilized to save it. They were successful. The stately complex now houses agencies of the State Department.

Fort Detrick, the Maryland base where Frank Olson and his comrades in the Special Operations Division once produced their toxins, remains the army's principal center for biological research. Rows of greenhouses stand near sealed chambers where scientists cultivate and study deadly bacteria. Exotic medicines are kept in storage depots for emergency deployment to disaster zones. The giant spherical "Eight Ball," once used for testing aerosolized gases on human and animal subjects, sits unused, rusting and forgotten.

The apartment buildings where Gottlieb maintained his New York "safe house" and his San Francisco "pad" have been torn down. So has the Manhattan brownstone where Harold Abramson conducted early LSD experiments—and where he counseled Frank Olson during his final days. The Statler Hotel from which Olson plunged to his death remains standing, towering over Penn Station and renamed the Hotel Pennsylvania, as it was christened in 1919.

Blackwater Homestead, the Virginia retreat where Gottlieb lived for most of his later life, still sits perched atop a remote hill, looking strikingly modern against the surrounding wilderness. "It was about as solar as you could get back then," the man who bought it from Gottlieb in the late 1990s told a visitor twenty years later. He said he remembered Gottlieb well, had been friendly with his widow, and considered them "two of the finest people you'd ever want to meet."

The installations in Germany where Artichoke and MK-ULTRA interrogators conducted intense experiments either no longer exist or serve entirely different purposes. Camp King, where the "rough boys" abused prisoners alongside Gottlieb's men and their ex-Nazi advisers, closed in 1993. Villa Schuster remains standing and looks much as it did when suspected spies and other unfortunates were tormented there. It was briefly in the news after two German researchers published a heavily documented study in 2002 entitled *Code Name Artichoke: Secret Human Experimentation by the CIA*. One newspaper called it "a villa with dark secrets where the CIA once conducted experiments on human beings . . . a vivid monument to the madness of that era." The country's largest news magazine, *Der Spiegel*, investigated CIA operations in Germany and concluded that "the worst things happened at Villa Schuster, a turn-of-the-century villa in Kronberg . . . There were deaths, but the number is not known."

After the CIA shut its secret prison at Villa Schuster in the mid-1950s, the villa passed into the hands of the West German government. It became a retreat for government employees. In 2016 it was sold to a young German businessman. He renovated it, divided it into rental apartments, and built a gate across the driveway. Basement chambers where victims were drugged and electroshocked are now storage rooms.

"In this house, the CIA did experiments like the ones the Nazis did in concentration camps," the new owner said as he showed the house to a visitor. "It's no secret. People in the neighborhood all know the story. They say that bodies of the victims were buried in fields or forests around here—places where shopping centers and apartment houses have been built since then. A little while after I bought the place, I was doing some yard work and an elderly lady who lives up the road came to see me. She offered to do some kind of cleansing ritual where we would burn herbs or something to chase away evil spirits in the house. I told her I don't believe in any of that nonsense."

ONE OF THE most famous fictional assassins of the twenty-first century, Jason Bourne, speaks many languages and knows even more ways to kill. He has no idea, however, how or why he acquired these skills. Slowly and painfully he recalls that he had once worked for Operation Treadstone, a secret CIA project that developed a technique for wiping away memory.

Around the same time this assassin emerged, another fictional operative was assigned to find Americans who had witnessed alien landings and make them forget what they saw. He cleansed their minds by flashing a burst of light from a pocket-sized gadget into their eyes. Then he implanted false memories to replace the ones he blasted away. His sidekick, the newest recruit for Men in Black, was impressed.

"When do I get my own flashy memory-messer-upper thing?" he asked.

When Sidney Gottlieb brought MK-ULTRA to its end in the early 1960s, he told his CIA superiors that he had found no reliable way to wipe away memory, make people abandon their consciences, or commit crimes and then forget them. Later he repeated his conclusion in congressional testimony. That did nothing, however, to stifle the imagination of screenwriters and other purveyors of popular culture. On the contrary, revelations about MK-ULTRA grabbed their attention. Once it became clear that the CIA had spent years searching for mind control techniques, and that it had conducted bizarre experiments as part of its search, creative imaginations began to churn. Plots that would once have seemed over-imaginative became plausible. Mind control experiments, attempts to "brainwash" human subjects, government efforts to create programmed killers, and other plots that emerged from MK-ULTRA appear in the works of writers as diverse as Thomas Pynchon, E. L. Doctorow, Joseph Heller, and Ishmael Reed.

MK-ULTRA was nourished by fantasies taken from fiction. Decades later the process was reversed. Revelations about MK-ULTRA inspired a new sub-genre of novels, stories, films, television shows, and video games. They reflect the same fascination with mind control that has gripped imaginations for centuries, but with a twist. Modern incarnations of Svengali and Dr. Caligari were even more terrifying than the originals because they worked for the government.

In David Foster Wallace's *Infinite Jest*, one character produces tablets that were "used in certain shady CIA-era military experiments." When he is asked if the experiments were aimed at finding techniques of mind control, he replies, "More like getting the enemy to think their guns are hydrangea, the enemy's a blood relative, that sort of thing." Another contemporary novelist, Kathy Acker, portrays the experiments differently in *Empire of the Senseless*: "Subjects whom the CIA questioned, unfortunately for the CIA, remembered the questions, that they had blabbed, and whom they should tell that they had blabbed. The CIA had to destroy this human memory. Murder, in many cases, was an impractical solution because it tended to be public. The same with lobotomy . . . MK-ULTRA was designed to find ways to cause total human amnesia."

Films brought the idea of mind control even more vividly into America's consciousness. *The Bourne Identity*, which starred Matt Damon as the disoriented Operation Treadstone operative, was released in 2002 and quickly followed by two sequels. *Men in Black*, featuring Tommy Lee Jones and Will Smith, was equally popular, partly because of its ingenious introduction of the "memory-messer-upper thing," which could be set to wipe away memories of recent minutes, days, or years, and then implant new ones. Devices like this began turning up regularly on-screen. In an episode of *The Simpsons*, Vice President Dick Cheney blasted away the memory of a subordinate who was leaving his job. Characters in the animated sitcom *Family Guy* and the role-playing video game *Marvel Heroes* worked the same trick.

A relatively benign use of the "memory-messer-upper" technique is at the heart of the 2004 film *Eternal Sunshine of the Spotless Mind*, in which lovers played by Jim Carrey and Kate Winslet wipe away memories of their romance. In the trippy 2010 blockbuster *Inception*, a corporate thief played by Leonardo DiCaprio tries to steal secrets by infiltrating his victims' subconscious minds. The video game *Remember Me* allows players to direct the "remixing" of characters' minds. A corporate consultant played by Ben Affleck in *Paycheck* commits industrial espionage and subjects himself to a "memory wipe" so he forgets his crimes. Revelations about MK-ULTRA fed the imaginations that produced these works.

In the decades after Sidney Gottlieb's death, cultural references to MK-ULTRA became steadily more explicit. A character played by Jesse Eisenberg in the film *American Ultra* discovers that his memory was wiped away after he became an unwitting subject in the CIA's "Project Ultra." MK-ULTRA was mentioned by name in episodes of several television drama series, including *Fringe*, *The X Files*, and *Stranger Things*. In the film *Conspiracy Theory*, a character played by Mel Gibson tells another, played by Julia Roberts, about his past.

"Years ago I worked for the CIA, on the MK-ULTRA program. Are you familiar with it?"

"It was mind control. *Manchurian Candidate* kind of stuff."

"That's a vulgar generalization. But yes, you take an ordinary man and turn him into an assassin. That was our goal."

In the 1990s a rock band called MK-ULTRA emerged in Chicago, but it encountered legal troubles and changed its name. The British band Muse had better luck. Its Grammy-winning album *The Resistance* contains a song called "MK-ULTRA" that asks: "How much deception can you take? How many lies will you create? How much longer until you break?"

In 2003 the Cannabis Cup, given in Amsterdam for the world's best marijuana, went to a hybrid called MK-ULTRA. "The *indica cannabis* strain named MK-ULTRA derives its name from the CIA's Project MK-ULTRA, which aimed to influence mental manipulation through strategic methods," one reviewer wrote. "MK-ULTRA produces extreme cerebral effects, which is how it relates to the CIA's project."

A remarkable Canadian artist, Sarah Anne Johnson, is the granddaughter of Velma Orlikow, the Winnipeg woman whose lawsuit against Dr. Ewen Cameron made her one of the best-known MK-ULTRA victims. Johnson has devoted herself to telling her grandmother's story. One of her sculptures depicts her grandmother hooded and gloved, as patients were in Cameron's "psychic driving" experiments. Another tribute is a web of dreamy images drawn onto the page of a newspaper that recounts her grandmother's ordeal. The headline says INSIDE MONTREAL'S HOUSE OF HORRORS: CIA-FUNDED PSYCHIATRIST TURNED PATIENTS INTO BRAINWASH VICTIMS.

That work hung alongside wildly imaginative images of Lee Harvey Oswald, J. Edgar Hoover, and Martin Luther King Jr. in a 2018 exhibition at the Metropolitan Museum of Art in New York called "Everything Is Connected: Art and Conspiracy." MK-ULTRA has entered and come to permeate popular culture. It not only exists in history but richly nurtures the creative imagination. This is Sidney Gottlieb's most unexpected legacy.

THE CLOSING OF Villa Schuster, Camp King, and other sites where CIA officers interrogated and experimented on prisoners did not pull the United States out of the torture business. Quite to the contrary, Bluebird, Artichoke, and MK-ULTRA produced rich progeny. Gottlieb's work contributed decisively to the development of techniques that Americans and their allies used at detention centers in Vietnam, Latin America, Afghanistan, Iraq, Guantanamo Bay, and secret prisons around the world.

In the early 1960s, as the Vietnam War intensified and leftist insurrections erupted in Latin America, the CIA set out to produce a manual for interrogators. It emerged in 1963, entitled *KUBARK Counter-Intelligence Interrogation*—KUBARK being the CIA's cryptonym for itself. This 128-page manual, not fully declassified until 2014, codified everything that the CIA had learned about what it calls "coercive counterintelligence interrogation of resistant sources." It includes references to academic papers and "scientific inquiries conducted by specialists," including those directed by Ewen Cameron, the enthusiastic MK-ULTRA contactor at the Allan Memorial Institution in Montreal. During the 1960s it was the essential text for CIA interrogators and their partners in "allied services" around the world. It shaped the Phoenix program in Vietnam, under which suspected Communists were interrogated and at least twenty thousand killed. Most of the techniques it describes, and most of its insights into how prisoners react to various forms of abuse, come from MK-ULTRA.

- A man's sense of identity depends upon a continuity in his surroundings, habits, appearance, actions, relations either others, etc. Detention permits the interrogator to cut through these links.
- Control of the source's environment permits the interrogator to determine his diet, sleep pattern and other fundamentals. Manipulating these into irregularities, so that the subject becomes disoriented, is very likely to create feelings of fear and helplessness.
- The chief effect of arrest and detention, and particularly of solitary confinement, is to deprive the subject of many or most of the sounds, tastes, smells, and tactile sensations to which he has grown accustomed.
- Results produced only after weeks or months of imprisonment in an ordinary cell can be duplicated in hours or days in a cell which has no light (or artificial light which never varies), which is sound-proofed, in which odors are eliminated, etc. An environment still more subject to control, such as a water-tank or iron lung, is even more effective.
- Drugs can be effective in overcoming resistance not dissolved by other techniques.
- The principal coercive techniques are arrest, detention, the deprivation of sensory stimuli, threats and fear, debility, pain, heightened suggestibility and hypnosis, and drugs.
- The usual effect of coercion is regression. The interrogatee's mature defenses crumble as he becomes more childlike.
- The electric current should be known in advance, so that transformers and other modifying devices will be on hand if needed.
- The profound moral objection to applying duress past the point of irreversible psychological damage has been stated. Judging the validity of other ethical arguments about coercion exceeds the scope of this paper.

In 1983, twenty years after the *KUBARK* manual was written, the CIA produced a new version called *Human Resources Exploitation Training Manual*. It was intended specifically for use by military-dominated governments in Latin America. Among the first police forces to receive it were those in Honduras and El Salvador, both then known for extreme brutality. Green Beret trainers later brought it to other countries where torture was commonly practiced. It became the basis for seven texts tailored to individual countries, all based on the principle that interrogators should "manipulate the subject's environment" in order to create "intolerable situations to disrupt patterns of time, space, and sensory perception . . . The more complete the deprivation, the more rapidly and deeply the subject is affected." Techniques described in the *Human Resources Exploitation Training Manual* are strikingly similar to those in the *KUBARK* manual.

"While we do not stress the use of coercive techniques," the manual says, "we do want to make you aware of them and the proper way to use them."

One CIA officer who trained Latin American interrogators in techniques described in these manuals—his name has not been declassified—went on to become chief of interrogations for the CIA Rendition Group, which was formed after the 9/11 terror attacks in 2001 and charged with kidnapping suspected terrorists and sending them to secret prisons for interrogation. His presence personified the continuity between interrogation techniques that the CIA used in Latin America during the 1980s and those that became notorious in the twenty-first century. Among them were shackling, sleep deprivation, electroshock, cramped confinement, and hooding for sensory deprivation. Psychologists who helped design these techniques emphasized the need to reduce a prisoner to a state of dependence on the interrogator—precisely what the overseers of MK-ULTRA and the authors of the *KUBARK* manual recommended.

When American leaders decided after the 9/11 attacks that "the gloves come off," as CIA counterintelligence chief Cofer Black put it, they were able to draw on a full store of experience. Designing a set of techniques for "extreme interrogation" of Muslim prisoners required nothing more than pulling old manuals out of the drawer, tweaking their recommendations, and passing them on to interrogators. The handoffs are clear: from Kurt Blome and Shiro Ishii to the directors of the Bluebird project, later renamed Artichoke; from Artichoke to Gottlieb and MK-ULTRA; from MK-ULTRA to *KUBARK Counter-Intelligence Interrogation*; from there to the *Human Resources Exploitation Training Manual*; and from those manuals to Guantanamo Bay, Abu Ghraib, and CIA "black sites" around the world. Gottlieb is an indispensable link in this grim chain.

HISTORY AND MORALITY loom like threatening clouds over any attempt to assess Sidney Gottlieb's life and work. He can be fairly praised as a patriot, and just as fairly abhorred as demonic. Judging him requires a deep dive into the human mind and the human soul.

Gottlieb was, as is everyone, a product of his world. His parents and the parents of most of his schoolmates were Jews who fled oppression in Europe. America saved them from the Holocaust. To them it was a country where, as one son of Jewish immigrants wrote, "the dreams that you dare to dream really do come true." Gottlieb could not help being caught up in the patriotic fervor that followed the 1941 attack on Pearl Harbor, or being crushed when he was deemed unfit to join the army. The CIA gave him a chance to serve. Many of America's "very best men" jumped at that chance, so Gottlieb cannot be judged harshly for doing the same. On the contrary, he may be admired for choosing to join a secret elite dedicated to defending the United States against what seemed a fanatic and pitiless enemy.

Nor can Gottlieb rightly be censured for his seven years as chief of the CIA's Technical Services Division. If nations need spies, someone must make the tools that spies use. Gottlieb had the array of talents to excel at that strange job.

Another aspect of Gottlieb's work, the preparation of poisons to kill foreign leaders, led to his brief burst of notoriety in the 1970s. This was the dirtiest of jobs. Presidents may be harshly condemned for their decisions to seek the assassination of foreign leaders. All CIA officers who participated in those plots, including Gottlieb, moved in dubious moral territory. They share responsibility with Eisenhower and Kennedy.

The weightiest case against Gottlieb is his work running MK-ULTRA. Under someone else's leadership, it might have been far less extreme. Gottlieb not only refused to limit its work but pushed his contractors to reach and exceed every limit they could imagine. His gruesome "subprojects" and his work directing "special interrogation" at secret prisons around the world resulted in immense human suffering. He was a talented scientist and a faithful civil servant, but also his generation's most prolific torturer.

One especially arresting aspect of Gottlieb's ethical calculation was his willingness to work with Nazi scientists who he knew were connected to the torture and murder of Jews in concentration camps. Many of the Americans who worked with those scientists had only general or theoretical reasons to detest Nazism, and easily put their doubts aside as soon as World War II ended and Communism emerged as the new enemy. Gottlieb, though, was not simply Jewish but just one generation removed from the shtetl. If his parents had not left Europe at the beginning of the twentieth century, he might well have been forced into a ghetto as a young man and then arrested, sent to a concentration camp, and killed during a lethal experiment. Nonetheless he worked with the scientists who conducted those experiments.

Gottlieb was not a sadist, but he might as well have been. MK-ULTRA gave him life-or-death power over other people's minds and bodies. He was a master manipulator, enthralled by the role he played and what it allowed him to do. Carried away by forces from within himself as well as by those that swirled around him, he justified every sort of brutality. He developed an extraordinary level of psychic tolerance for the violent abuse of other human beings. Death squad leaders in Latin America sometimes tucked their children tenderly into bed before leaving for nighttime missions of torture and murder. In much the same way, Gottlieb's cheerfulness and community spirit were a façade that covered his day-to-day work overseeing experiments in which human lives were destroyed.

Cold War historians now agree that America's fear of Soviet attack was greatly exaggerated. At the time, though, it seemed vividly real. Some intelligence officers have argued that the perceived imminence of that threat justified the CIA's excesses. "What you were made to feel was that the country was in desperate peril and we had to do whatever it took to save it," one said. Another recalled being "totally absorbed in something that has become misunderstood now, but the Cold War in those days was a very real thing with hundreds of thousands of Soviet troops, tanks, and planes poised on the East German border, capable of moving to the English Channel in forty-eight hours."

Commitment to a cause provides the ultimate justification for immoral acts. Patriotism is among the most seductive of those causes. It posits the nation as a value so transcendent that anything done in its service is virtuous. This brings into sharp relief what the essayist Jan Kott called the "discrepancy between the moral order and the order of practical behavior."

"He hears the voice of conscience," Kott wrote about a murderer, "but at the same time realizes that conscience cannot be reconciled with the laws and order of the world he lives in—that it is something superfluous, ridiculous and a nuisance."

Gottlieb faced a question that cuts to the human heart: Are there limits to the amount of evil that can be done in a righteous cause before the evil outweighs the righteousness? Even if he believed that such limits might exist in theory, or in other cases, he never observed them in his own work. He persuaded himself that he was defending nothing less than the survival of the United States and human freedom on earth. That allowed him to justify grave assaults on human life and dignity. He assumed the role of God, freely destroying the lives of innocents for what he believed were good reasons. That sin was deep. Gottlieb lived with it uncomfortably in his later years.

The great mechanism in which Gottlieb was a cog gave birth to MK-ULTRA and nurtured it through waves of suffering. Something like it would have existed even if Gottlieb, Helms, Dulles, and Eisenhower had never been born. Behind it lies a quintessential moral trap. Most people are able to distinguish right from wrong. Some do things they know are wrong for what they consider good reasons. No one else of Gottlieb's generation, however, had the government-given power to do so many things that were so profoundly and horrifically wrong. No other American—at least, none that we know of—ever wielded such terrifying life-or-death power while remaining so completely invisible.

Gottlieb saw himself as a spiritual person. By most definitions, though, true spirituality means that a measure of compassion and mindfulness informs every aspect of a person's life. That was not the case with Gottlieb. Neither his scientific curiosity, his sense of patriotism, or his acts of private charity justify his years of heinous assaults on the lives of others.

The last quarter century of Gottlieb's life was exemplary. He became what he liked to believe was the true Sidney Gottlieb: a caring, selfless community leader always ready to help the needy or afflicted. But although he refused to speak about MK-ULTRA, he could not pretend it had not existed. Memory would have plagued him even if he had not faced investigations and lawsuits. Anyone who believes in divine judgment or karmic payback would be disturbed to look back on a career like his.

Gottlieb searched relentlessly for inner peace while just as relentlessly laying waste to other people's minds and bodies. He was a jumble of contradictory archetypes: a creator and destroyer, an outlaw who served power, a gentle-hearted torturer. Above all he was an instrument of history. Understanding him is a deeply disturbing way of understanding ourselves.

Afterword to the Paperback Edition

In the months following the initial publication of this book, I received notes from people who believe that they or their relatives may have been victims of MK-ULTRA or some similar program. More than a few had the ring of truth. Often they ended with a poignant plea, like this one from a woman born in 1947: "Any response would be appreciated as I am still seeking answers as to why I was treated in this way." Neither I nor anyone else can offer much succor to these possible victims. Records identifying the human subjects of MK-ULTRA were destroyed, so it is all but impossible to know whether any particular individual was victimized.

I also heard from several people who knew Sidney Gottlieb and wanted to share their recollections. They shed some rays of light onto a life that was lived in the deepest secrecy.

The most remarkable response came from a retired CIA officer who was Gottlieb's right-hand man—not while he ran MK-ULTRA during the 1950s, but later in his career, when he was chief of the Technical Services Staff. His review on this book's Amazon page stunned me. It was headed, "Carlos Luria—I was his chief of staff." Luria described his former boss as "a brilliant biochemist and a deeply sensitive humanist." After MK-ULTRA "spun out of control," he said, others at the CIA "were content to distance themselves and leave Dr. Gottlieb holding the bag."

"Stephen Kinzer's book deftly captures the conundrum: How could so kindly and devout a humanist as Sidney Gottlieb have so grimly and mindlessly pursued brain-altering methods?" Luria wrote. "Was his a Jekyll/Hyde personality? *Poisoner in Chief* somewhat over-exploits the sensational, in my view. . . . It mentions but fails to capture the paranoia that gripped America in the 1950's [*sic*], when International Communism was on a roll, winning local, regional and even some national elections. . . . But most profoundly, it overlooks a common human trait: When our security is challenged, we demand protection. No matter the cost; no matter the consequences. And if a few bones get broken, or principles trampled in the process—well, that's the price of liberty, isn't it? But once the crisis is over, principles return—and with a vengeance: 'How could they have done that?'"

This review startled me because during my research and writing, I had concluded that none of Gottlieb's close CIA comrades remained alive. I managed to locate Luria, who was living in quiet retirement and in apparent good health despite advanced age. He agreed to answer a few questions. This is what he told me:

One thing you can really criticize is the era, the atmosphere of fear that existed in America during the 1950s. As a country, we overreacted to a foreign threat just the way we did after 9/11. We projected our enemy as ten feet tall. We have that tendency, as a country, to go after flies not with a flyswatter but with a bazooka. Now we can look back and see all the trouble that caused. So all of that criticism is valid, but what I think Gottlieb saw as unfair is that he became the symbol of that era. He became the point of focus. Everything seemed to be his fault. Too much was blamed on him.

He was torn by it. That was very clear. . . . He felt he had not been treated fairly, that he been abandoned by a system he had served faithfully. Already at that point, while he was still at the Agency, he felt that management was backing away from him, leaving him out to dangle in the wind to the point of victimizing him. People would say, "That Gottlieb, he really went around the bend." This troubled him deeply. It was something he carried with him to the grave. . . . My wife and I really loved him and respected him immensely. I have such trouble reconciling the Sidney Gottlieb we knew with Sidney

Gottlieb as he's now being depicted. He's a tragic figure. He is one who had the tiger by the tail. He couldn't hold onto the tail, so the tiger turned around and ate him. I see him as a victim of his own brilliance and naïvete.

Because Luria had been one of Gottlieb's longtime friends, I ventured to ask whether he shared suspicions that Gottlieb committed suicide rather than face a trial in which he was likely to be cross-examined about MK-ULTRA. "It's not unreasonable," he replied. "I think he'd had it—as they say in German, '*Ich habe die Schnauze voll.*' The idea of a trial and more publicity in the newspapers was too much for him. I don't know the answer, but I wouldn't be surprised."

While I was corresponding with Luria, I received a note from a New York clergyman, Andrew Kadel, who told me he had crossed paths with Gottlieb and that the experience "has stuck with me for the rest of my life." In the late 1970s, Kadel recalled, he was a seminary student in Berkeley when his wife discovered that Gottlieb, with whom she had a family connection, was living in nearby Santa Cruz. They arranged to pay a visit. Sid and Margaret, he recalled, were "extremely gracious hosts, unpretentious, attentive, intelligent, good-humored . . . pretty typical of Jewish middle class intelligentsia at the time: liberal, broad in their interests, not particularly religious."

He was in his early 60s, a bit younger than I am now, so it was unusual for a man of that age to take retirement then. At some point the question of leaving & changing careers came up—he kind of shrugged his shoulders, or at least indicated that "these things happen," but his wife was clearly angry and outraged at what the Church Committee had done to her husband. I have no reason to doubt any of the things reported in your book and elsewhere, but for her, the construction of them described someone entirely different than the man she had spent her life with . . .

About the time we were about to leave, Mrs. Gottlieb got a phone call which upset her. I only heard a few phrases. "Dr. Strangelove" was one of them, and I gleaned that this was about the cover story of *Psychology Today* that was supposed to come out that day or the next day. When we got back to Berkeley, I went to a bookstore and found the issue of *Psychology Today* and indeed it was about the CIA drug experiments and it used Gottlieb's stutter as part of his description of him as "The Doctor Strangelove of the CIA drug experiments."

The dissonance between the historic facts and my experience of these gracious people has always affected me. . . . There's no doubt that the things that Gottlieb did for the CIA were filled with evil. It is also clear that the anti-Communism that motivated most government actions during the Cold War was itself psychological manipulation, based on mistaken and undemocratic ideas. But that was the consensus of both political parties and virtually all factions, to one degree or another, it wasn't just one set of interested parties . . .

I would guess that Sidney Gottlieb had his CIA work compartmented off from the rest of his life. At work, he was apparently able to ignore the humanity of his subjects. . . . Yet coming home, he was the very humane guy that his wife knew and loved.

Around the same time I received that note, another email arrived. The subject line was arresting: "I worked with Sid Gottlieb, and my husband and I thought we knew him pretty well. . . . Wow!" So was the first sentence: "I heard your interview with Pat Thurston on KGO the other day and was shocked beyond belief."

The woman who wrote this account, Lynn Woolhouse, reported that in 1980 she had been a fourth-grade teacher at a school in Santa Cruz, California, where Sidney Gottlieb worked as a speech therapist. The two of them shared responsibility for helping a deaf student. "Sid was really wonderful with the boy, and according to other teachers in the school, he was great with the other children he worked with as well," she recalled. "We spent a lot of time practicing and chatting. Sid had a great sense of humor and he was one of the kindest people I've ever known." Then the plot thickened.

I had a new boyfriend, Geoff, and Sid and Margaret, his wife, had us over for dinner. (Geoff and I got married about a year after that, but if I had paid attention to Sid's advice I probably wouldn't have married him.) Geoff has mild bipolar and the night we went to dinner he was in his "up" or as he called it, his "short sleep" phase. We had a really good time with them and we played Boggle, a game we hadn't known about before and talked so much about everything—but obviously not quite everything. . . . As it approached midnight, I started giving Geoff the "Maybe we should get going" look but he was having so much fun, he ignored me. Everything seemed very funny and as far as I could tell, the four of us were really enjoying each other. When it got close to 2 am I finally insisted that we leave. Sid and Margaret were about 30 years older than we were and surely wanted to be rid of us!

The following Monday at school, Sid came to me with quite a serious look and said we needed to talk. I've never forgotten what he said: "I've been around a lot, and I've known a lot of different people. I know you like Geoff a lot and he seems like a great guy, but before you two get too serious, I just want you to think seriously about what being around someone like that would be like for the long run." Knowing what I do now about Sid makes me think, "OK, yeah, you were around a lot, that's for sure." 38 years ago I felt kind of resentful—I had my own parents to warn me about Geoff. Luckily I didn't heed his advice and we've been married (ups and downs for sure but the bipolar wasn't ever out of control) for close to 40 years and have two great children.

I have nothing but warm memories of both Gottliebs. Geoff and I really liked them a lot. The more I've thought about the things in your book the more astounded I feel.

Unlike Gottlieb, Ms. Woolhouse saved records of her past. Among them she found a Christmas card that she and her husband received from "Sid and Margaret" in 1984. It qualifies as a historical artifact because on the front is a drawing that shows how the couple looked a decade after Gottlieb retired:

Courtesy of Lynn Woolhouse

Not all of the recollections that readers sent me were about Gottlieb. To my astonishment, I heard from a man who grew up in Ojai, California, where the substitute math and chemistry teacher at his high school was Robert Lashbrook, Gottlieb's deputy during the decade he ran MK-ULTRA. Other than Gottlieb himself, Lashbrook knew more about MK-ULTRA than anyone. Inside his head were secrets that could have shaken the CIA, the United States government, and the world. Not least among them was the truth about Frank Olson's plunge to his death from a New York hotel room in 1953, since Lashbrook shared the room and was the last person to see Olson alive. It is disorienting to realize that this shadowy and bloodstained chemist wound up as a substitute teacher in a small-town high school.

What else, though, could a man like Lashbrook do after retiring? Years of helping to supervise a global network of medical torture centers is not an obvious qualification for many jobs. From the CIA, Lashbrook went to work for the aircraft manufacturer Northrop, but he lost his job after a few years. In 1975, when new revelations brought the Frank Olson case back into the news, reporters found him living in Ojai. When one pressed him for comment about the case, he memorably replied, "I don't really know what I should say and what I shouldn't."

No one at Nordhoff High School could have had the slightest idea that their mild-mannered substitute chemistry teacher had spent years at the CIA wielding life-or-death power over ill-fated "expendables." In fact, as this recollection suggests, Lashbrook suffered the fate of many substitute teachers: ridicule at the hands of pimply-faced teenagers. Few men who shook the world from positions of great power in Washington spent their last years in a condition so entirely divorced from the lives they had once lived.

The former student who wrote this recollection surmises that Lashbrook would have been in his late fifties during his substitute-teacher years. "I do remember thinking he looked and acted old at the time," he recalled. "He had thinning, kind of longish unkempt white hair. He also wore glasses. He was a fairly slight man, and thin. . . . He was very soft spoken, and seemed almost shy—kind of timid, really. . . . He was uncomfortable in the role, as many are. I'm guessing he was between jobs, so it was something he had to do to make ends meet. And as I now know, the Rockefeller Commission hearings were going on right about this time as well, so I suspect he was under a ton of stress as many of his past activities were coming to light."

One of the other reasons I remember him so clearly is because of an incident that happened one of the times he was subbing in my math class as a freshman. . . . At the time I was in the upper level math class for ninth graders, which meant there were also some older kids also in there who had to retake the class, or who needed it to graduate as their last math class. So the older kids tended to be jerks to any sub, and to Mr. Lashbrook they were particularly unruly.

On this day, Mr. Lashbrook was writing something on the board with his back to the class, and an older student basically made a spit wad out of a full sheet of paper. The saliva-soaked sheet was about the size of a golf ball, which he then hurled at the chalkboard in the general direction of Mr. Lashbrook. Thankfully it didn't hit him, but it struck the wall to the left and exploded upon impact. It was disgusting to say the least, and super disrespectful and out of line.

Lashbrook was surprised and stunned, and it was obvious that he clearly didn't know what to do in that moment. He didn't really see who threw it, and even the other kids were kind of shocked it happened. The room was awkwardly silent. I sat there and felt soooooo sorry for the guy. He really looked hurt. I had never seen an incident like that, nor seen a teacher kind of freeze and not really know how to react. I now know that as a complete lack of class management, but at the time I just found it incredibly hard to watch, and I haven't really forgotten about it. In the end he just turned around and started writing the board again.

It's hard to imagine his previous life and activities with the CIA and equate it to the person I came into contact with 20 years later. A man who seemed to be gentle and decent, and a family man whose children were good kids—much like Gottlieb, ironically. Maybe he was also haunted by his past?

After a covert career concocting poisons and helping to oversee brutal CIA experiments across three continents, Lashbrook wound up being intimidated by a teenager who threw a spitball at him. It is an apt foot-note to the madness that propelled MK-ULTRA. Decades after Sidney Gottlieb's death, footnotes may be all that remain to be discovered.

Some may be drawn from Gottlieb's personnel file, which the CIA released to me soon after this book was published. I had submitted a Freedom of Information Act request for that file soon after beginning my research. A year later, I wrote to inquire about its status. I received a letter telling me that my request had been received and was being processed, and that I should not inquire again. Another year passed. In that interim, the CIA rejected my request to declassify information about Gottlieb's work in Germany, where he spent two years in the late 1950s, but did agree to release several portrait photos. As I completed the book, I wondered if the CIA would ever declassify his personnel file. Soon after the book was published—less than ideal timing—a fat envelope arrived in my mail. There was the file, heavily redacted but studded with tidbits that illuminate the career of this most extraordinary American.

Some are little more than curiosities that enriched what I already knew. When asked to list his hobbies on one form, for example, Got-tlieb wrote, "Folk Dancing—have been collector and teacher for 17 years. Goat raising—great proficiency." More revealing were Gottlieb's repeated assertions that he was in full control of the Chemical Division of the Technical Services Staff, whose main project in the 1950s was MK-ULTRA. When asked to summarize his duties at various points during the 1950s, he wrote that he was "directly responsible for the overall activities of CD/TSS," took "responsibility for all activities of TSS/CD," and was assigned "to administer overall activities of the Chemical Division, TSS." This is clear acknowledgment, in Gottlieb's own words, that MK-ULTRA was all his.

Perhaps the most tantalizing page in this trove is a smudged and redacted list of Gottlieb's foreign travels. I knew that he and other MK-ULTRA scientists had made trips to Europe and East Asia to direct or monitor experiments, but this page, dated 1967, lists them. Gottlieb is reported to have made seven business trips to the "European Area," two to the "Asia Area," and one to "Western Hemisphere." Information on three other trips is redacted. One destination is listed as "Around the

World." The date appears to coincide with the mission Gottlieb made to the Congo in 1960, carrying poison for use in assassinating Prime Minister Patrice Lumumba.

Gottlieb's personnel file also contains a few notes about his two years as a CIA officer in Germany. In 1957 he signed an agreement "to serve outside the continental United States for a minimum tour of 24 months." A notation on another form shows that he left Washington that September for an assignment as "DDP/EE/GerSta/MOB/Ch, S&T," which decodes as "Deputy Directorate for Plans/Eastern Europe/Germany Station/Munich Operating Base/Chief, Science and Technology." After he had been in Germany for a year, one of his supervisors wrote a highly favorable appraisal of his work:

> Subject is a very mature and highly intelligent officer. Prior to his assignment to [redacted] his entire agency career had been technical in nature. . . . The period covered by this report involves Subject's first indoctrination to operational activities. The high degree of competence plus the facility for adapting himself to a completely new field of endeavor strongly indicate that Subject will become a very competent case officer. Subject's keen desire to learn coupled with his complete willingness to undertake all types of operational assignments are worthy of special note. . . . Subject's only apparent weakness is a tendency to let his enthusiasm carry him into more precipitous action than the operational situation will bear.

Another form that refers to Gottlieb's foreign travel offers a fleeting glimpse of his self-image. In 1960 he was issued one of the fictitious "special" passports that CIA officers sometimes use. On the space where he had to state his profession, Gottlieb wrote "Ecologist." That may have been a wry joke, a nod to his interest in back-to-the-earth environmentalism, or a declaration, at least to himself, that MK-ULTRA was legitimate research into the ecology of the mind.

The personnel file also reveals that Gottlieb was involved in development of the U-2 spy plane, which was not previously known. Forms dated 1960 and 1961 give him security clearance to participate in four projects—ARGON, CHALICE, CORONA, and OXCART—that were related to aerial surveillance, analysis of satellite imagery, and photographic mapping. He was also cleared to work on the HTLINGUAL project, under which the CIA intercepted mail sent to the Soviet Union or China.

Evaluations of Gottlieb's work at the CIA, contained in annual fitness reports, suggest that he was a valuable officer. One describes him as "dependable, loyal and conscientious" and notes: "There is no lack of initiative on his part." Another calls him an "exceptionally strong and versatile individual." Not every line is positive, though. In 1955, when MK-ULTRA was at its peak, one of his fellow officers was asked to rate him on various scales. He scored well for memory, analytical ability, and stamina, but received the lowest possible rating for being "able to see another's point of view."

"Could be somewhat more deliberate and unemotional," the evaluation concludes. "However, Dr. Gottlieb realizes this and makes adequate compensation."

Notes

1. I Needed More of a Challenge

2 "I was in contact with Dr. Death himself": Terry Lenzner, *The Investigator: Fifty Years of Uncovering the Truth* (New York: Penguin Random House / Blue Rider Press, 2013), p. 190.

2 SIDNEY GOTTLIEB, 80, DIES: Tim Weiner, "Sidney Gottlieb, 80, Dies; Took LSD to C.I.A.," *New York Times*, April 10, 1999.

3 "James Bond had Q": Elaine Woo, "CIA's Gottlieb Ran LSD Mind Control Testing," *Los Angeles Times*, April 4, 1999.

3 PUSHER, ASSASSIN & PIMP: Ken Hollington, *Wolves, Jackals, and Foxes: The Assassins Who Changed History* (New York: Thomas Dunne Books, 2008), p. 397; Jeffrey St. Clair and Alexander Cockburn, "Pusher, Assassin & Pimp: US Official Poisoner Dies," *Counterpunch*, June 15, 1999.

3 "takes his place among the Jekyll and Hydes": Elsa Davidson, "Polarity of Sidney Gottlieb," *Feed*, March 18, 1999.

3 "everything you have dreamed of in a mad scientist": Rupert Cornwell, "Obituary: Sidney Gottlieb," *Guardian*, March 10, 1999.

3 "living vindication for conspiracy theorists": *Independent*, April 4, 1999.

3 "When Churchill spoke of a world": "Sidney Gottlieb," *Times*, March 12, 1999.

3 "known to some as the 'dark sorcerer'": Gordon Corera, *The Art of Betrayal: The Secret History of MI6* (New York: Pegasus, 2012), p. 123.

4 The author gives him grudging credit: Mark Frauenfelder, *The World's Worst:*

A Guide to the Most Disgusting, Hideous, Inept and Dangerous People, Places, and Things on Earth (Vancouver: Raincoast, 2005), p. 86.

4   "a scientist named Dr. Gottlieb was hired": Barbara Kingsolver, *The Poisonwood Bible* (New York: Harper Perennial Modern Classics, 2008), p. 319.

4   "cosmic in scope, interested in everything": Norman Mailer, *Harlot's Ghost* (New York: Random House, 1992), p. 331.

4   from a rubber airplane to an escape kit: Robert Wallace and H. Keith Melton, with Henry Robert Schlesinger, *Spycraft: The Secret History of the CIA's Spytechs from Communism to Al-Qaeda* (New York: Dutton, 2008), pp. 290, 297.

4   "Under Gottlieb's leadership": Ibid., pp. 379–80.

5   At the age of twelve: Ted Gup, "The Coldest Warrior," *Washington Post*, December 16, 2001. "I was born with a pair of clubbed feet that were corrected, as best they could in those days, very early in my life, in the first year or two. And I wore braces to continue the therapeutic process . . . I wore special shoes at various parts of my life"; U.S. District Court of Appeals for the Second Circuit, *Gloria Kronisch, Executrix of the Estate of Stanley Milton Glickman, against United States of America, Sidney Gottlieb, et al.*, "Deposition of Sidney Gottlieb," September 19, 1995, Cr62448.0-Cr62451, pp. 6–7.

5   "viciously harassed": H. P. Albarelli Jr., *A Terrible Mistake: The Murder of Frank Olson and the CIA's Secret Cold War Experiments* (Walterville, OR: Trine Day, 2009), p. 102.

6   He studied advanced German: Sidney Gottlieb Admissions Papers, Series 19/12/2/1, University of Wisconsin–Madison Archives.

6   He received a short but cordial reply: Ibid.

6   he was able to take the courses he wanted: Ibid.

6   He sang in the Glee Club: *Agricola* (Russellville: Arkansas Polytechnic College, 1938).

6   "a Yankee who pleases the southerners": Ibid.

6   "I have been keeping up an A average": Gottlieb Admissions Papers.

7   he joined the campus chapter of the Young People's Socialist League: Weiner, "Sidney Gottlieb, 80, Dies"; Gup, "Coldest Warrior."

7   Baldwin gave him a glowing recommendation: Accession 1990/061, College of Agriculture, student folders, University of Wisconsin–Madison Archives.

7   "Grad students were not supposed to get married": Margaret Moore Gottlieb, "Autobiographical Essays" (Box 1, Folder 24—Call No. RG 489), Presbyterian Historical Society, Philadelphia, PA.

8   "We were very excited to get the cable": Ibid.

8   "I wanted to do my share in the war effort": Albarelli, *Terrible Mistake*, p. 102.

8   "I enjoyed my FDA time": Ibid., p. 103.

9   "By this time we had found a very old and primitive cabin": Margaret Gottlieb, "Autobiographical Essays."

9   A relative who spent four days with the young family: Ibid.

9   "Sid is pitching in more": Ibid.

2. Dirty Business

11   On a wall near Odeonsplatz: "Munich City 1945 in Colour—Old City," YouTube video, 3:22, posted by Timeline, February 24, 2014, https://www .youtube.com/watch?v=idiJegt7tFw.

11   Blome was, according to one report, "a well-dressed man": Annie Jacobsen, *Operation Paperclip: The Secret Intelligence Program That Brought Nazi Scientists to America* (New York: Back Bay, 2014), p. 75; Egmont R. Koch and Michael Wech, *Deckname Artischocke: Die Geheimen Menschenversuche der CIA* (Munich: Bertelsmann, 2002), p. 28.

12   Blome's complex was surrounded by ten-foot walls: Ute Deichmann, *Biologists under Hitler* (Cambridge, MA: Harvard University Press, 1996), p. 283; Linda Hunt, *Secret Agenda: The United States Government, Nazi Scientists, and Project Paperclip, 1944–1990* (New York: St. Martin's Press, 1991), p. 180; Jacobsen, *Operation Paperclip*, pp. 159–64.

13   "very concerned that the installations for human experiments": Deichmann, *Biologists under Hitler*, p. 287.

13   Interrogators from the Counterintelligence Corps confronted Blome: Jacobsen, *Operation Paperclip*, pp. 160–65.

13   "In 1943 Blome was studying bacteriological warfare": Operation Paperclip Info, "Kurt Blome," http://www.operationpaperclip.info/kurt-blome.php.

14   "The best defense is offense": Ed Regis, *The Biology of Doom: The History of America's Secret Germ Warfare Project* (New York: Henry Holt / Owl Books, 1999), p. 21.

14   "Biological warfare is of course a 'dirty business'": Ibid., p. 25.

14   "The value of biological warfare": Ernest T. Takafuji, *Biological Weapons and Modern Warfare* (Washington, DC: National Defense University Press, 1991), p. ii.

15   Churchill asked the Americans for help: PBS *American Experience*, "The Living Weapon," https://www.dailymotion.com/video/x35q3xt; Regis, *Biology of Doom*, p. 69.

15   "Practically all of the people there": University of Wisconsin Oral History Program, "Interview with Ira L. Baldwin, 1974. First Interview of Three," http:// www.worldcat.org/title/oral-history-program-interview-with-ira-l-baldwin -1974-first-interview-of-three/oclc/227181167&referer=brief_results.

16   "To understand the biological warfare program": Ibid.

16   "If I said 'I want that man'": Ibid.

17   Baldwin and a couple of Chemical Warfare Service officers: History Net, "Dr. Ira Baldwin: Biological Weapons Pioneer," http://www.historynet.com/dr -ira-baldwin-biological-weapons-pioneer.htm; PBS, "The Living Weapon"; Regis, *Biology of Doom*, pp. 38–39.

17   The Office of Strategic Services, America's wartime intelligence agency: Albarelli, *Terrible Mistake*, pp. 46–47.

17   On March 9, 1943, the army announced: Regis, *Biology of Doom*, p. 41.

17   The first commandant immediately ordered: Ibid., p. 79; Peter Williams and David Wallace, *Unit 731: The Shattering Exposé of the Japanese Army's Secret of Secrets* (London: Grafton, 1989), p. 160.

18   Everything Baldwin requisitioned was immediately supplied: Regis, *Biology of Doom*, p. 80.

18   "I remember one time we had a party": PBS, "The Living Weapon."

18   Ultimately about fifteen hundred came to work at Camp Detrick: Oral History, "Interview with Ira L. Baldwin."

18   "They were passionate about their science": PBS, "The Living Weapon."

18   "In the event of my death": Albarelli, *Terrible Mistake*, p. 41.

18   New arrivals at Camp Detrick: Regis, *Biology of Doom*, pp. 66–67.

19   Early in 1944, Winston Churchill abruptly changed: *American History*, "Dr. Ira Baldwin: Biological Weapons Pioneer," http://www.historynet.com/dr-ira -baldwin-biological-weapons-pioneer.htm; PBS, "The Living Weapon."

20   Hundreds of scientists: Norman Covert, *Cutting Edge: A History of Fort Detrick, Maryland 1943–1993* (Fort Detrick, MD: Headquarters U.S. Army Garrison Public Affairs Office, 1993), p. 19.

20   Baldwin also built two field testing stations: Regis, *Biology of Doom*, pp. 79–80; Oral History, "Interview with Ira L. Baldwin."

20   Donovan wanted authority to grant them immunity: Hunt, *Secret Agenda*, pp. 9–10.

21   At the Kransberg Castle interrogation center: Jacobsen, *Operation Paperclip*, p. 227.

21   President Harry Truman set it in motion: Hunt, *Secret Agenda*, pp. 38–40.

21   Ultimately more than seven hundred scientists: Estimates range from 765 (Linda Hunt, "U.S. Coverup of Nazi Scientists," *Bulletin of the Atomic Scientists*, April 1985) to more than 1,600 (Annie Jacobsen, "What Cold War CIA Interrogators Learned from the Nazis," *Daily Beast*, February 11, 2014, https://www.thedailybeast.com/what-cold-war-cia-interrogators-learned -from-the-nazis?ref=author).

22   Part of their assignment was to teach Americans: Hunt, *Secret Agenda*, pp. 160–61.

22   They systematically expunged references: Ibid., p. 108; Ralph Blumenthal, "Nazi Whitewash in 1940s Charged," *New York Times*, March 11, 1985.

22   Applicants who had been rated by interrogators: Hunt, *Secret Agenda*, pp. 118–19.

22   "In effect . . . the scientific teams wore blinders": Ibid., p. 10.

23   At home, the Federal Bureau of Investigation: Ibid., p. 112.

23   The American Federation of Scientists wrote to President Truman: Ibid., p. 113.

23   Newspapers reported that one of the first Paperclip contracts: United Nations War Crimes Commission, *Law Reports of Trials of War Criminals*, vol. 10: *The I. G. Farben and Krupp Trials* (London: His Majesty's Stationery Office),1949, p. 1.

23   Captain Bosquet Wev: Hunt, *Secret Agenda*, p. 110; Hunt, "U.S. Coverup"; Blumenthal, "Nazi Whitewash."

23   Recalcitrant diplomats were pilloried: Hunt, *Secret Agenda*, p. 123.

23   Press reports portrayed the conflict: Ibid., p. 122.

24   As a reward, and a sign of respect: Author's interview with Oberursel historian Manfred Kopp, 2017; Koch and Wech, *Deckname Artischocke*, p. 54.

24   They discovered that the army surgeon who ran Unit 731: Ibid., p. 55.

24   Two obsessions . . . shaped Shiro Ishii: Daniel Barenblatt, *A Plague upon Humanity: The Hidden History of Japan's Biological Warfare Program* (New York: Harper Perennial, 2005), pp. 10–20; Sheldon H. Harris, *Factories of Death: Japanese Biological Warfare, 1932–45, and the American Cover-up* (New York: Routledge, 1994), pp. 13–22; Hal Gold, *Unit 731 Testimony: Japan's Wartime Human Experimentation Program* (Clarendon, VT: Tuttle Publishing, 2004), pp. 23–25.

24   In 1928, after finishing medical school: Harris, *Factories of Death*, pp. 40–49; Williams and Wallace, *Unit 731*, pp. 39–45.

25   "a swashbuckling womanizer": Christopher Hudson, "Doctors of Depravity," *Daily Mail*, March 2, 2007.

25   "Our God-given mission as doctors": Regis, *Biology of Doom*, pp. 40–41.

25   Japanese soldiers began sweeping up "bandits": Gold, *Unit 731 Testimony*, pp. 40–42; Hudson, "Doctors of Depravity;" Williams and Wallace, *Unit 731*, pp. 81–82.

25   For the brave of heart and strong of stomach: Gold, *Unit 731 Testimony*, pp. 83–85; Harris, *Factories of Death*, pp. 41–82; Robert Harris and Jeremy Paxman, *A Higher Form of Killing: The Secret Story of Chemical and Biological Warfare* (New York: Noonday, 1982), pp. 57–82; Nicholas D. Kristof, "Unmasking Horror: Japan Confronting Gruesome War Atrocity," *New York Times*, March 17, 1995; Keiichi Tsuneishi, *The Germ Warfare Unit That Disappeared: The Kwangtung Army's 731st Unit* (Tokyo: Kai-mei-sha, 1982), pp. 1–166; Williams and Wallace, *Unit 731*, pp. 50–101.

26   In the last days of the war: Gold, *Unit 731 Testimony*, p. 10; Williams and Wallace, *Unit 731*, pp. 144–51.

26   "He literally begged my father": Williams and Wallace, *Unit 731*, p. 227.

27   Ishii admitted no crimes: Ibid., pp. 228–52; Koch and Wech, *Deckname Artischocke*, p. 56; Regis, *Biology of Doom*, pp. 104–11.

27   the Americans were interested in "technical and scientific information": Regis, *Biology of Doom*, p. 109.

27   "The value to the US of Japanese biological weapons data": Williams and Wallace, *Unit 731*, p. 314.

27   "Statements from Ishii . . . can probably be obtained": Gold, *Unit 731 Testimony*, p. 109.

28   "Chalking that up to simple racism": Lee Nisson, "Acknowledging Plunder: The Consequences of How the United States Acquired Japanese and German Technological Secrets after WWII," senior thesis, Brandeis University, 2014, p. 143.

28   Each slide contained a sliver of tissue: Regis, *Biology of Doom*, pp. 126–27.

28   "Information has accrued": Harris and Paxman, *Higher Form of Killing*, p. 154.

28   Over the following years: Howard Brody et al., "United States Responses to Japanese Wartime Inhuman Experimentation after World War II: National Security and Wartime Exigency," *Cambridge Quarterly of Health Care Ethics*, vol. 23, no. 2 (April 2014), https://www.ncbi.nlm.nih.gov/pmc/articles /PMC4487829/; Ralph Blumenthal, "Revisiting World War II Atrocities: Comparing the Unspeakable to the Unthinkable," *New York Times*, March 7, 1999.

29   Evidence later emerged: Nisson, "Acknowledging Plunder," p. 154.

29   Designs of their medical torture centers: Christian W. Spang and Rolf-Harald Wippich, eds., *Japanese-German Relations, 1895–1945: War, Diplomacy and Public Opinion* (New York: Routledge, 2008), p. 208.

29   The bang of the gavel: Vivien Spitz, *Doctors from Hell: The Horrific Account of Nazi Human Experiments* (Boulder, CO: Sentient, 2005), pp. 42–45.

30   Blome put up a spirited defense: Jacobsen, *Operation Paperclip*, pp. 273–74; Nisson, "Acknowledging Plunder," pp. 68–69; Douglas O. Lindor, "The Nuremberg Trials: The Doctors Trial," *Famous Trials*, https://www.famous-trials.com /nuremberg/1903-doctortrial.

30   Blome's testimony was not all that helped his case: "Operation Paperclip Nazi Rogues Page," http://ahrp.org/operation-paperclip-nazi-rogues-page/; "Operation Paperclip: Kurt Blome," http://www.operationpaperclip.info/kurt -blome.php.

30   "The deck was clearly stacked": Koch and Wech, *Deckname Artischocke*, p. 54.

31   "Available now for interrogation": Jacobsen, *Operation Paperclip*, p. 292.

31   At one session, though, he mentioned: Ibid., p. 295.

33   In the spring of 1949 they created a secret team: Scott Shane, "Buried Secrets of Bio-Warfare," Baltimore *Sun*, August 1, 2004.

33   "a little Detrick within Detrick": Ibid.

3. Willing and Unwilling Subjects

34   For the next two hours he careened: Robert Campbell, "The Chemistry of Madness," *Life*, November 26, 1971.

35   "I had great difficulty in speaking coherently": Julian B. Rotter, *Psychology* (Glenview, IL: Scott, Foresman, 1975), p. 183.

35   Hofmann reported what he called: Albert Hofmann, "The Discovery of LSD and Subsequent Investigations on Naturally Occurring Hallucinogens," *Psychedelic Library*, http://www.psychedelic-library.org/hofmann.htm.

35   He collected all the information he could find: Hunt, *Secret Agenda*, p. 162.

36   "Their will to resist would be weakened": Jacobsen, *Operation Paperclip*, p. 289.

36   "Throughout recorded history, wars have been characterized": Armin Krishnan, *Military Neuroscience and the Coming Age of Neurowarfare* (Abingdon, UK: Routledge, 2018), p. 26.

36   Under this "informal agreement": Albarelli, *Terrible Mistake*, p. 65.

37 "Under MK-NAOMI": John Marks, *The Search for the "Manchurian Candidate": The CIA and Mind Control* (New York: W. W. Norton, 1978), pp. 80–81.

37 Some observed bio-weapons tests: Albarelli, *Terrible Mistake*, p. 73; "Deckname Artischocke—Geheime Menschenversuche," YouTube video, 44:47, posted by Taurus322, June 15, 2011, https://www.youtube.com/watch?v=O7xD7_IJIrk&t =145s.; BBC, "Germ Warfare Fiasco Revealed," November 19, 1999, http://news .bbc.co.uk/2/hi/uk_news/politics/526870.stm; "Operation Harness, 1948–1949 [Allocated Title]," video, posted by the Imperial War Museum, catalog no. DED 85, https://www.iwm.org.uk/collections/item/object/1060017887.

37 That same year, six members: Albarelli, *Terrible Mistake*, p. 117.

37 They chose San Francisco: Jim Carlton, "Of Microbes and Mock Attacks: Years Ago, the Military Sprayed Germs on U.S. Cities," *Wall Street Journal*, October 22, 2001; Leonard A. Cole, *Clouds of Secrecy: The Army's Germ-Warfare Tests over Populated Areas* (Totowa, NJ: Rowman and Littlefield, 1988), pp. 75–84.

38 "It was noted that a successful BW attack": Rebecca Kreston, "Blood and Fog: The Military's Germ Warfare Tests in San Francisco," *Discovery*, June 28, 2015.

38 The program was code-named Bluebird: Albarelli, *Terrible Mistake*, pp. 28, 208; Marks, *Search for the "Manchurian Candidate,"* p. 24.

38 One of the first Bluebird memos: Albarelli, *Terrible Mistake*, p. 208; Marks, *Search for the "Manchurian Candidate,"* p. 24.

38 Experiments would be aimed at: William Bowart, *Operation Mind Control* (New York: Delacorte, 1977), p. 104.

38 Barely six months after it was launched: Albarelli, *Terrible Mistake*, pp. 208–9.

40 "In our conversation of 9 February 1951": Jacobsen, *Operation Paperclip*, p. 366.

40 Other memos from this period: Albarelli, *Terrible Mistake*, pp. 208–9.

40 Camp King was home base for the "rough boys": Author's interview with Manfred Kopp; Alfred W. McCoy, "Science in Dachau's Shadow: Hebb, Beecher, and the Development of CIA Psychological Torture and Modern Medical Ethics," *Journal of the History of the Behavioral Sciences*, vol. 43(4) (Fall 2007).

41 "The unit took great pride in their nicknames": H. P. Albarelli Jr. and Jeffrey S. Kaye, "The CIA's Shocking Experiments on Children Exposed: Drugging, Electroshocks and Brainwashing," *Alternet*, https://www.alternet.org /story/147834/the_cia's_shocking_experiments_on_children_exposed_—_drugging,_electroshocks_and_brainwashing.

41 "disposal of body would be no problem": Marks, *Search for the "Manchurian Candidate,"* p. 42.

41 A few miles from Camp King: Koch and Wech, *Deckname Artischocke*, pp. 98–100.

42 "This villa on the edge of Kronberg": WDR German Television, "Deckname Artischocke: Geheime Menschenversuche," https://www.youtube.com/watch ?v=O7xD7_IJIrk&t=145s.

42   "usually resulted in a slow and agonizing death": Hunt, *Secret Agenda*, pp. 151–52; Koch and Wech, *Deckname Artischocke*, pp. 29–30; Jacobsen, *Operation Paperclip*, pp. 303–4.

43   "The former chief physician of the German army": Koch and Wech, *Deckname Artischocke*, p. 91.

43   One CIA-connected researcher: SWR German Television, *Folterexperten— Die Geheimen Methoden der CIA* (film), https://www.dailymotion.com/video /xvzl7j; "Henry K. Beecher," *Enacademic*, http://enacademic.com/dic.nsf /enwiki/2224000.

43   German researchers would later identify other secret prisons: Albarelli, *Terrible Mistake*, p. 79; WDR German Television, *Deckname Artischocke* (film).

44   Bluebird interrogation teams injected captured North Korean soldiers: Bowart, *Operation Mind Control*, pp. 102–5; Marks, *Search for the "Manchurian Candidate,"* p. 25; Dominic Streatfeild, *Brainwash: The Secret History of Mind Control* (New York: Thomas Dunne Books, 2007), p. 50.

45   He had rubber-stamped dozens of others: Hunt, *Secret Agenda*, pp. 180–81; Jacobsen, *Operation Paperclip*, pp. 344–45; Koch and Wech, *Deckname Artischocke*, pp. 28–30.

45   Fortunately, the ideal job had just become available: Jacobsen, *Operation Paperclip*, pp. 347, 364–65; Koch and Wech, *Deckname Artischocke*, pp. 106–8.

46   Answers to these questions, they asserted in a memo: Declassified CIA document, MORI #140401, "Special Research, Bluebird," https://www.wanttoknow .info/mind_control/foia_mind_control/19520101_140401.

4. The Secret That Was Going to Unlock the Universe

48   Waves of damp heat enveloped Washington: Albarelli, *Terrible Mistake*, p. 103; *Weather Underground*, "Weather for KDCA—July 1951," https://english .wunderground.com/history/airport/KDCA/1951/7/13/DailyHistory .html?req_city=&req_state=&req_statename=&reqdb.zip=&reqdb.magic =&reqdb.wmo=. According to Wallace et al., *Spycraft*, Gottlieb's Technical Services Staff then operated from a "covert building on 14th Street near the Department of Agriculture" (p. 47).

48   "Do you know why they recruited you?": U.S. District Court 2nd Circuit, "Deposition of Sidney Gottlieb," September 19, 1995, p. 11.

49   he "continued his work": Koch and Wech, *Deckname Artischocke*, p. 63.

49   Several years earlier, Baldwin had guided: Gordon Thomas, *Secrets and Lies: A History of CIA Mind Control and Germ Warfare* (Old Saybrook, CT: Konecky and Konecky, 2007), p. 42.

50   "It's pretty amazing": H. P. Albarelli, "The Mysterious Death of Frank Olson," *Crime*, May 19, 2003, http://www.crimemagazine.com/part-two-mysterious -death-cia-scientist-frank-olson.

50   He confessed to the CIA psychologist assigned to screen him: Gup, "Coldest Warrior"; Weiner, "Sidney Gottlieb, 80, Dies."

51   Neither ever walked normally: Thomas, *Secrets and Lies*, p. 63.

51   "a strong but never mentioned bond": Albarelli, *Terrible Mistake*, p. 103.

51   Gottlieb's first assignment at the CIA: U.S. District Court 2nd Circuit, "Deposition of Sidney Gottlieb," September 19, 1995, p. 311.

51   On August 20, 1951, he directed that Bluebird be expanded: Tani M. Linville, "Project MKULTRA and the Search for Mind Control: Clandestine Use of LSD within the CIA," *Digital Commons*, April 26, 2016, https://digitalcommons .cedarville.edu/cgi/viewcontent.cgi?article=1005&context=history_capstones; Susan Maret, "Murky Projects and Uneven Information Policies: A Case Study of the Psychological Strategy Board and CIA," *Secrecy and Society*, vol. 1, no. 2, February 2018, https://scholarworks.sjsu.edu/cgi/viewcontent .cgi?referer=https://www.google.com/&httpsredir=1&article=1034&context =secrecyandsociety; Colin Ross, *The CIA Doctors: Human Rights Violations by American Psychiatrists* (Richardson, TX: Manitou, 2006), p. 34.

51   Supposedly he chose that name: Albarelli, *Terrible Mistake*, p. 226; Richard Gilbride, *Matrix for Assassination: The JFK Conspiracy* (Bloomington, IN: Trafford, 2009), p. 31.

52   The first directives sent to Artichoke teams: John Ranelagh, *The Agency: The Rise and Decline of the CIA* (New York: Simon and Schuster, 1986), pp. 211–13.

52   "Our principal goal": Ibid., p. 214.

52   "drugs are already on hand": Martin A. Lee and Bruce Shlain, *Acid Dreams: The Complete Social History of LSD: The CIA, the Sixties, and Beyond* (New York: Grove, 1985), p. 13.

52   The first subject was a prisoner called Kelly: Jeffrey Kaye and H. P. Albarelli, "The Real Roots of the CIA's Rendition and Black Sites Program," *Truthout*, February 17, 2010, https://truthout.org/articles/the-real-roots-of-the-cias -rendition-and-black-sites-program/.

53   Hunter had been a militantly anti-Communist journalist: Albarelli, *Terrible Mistake*, pp. 187–90; Marcia Holmes, "Edward Hunter and the Origin of 'Brainwashing,'" May 26, 2017, http://www.bbk.ac.uk/hiddenpersuaders/blog /hunter-origins-of-brainwashing/; *New World Encyclopedia*, "Brainwashing," http://www.newworldencyclopedia.org/entry/Brainwashing; Matthew W. Dunne, *A Cold War State of Mind: Brainwashing and Postwar American Society* (Amherst: University of Massachusetts Press, 2003), pp. 3–56; Kathleen Taylor, *Brainwashing: The Science of Thought Control* (Oxford: Oxford University Press, 2004), pp. 3–11, 101–4.

54   "psychological warfare on a scale": Timothy Melley, *The Covert Sphere: Secrecy, Fiction, and the National Security State* (Ithaca: Cornell University Press, 2012), p. 48.

54   "The Reds have specialists": Tim Weiner, "Remembering Brainwashing," *New York Times*, July 6, 2008.

54   "There was deep concern over the issue of brainwashing": Central Intelligence Agency, "An Interview with Richard Helms," https://www.cia.gov/library /center-for-the-study-of-intelligence/kent-csi/vol44no4/html/v44i4a07p _0020.htm.

55   "Specific research should be undertaken": Central Intelligence Agency, "Special Research for Artichoke," April 24, 1952, https://mikemcclaughry .wordpress.com/the-reading-library/cia-declassified-document-library /project-artichoke-special-research-areas-april-24-1952/.

56   Each Artichoke team included a "research specialist": Albarelli, *Terrible Mistake*, pp. 228–29; Koch and Wech, *Deckname Artischocke*, p. 75; Marks, *Search for the "Manchurian Candidate,"* pp. 31–36, 40–47.

56   "As a rule": Albarelli, *Terrible Mistake*, pp. 228–30.

57   In 1950 they completed more than two years of work: Chris Heidenrich, *Frederick: Local and National Crossroads* (Mount Pleasant, SC: Arcadia, 2003), p. 144; Jacobsen, *Operation Paperclip*, p. 291.

57   "aerobiological studies of agents": U.S. Department of the Interior, "National Register of Historic Places Registration Form: One-Million-Liter Test Sphere," https://mht.maryland.gov/secure/medusa/PDF/Frederick/F-3-46.pdf.

57   He pushed for wider use of polygraphs: Marks, *Search for the "Manchurian Candidate,"* pp. 26–28.

57   "dangerous combinations of drugs": Alfred W. McCoy, *Torture and Impunity: The U.S. Doctrine of Coercive Interrogation* (Madison: University of Wisconsin Press, 2012), p. 77.

58   After taking a four-day course: Streatfeild, *Brainwash*, pp. 151–54.

58   "If hypnotic control can be established over any participant": Ibid., p. 154.

58   The first drug they hoped would work: Lee and Shlain, *Acid Dreams*, p. 4; Marks, *Search for the "Manchurian Candidate,"* p. 7.

59   Cocaine was the next candidate: Lee and Shlain, *Acid Dreams*, pp. 11–12.

59   "frequently used by police and intelligence": Ibid., p. 12.

59   At the end of 1950 the U.S. Navy: Marks, *Search for the "Manchurian Candidate,"* pp. 39–42.

59   Could mescaline . . . be the answer?: Lee and Shlain, *Acid Dreams*, p. 5; Marks, *Search for the "Manchurian Candidate,"* pp. 4, 11; McCoy, "Science in Dachau's Shadow."

60   The MK-NAOMI project: Regis, *Biology of Doom*, p. 158.

60   "I happened to experience an out-of-bodyness": U.S. District Court 2nd Circuit, "Deposition of Sidney Gottlieb," September 19, 1995, p. 86.

60   Later, Agency trainees were given LSD without forewarning: Streatfeild, *Brainwash*, p. 68; "They were witting in the sense people knew that this was going to happen when they got there. Perhaps at the particular moment they were given was not witting." U.S. District Court for the District of Columbia, Civil Action No. 80–3163, "Deposition of Sidney Gottlieb," April 19, 1983, p. 156.

60   "There was an extensive amount of self-experimentation": Lee and Shlain, *Acid Dreams*, p. 29.

61   "We had thought at first": Marks, *Search for the "Manchurian Candidate,"* p. 110.

61   As part of his effort to mold a coherent team: Albarelli, *Terrible Mistake*, p. 60.

61   "Needless layers of interplay and approval": Ibid., p. 66.

62   "There were CIA people who infiltrated": Ibid., p. 76.

62   Greene, whose advocacy of LSD had been secret: Ibid., pp. 63–64.

63   "I was fascinated by the ideas Greene was advancing": Ibid., p. 61.

63   "the most fascinating thing about it": Marks, *Search for the "Manchurian Candidate,"* p. 58.

63   "Although no Soviet data are available on LSD-25": Lee and Shlain, *Acid Dreams*, pp. 14–16.

64   to identify themselves only as a "staff support group": Testimony of Charles Senseney to Church Committee, https://www.aarclibrary.org/publib/church /reports/vol1/pdf/ChurchV1_6_Senseney.pdf, pp. 160–61.

64   "Do you know what a 'self-contained'": Albarelli, *Terrible Mistake,* p. 76.

64   "In 1951 a team of CIA scientists": Thomas, *Secrets and Lies*, pp. 66–67.

65   For more than a year, under the terms of MK-NAOMI: Albarelli, *Terrible Mistake*, p. 65; Marks, *Search for the "Manchurian Candidate,"* p. 32.

65   "Under an agreement reached with the Army in 1952": Letter from Stansfield Turner to Sen. Daniel Inouye, cited in Wayne Madsen, "The US Continued Biological Weapons Research Until 2003," *Strategic Culture*, August 28, 2016, https://www.strategic-culture.org/news/2016/08/23/us-continued-biological -weapons-research-until-2003.html.

65   "Arrived back in Frankfurt from Paris": "Letters Home: Joan Eisenmann to Elmer and Frances Eisenmann," https://www.yumpu.com/en/document /view/3767896/letters-home-joan-eisenmann-to-elmer-frances-eisenmann.

65   Bohemian expatriates in Paris: Noel Riley Fitch, *Paris Café: The Select Crowd* (New York: Soft Skull, 2007), pp. 57–104.

66   Stanley Glickman had shown artistic talent: Albarelli, *Terrible Mistake*, pp. 643–45; Alliance for Human Research Protection, "Stanley Glickman Was Another Human Casualty of Sidney Gottlieb's LSD Antics," http://ahrp.org /1952-stanley-glickman-was-another-human-casualty-of-sidney-gottliebs -lsd-antics/; Russ Baker, "Acid, Americans and the Agency," *Guardian*, February 14, 1999; *Glickman v. United States*, https://law.justia.com/cases/federal /district-courts/FSupp/626/171/1398799/; José Cabranes, *Kronisch v. United States*, July 9, 1998, https://caselaw.findlaw.com/us-2nd-circuit/1364923 .html.

67   "Even in an area known for street characters": Baker, *Guardian*, February 14, 1999.

67   "Subjects in whom even a slight modification": Ibid.

68   Beginning on December 5, 1952, one of Hoch's assistants: Albarelli, *Terrible*

Mistake, pp. 161–62; Alliance for Human Research Protection, "NYPSI an Early CIA-Contracted Academic Institution under MK-NAOMI," http://ahrp.org/nypsi-an-early-cia-contracted-academic-institution-under-mk-naomi/; Harris and Paxman, *Higher Form of Killing*, p. 191; J. Francis Wolfe, "10 Real Victims of the CIA's MKULTRA Program," *Listverse*, May 28, 2015, http://listverse.com/2015/05/28/10-real-victims-of-the-cias-mkultra-program/.

70   On the evening of March 30, 1953, Allen Dulles sat down for dinner: Albarelli, *Terrible Mistake*, pp. 132–34; William R. Corson, Susan B. Trento, and Joseph John Trento, *Widows: Four American Spies, the Wives They Left Behind, and the KGB's Crippling of American Intelligence* (New York: Crown, 1989), pp. 11–13; David Talbot, *The Devil's Chessboard: Allen Dulles, the CIA, and the Rise of America's Secret Government* (New York: HarperCollins, 2015), pp. 297–300; Paul Vidich, "An Honorable Man: Backstory," http://paulvidich.com/books/an-honorable-man/backstory/.

70   "Allen probably had a special potion prepared": Peter Janney, *Mary's Mosaic: The CIA Conspiracy to Murder John F. Kennedy, Mary Pinchot Meyer, and Their Vision for World Peace* (New York: Skyhorse, 2016), p. 379.

70   A redacted version of this memo: Central Intelligence Agency, "Project MK-ULTRA: Extremely Sensitive Research and Development Programs," https://cryptome.org/mkultra-0003.htm (Tab A).

71   On April 10, 1953, as Dulles was considering this proposal: "Summary of Remarks by Mr. Allen W. Dulles at the National Alumni Conference of the Graduate Council of Princeton University, Hot Springs, Va., on Brain Warfare," https://www.cia.gov/library/readingroom/docs/CIA-RDP80R01731R001700030015-9.pdf.

72   "It was fashionable among that group": Marks, *Search for the "Manchurian Candidate*," p. 61.

73   He set to work with three assets: Gary Kamiya, "When the CIA Ran a LSD Sex-House in San Francisco," *San Francisco Chronicle*, April 1, 2016; Marks, *Search for the "Manchurian Candidate*," p. 61; Kim Zettler, "April 13, 1953: CIA OKs MK-ULTRA Mind-Control Tests," *Wired*, April 13, 2010.

5. Abolishing Consciousness

74   "fat and bull-like": Douglas Valentine, "Sex, Drugs and the CIA," *Counterpunch*, June 19, 2002, https://www.counterpunch.org/2002/06/19/sex-drugs-and-the-cia-2/.

74   "a vastly obese slab of a man": Johann Hari, "The Hunting of Billie Holiday," *Politico*, January 17, 2015, https://www.politico.com/magazine/story/2015/01/drug-war-the-hunting-of-billie-holiday-114298_Page3.html.

74   "an extremely menacing bowling ball": Marks, *Search for the "Manchurian Candidate*," p. 96.

74   His first wife, who divorced him in 1945: Valentine, "Sex, Drugs and the CIA."

75   His consumption of alcohol . . . was legendary: Marks, *Search for the "Manchurian Candidate,"* p. 97.

75   His other appetite was sexual fetish: Albarelli, *Terrible Mistake*, p. 411; Valentine, "Sex, Drugs and the CIA."

75   "Poor little bastard just couldn't make it": John Jacobs, "The Diaries of a CIA Operative," *Washington Post*, September 5, 1977.

75   The men's magazine *True* lionized him: *True*, December 1959.

75   He was sent for paramilitary training: "The LSD Chronicles: George Hunter White, Part One," http://visupview.blogspot.com/2012/12/the-lsd-chronicles-george-hunter-white.html.

75   Several of his trainees went on to long careers at the CIA: Ibid.

75   In 1949 he made national headlines: Hari, "The Hunting of Billie Holiday."

77   They talked about the OSS: Albarelli, *Terrible Mistake*, p. 67.

77   "really gave us a chance to discuss": Ibid., p. 217.

77   "We were Ivy League, white, middle class": Marks, *Search for the "Manchurian Candidate,"* p. 98.

77   She shared many of his interests: Valentine, "Sex, Drugs and the CIA."

77   In 1952 the Whites hosted a Thanksgiving dinner party: Albarelli, *Terrible Mistake*, p. 240.

78   "Gottlieb proposes I be a CIA consultant": Jacobs, "Diaries"; Marks, *Search for the "Manchurian Candidate,"* p. 96.

78   "A couple of crew-cut, pipe-smoking punks": Ibid., p. 97.

78   "CIA—got final clearance": Jacobs, "Diaries."

79   "He posed alternately as a merchant seaman": Valentine, "Sex, Drugs and the CIA."

79   "I was angry at George for that": Ibid.

79   Episodes like these were kept quiet: Ibid.

79   "mostly rich boys, trust fund snobs": Albarelli, *Terrible Mistake*, p. 98.

80   "A confidential informant of this office": Internet Archive, "Full Text of George Hunter White," https://archive.org/stream/GeorgeHunterWhite/FBI_white-george1_djvu.txt.

80   White had taken up leatherworking: Albarelli, *Terrible Mistake*, p. 413.

80   Gottlieb taught him to dance a jig: Marks, *Search for the "Manchurian Candidate,"* p. 99.

80   "That period, up until about 1954": Author's interview with retired CIA officer "BD."

81   "You can look around the whole circle of the world": "John Foster Dulles Interview: U.S. Secretary of State under Dwight D. Eisenhower (1952)," YouTube video, 12:16, posted by the Film Archives, May 23, 2012, https://www.youtube.com/watch?v=7EJZdikc6OA.

82   He sent the chief of his Tehran station: James Risen, "Secrets of History: The CIA in Iran, a Special Report," *New York Times*, April 16, 2000.

82 Worthwhile results . . . "could not be obtained": Albarelli, *Terrible Mistake*, pp. 365–66.

83 "SOD developed darts coated with biological agents": Redfern, *Secret History*, p. 158; U.S. Senate, *Final Report of the Select Committee to Study Governmental Operations with Respect to Intelligence Activities, Book I: Foreign and Military Intelligence* (Washington, DC: Government Printing Office, 1976), p. 361, https://www.maryferrell.org/showDoc.html?docId=1157&relPageId=369; U.S. Senate, *Joint Hearing before the Select Committee on Intelligence and the Subcommittee on Health and Scientific Research of the Committee on Human Resources: Project MK-ULTRA, the CIA's Program of Research on Behavioral Modification* (Washington, DC: Government Printing Office, 1977), p. 389.

83 Americans should have been able to celebrate: Lorraine Boissoneault, "The True Story of Brainwashing and How It Shaped America," *Smithsonian .com*, May 22, 2017, https://www.smithsonianmag.com/history/true-story -brainwashing-and-how-it-shaped-america-180963400/; Marks, *Search for the "Manchurian Candidate,"* p. 134; Thomas, *Journey into Madness*, p. 157; Charles S. Young, "Missing Action: POW Films, Brainwashing and the Korean War, 1954–1968," *Historical Journal of Film, Radio and Television* 18, no. 1, 1998, https://www.tandfonline.com/doi/abs/10.1080/01439689800260021.

83 "The most-used germ bomb was a 500-pounder": Thomas, *Secrets and Lies*, p. 59.

84 In it, two "acknowledged independent experts": Ibid., p. 85.

84 "shifty-eyed and groveling": "Korea: The Sorriest Bunch," *Newsweek*, February 8, 1954.

84 COMMUNIST BRAINWASHING—ARE WE PREPARED?: *New Republic*, June 8, 1953.

84 "Interrogations of the individuals who had come out of North Korea": Ross, *CIA Doctors*, p. 35.

85 "There is ample evidence in the reports": Michael Otterman, *American Torture: From the Cold War to Abu Ghraib and Beyond* (London: Pluto, 2007), p. 21.

85 "[It] is awfully hard in this day and age": Ibid., p. 22.

86 Other early "subprojects" were aimed at studying: Ross, *CIA Doctors*, p. 60.

86 "hypnotize a man—without his knowledge": Bowart, *Operation Mind Control*, p. 59; McCoy, *Question of Torture*, p. 24.

86 After MK-ULTRA was launched, Estabrooks wrote a memo: Ross, *CIA Doctors*, pp. 152–53.

87 In 1953, Morse Allen, who also believed fervently: Streatfeild, *Brainwash*, p. 160.

87 This contradicted what many scientists believed: Albarelli, *Terrible Mistake*, p. 270.

87 One of his first ventures was MK-ULTRA Subproject 5: Ross, *CIA Doctors*, pp. 63–66.

88 West was researching ways to create: Ibid., pp. 106–17, 289.

6. Any Effort to Tamper with This Project, MK-ULTRA, Is Not Permitted

89   A birdcage disappears into thin air: John Mulholland, *John Mulholland's Book of Magic* (New York: Charles Scribner's Sons, 1963), pp. 29–57.

89   His circle of friends and admirers: Ben Robinson, *The Magician: John Mulholland's Secret Life* (Lybrary.com: 2008), p. 53.

89   His library on these and related subjects: Michael Edwards, "The Sphinx and the Spy: The Clandestine World of John Mulholland," *Genii: The Conjurer's Magazine*, April 2001.

89   After his death: Robinson, *Magician*, pp. 202–3.

89   When not writing or performing: Tatiana Kontou, *The Ashgate Research Companion to Nineteenth-century Spiritualism and the Occult* (New York: Routledge, 2012), p. 257; Robinson, *Magician*, p. 54.

90   On April 13, 1953—the day MK-ULTRA: Robinson, *Magician*, p. 96.

90   "the psychology of deception": Ibid., p. 77.

90   "John was an American and he loved his country": Ibid., p. 85.

90   "He said yes because his government asked him to": Edwards, "Sphinx and the Spy."

90   "Our interest was in sleight-of-hand practices": Albarelli, *Terrible Mistake*, p. 271.

91   "in the form of a concise manual": Edwards, "Sphinx and the Spy."

91   One item in Mulholland's personal background: Robinson, *Magician*, pp. 62–63.

91   Few at the CIA were that open-minded: Albarelli, *Terrible Mistake*, p. 253.

91   The letterhead said "Chemrophyl Associates": Robinson, *Magician*, pp. 88–92.

92   Mulholland was asked to sign a pledge: Ibid., pp. 98–99.

92   "Dear Sherman": Edwards, "Sphinx and Spy."

93   "The purpose of this paper is to instruct the reader": Ibid.

93   It was published with an apt title: Ki Mae Heussner, "Secret CIA 'Magic' Manual Reveals Cold War Spy Tricks," *ABC News*, December 4, 2009, https://abcnews.go.com/Technology/secret-cia-magic-manual-reveals-cold-war-spy/story?id=9229248; Noah Shachtman, "CIA's Lost Magic Manual Resurfaces," *Wired*, November 24, 2009; Robert Wallace and Keith Melton, eds., *The Official CIA Manual of Trickery and Deception* (New York: William Morrow, 2010).

93   "The fact that he was asked to contemplate such things": Wallace and Melton, eds., *Official CIA Manual of Trickery and Deception*, p. xiii.

94   Early in 1953 he wrote to ask: Albarelli, *Terrible Mistake*, p. 312.

94   Carefully observing bureaucratic protocol: Ibid., pp. 311–12.

95   "The deal was pretty simple": Streatfeild, *Brainwash*, p. 66.

95   Isbell's MK-ULTRA contracts included: Central Intelligence Agency, "MKULTRA Briefing Book: Containing Brief Summaries of Each of the 149 MKULTRA Subprojects," January 1, 1976, https://ia600206.us.archive.org/31/items/MKULTRABriefingBookListOfSubprojectsWithBriefDescriptions

January1976/MKULTRA%20Briefing%20Book%20-%20List%20of%20sub projects%20with%20brief%20descriptions%20-%20January%201976.pdf; Ross, *CIA Doctors*, pp. 291, 296.

95 One of his articles refers to a volunteer: Harris Isbell et al., "Studies on Lysergic Acid Diethylamide (LSD-25): Effects in Former Morphine Addicts and Development of Tolerance During Chronic Intoxication," *Archives of Neurology and Psychiatry*, November 1956, https://jamanetwork.com/journals /archneurpsyc/article-abstract/652297.

95 "I feel sure you will be interested": Albarelli, *Terrible Mistake*, p. 312.

95 A month later Isbell provided an update: Ibid., pp. 313–14.

96 Sometimes he brought Frank Olson: Ibid., p. 311.

96 "What Harris Isbell did to my father": William Henry Wall, *From Healing to Hell* (Montgomery, AL: NewSouth, 2011), p. 186.

96 "I have 7 patients who have been taking the drug": Streatfeild, *Brainwash*, p. 67.

96 "It was the worst shit I ever had": Marks, *Search for the "Manchurian Candidate,"* pp. 68–69.

97 The most enthusiastic of these doctors: CIA, "MKUKTRA Briefing Book," https://archive.org/stream/DOC_0000190090/DOC_0000190090_djvu.txt.

97 "epileptic-type seizures": Albarelli, *Terrible Mistake*, p. 235.

97 "produced a model psychosis": Ibid., pp. 303–4.

97 "We learned a lot from the Atlanta experiments": Ibid., p. 302.

97 That conclusion is richly confirmed: Dick Lehr and Gerard O'Neill, *Whitey: The Life of America's Most Notorious Mob Boss* (New York: Broadway, 2013), pp. 102–22; Wolfe, "10 Real Victims."

98 In a notebook that he wrote: Kathy Curran, "Whitey Bulger's Notebook Chronicles LSD Prison Testing," WBZ-TV, July 7, 2011, https://boston .cbslocal.com/2011/07/07/i-team-whitey-bulger-volunteered-for-lsd-testing -while-in-prison-in-1950s/.

98 "In 1957, while a prisoner": James "Whitey" Bulger, "Whitey Bulger: I Was a Guinea Pig for CIA Drug Experiments," *Oxy*, May 9, 2017, https:// www.ozy.com/true-story/whitey-bulger-i-was-a-guinea-pig-for-cia-drug -experiments/76409.

99 His first assignment, which Gottlieb called Subproject 2: Albarelli, *Terrible Mistake*, pp. 283–84; CIA, "MKULTRA Briefing Book"; Marks, *Search for the "Manchurian Candidate,"* p. 215; Ross, *CIA Doctors*, p. 286.

99 Hyde had a unique credential: Marks, *Search for the "Manchurian Candidate,"* p. 180; Ryan H. Walsh, *Astral Weeks: A Secret History of 1968* (New York: Penguin, 2018), p. 191.

99 Colleagues considered him: Albarelli, *Terrible Mistake*, p. 299.

99 As soon as the CIA began funding LSD research: Walsh, *Astral Weeks*, p. 192.

99 Each was paid $15 to drink: Albarelli, *Terrible Mistake*, p. 299.

100   "none of those involved in the experiments": Walsh, *Astral Weeks*, p. 192.

100   Gottlieb's assignments to him were remarkably broad: Central Intelligence Agency, "List of MKULTRA Subprojects," https://www.illuminatirex.com/list-of-mkultra-subprojects/.

100   "wild and crazy": Albarelli, *Terrible Mistake*, p. 286.

100   In mid-1953 Gottlieb gave Abramson $85,000: Marks, *Search for the "Manchurian Candidate,"* p. 66.

100   More disturbing, he developed a special curiosity: Albarelli, *Terrible Mistake*, p. 285.

101   "It was done with great secrecy": Marks, *Search for the "Manchurian Candidate,"* p. 136.

101   "Within the agency, Dr. Gottlieb": Thomas, *Journey into Madness*, p. 237.

102   "I am impatient when I hear people equate": Margaret Gottlieb, "Autobiographical Essays."

102   To reinforce that mystique: Albarelli, *Terrible Mistake*, p. 103.

102   "Don't you know how foreign diplomats live in Moscow?": George Kennan, *Encounters with Kennan: The Great Debate* (New York: Routledge, 1979), p. 42.

102   Soviet leaders could not abide: George F. Kennan, *Memoirs, 1925–1950* (New York: Pantheon, 1967), pp. 145–67.

103   Kennan told friends in the State Department: Walter L. Hixon, *George F. Kennan: Cold War Iconoclast* (New York: Columbia University Press, 1991), p. 128.

103   Inside the CIA, a darker theory emerged: Albarelli, *Terrible Mistake*, p. 104; CIA, "Interview with Richard Helms."

103   Allen Dulles was a member: Streatfeild, *Brainwash*, p. 23.

104   The number of people who knew even its general outlines: Albarelli, *Terrible Mistake*, p. 91; McCoy, *Question of Torture*, p. 28.

104   "Knowledge was a danger": Don DeLillo, *Libra* (New York: Penguin, 1991), p. 21.

105   "Sometime during the fall of 1953": Albarelli, *Terrible Mistake*, pp. 176–77.

106   "Some individuals at the Agency": Streatfeild, *Brainwash*, pp. 223–24.

106   "There is nothing such as a witting P-1 interrogation": U.S. District Court 2nd Circuit, "Deposition of Sidney Gottlieb," September 19, 1995, p. 195.

106   "Sid got back from Manilla": Margaret Gottlieb, "Autobiographical Essays."

7. Fell or Jumped

108   Glass shattered high above Seventh Avenue: Albarelli, *Terrible Mistake*, pp. 17–35; Bob Coen and Eric Nadler, *Dead Silence* (Berkeley: Counterpoint, 2009), pp. 83–102; Mary A. Fischer, "The Man Who Knew Too Much," *Gentleman's Quarterly*, January 2000, http://stevenwarranresearch.blogspot.com/2014/10/january-2000-gentlemans-quarterly-man.html; Michael Ignatieff, "Who Killed Frank Olson?," *New York Review of Books*, February 22, 2018, https://

www.nybooks.com/articles/2018/02/22/who-killed-frank-olson/; Regis, *Biology of Doom*, pp. 178–79; James Starrs and Katherine Ramsland, *A Voice for the Dead: A Forensic Investigator's Pursuit for Truth in the Grave* (New York: Putnam, 2005), pp. 105–55.

109   "In all my years in the hotel business": Albarelli, *Terrible Mistake*, p. 14.

109   "Well, he's gone," the caller had said: "Frank Olson," https://unsolved.com /gallery/frank-olson/.

110   He was in training there: Jacobsen, *Operation Paperclip*, p. 371; Frank Olson Project, "Frank Olson Is Recruited to Camp Detrick," https://frankolsonproject .org/timeline/.

111   "Just as we speculated about the atom bomb project": Albarelli, *Terrible Mistake*, p. 41.

111   Olson was discharged from the army in 1944: Ibid., p. 75.

111   He co-authored a 220-page study: Ibid., pp. 55–56.

111   In 1949 he was one of several scientists: Ibid., p. 73.

111   He regularly traveled to Fort Terry: Ibid., p. 75.

112   Olson learned of it: Ibid., p. 88.

112   His job description was vague but tantalizing: Ibid., p. 60.

112   "the airborne distribution of biological germs": Thomas, *Journey into Madness*, p. 241.

112   "He'd come to work in the morning": Author's interview with Eric Olson, 2018.

112   "In CIA safe-houses in Germany": Richard Belzer and David Wayne, *Dead Wrong: Straight Facts on the Country's Most Controversial Coverups* (New York: Skyhorse, 2012), pp. 7–8.

113   It was headlined: "Deep Creek Rendezvous," https://frankolsonproject.org /staging01/wp-content/uploads/2018/01/deep-creek-memo-1.jpg.

113   Lashbrook . . . produced a bottle of Cointreau: Albarelli, *Terrible Mistake*, pp. 28, 259–60; Regis, *Biology of Doom*, pp. 153–54.

114   "boisterous and laughing": Albarelli, *Terrible Mistake*, p. 28.

114   "I've made a terrible mistake": Author's interview with Eric Olson, 2018.

114   "I think what happened was that at the Deep Creek meeting": Ibid.

115   "I think we made a poor choice of movie": Ibid.

115   "the most frightening experience": Corey Ransom, "Paper on the Death of Frank Olson," Seminar on American History since 1865, University of Delaware, fall semester 1999, part 6, pp. 5–6.

115   "He appeared to be agitated": Albarelli, *Terrible Mistake*, p. 108; Regis, *Biology of Doom*, p. 158.

115   "tighter than tight": Albarelli, *Terrible Mistake*, p. 59.

116   He had repeatedly visited Germany: Ibid., pp. 78, 681.

116   He was one of several Special Operations Division scientists: Ibid., pp. 350–57; Loïc Chauvin, "En 1951, un village français a-t-il été arrosé de LSD par la CIA ?," *Rue 89*, March 8, 2010, https://www.nouvelobs.com/rue89/rue89-nos -vies-connectees/20100308.RUE5429/en-1951-un-village-francais-a-t-il-ete

-arrose-de-lsd-par-la-cia.html; Mike Thomson, "Pont-Saint-Esprit Poisoning: Did the CIA Spread LSD?," *BBC News*, August 23, 2010, https://www.bbc.com/news/world-10996838; TootlaFrance, "The Idyllic French Village That Went Insane," July 29, 2014, http://www.tootlafrance.ie/features/the-idyllic-french-village-that-went-insane.

116   "He was very, very open": Belzer and Wayne, *Dead Wrong*, p. 7.

116   On May 6 a volunteer subject: Anthony Barnett, "Final Agony of RAF Volunteer Killed by Sarin—in Britain," *Guardian*, September 28, 2003, https://www.theguardian.com/uk/2003/sep/28/military.antonybarnett; Rob Evans, "The Past Porton Down Can't Hide," *Guardian*, May 6, 2004, https://www.theguardian.com/science/2004/may/06/science.research.

116   A month later Olson was back in Germany: Thomas, *Secrets and Lies*, p. 155.

116   according to records that were later declassified: *Deckname Artischocke* (film).

116   "visited a CIA 'safe house' near Stuttgart": Gordon Tomas, "US Vice President Dick Cheney and Secretary of Defense Donald Rumsfeld Linked to 'Murder of CIA Scientist,'" *Rence.com*, June 25, 2004, https://rense.com/general54/ewerwopr.htm.

117   After stops in Scandinavia and Paris: Albarelli, "Mysterious Death"; Frank Olson Project, "Frank Olson Travels to Berlin," https://frankolsonproject.org/timeline/; *Deckname Artischocke* (film).

117   Immediately after their meeting, Sargant wrote a report: Thomas, *Secrets and Lies*, pp. 155–56.

117   Soon after Olson returned home: Belzer and Wayne, *Dead Wrong*, p. 8.

117   "just got involved in it": Albarelli, *Terrible Mistake*, p. 681.

117   "seemed to me to be confused": Ibid., p. 119.

117   "I've consented to take psychiatric care": Ibid., pp. 107–9.

118   He said he felt "all mixed up": Regis, *Biology of Doom*, p. 158.

118   Alice Olson had been told that Abramson was chosen: Albarelli, *Terrible Mistake*, p. 109.

119   Later that evening, Abramson joined them: Ibid., p. 111.

119   "You know, I feel a lot better": Regis, *Biology of Doom*, p. 159.

119   According to a later report: Michael Ignatieff, "What Did the CIA Do to His Father?," *New York Times*, April 1, 2001.

119   "became agitated when he thought": Albarelli, "Mysterious Death."

119   He reported that he had been wandering: Regis, *Biology of Doom*, p. 159.

120   "What's wrong?" Ruwet asked: Albarelli, *Terrible Mistake*, pp. 109–19.

120   The next morning, Abramson, Lashbrook, and Olson drove back to Manhattan: Marks, *Search for the "Manchurian Candidate,"* p. 87.

121   "Would you happen to know where Mr. Olson's wallet is?": Ibid., p. 23.

122   Immediately after Olson crashed: Albarelli, "Mysterious Death."

123   "Your father had an accident": Author's interview with Eric Olson.

123   "For years after that, I was completely stumped": "Frank Olson: Did a Government Scientist Jump to His Death from a New York Hotel? Or Was He Pushed?," https://unsolved.com/gallery/frank-olson/.

124   Later he was identified as James McCord: Albarelli, *Terrible Mistake*, pp. 86–92.

124   "Upon closing the door, Dr. Abramson and Lashbrook": Ibid., pp. 93–94.

125   The investigating police detective concluded: Regis, *Biology of Doom*, p. 180.

125   "A bacteriologist from the Army": "Army Bacteriologist Dies in Plunge from NY Hotel," *Frederick News-Post*, November 29, 1953, https://stevenwarran .blogspot.com/2014/10/.

125   "That was Bob Lashbrook and his boss": Albarelli, *Terrible Mistake*, p. 169.

125   Later that week, "Lashbrook and his boss": Ibid.

125   "It was probably to check me out": *ABC Closeup*, "Mission Mind Control," 1979, https://boingboing.net/2015/07/21/tv-documentary-about-mkultra.html.

126   "Conspiracy theories aside": Ransom, "Paper on the Death," part 9, p. 7.

126   The CIA's general counsel, Lawrence Houston: Albarelli, *Terrible Mistake*, pp. 145–46.

127   "I attempted to confirm what I had heard": Ibid., p. 139.

127   "There should be immediately established": Ibid., p. 143.

127   "Hand carry to Gibbons, Drum, and Gottlieb": Ibid., p. 144.

127   In the first two letters, Dulles said: Ibid.

128   "I have personally reviewed the files": Bowart, *Operation Mind Control*, p. 102.

8. Operation Midnight Climax

129   Senator Joseph McCarthy declared that "twenty years of treason": William H. Chafe, *The Unfinished Journey: America Since World War II* (Oxford: Oxford University Press, 2014), p. 127.

129   Congress passed the Communist Control Act: Richard Alan Schwartz, *The 1950s* (New York: Facts on File, 2002), p. 230.

130   On December 15 the ever vigilant Office of Security: Lee and Shlain, *Acid Dreams*, p. 29; Streatfeild, *Brainwash*, p. 68.

130   "Chemists of the Eli Lilly Company": Albarelli, *Terrible Mistake*, p. 153.

130   Assured of a steady supply: Marks, *Search for the "Manchurian Candidate,"* pp. 70–71; Ross, *CIA Doctors*, p. 59.

131   "Almost overnight . . . a whole new market": Lee and Shlain, *Acid Dreams*, p. 19.

131   Many conducted their CIA-sponsored "subprojects": Darla Jones, "MK-Ultra Involved Hospitals, Universities and Government Facilities," *Zodiac Killer Site*, November 10, 2012, http://www.zodiackillersite.com/viewtopic.php?f =102&t=2025; "List of Agencies, Institutions, and Individuals Involved in Mind Control," *Global Village*, http://grahamhancock.com/phorum/read .php?2,507101,507101; Colin Ross, *Bluebird: Deliberate Creation of Multiple Personality by Psychiatrists* (Richardson, TX: Manitou, 2000), p. 70. "Three types of institutions surfaced as part of the MKULTRA program:

academic institutions, legitimate business enterprises, and federal/state institutions. In the past several weeks, the General Counsel has notified 76 institutions of their involvement in Agency drug testing programs." Central Intelligence Agency, "Memorandum for Director of Central Intelligence," September 16, 1977, https://www.cia.gov/library/readingroom/docs/CIA -RDP79M00983A002200070014-3.pdf.

131   Some of these drug experiments required risking the health of participants: J. Samuel Walker, *Permissible Dose: A History of Radiation Protection in the Twentieth Century* (Berkeley: University of California Press, 2000), p. 17; Zareena Hussain, "MIT to Pay Victims $1.85 Million in Fernald Radiation Settlement," *Tech*, January 7, 1998, http://tech.mit.edu/V117/N65/bfernald .65n.html.

131   Soon after Dr. Robert Hyde began giving LSD: Marks, *Search for the "Manchurian Candidate,"* p. 64.

132   Early in 1955 he wrote a memo: Nick Redfern, *Secret History: Conspiracies from Ancient Aliens to the New World Order* (Canton Township, MI: Visible Ink, 2005), pp. 159–60; U.S. Senate, *Project MK-ULTRA*, p. 123.

133   "CIA investigators let their imaginations run": "Mind-Control Studies Had Origins in Trial of Mindszenty," *New York Times*, August 2, 1977.

133   "We did do LSD-related operations in the Far East": U.S. District Court 2nd Circuit, "Deposition of Sidney Gottlieb," September 20, 1995, pp. 249, 286.

133   In 1955, Gottlieb was drafted into a plot: Harvey Ferguson, *The Last Cavalryman: The Life of General Lucian Truscott, Jr.* (Norman: University of Oklahoma Press, 2015), p. 351; Joseph J. Trento, *The Secret History of the CIA* (New York: MJF, 2001), p. 194.

134   His biographer wrote that he was "outraged": H. Paul Jeffers, *Command of Honor: General Lucian Truscott's Path to Victory in World War II* (Open Library: NAL Hardcover, 2008), p. 293.

134   A platoon of U.S. Marines trudging along a mountain path: Abraham Lincoln Presidential Library Veterans Remember Oral History project, "An Interview with Allen M. Dulles," https://www2.illinois.gov/alplm/library/collections /oralhistory/VeteransRemember/koreanwar/Documents/DullesAllen /Dulles_All_4FNL.pdf.

135   He wrote several research proposals for Gottlieb: Marks, *Search for the "Manchurian Candidate,"* pp. 158–59.

135   "changes in behavior due to stress": CIA, "MKULTRA Briefing Book."

135   It emerged as the Society for the Investigation of Human Ecology: Thomas, *Secrets and Lies*, p. 72.

136   Soon after establishing this bogus foundation: Harvey Weinstein, *Father, Son and CIA: The Riveting Account of the Destruction of One Man's Life by Secret Mind Control Experiments Funded by the CIA* (Halifax: Goodread, 1990), p. 139.

136   "the areas of influencing human behavior": Albarelli, *Terrible Mistake*, p. 194.

136   One of the first "subprojects" the society commissioned: Marks, *Search for the "Manchurian Candidate,"* pp. 160–69.

137   "effects of radical isolation upon intellectual function": Alfred W. McCoy, *A Question of Torture: CIA Interrogation, from the Cold War to the War on Terror* (New York: Henry Holt / Owl Books, 2006), p. 35.

137   Student volunteers in these experiments: Ross, *CIA Doctors*, pp. 286–96.

137   The paper's principal author, Dr. James Hebb: Ibid., p. 36.

137   The Office of Security issued a memo telling interrogators: Central Intelligence Agency, "Memorandum for the Record," January 31, 1975, in Robert Clayton Buick, *Assassination* (Bloomington, IN: XLibris, 2012), p. 99.

137   In 1955 the CIA mind control enthusiast Morse Allen: Streatfeild, *Brainwash*, p. 117.

137   That experiment, he wrote in reply, suggested: McCoy, *A Question of Torture*, pp. 37–38.

137   In 1956 this remarkable physician, Ewen Cameron: Ibid., p. 43.

138   "If we can succeed in inventing means": Weinstein, *Father, Son and CIA*, p. 100.

138   "not only a loss of the space-time image": "MK-ULTRA Violence: How McGill Pioneered Psychological Torture," *McGill Daily*, September 6, 2012.

138   To cleanse unwanted thoughts from a patient's mind: Alliance for Human Research Protection, "Dr. Ewen Cameron Destroyed Minds at Allan Memorial Hospital in Montreal," http://ahrp.org/1950s-1960s-dr-ewen-cameron-destroyed-minds-at-allan-memorial-hospital-in-montreal/; McCoy, *Question of Torture*, p. 44; *McGill Daily*, September 12, 2012; Weinstein, *Father, Son and CIA*, pp. 108–30.

139   "the shock treatment turned the then-19-year-old honors student": Alliance for Human Research Protection, "Dr. Ewen Cameron," http://ahrp.org/1950s-1960s-dr-ewen-cameron-destroyed-minds-at-allan-memorial-hospital-in-montreal/.

139   "Although the patient was prepared": Sid Taylor, "A History of Secret CIA Mind Control Research," *Nexus*, April–May 1992, http://all.net/journal/deception/MKULTRA/www.profreedom.free4all.co.uk/skeletons_1.html.

139   Like many other MK-ULTRA collaborators: Streatfeild, *Brainwash*, p. 231.

139   Their contract specified what it would entail: McCoy, *A Question of Torture*, p. 43.

140   "approximately one hundred patients": Ibid., p. 44.

140   "Dr. G made clear my job was to ensure": Thomas, *Secrets and Lies*, p. 91.

140   A review conducted decades later: Alliance for Human Research Protection, "Dr. Ewen Cameron."

140   While the experiments were underway: Streatfeild, *Brainwash*, pp. 212–15; Thomas, *Secrets and Lies*, pp. 86–93.

141   "A chemist who is not a mystic": Roman Katzer, "Albert Hofmann und sein LSD: We eine Droge unser Weltbild revolutionierte," *Newsage* 2, 2012, https://www.newsage.de/2012/04/albert-hofmann-und-sein-lsd/.

141   White plunged into his new assignment: Darien Cavanaugh, "The CIA's Operation 'Midnight Climax' Was Exactly What It Sounded Like: Agents Lured

Johns to Brothels for Drug-Laced Encounters," *War Is Boring*, September 17, 2016, https://medium.com/war-is-boring/the-cias-operation-midnight -climax-was-exactly-what-it-sounded-like-fa63f84ad015; Channel 2 KTVU, *11 PM News* (Oakland), https://www.cia.gov/library/readingroom/docs/CIA -RDP88-01315R000200230006-5.pdf; Marks, *Search for the "Manchurian Candidate,"* pp. 101–4; U.S. Senate, *Joint Hearing*, p. 48; Jim Wood, "CIA Chief Deplores CIA Brothels," *San Francisco Examiner*, August 5, 1977.

142   "was so wired that if you spilled a glass of water": Streatfeild, *Brainwash*, p. 84.

142   "We had a comprehensive library on Chestnut Street": Behmke Reporting and Video Services, *Transcript of Consensually Monitored Conversation: Conversation Between Ike Feldman and Unidentified Speakers*, Investigation No. C00-3940 MHP, January 26, 2003, pp. 66–67.

142   among documents that the CIA later declassified: Black Vault, MKULTRA/ Mind Control Collection, pp. 42–179, http://documents.theblackvault.com /documents/mkultra/mkultra4/DOC_0000017440/DOC_0000017440 .pdf.

142   He listed more than a hundred: Ibid., pp. 42–144.

142   "Due to the highly unorthodox nature of these activities": Marks, *Search for the "Manchurian Candidate,"* p. 107.

143   "Before long, I get a call, this time from White": Richard Stratton, "Altered States of America," *Spin*, March 1994, http://mirror.macintosharchive.org/ca.cdn .preterhuman.net/texts/thought_and_writing/mind_control/MKULTRA /Stratton%20-%20Altered%20States%20of%20America%20(Spin%201994).pdf.

143   He ran a sting operation in which he posed as a pimp: Marks, *Search for the "Manchurian Candidate,"* p. 102; Stratton, "Altered States."

143   "One day, White calls me into his office": Stratton, "Altered States."

143   The next time Gottlieb was in San Francisco: Behmke Reporting Services, *Transcript of Consensually Monitored Conversation*, pp. 22–25.

144   Each time one of them brought a client: Alliance for Human Research Protection, "1953–1964: Operation Midnight Climax—CIA's Lurid Ventures into Sex, Hookers and LSD," http://ahrp.org/1953-1964-operation-midnight -climax-cias-lurid-ventures-into-sex-hookers-and-lsd/; Lee and Shlain, *Acid Dreams*, p. 32; Stratton, "Altered States."

144   "I would go to various bars": "Mind Control Murder," YouTube video, 45:12, posted by Capitan Black, March 18, 2016, https://www.youtube.com/watch?v =e2ot9noqQUw.

145   "We were interested in the combination of certain drugs with sex acts": "The LSD Chronicles: George Hunter White," http://thegipster.blogspot.com/2012 /12/the-lsd-chronicles-george-hunter-white_1757.html.

145   "certain individuals who covertly administered": Marks, *Search for the "Manchurian Candidate,"* p. 107.

145   "If we were scared enough of a drug": Ibid., p. 105.

145   "He always wanted to try everything himself": Stratton, "Altered States."

145   While his prostitutes and their clients had sex: Streatfeild, *Brainwash*, p. 84.

145   "If it was a girl, you put her tits in a drawer": Stratton, "Altered States."

146   "To find a prostitute who is willing to stay": "Mind Control Murder," You-Tube video, https://www.youtube.com/watch?v=e2ot9noqQUw.

146   a second safe house outside city limits: Jo Thomas, "CIA Sought to Spray Drug on Partygoers," New York Times, September 21, 1977.

146   Among the compounds he fabricated: Marks, Search for the "Manchurian Candidate," p. 107; U.S. Senate, Hearings before the Subcommittee on Health and Scientific Research of the Committee on Human Resources: Human Drug Testing by the CIA (Washington, DC: Government Printing Office, 1977), pp. 107–8.

146   Gottlieb wanted to see if he could dose a roomful of people: U.S. Senate, Human Drug Testing, pp. 101, 107–8; Jo Thomas, "CIA Sought to Spray Drug."

147   "When he wasn't operating a national security whorehouse": Lee and Shlain, Acid Dreams, p. 33.

147   At the end of 1957, a deputy federal marshal: Wolfe, "10 Real Victims."

148   "I didn't do any follow-up": U.S. District Court, District of California, San Francisco Division, Wayne A. Ritchie, Plaintiff, against United States of America, Defendant, Continued Videotaped Deposition of Ira Feldman, February 7, 2003, p. 428.

148   Ultimately a judge denied Ritchie's claim: U.S. District Court, District of California, San Francisco Division, Wayne Ritchie, Plaintiff-Appellant, v. United States of America et al., 451 F.3d 1019 (9th Cir. 2006), June 26, 2006, https://law.justia.com/cases/federal/appellate-courts/F3/451/1019/627287/.

148   "White was a son of a bitch": Stratton, "Altered States."

149   "He was cock crazy": U.S. District Court, Ritchie v. US, Continued Videotape Deposition of Ira Feldman, February 7, 2003, pp. 20, 26.

149   "Anytime that fuck came to San Francisco": Ibid., pp. 449–50.

149   "Gottlieb was humping his wife": Behmke Reporting and Video Services, Transcript of Consensually Monitored Conversation, Investigation No. C00-3940 MHP, pp. 21–25.

149   In a memo to his superiors, he proposed: Central Intelligence Agency, Subproject 35 MKULTRA, https://cryptome.org/mkultra-0005.htm.

151   "took it to President Eisenhower's special committee": Marks, Search for the "Manchurian Candidate," p. 217.

151   Little is known about the experiments: U.S. Senate, Joint Hearing, pp. 40, 120, 126–33.

151   Pressed for details two decades later: Ibid., p. 21.

151   He liked to tell a story about the time: Nicholas M. Horrock, "Destruction of LSD Data Laid to C.I.A. Aide in '73," New York Times, July 18, 1975.

151   "For the past four years": "Memorandum from Director of Central Intelligence Dulles to Secretary of Defense Wilson," https://history.state.gov/historicaldocuments/frus1950-55Intel/d244.

9. The Divine Mushroom

153   "Because of the very nature of the Central Intelligence Agency": *Congressional Quarterly*, "CIA 'Watchdog' Committee," in *CQ Almanac 1956*, http://library.cqpress.com/cqalmanac/cqal56-1349665.

153   Mansfield proposed to create a twelve-member congressional committee: *Congressional Record—Senate*, April 9, 1956, p. 5930.

154   The headline over one *Washington Star* article: Richard Fryklund, "CIA Leaders Are Cool to Watchdog Proposal," *Washington Star*, February 20, 1956.

154   "over my dead body": James Reston, "Washington: File and Forget?," *New York Times*, July 22, 1987.

154   "If there is one agency of the government": Central Intelligence Agency, "How Intelligence-Sharing with Congress Has Evolved," March 19, 2007, https://www.cia.gov/library/center-for-the-study-of-intelligence/csi-publications/books-and-monographs/sharing-secrets-with-lawmakers-congress-as-a-user-of-intelligence/1.htm#rft4.

155   "As a member of the Armed Services and Appropriations committees": *Congressional Record—Senate*, April 9, 1956, pp. 5923–24.

155   Senator Russell asserted in a speech: *Congressional Quarterly*, "CIA 'Watchdog' Committee."

155   "I am beginning to feel like David facing Goliath": *Congressional Record—Senate*, April 11, 1956, p. 5939.

155   "Let's get into the technology of assassinations": Albarelli, *Terrible Mistake*, p. 323.

156   Morse Allen learned of a Mexican plant: Marks, *Search for the "Manchurian Candidate,"* pp. 114–16; Streatfeild, *Brainwash*, pp. 77–78.

156   "Very early accounts of the ceremonies": Marks, *Search for the "Manchurian Candidate,"* p. 115.

156   "If I had thought I was participating": Ibid., p. 117.

157   On their honeymoon, Valentina shocked him: Jan Irvin, "R. Gordon Wasson: The Man, the Legend, the Myth," in John Rush, ed., *Entheogens and the Development of Culture: The Anthropology and Neurobiology of Ecstatic Experience* (Berkeley: North Atlantic, 2013), pp. 565–616.

157   led them to the home of a Mazatec woman: R. Gordon Wasson, "Seeking the Magic Mushroom," *Life*, June 10, 1957, http://www.imaginaria.org/wasson/life.htm.

157   "I am the woman who shepherds the immense": "María Sabina Documental," YouTube video, 1:20:47, posted by Soy Eus, July 16, 2016, https://www.youtube.com/watch?v=30s3ZCF7E3A.

157   "We were never more wide awake": Wasson, "Seeking the Magic Mushroom."

158   A deal was struck: Marks, *Search for the "Manchurian Candidate,"* p. 122; Streatfeild, *Brainwash*, pp. 80–81.

158   The mushrooms, he wrote afterward: Marks, *Search for the "Manchurian Candidate,"* p. 123.

158   Gottlieb cautioned, however, that research: Jay Stevens, *Storming Heaven: LSD and the American Dream* (New York: Harper and Row, 1987), p. 83.

158   The result was a seventeen-page spread: Wasson, "Seeking the Magic Mushroom."

159   "Throughout the 1950s and for some time beyond": H. P. Albarelli and Jeffrey Kaye, "Cries from the Past: Torture's Ugly Echoes," *Truthout*, May 23, 2010, https://truthout.org/articles/cries-from-the-past-tortures-ugly-echoes/.

160   A report on his MK-ULTRA work: Streatfeild, *Brainwash*, p. 86; *Orlikow v. United States*, U.S. District Court, September 12, 1988, p. 5, http://breggin.com/wp-content/uploads/2008/03/civilDOrlikowPretrialstatmnt.pdf.

160   "Gottlieb had wanted to apply his black arts": Joseph J. Trento, *The Secret History of the CIA* (New York: MJF, 2001), p. 195. "I went into training to go overseas in the spring of 1957. I actually went overseas—I think we departed these shores in about August or September," US District Court for the District of Columbia, "Deposition of Sidney Gottlieb," April 19, 1983, p. 77; "When did you return to Washington from overseas?" "In 1959," Ibid., p. 172; "What were your duties there?" "I am not at liberty to say that," Ibid., p. 15.

161   a Ukrainian exile leader . . . collapsed and died: Christopher Andrew, *The Sword and the Shield: The Mitrokhin Archive and the Secret History of the KGB* (New York: Basic Books, 1999), p. 362.

161   "When it came to spying": John le Carré, *The Secret Pilgrim* (New York: Ballantine, 2008), p. 132.

161   "without the knowledge of German authorities": Klaus Wiegrefe, "Das Geheimnis der Villa im Taunus," *Der Spiegel*, December 12, 2015, http://www.spiegel.de/spiegel/print/d-140390016.html.

161   "For two years he worked under cover": Gup, "Coldest Warrior."

162   "When he lectured to our group": Author's interview with retired CIA officer "BD."

164   Dictionaries define a "svengali": *Dictionary.com*, https://www.dictionary.com/browse/svengali; *Merriam-Webster*, https://twitter.com/merriamwebster/status/404308437888421888; *Oxford Living Dictionaries*, https://en.oxforddictionaries.com/definition/svengali.

164   "horrible improbabilities seem near and familiar": John Henry Ingram, *Elizabeth Barrett Browning* (CreateSpace, 2017), p. 144.

165   "Gaslighting is a form of persistent manipulation": Preston Ni, "8 Signs That Someone Is in a Relationship with a Gaslighter," *Psychology Today*, February 15, 2017.

166   more than two hundred articles on these subjects: Timothy Melley, *The Covert Sphere: Secrecy, Fiction, and the National Security State* (Ithaca: Cornell University Press, 2012), p. 148.

167   "a wild, vigorous, curiously readable mélange": Frederick Morton, "One Thing Led to Another," *New York Times Book Review*, April 26, 1959.

168   "Postwar conspiracy theory is deeply influenced": Timothy Melley, "Brainwashed! Conspiracy Theory and Ideology in the Postwar United States," *New*

German Critique 103 (Winter 2008), https://www.jstor.org/stable/27669224?seq=1#page_scan_tab_contents.

168   "By 1961, 1962, it was at least proven": U.S. Senate, *Joint Hearing*, p. 62.

10. Health Alteration Committee

170   Thirteen miles above the Ural Mountains: Christopher Moran, *Company Confessions: Secrets, Memoirs and the CIA* (New York: St. Martin's Press, 2015), pp. 89–90; Francis Gary Powers and Curt Gentry, *Operation Overflight: A Memoir of the U-2 Incident* (Lincoln, NE: Potomac, 2003), pp. 61–63; Villon Films, "Counterpoint: The U-2 Story," http://www.villonfilms.ca/counterpoint-the-u-2-story/.

170   "tortures and unknown horrors": Michael Dobbs, "Gary Powers Kept a Secret Diary with Him After He Was Captured by the Soviets," *Smithsonian*, October 15, 2015, https://www.smithsonianmag.com/smithsonian-institution/gary-powers-secret-diary-soviet-capture-180956939/.

171   One of those pilots, Carmine Vito: Norman Polmar, *Spyplane: The U-2 History Declassified* (Minneapolis: Zenith, 2001), pp. 103–4.

172   "Inside the dollar was what appeared to be": Powers and Gentry, *Operation Overflight*, p. 50.

173   Powers later testified: Dobbs, "Gary Powers Kept a Secret Diary."

173   "There was absolutely no—N-O, no": Howard Jones, *Crucible of Power: A History of American Foreign Relations from 1945* (Lanham, MD: Rowman and Littlefield, 2008), p. 94.

174   "To cover up the tracks of the crime": Union of Journalists of the USSR, "Aggressors Must Be Sent to the Pillory: The Truth about the Provocative Intrusion of the American Plane into the Air Space of the USSR" [CIA Translation], https://www.cia.gov/library/readingroom/docs/CIA-RDP80T00246A074400420001-9.pdf.

174   "If the assignments received by Powers": Powers and Gentry, *Operation Overflight*, p. 152.

174   "The following was established during the investigation of the pin": Francis Gary Powers, *The Trial of the U2: Exclusive Authorized Account of the Court Proceedings of the Case of Francis Gary Powers* (Whitefish, MT: Literary Licensing, 2011), p. 93; Powers and Gentry, *Operation Overflight*, p. 151.

175   "surpass by many times such known substances": Neil Edwards, "Saxitoxin: From Food Poisoning to Chemical Warfare," *The Chemical Laboratories* (University of Sussex at Brighton), http://www.bris.ac.uk/Depts/Chemistry/MOTM/stx/saxi1.htm; Vladyslav V. Goncharuk, *Drinking Water: Physics, Chemistry and Biology* (New York: Springer, 2014), p. 13.

175   "performed his duty in a very dangerous mission": Powers and Gentry, *Operation Overflight*, p. 296.

175   "Will announce himself as Joe from Paris": Loch Johnson, ed., *Strategic Intelligence: Understanding the Hidden Side of Government* (Westport, CT: Praeger, 2007), p. 209.

176   "He was a senior officer, a highly respected chemist": Larry Devlin, *Chief of Station, Congo: Fighting the Cold War in a Hot Zone* (New York: Public Affairs, 2007), p. 95.

176   During this period he was also part: Leonard Mosley, *Dulles* (New York: Dial, 1978), p. 459; David Wise, "The CIA, Licensed to Kill," *Los Angeles Times*, June 22, 2009.

176   At mid-morning on August 18, 1960: The President's Appointments, July–December, 1960, *President's Daily Appointment Schedules: Dwight D. Eisenhower: Records as President, 1953–1961*, Dwight D. Eisenhower Library.

176   "Embassy and station believe Congo experiencing": William H. Worger et al., *Africa and the West: A Documentary History*, vol. 2, *From Colonialism to Independence, 1875 to the Present* (New York: Oxford University Press, 2010), p. 136.

177   "There was stunned silence for about 15 seconds": Martin Kettle, "President 'Ordered Murder' of Congo Leader," *Guardian*, August 9, 2000.

177   "hunting good here when light is right": Johnson, *Strategic Intelligence*, p. 219.

177   "Gottlieb suggested that biological agents were perfect": Regis, *Biology of Doom*, p. 183.

178   "Jesus H. Christ!": Devlin, *Chief of Station*, p. 95.

178   "anything he could get to his mouth": U.S. Senate, *An Interim Report of the Select Committee to Study Governmental Operations with Respect to Intelligence Activities: Alleged Assassination Plots Involving Foreign Leaders* (Washington, DC: Government Printing Office, 1975), p. 25.

179   "normal traces found in people who die of certain diseases": Ibid.

179   "act as inside man": Ibid., p. 27.

179   "certain items of continuing usefulness": Ibid., p. 29.

179   On January 17, 1961, a squad of six Congolese: Brian Urquhart, "The Tragedy of Lumumba," *New York Review of Books*, October 4, 2001.

179   "my mind was racing": Devlin, *Station Chief*, pp. 96–97.

180   Roselli said he would prefer something "nice and clean": U.S. Senate, *Alleged Assassination Plots*, p. 80.

180   President Eisenhower ordered Castro "sawed off": Jim Rasenberger, *The Brilliant Disaster: JFK, Castro, and America's Doomed Invasion of Cuba's Bay of Pigs* (New York: Scribner, 2011), p. 83.

180   He did not use . . . "bad words": Central Intelligence Agency, "Memorandum for the Record, Subject: Report on Plots to Assassinate Fidel Castro," May 22, 1967, in Fabian Escalante (Introduction), *CIA Targets Fidel: The Secret Assassination Report* (Melbourne: Ocean, 2002), p. 34.

180   Since it would entail making poison: Thomas Powers, *The Man Who Kept the Secrets: Richard Helms and the CIA* (New York: Pocket, 1979), p. 184.

180   The first grew from Gottlieb's long fascination with LSD: U.S. Senate, *Alleged Assassination Plots*, p. 72.

181   Gottlieb's team then came up with: Ibid.

181   "did contaminate a full box of fifty cigars": Escalante, *CIA Targets Fidel*, p. 37.

181   "Sidney Gottlieb of TSD claims to remember": Ibid., p. 30.

182   The poisoned Cohiba cigars: Ibid., p. 37.

183   These included, according to a Senate investigation: U.S. Senate, *Alleged Assassination Plots*, p. 71.

183   Samuel Halpern, who served at the top level: Seymour Hersh, *The Dark Side of Camelot* (Boston: Back Bay, 1998), p. 268.

183   "There was a flat-out effort ordered by the White House": Central Intelligence Agency, "Summary of Facts: Investigation of CIA Involvement in Plans to Assassinate Foreign Leaders," p. 54, https://www.fordlibrarymuseum.gov/library/document/0005/7324009.pdf.

184   "None of the shells that might conceivably be found": Escalante, *CIA Targets Fidel*, p. 77.

184   "TSD bought a diving suit": Wallace et al., *Spycraft*, p. 275.

184   "four possible approaches were considered": Escalante, *CIA Targets Fidel*, p. 38.

185   During 1961 and 1962, intermediaries working for the CIA: Ibid., pp. 55–57.

185   "a pencil designed as a concealment device": Ibid., p. 40.

185   "a ballpoint pen which had a hypodermic needle inside": CIA, "Summary of Facts," p. 63.

185   "designed to be so fine": Wallace et al., *Spycraft*, p. 275.

185   "we had been operating a goddamn Murder Inc.": Evan Thomas, "The Real Cover-Up," *Newsweek*, November 21, 1993.

11. We Must Always Remember to Thank the CIA

186   "Capture green bug for future reference": Jefferson Morley, "Clare Boothe Luce's Acid Test," *Washington Post*, October 22, 1997.

186   "Harold A. Abramson of the Cold Spring Harbor Biological Laboratory": "Medicine: Artificial Psychoses," *Time*, December 19, 1955, http://content.time.com/time/subscriber/article/0,33009,861768-2,00.html.

187   LSD had become "all the rage": Morley, "Clare Boothe Luce's Acid Test."

187   got her LSD from Sidney Cohen: Online Archives of California, Sidney Cohen Collection, 1910–1987, https://oac.cdlib.org/findaid/ark:/13030/kt0d5nf1w1/entire_text/.

187   The first celebrity to speak publicly about LSD: Stevens, *Storming Heaven*, pp. 64–65; Geoffrey Wansell, *Haunted Idol: The Story of the Real Cary Grant* (New York: William Morrow, 1984), pp. 232–33.

187   "After my series came out": Bob Gaines, "LSD: Hollywood's Status Symbol Drug," *Cosmopolitan*, November 1963.

187   "Researchers were growing lax in controlling the drug": Steven J. Novak, "LSD before Leary: Sidney Cohen's Critique of 1950s Psychedelic Research," *Isis* 88, no. 1 (March 1997), https://www.jstor.org/stable/235827?seq=1#page_scan_tab_contents.

187   Among the students who took LSD: Lee and Shlain, *Acid Dreams*, pp. 119–26; Stevens, *Storming Heaven*, pp. 226–51; Wolfe, "10 Real Victims."

187   "turned into a twenty-four-hour psychedelic party": Lauren Marie Dickens, "Driving Further into the Counterculture: Ken Kesey On and Off the Bus in the 1960s," Master of Arts thesis, Middle Tennessee State University, 2015, http://jewlscholar.mtsu.edu/bitstream/handle/mtsu/4737/Dickens_mtsu_0170N_10481.pdf?sequence=1.

188   The music of the Grateful Dead: Steven Gimbel, ed., *The Grateful Dead and Philosophy: Getting High-Minded About Love and Haight* (Chicago: Open Court, 2007), pp. 52–54.

188   Hunter was another of the psychedelic voyagers: *Acid Dreams*, p. 143.

188   "He'd been making some money": Dennis McNally, *A Long Strange Trip: The Inside History of the Grateful Dead* (New York: Three Rivers Press, 2003), pp. 42–43.

188   Later he said the experiments seemed aimed: David Browne, "Robert Hunter on Grateful Dead's Early Days, Wild Tours, 'Sacred' Songs," *Rolling Stone*, March 9, 2015, https://www.rollingstone.com/music/music-news/robert-hunter-on-grateful-deads-early-days-wild-tours-sacred-songs-37978/.

189   "Sit back picture yourself swooping": McNally, *Long Strange Trip*, p. 42.

189   "Psychiatrists who had worked for the US Navy": John L. Potash, *Drugs as Weapons against Us: The CIA's Murderous Targeting of SDS, Panthers, Hendrix, Lennon, Cobain, Tupac, and Other Leftists* (Waterville, OR: Trine Day, 2015), pp. 58–59.

189   "He volunteered to become an experimental subject": Steve Silberman, "The Plot to Turn On the World: The Leary/Ginsberg Acid Conspiracy," *Neuro-Tribes*, April 21, 2011, https://blogs.plos.org/neurotribes/2011/04/21/the-plot-to-turn-on-the-world-the-learyginsberg-acid-conspiracy/.

189   During his first sessions, Ginsberg listened: Lee and Shlain, *Acid Dreams*, p. 59.

189   "healthy personal adventure": Don McNeill, "Why Leading Beatnik Poet Allen Ginsberg Was a Crusader for Legalizing LSD," *Alternet*, March 8, 2017, https://www.alternet.org/books/why-leading-beatnik-poet-allen-ginsberg-was-crusader-legalizing-lsd.

189   "It was above all and without question": "Playboy Interview: Timothy Leary," *Playboy*, September 1966, https://archive.org/details/playboylearyinte00playrich.

189   "the most dangerous man in America": Ari Shapiro, "Nixon's Manhunt for the High Priest of LSD in 'The Most Dangerous Man in America,'" NPR, January 5, 2018, https://www.npr.org/2018/01/05/575392333/nixons-manhunt-for-the-high-priest-of-lsd-in-the-most-dangerous-man-in-america.

190   "early use was among small groups of intellectuals": Marks, *Search for the "Manchurian Candidate,"* p. 129.

190   "The authors seem to have correctly analyzed": Ibid.

190   "The United States government was in a way responsible": Gimbel, *Grateful Dead and Philosophy*, p. 53.

190   "Am I, Allen Ginsberg, the product": Allen Ginsberg, *Poems All Over the Place* (Cherry Valley, NY: Cherry Valley Editions, 1978), p. 53.

190   "It was being done to make people insane": David Bianculli, "Ken Kesey on Misconceptions of the Counterculture," *NPR*, August 12, 2011, https://www .npr.org/templates/transcript/transcript.php?storyId=139259106.

190   "The LSD movement was started by the CIA": Lee and Shlain, *Acid Dreams*, p. xx.

190   "We must always remember to thank the CIA": "Playboy Interview: John Lennon," *Playboy*, January 1981, http://www.beatlesinterviews.org/dbjypb .int3.html.

191   Under a staircase in a faded Moscow apartment block: Jeremy Duns, *Dead Drop: The True Story of Oleg Penkovsky and the Cold War's Most Dangerous Operation* (London: Simon and Schuster, 2013), p. 169; Wallace et al., *Spycraft*, pp. 25–34.

191   Some post-mortems on Penkovsky's loss: Wallace et al., *Spycraft*, p. 37.

191   McCone began by shaking up the team: Marks, *Search for the "Manchurian Candidate,"* p. 210; Jeffrey T. Richelson, *The Wizards of Langley: Inside the CIA's Directorate of Science and Technology* (Boulder, CO: Westview, 2001), pp. 42–46.

192   "TSD leadership had mountains to climb": Wallace et al., *Spycraft*, p. 58.

192   The complex was spacious: U.S. Department of the Interior, "National Register of Historic Places Registration Form: E Street Complex (Office of Strategic Services and Central Intelligence Agency Headquarters)," p. 33, https://osssociety.org/pdfs/oss_nr_final_to_hpo.pdf.

192   He recognized that technology was becoming steadily more important: Wallace et al., *Spycraft*, p. 54.

193   Are Soviet diplomats in a Latin American country: Ibid., pp. 197–98.

193   Technical Services invented a "subminiature" camera: Ibid., pp. 89–90.

193   Does a spy say he will take risks: Eyeglasses displayed at International Spy Museum, Washington, DC, 2017.

194   "a special research study of handwriting analysis": Marks, *Search for the "Manchurian Candidate,"* pp. 182–83.

194   "Graphologists will categorize a number of handwriting samples": Central Intelligence Agency, "Memorandum for the Record," December 16, 1958, pp. 83–91, https://ia601202.us.archive.org/33/items/DOC_0000017485/DOC _0000017485.pdf.

194   "[Redacted] has conducted a detailed study": Sidney Gottlieb, "Memorandum for the Record," April 18, 1958, http://www.all.net/journal/deception /MKULTRA/64.224.212.103/Mkultra/subproject.html.

195   "As of 1960 no effective knockout pill": Central Intelligence Agency, *Report of Inspection of MKULTRA/TSD*, https://cryptome.org/mkultra-0003.htm.

195   "The possibility of creating a 'Manchurian Candidate'": Streatfeild, *Brainwash*, p. 169.

195   They managed to persuade McCone: Powers, *Man Who Kept the Secrets*, pp. 436–37.

196   Earman submitted his report: J. S. Earman, "Memorandum for Director of Central Intelligence," July 26, 1963, https://cryptome.org/mkultra-0003.htm.

198   "It has become increasingly obvious": Hilary Evans and Robert E. Bartholomew, *Outbreak!: The Encyclopedia of Extraordinary Social Behavior* (Charlottesville, VA: Anomalist, 2015), p. 411.

198   "I remember him saying that the Soviets were doing": Author's interview with retired CIA officer "HD."

12. Let This Die with Us

199   "The way we thought about our children's upbringing": Margaret Gottlieb, "Autobiographical Essays."

200   "I was a smart kid": Author's interview with "Elizabeth."

201   Silent CIA officers watched intently: Richelson, *Wizards of Langley*, p. 145; Wallace et al., *Spycraft*, pp. 200–201.

202   "Listen to those two guys": Charlotte Edwardes, "CIA Recruited Cat to Bug Russians," *Telegraph*, November 4, 2001, https://www.telegraph.co.uk/news/worldnews/northamerica/usa/1361462/CIA-recruited-cat-to-bug-Russians.html.

202   "Technically the audio system worked": Wallace et al., *Spycraft*, p. 201.

203   "The work done on this problem over the years": Edwardes, "CIA Recruited Cat."

203   "to develop a capability to manipulate human behavior": General Counsel of the Department of Defense, "Memorandum for the Secretary of Defense," September 20, 1977, http://www.unwittingvictim.com/DeclassifiedHumanExperimentationMKULTRAAndMore.pdf.

203   "that clubfooted Jew": Author's interview with retired CIA officer "LD."

204   Gottlieb hesitated: Regis, *Biology of Doom*, pp. 213–17.

204   Nathan Gordon later testified that he ordered this operation himself: Nicholas M. Horrock, "A Mass Poison, Linked to C.I.A., Reported Found at Army Base," *New York Times*, September 9, 1975; U.S. Senate, Select Committee to Study Governmental Operations with Respect to Intelligence Activities, *Unauthorized Storage of Toxic Agents* (Washington, DC: Government Printing Office, 1975), pp. 52–91, https://www.intelligence.senate.gov/sites/default/files/94intelligence_activities_I.pdf.

205   Gottlieb's men and women provided them: Wallace et al., *Spycraft*, pp. 74, 285, 393, 418.

205   Gottlieb's "concealment engineers" also provided: Christopher Moran, *Company Confessions: Secrets, Memoirs, and the CIA* (New York: St. Martin's Press, 2015), p. 125; Christopher Moran, "Turning Against the CIA: Whistleblowers During the 'Time of Troubles,'" *History: The Journal of the Historical Association*, March 27, 2015, https://onlinelibrary.wiley.com/doi/full/10.1111/1468-229X.12099; Wallace et al., *Spycraft*, pp. 195–96.

206   "Could *you* do that?": Wallace et al., *Spycraft*, p. 112.

206   "thirty to forty missions a day": Ibid., p. 295.

206   Engineers from Technical Services designed: Ibid., pp. 279–84.

206   "Throughout 1968, Dr. Gottlieb continued to preside": Thomas, *Journey into Madness*, pp. 399–400.

207   "The Israelis spent three months in 1968 trying to transform": Ronen Bergman, "How Arafat Eluded Israel's Assassination Machine," *New York Times Magazine*, January 28, 2018.

207   At lunchtime he snacked on food he brought from home: Thomas, *Secrets and Lies*, pp. 29, 34–35.

207   "It sounds hokey, but he had a touch": Wallace et al., *Spycraft*, p. 83.

208   Gottlieb's Technical Services Division had prepared false identity papers: Richelson, *Wizards of Langley*, p. 164; Harry Rositzke, *CIA's Secret Operations: Espionage, Counterespionage, and Covert Action* (Pleasantville, NY: Reader's Digest Press, 1977), pp. 220–21.

208   "Early in 1973, Dr. Gottlieb, then C/TSD": Central Intelligence Agency, "Memorandum for Director, OTS," August 19, 1975, https://www.cia.gov/library/readingroom/docs/DOC_0005444840.pdf.

209   "Over my stated objections, the MK-ULTRA files were destroyed": Bowart, *Operation Mind Control*, p. 108.

209   Around the same time, Gottlieb directed his secretary: Albarelli, *Terrible Mistake*, pp. 451–52; U.S. District Court 2nd Circuit, "Deposition of Sidney Gottlieb," September 22, 1995, p. 623; Marks, *Search for the "Manchurian Candidate,"* pp. 219–20; Powers, *Man Who Kept the Secrets*, p. 348.

209   "Schlesinger came on strong": William Colby with Peter Forbath, *Honorable Men: My Life in the CIA* (New York: Simon and Schuster, 1978), p. 329.

209   One afternoon in April, Schlesinger telephoned: Central Intelligence Agency History Staff Oral History Program, "Tough, Unconventional, and Effective: An Interview with Former DDCI John N. McMahon," https://www.cia.gov/library/readingroom/docs/DOC_0001407025.pdf; Richelson, *Wizards of Langley*, p. 164; U.S. Congress, Select Committee on Intelligence, *Nomination of John N. McMahon* (Washington, DC: Government Printing Office, 1982), p. 18; Wallace et al., *Spycraft*, p. 460.

211   Sidney Gottlieb retired from the CIA: U.S. Senate, *Hearings before the Subcommittee on Health and Scientific Research*, p. 208.

211   Before departing he was awarded one of the Agency's highest honors: Scott C. Monje, *The Central Intelligence Agency: A Documentary History* (Westport, CT: Greenwood, 2008), pp. 133–38.

13. Some of Our People Were Out of Control in Those Days

212   "I am determined that the law shall be respected": Monje, *Central Intelligence Agency*, p. 174.

213   "He was a Roman Catholic": Ranelagh, *Agency*, pp. 554, 557.

213   "In January 1973, Dr. Sidney Gottlieb": Albarelli, *Terrible Mistake*, p. 468.

214   "The Central Intelligence Agency, directly violating its charter": Seymour Hersh, "Huge CIA Operation Reported in US Against Antiwar Forces, Other Dissidents in Nixon Years," *New York Times*, December 22, 1974.

214   "Unnecessary disclosures would almost certainly result": Gerald R. Ford, *A Time to Heal: The Autobiography of Gerald Ford* (Harper and Row, 1979), p. 224.

215   "beset by continuing threats to our national security": Gerald R. Ford, "Statement Announcing Establishment of a Commission on CIA Activities within the United States," January 4, 1975, https://www.presidency.ucsb.edu /documents/announcing-establishment-commission-cia-activities-within -the-united-states.

215   "Frankly, we are in a mess": Jussi M. Hanhimaki and Odd Arne Westad, eds., *The Cold War: A History in Documents and Eyewitness Accounts* (Oxford: Oxford University Press, 2004), p. 477.

215   "A lot of dead cats will come out": White House, *Memorandum of Conversation*, January 4, 1975, https://www.fordlibrarymuseum.gov/library /document/0314/1552899.pdf.

216   "Bill, do you really have to present all this material": Colby, *Honorable Men*, p. 400.

216   The Rockefeller Commission's report: *Report to the President by the Commission on CIA Activities within the United States*, June 1975, p. 227, https:// www.fordlibrarymuseum.gov/library/document/0005/1561495.pdf.

217   One was headlined SUICIDE REVEALED: Thomas O'Toole, "Suicide Revealed," *Washington Post*, June 11, 1975.

217   "Have you seen today's *Washington Post*?": Albarelli, *Terrible Mistake*, p. 478.

217   "It was amazing": *Crazy Rulers of the World: Episode 3, The Psychic Foot-Soldiers* (film), https://www.youtube.com/watch?v=EQKTMjApnkI&t=1029s.

218   "This must be the most goddamn incurious family": *Wormwood* (film), https://www.netflix.com/title/80059446.

218   "Since 1953, we have struggled to understand": Eric Olson et al., "August 8, 2002, Press Conference, Family Statement on the Murder of Frank Olson," http://stevenwarran-backstage.blogspot.com/2014/11/august-8-2002-press -conference.html.

218   "to look at the whole matter": Albarelli, *Terrible Mistake*, p. 500.

218   "I don't really know what I should say": "Former CIA Agent Tells of Olson's Last Days," *News* (Frederick, MD), https://newspaperarchive.com/news-jul -18-1975-p-1/.

219   On the same day the *Post* ran that interview: Horrock, "Destruction of LSD Data."

219   "President Ford's chief of staff, Donald Rumsfeld": Maureen Farrell, "Dick Cheney, Donald Rumsfeld and the Manchurian Candidate," May 18, 2004, https://www.scribd.com/document/61308378/Dick-Cheney-Donald

-Rumsfeld-and-the-Manchurian-Candidate; Thomas, "US Vice President."

220   "With deepest sincerity and conviction": Edward C. Schmultz files, "Olson, Frank, Meeting with Olson's Family 7/22/75," Gerald Ford Presidential Library.

220   "Some of our people were out of control in those days": Albarelli, *Terrible Mistake*, p. 511.

220   He wrote that he was fifty-five years old: U.S. Civil Service Commission, "Security Investigation Data for Sensitive Position—Sidney Gottlieb," released by National Personnel Records Center, May 15, 2016.

220   Gottlieb spent seven months at the Drug Enforcement Administration: Horrock, "Destruction of LSD Data."

221   "Sid retired from government at an early age": Margaret Gottlieb, "Autobiographical Essays."

221   "I never wanted to go back to India": Ibid.

222   In a secluded glen a few miles from the White House: Lenzner, *The Investigator*, 2013), pp. 190–92.

224   "Look, Sid, the goal here is to keep you out of the newspapers": Ibid., p. 196.

224   "Because of his expertise in poisons": Ibid., pp. 194–95.

225   He produced a summary of its work: Redfern, *Secret History*, p. 158.

225   Colby testified that despite having spent: Nicholas M. Horrock, "Colby Describes CIA Poison Work," *New York Times*, September 17, 1975.

225   "General Patton on steroids": Richard Leiby, "Terry Lenzner, the Private Eye Who Has Seen It All, from Watergate to Microsoft," *Washington Post*, October 9, 2013.

225   "forty-odd hours of testimony": U.S. Senate, *Human Drug Testing*, p. 170.

225   The lithograph shows a hooded monk: "The Left Bower Smoking Tobacco Manufactured by Joseph Scheider, 100 Walker St., N.Y.," Pickryl, https://picryl.com/media/the-left-bower-smoking-tobacco-manufactured-by-joseph-scheider-100-walker-st.

225   "Joseph Scheider testified that he had 'two or three conversations'": U.S. Senate, *Alleged Assassination Plots*, pp. 20–24.

226   "Sid said he was charged with implementing a program": Lenzner, *The Investigator*, p. 198.

226   Questioning was proceeding methodically: Ibid., pp. 198–200.

227   "claimed to have forgotten virtually everything": Streatfeild, *Brainwash*, p. 65.

227   "When you were asked to kill Lumumba": Testimony of "Joseph Scheider," October 9, 1975, cited in Loch Johnson, *Strategic Intelligence: Covert Action; Behind the Veils of Secret Foreign Policy* (Westport, CT: Praeger, 2006), p. 208.

227   "My view of the job at the time": Ranelagh, *Agency*, p. 343.

228   "Sources said Dr. Sidney Gottlieb . . . returned here recently": Bill Richards, "Ex-CIA Aide Set to Talk of Drug File," *Washington Post*, September 2, 1975.

228   On October 14, 1975, FBI director Clarence Kelley: Federal Bureau of

Investigation, "Airtel to SAC, Alexandria," October 14, 1975, FBI Release #52-101074-13, http://documents.theblackvault.com/documents/fbifiles /historical/sidneygottlieb-FBI1.pdf.

229   The FBI tried one last gambit: Ibid.

229   Once the testimony was finished, he withdrew his offer: Federal Bureau of Investigation, "Doctor Sidney Gottlieb: Destruction of Government Property," November 3, 1975, FBI Release #52-2392-28; Federal Bureau of Investigation, "Doctor Sidney Gottlieb: Destruction of Government Property," January 14, 1976, FBI Release #52-101074-18, http://documents .theblackvault.com/documents/fbifiles/historical/sidneygottlieb-FBI1.pdf.

229   An internal FBI memo dated December 8: Federal Bureau of Investigation, "Airtel to Director, FBI," December 8, 1975, FBI Release #52-101074-16, http:// documents.theblackvault.com/documents/fbifiles/historical/sidneygottlieb -FBI1.pdf.

229   "The Criminal Division of the Department of Justice": Federal Bureau of Investigation, "Airtel to SAC, Alexandria," January 21, 1976, FBI Release #52-2392-84, http://documents.theblackvault.com/documents/fbifiles/historical /sidneygottlieb-FBI1.pdf.

229   "I argued that no, he is sufficiently high": Katherine A. Scott, ed., *Church Committee Members and Staff, 1975–1976, Oral History Interviews* (Washington, DC: U.S. Senate Historical Office, 2016), p. 462.

229   The Senate report, issued a few days later: U.S. Senate, *Alleged Assassination Plots*, p. 20.

229   "They declined to identify their client": Nicholas M. Horrock, "Bid to Cut Name in Report on C.I.A. Fails," *New York Times*, November 18, 1975.

14. I Feel Victimized

231   Over a fifteen-month period the Church Committee: Moran, *Company Confessions*, p. 108.

231   "Intelligence agencies have undermined the constitutional rights": U.S. Senate, "Select Committee to Study Governmental Operations with Respect to Intelligence Activities," https://www.senate.gov/artandhistory/history /common/investigations/ChurchCommittee.htm.

231   Tucked away in the committee's six-volume final report: U.S. Senate, *Final Report of the Select Committee to Study Government Operations with Respect to Intelligence Activities* (Washington, DC: Government Printing Office, 1976), pp. 39–97.

232   The report also summarized what the committee had discovered: Ibid., pp. 385–95.

233   "did a very diligent job of Sherlock Holmesing": U.S. Senate, *Human Drug Testing*, p. 124.

233   "Central Intelligence Agency documents released yesterday": John Jacobs,

"CIA Papers Detail Secret Experiments on Behavior Control," *Washington Post*, July 21, 1977.

233   MK-ULTRA, he began, was "an umbrella project": U.S. Senate, *Joint Hearing before the Select Committee on Intelligence and the Subcommittee on Health and Scientific Research*, pp. 8–15.

233   "Admiral Turner, this is an enormously distressing report": Ibid., pp. 15–16.

234   "The overall agent, Mr. Gottlieb, has indicated a fuzzy memory": Ibid., pp. 45–47.

234   "I don't see how we can fulfill our responsibility": Nicholas M. Horrock, "80 Institutions Used in CIA Mind Studies," *New York Times*, August 4, 1977.

235   "As part of the ongoing investigation": U.S. Senate, *Project MKULTRA*, p. 49.

235   "The word went out to the subcommittee staff": "Key Witness in C.I.A. Inquiry," *New York Times*, September 20, 1977.

235   "Because the drug testing programs involved": John Crewdson and Jo Thomas, "Ex-CIA Aide Asks Immunity to Testify," *New York Times*, September 7, 1977.

235   While Senate lawyers were weighing their options: Jacobs, "Diaries."

236   For a time he served as the fire marshal: Valentine, "Sex, Drugs and the CIA."

236   "I was a very minor missionary": U.S. Court of Appeals 2nd Circuit, Plaintiff's Confidential Exhibits, Volume III of III, p. E1383; Troy Hooper, "Operation Midnight Climax: How the CIA Dosed S.F. Citizens with LSD," *SFWeekly*, March 14, 2010.

236   "I insisted that the hearing be held in executive session": Lenzner, *The Investigator*, p. 201.

236   "the first public emergence of the distinguished-looking scientist": *New York Times*, "Key Witness."

237   "Dr. Sidney Gottlieb, a key but shadowy figure": Jo Thomas, "Key Figure Testifies in Private on C.I.A. Drug Tests," *New York Times*, September 22, 1977.

237   He began with a few sentences about MK-ULTRA: U.S. Senate, *Human Drug Testing*, pp. 170–71.

238   "I would like this committee to know": Ibid., p. 174.

238   "That was a traumatic period": Ibid., p. 185.

238   "The decision was, 'Don't change anything'?": Ibid., p. 188.

238   the conclusion he had reported to his CIA superiors: Ibid., p. 190.

239   He said that before leaving the CIA in 1973: Ibid., pp. 195–96.

239   "I feel victimized and appalled by the CIA's policy": Ibid., p. 173.

239   "There was a policy review of this project": Ibid., pp. 179–80.

240   "given the number of informal conversations that Eisenhower had": William L. d'Ambruoso, "The Persistence of Torture: Explaining Coercive Interrogation in America's Small Wars," doctoral dissertation, University of Washington, 2015, p. 114, https://digital.lib.washington.edu/researchworks/bitstream/handle/1773/37225/DAmbruoso_washington_0250E_16413.pdf?sequence=1.

240   "To answer the question precisely": U.S. Senate, *Human Drug Testing*, p. 204.

240   "remarkable skill in answering questions": Jeremiah O'Leary, "CIA's Drug Tests Are Defended in Cold War Context," *Washington Star*, September 22, 1977.

240   "There was tangible evidence that both the Soviets": U.S. Senate, *Human Drug Testing*, p. 170.

240   "There was no advance knowledge or protection": Ibid., p. 172.

241   "They steered us away": Author's interview with Burton Wides, 2018.

241   One prominent member of the Church Committee: Author's interview with Gary Hart, 2018.

242   Robert Lashbrook admitted that he had been Gottlieb's deputy: U.S. Senate, *Human Drug Testing*, p. 114.

242   "not the slightest idea": U.S. Senate, *Project MKULTRA*, p. 62.

242   "a rich variety of twits": Mary McGrory, "Getting Absurdity Out of the CIA," *Sarasota Herald-Tribune*, September 24, 1977.

15. If Gottlieb Is Found Guilty, It Would Be a Real First

243   "Damn!" Secretary of Defense Harold Brown shouted: Albarelli, *Terrible Mistake*, p. 552.

244   The intelligence historian Thomas Powers: Marks, *Search for the "Manchurian Candidate,"* pp. xvii–xviii.

244   "Only 33 years old when he took over the Chemical Division": Ibid., pp. 59–60.

245   "Unfortunately, the files available to date": Central Intelligence Agency, "Memorandum for Director of Central Intelligence," September 16, 1977, Approved for Release January 5, 2002.

245   Turner reported to Attorney General Griffin Bell: H. P. Albarelli, "Government-Linked 'Suicide' Probed," *WND*, September 8, 2002, https://www.wnd.com/2002/09/15128/amp/.

245   "Unwitting testing was performed": Albarelli, *Terrible Mistake*, p. 577.

245   "I didn't read that book": U.S. District Court 2nd Circuit, "Deposition of Sidney Gottlieb," September 22, 1995, p. 546.

246   "Sid is going to school in San Jose": Margaret Gottlieb, "Autobiographical Essays."

246   "The entire place was powered by the sun": Author's interview with retired CIA officer "LD."

246   He and his wife: Gup, "Coldest Warrior."

247   "The transformation was complete": Ibid.

247   "Since suburbia had taken over our former haunts": Margaret Gottlieb, "Autobiographical Essays."

248   "I have accumulated a number of honors": "David Gottlieb, 1911–1982," https://www.apsnet.org/publications/phytopathology/backissues/Documents/1983Articles/phyto73n01_32.pdf; P. D. Shaw and R. E. Ford, "David Gottlieb, 1911–1982," *Mycologia*, 75 (2), March–April 1983, https://www.jstor.org/stable/3792802?seq=1#page_scan_tab_contents.

248   issued a public "Statement on MK-ULTRA": Central Intelligence Agency, "Statement on MKULTRA," March 1, 1984, https://www.cia.gov/library /readingroom/docs/CIA-RDP86M00886R000800010039-4.pdf.

248   "Years later, a television reporter ambushed Gottlieb": Albarelli, "Mysterious Death"; *Crazy Rulers of the World* (film).

248   "I'm so happy you don't have a weapon": Author's interview with Eric Olson, 2018.

249   "what would happen if a scientist were taken prisoner": Albarelli, *Terrible Mistake*, p. 593.

249   "Your father and I were very much alike": Author's interview with Eric Olson.

249   "There was a tautness to him": Ibid.

249   "You say that you've been through a change of consciousness": Ibid.

249   "Look, if you don't believe me": Albarelli, *Terrible Mistake*, p. 594.

250   As the family was rising to leave: Ibid.

250   "I didn't have the confidence then in my skepticism": Ibid.

250   "I don't know if we're going to find out": Brian Mooar, "Digging for New Evidence," *Washington Post*, June 3, 1994.

250   "I would venture to say that this hematoma": National Geographic Channel, *CIA Secret Experiments* (film), https://www.youtube.com/watch?v=7Afjf2ZgGZE.

251   Starrs later wrote that it was "the most perplexing": Starrs and Ramsland, *Voice for the Dead*, p. 144.

252   It is unsigned: Thomas, *Secrets and Lies*, p. 17.

252   "The contrived accident is the most effective technique": Central Intelligence Agency, "A Study of Assassination," https://archive.org/details /CIAAStudyOfAssassination1953.

252   "The death of Frank Olson": "Family Statement on the Murder of Frank Olson," https://frankolsonproject.org/descent/; Stephanie Desmon, "In Reburial, Olsons Hope to Lay Saga of Father to Rest," *Baltimore Sun*, August 9, 2002.

252   Gottlieb appears dapper and white-haired: National Geographic Channel, *CIA Secret Experiments.*

253   it was Lashbrook: U.S. District Court for the District of Columbia, "Deposition of Sidney Gottlieb," April 19, 1983, p. 192: "Who put the LSD?" "Dr. Lashbrook." "Under your instructions?" "Yes, under my general instructions."

253   Gottlieb also makes extended appearances: *Wormwood* (film).

253   In 2017, Stephen Saracco: Science Channel, *CIA Drug Conspiracy* (film), https://www.sciencechannel.com/tv-shows/deadly-intelligence/full -episodes/cia-drug-conspiracy.

254   He charged that, at the Agency's direction: Thomas, *Journey into Madness*, pp. 257–63; Thomas, *Secrets and Lies*, pp. 185–90; Kristin Annable, "'She Went Away, Hoping to Get Better': Family Remembers Winnipeg Woman Put through CIA-Funded Brainwashing," *CBC News*, December 15, 2017, https://www.cbc.ca/news/canada/manitoba/mkultra-cia-velma-orlikow-1 .4449922; *Toronto Star*, May 25, 1990.

254   "I really can't remember that level of detail": U.S. District Court for the District of Columbia, "Deposition of Sidney Gottlieb," April 19, 1983, p. 10.

254   Did he conduct research into the effects: Ibid., p. 333.

254   "I may be having a mental block": Ibid., p. 213.

254   "My memory is hazy about that": Ibid., p. 70.

255   "I don't remember what Mr. Helms's job was": Ibid., p. 132.

255   "What Dr. Gottlieb has done is to show a reckless disregard": Ibid., p. 44.

255   "You are badgering the witness!": Ibid., p. 41.

255   "You are doing nothing but abusing this man": Ibid., p. 207.

255   "MK-ULTRA was a project to investigate": Ibid., p. 107.

255   He admitted that he had felt "somewhat abused": Ibid., p. 204.

255   "quite angry" when the CIA declassified: Ibid., p. 43.

255   "I was very upset that a human being had been killed": Ibid., p. 206.

255   Gottlieb admitted that some CIA officers had been "disinclined": U.S. District Court for the District of Columbia, "Deposition of Sidney Gottlieb," May 17, 1983, p. 263.

255   "I find it very difficult to answer that question": Ibid., p. 363.

255   "Did you ever consider you should adopt something analogous": U.S. District Court for the District of Columbia, "Deposition of Sidney Gottlieb," April 19, 1983, p. 149.

255   The CIA agreed to pay the Orlikow family: Helen L. McGonigle, "The Law and Mind Control: A Look at the Law and Government Mind Control through Five Cases," *Smart*, August 15, 1999, https://ritualabuse.us/mindcontrol/articles-books/the-law-and-mind-control-a-look-at-the-law-and-goverment-mind-control-through-five-cases/.

256   "The word Bluebird totally confuses me": U.S. District Court 2nd Circuit, "Deposition of Sidney Gottlieb," September 22, 1995, p. 648.

256   "Was he your deputy?": U.S. District Court 2nd Circuit, "Deposition of Sidney Gottlieb," September 21, 1995, p. 492.

256   He said he had never set foot in Paris: U.S. District Court 2nd Circuit, "Deposition of Sidney Gottlieb," September 22, 1995, p. 557.

256   "It never happened": Ibid., p. 610.

257   "Assuming that a jury would find": U.S. Court of Appeals 2nd Circuit, *Gloria Kronisch, Executrix of the Estate of Stanley Milton Glickman, Plaintiff-Appellant, v. United States of America, Sidney Gottlieb, in his individual and in his official capacities, Richard Helms, in his individual and in his official capacities, and John Does, unknown agents of the Central Intelligence Agency*, no. 97-6116, July 9, 1998, https://caselaw.findlaw.com/us-2nd-circuit/1364923.html.

257   "If Gottlieb is found guilty, it would be a real first": Sarah Foster, "Meet Sidney Gottlieb—CIA Dirty Trickster," *WND*, November 19, 1998, https://www.wnd.com/1998/11/3426/.

257   Gottlieb met one of his old college friends: Gup, "Coldest Warrior."

258   "Money is tight these days": Margaret Gottlieb, "Autobiographical Essays."

258   The journalist Seymour Hersh . . . visited Gottlieb: Author's interview with Seymour Hersh, 2018.

258   "A lot of Sid's later life was spent atoning": Gup, "Coldest Warrior."

258   "I felt that he was on a path of expiation": Ibid.

259   Gottlieb died on March 7, 1999: Weiner, "Sidney Gottlieb, 80, Dies."

259   "We were in a World War II mode": Ibid.

259   The CIA officer who had been Gottlieb's boss: Gup, "Coldest Warrior."

259   "He was unquestionably a patriot": Weiner, "Sidney Gottlieb, 80, Dies."

259   "Given his altruistic hobbies": Davidson, "Polarity of Sidney Gottlieb."

260   "Besides the case I was pursuing": Author's interview with Sidney Bender, 2018.

260   "He was concerned that he might never find": Albarelli, "Mysterious Death."

260   "gradually became depressed": Gup, "Coldest Warrior."

260   Margaret asked the funeral home not to disclose: Thomas, *Secrets and Lies*, p. 37.

260   "Gottlieb's two worlds came together": Gup, "Coldest Warrior."

261   "Anyone who knew Sid knew he was haunted": Regis, *Biology of Doom*, p. 231; Thomas, *Secrets and Lies*, p. 36.

261   With Gottlieb gone, the already sluggish pace: CIA, "Interview with Richard Helms."

261   "Helms was a liar": Author's interview with Frederick Schwarz, 2018.

261   "Those who had talked to Gottlieb in the past few years": St. Clair and Cockburn, "Pusher, Assassin and Pimp."

16. You Never Can Know What He Was

262   A seven-thousand-pound bull elephant: Streatfeild, *Brainwash*, p. 67; *Tusko: The Elephant Who Died on LSD* (film), https://www.youtube.com/watch?v=hy1fD-0ZwtU.

263   he set off an intense controversy: Philip J. Hilts, "Louis J. West, 74, Psychiatrist Who Studied Extremes, Dies," *New York Times*, January 9, 1999.

263   "I sleep with the lights on 24 hours a day": Kyle Scott Clauss, "Whitey Bulger Disciplined for Pleasuring Himself in Prison," *Boston*, February 26, 2016, https://www.bostonmagazine.com/news/2016/02/26/whitey-bulger-masturbating/.

264   One Boston lawyer with experience representing gangsters: "The Defense That Sank Whitey Bulger," *Daily Beast*, August 13, 2012, https://www.thedailybeast.com/the-defense-that-sank-whitey-bulger.

265   "It was the custom in those days": U.S. Senate, *Joint Hearings before the Subcommittee on Health of the Committee on Labor and Public Welfare and the Subcommittee on Administrative Practice and Procedure of the Committee on the Judiciary: Biomedical and Behavioral Research* (Washington, DC: Government Printing Office, 1975), pp. 253–54.

265   "Anyone closely associated with Harold": J. Falliers, "In Memoriam: Harold A. Abramson, M.D., 1899–1980," *Journal of Asthma*, vol. 18, no. 1 (1981), https://

www.tandfonline.com/doi/abs/10.3109/02770908109118319?journalCode
=ijas20.

265   "he was found dead under mysterious circumstances": Jim Lewis, "Val Orlikow, 73, Was Victim of CIA Brainwashing Tests," *Toronto Star*, May 25, 1990.

266   "To the patients of Dr. Ewen Cameron": "MK-ULTRA Violence," *McGill
Daily*.

266   A brief note in the local newspaper: "California—Ventura Country—
Miscellaneous Obituaries," www.genealogybuff.com/ucd/webbbs_config.pl
/noframes/read/1929.

266   The *New York Times* obituary said: Christopher Marquis, "Richard Helms,
Ex-C.I.A. Chief, Dies at 89," *New York Times*, October 24, 2002.

266   Yet like all CIA officers, he had signed a secrecy agreement: *United States of
America, Appellee, v. Victor L. Marchetti, Appellant*, 466 F.2d 1309 (4th Cir.
1972), September 11, 1972, https://law.justia.com/cases/federal/appellate
-courts/F2/466/1309/424716/.

267   "I must say Colby has done a startlingly good job": Moran, *Company Confessions*, pp. 151–52.

267   The best Helms could say about his old colleague: CIA, "Interview with Richard Helms."

267   "I see no way to handle it": Gup, "Coldest Warrior."

267   "Ah, poor Sid Gottlieb": Ibid.

267   "In retrospect, it is clear that Gottlieb's work lit a fuse": Ranelagh, *Agency*, p.
208.

268   "My sense is that the new oversight procedures": Loch Johnson, *Spy Watching: Intelligence Accountability in the United States* (New York: Oxford University Press, 2018), pp. 431–32.

268   "I talked to my wife quite a bit about it": U.S. District Court for the District of
Columbia, "Deposition of Sidney Gottlieb," April 19, 1983, p. 66.

268   "You never get it right": Gup, "Coldest Warrior."

268   "She was an enthusiastic folk dancer": "Margaret Gottlieb," *Rappahannock
News*, December 11, 2011, https://www.pressreader.com/usa/rappahannock
-news/20111208/282815008071703.

269   Peter wrote a book about African American history: Peter Gottlieb, *Making
Their Own Way: Southern Blacks' Migration to Pittsburgh, 1916–30* (Cham-
paign: University of Illinois Press, 1996).

269   In 2013, Peter and Penny . . . joined a group of volunteers: Chris Mertes, "Sun
Prairie Resident Returns from El Salvador Trip," *Sun Prairie Star*, February
18, 2013, http://www.hngnews.com/sun_prairie_star/community/features
/article_8b72347e-7a1e-11e2-b7fa-001a4bcf6878.html.

269   "The family decided some time ago": Author's interview with Gottlieb relative, 2018.

270   "a villa with dark secrets": "Die Geheimnisse der Villa Schuster," *Taunus-
Zeitung*, January 11, 2016.

270   "the worst things happened at Villa Schuster": Klaus Wiegrefe, "Das Geheimnis," *Der Spiegel*, December 12, 2015.

270   "In this house, the CIA did experiments": Author's interview with owner of Villa Schuster.

272   one character produces tablets: David Foster Wallace, *Infinite Jest* (New York: Back Bay, 2006), p. 212.

272   "Subjects whom the CIA questioned": Kathy Acker, *Empire of the Senseless* (New York: Grove, 2018), p. 142.

273   A remarkable Canadian artist: Ashifa Kassam, "The Toxic Legacy of Canada's Brainwashing Experiments," *Guardian*, May 3, 2018; Douglas Eklund et al., *Everything Is Connected: Art and Conspiracy* (New York: Metropolitan Museum of Art, 2018), pp. 146–62; Murray White, "Sarah Anne Johnson Takes Grim Trip into Family Past," *Toronto Star*, April 14, 2016.

274   It emerged in 1963: Central Intelligence Agency, *KUBARK Counter-Intelligence Interrogation*, July 1963, https://nsarchive2.gwu.edu/NSAEBB/NSAEBB27/docs/doc01.pdf.

275   In 1983, twenty years after the *KUBARK* manual was written: Central Intelligence Agency, *Human Resources Exploitation Manual*, 1963, https://nsarchive2.gwu.edu/NSAEBB/NSAEBB122/CIA%20Human%20Res%20Exploit%20A1-G11.pdf; McCoy, *Question of Torture*, pp. 88–96; McCoy, *Torture and Impunity*, pp. 27–29.

276   One CIA officer who trained Latin American interrogators: Peter Foster, "Torture Report: CIA Interrogations Chief Was Involved in Latin American Torture Camps," *Telegraph*, December 11, 2014.

276   "the gloves come off": National Commission on Terrorist Attacks upon the United States, "Testimony of Cofer Black," April 14, 2004, https://fas.org/irp/congress/2002_hr/092602black.html.

278   Some intelligence officers have argued: Marks, *Search for the "Manchurian Candidate,"* p. 30.

279   This brings into sharp relief: Jan Kott, *Shakespeare Our Contemporary* (New York: W. W. Norton, 1974), pp. 17, 33.

Acknowledgments

337   "The name Sidney Gottlieb is but an obscure footnote": Gup, "Coldest Warrior."

Bibliography

Agee, Philip. *Inside the Company: CIA Diary*. San Francisco: Stonehill, 1975.

Albarelli, H. P., Jr. *A Terrible Mistake: The Murder of Frank Olson and the CIA's Secret Cold War Experiments*. Walterville, OR: Trine Day, 2009.

Alibeck, Ken, and Stephen Handelman. *Biohazard: The Chilling True Story of the Largest Covert Biological Weapons Program in the World—Told from Inside by the Man Who Ran It*. New York: Random House, 2000.

Allen, Michael T. *The Business of Genocide: The SS, Slave Labor, and the Concentration Camps*. Chapel Hill: University of North Carolina Press, 2002.

Andrew, Christopher. *For the President's Eyes Only: Secret Intelligence and the American Presidency from Washington to Bush*. New York: HarperCollins, 1995.

———. *The Sword and the Shield: The Mitrokhin Archive and the Secret History of the KGB*. New York: Basic Books, 1999.

Andrews, George. *MKULTRA: The CIA's Top Secret Program in Human Experimentation and Behavior Modification*. Winston-Salem, NC: Healthnet, 2001.

Bain, Donald. *The Control of Candy Jones*. London: Futura, 1979.

Barenblatt, Daniel. *A Plague upon Humanity: The Hidden History of Japan's Biological Warfare Program*. New York: Harper Perennial, 2005.

———. *A Plague upon Humanity: The Secret Genocide of Axis Japan's Germ Warfare Operation*. New York: HarperCollins, 2004.

Barrett, David M. *The CIA and Congress: The Untold Story from Truman to Kennedy*. Lawrence: University of Kansas Press, 2005.

Bar-Zohar, Michael. *The Hunt for German Scientists*. New York: Avon, 1970.

Beck, Melvin C. *Secret Contenders: The Myth of Cold War Counterintelligence*. New York: Sheridan Square, 1984.

Belzer, Richard, and David Wayne. *Dead Wrong: Straight Facts on the Country's Most Controversial Cover-ups*. New York: Skyhorse, 2012.

Bergen-Cico, Dessa K. *War and Drugs: The Role of Military Conflict in the Development of Substance Abuse*. New York: Routledge, 2012.

Bissell, Richard M., et al. *Reflections of a Cold Warrior: From Yalta to the Bay of Pigs*. New Haven: Yale University Press, 1996.

Blome, Kurt. *Artzt im Kampf*. Leipzig: Johann Ambrosius Barth, 1942.

Bowart, William. *Operation Mind Control*. New York: Delacorte, 1977.

Bower, Tom. *The Paperclip Conspiracy: The Hunt for Nazi Scientists*. Boston: Little, Brown, 1987.

Brackman, Arnold C. *The Other Nuremberg: The Untold Story of the Tokyo War Crimes Trials*. New York: William Morrow, 1987.

Braden, William. *The Private Sea: LSD and the Search for God*. Chicago: Quadrangle, 1967.

Breitman, Richard, et al. *U.S. Intelligence and the Nazis*. New York: Cambridge University Press, 2005.

Brown, Anthony Cave. *Wild Bill Donovan: The Last Hero*. New York: Times Books, 1982.

Buick, Robert Clayton. *Assassination*. Bloomington, IN: XLibris, 2012.

Burgess, Frank. *The Cardinal on Trial*. Daventry, UK: Sword, 1949.

Carl, Leo D. *International Dictionary of Intelligence*. McLean, VA: International Defense Consultant Services, 1990.

Carroll, Michael Christopher. *Lab 257: The Disturbing Story of the Government's Secret Plum Island Germ Laboratory*. New York: William Morrow, 2004.

Chafe, William H. *The Unfinished Journey: America since World War II*. New York: Oxford University Press, 2014.

Clendenin, Lt. Col. Richard M. *Science and Technology at Fort Detrick, 1943–1968*. Frederick, MD: Fort Detrick, 1968.

Cockburn, Alexander, and Jeffrey St. Clair. *Whiteout: The CIA, Drugs, and the Press*. London: Verso, 1998.

Coen, Bob, and Eric Nadle. *Dead Silence*. Berkeley: Counterpoint, 2009.

Cohen, Sidney. *The Beyond Within: The LSD Story*. New York: Atheneum, 1967.

Colby, William, with Peter Forbath. *Honorable Men: My Life in the CIA*. New York: Simon and Schuster, 1978.

Cole, Leonard A. *Clouds of Secrecy: The Army's Germ Warfare Tests over Populated Areas*. Totowa, NJ: Rowman and Littlefield, 1988.

Collins, Anne. *In the Sleep Room*. Toronto: Key Porter, 1988.

Condon, Richard. *The Manchurian Candidate*. New York: Pocket Star, 1987.

Constantine, Alex. *Virtual Government: CIA Mind Control Experiments in America*. Venice, CA: Feral House, 1997.

Corera, Gordon. *The Art of Betrayal: The Secret History of MI-6*. New York: Pegasus, 2012.

Cornwell, John. *Hitler's Scientists: Science, War and the Devil's Pact*. New York: Penguin, 2004.

Corson, William R., with Susan B. Trento and Joseph John Trento. *Widows: Four*

American Spies, the Wives They Left Behind, and the KGB's Crippling of American Intelligence. New York: Crown, 1989.

Covert, Norman. *Cutting Edge: A History of Fort Detrick, Maryland, 1943–1993*. Fort Detrick, MD: Headquarters U.S. Army Garrison Public Affairs Office, 1993.

d'Ambruoso, William L. "The Persistence of Torture: Explaining Coercive Interrogation in America's Small Wars." Doctoral dissertation, University of Washington, 2015.

Davis, Brion David, ed. *The Fear of Conspiracy: Images of Un-American Subversion from the Revolution to the Present*. Ithaca: Cornell University Press, 1971.

Deichmann, Ute. *Biologists under Hitler*. Cambridge, MA: Harvard University Press, 1996.

DeLillo, Don. *Libra*. New York: Penguin, 1991.

Devine, Frank, with Vernon Loeb. *Good Hunting: An American Spymaster's Story*. New York: Farrar, Straus and Giroux / Sarah Crichton, 2014.

Devlin, Larry. *Chief of Station, Congo: Fighting the Cold War in a Hot Zone*. New York: Public Affairs, 2007.

Dickens, Lauren Marie. "Driving Further into the Counterculture: Ken Kesey On and Off the Bus in the 1960s." Master of Arts thesis, Middle Tennessee State University, 2015.

DuBois, Josiah E. *The Devil's Chemists: 24 Conspirators of the International Farben Cartel Who Manufacture Wars*. Boston: Beacon, 1952.

Dunne, Matthew W. *A Cold War State of Mind: Brainwashing and Postwar American Society*. Amherst: University of Massachusetts Press, 2003.

Duns, Jeremy. *Dead Drop: The True Story of Oleg Penkovsky and the Cold War's Most Dangerous Operation*. London: Simon and Schuster, 2013.

Eklund, Douglas, et al. *Everything Is Connected: Art and Conspiracy*. New York: Metropolitan Museum of Art, 2018.

Endicott, Stephen. *The United States and Biological Warfare: Secrets from the Early Cold War and Korea*. Bloomington: Indiana University Press, 1999.

Escalante, Fabian (introduction). *CIA Targets Fidel: The Secret Assassination Report*. Melbourne: Ocean Press, 2002.

Estabrooks, George. *Hypnotism*. New York: E. P. Dutton, 1943.

Estrada, Alvaro. *María Sabina: Her Life and Chants*. Santa Barbara: Ross-Erikson, 1981.

Evans, Hilary, and Robert E. Bartholomew, *Outbreak! The Encyclopedia of Extraordinary Social Behavior*. Charlottesville, VA: Anomalist Books, 2015.

Ferguson, Harvey. *The Last Cavalryman: The Life of General Lucian Truscott, Jr.* Norman: University of Oklahoma Press, 2015.

Fitch, Noel Riley. *Paris Café: The Select Crowd*. New York: Soft Skull Press, 2007.

Ford, Gerald R. *A Time to Heal: The Autobiography of Gerald Ford*. New York: Harper and Row, 1979.

Forte, Robert, ed. *Timothy Leary: Outside Looking In*. Rochester, VT: Park Street Press, 1999.

Frauenfelder, Mark. *The World's Worst: A Guide to the Most Disgusting, Hideous, Inept and Dangerous People, Places, and Things on Earth*. Vancouver, BC: Raincoast Books, 2005.

Frost, Michael, and Michael Gratton. *Spyworld: Inside the Canadian and American Intelligence Establishments*. Toronto: Doubleday, 1994.

Gilbride, Richard. *Matrix for Assassination: The JFK Conspiracy*. Bloomington, IN: Trafford, 2009.

Gillmor, Don. *I Swear by Apollo: Dr. Ewen Cameron and the CIA-Brainwashing Experiments*. Montreal: Eden Press, 1987.

Gold, Hal. *Unit 731 Testimony: Japan's Wartime Human Experimentation Program*. Clarendon, VT: Tuttle Publishing, 2004.

Goncharuk, Vladyslav V. *Drinking Water: Physics, Chemistry and Biology*. New York: Springer, 2014.

Grim, Ryan. *This Is Your Country on Drugs: The Secret History of Getting High in America*. Hoboken, NJ: Wiley, 2009.

Grose, Peter. *Gentleman Spy: The Life of Allen Dulles*. New York: Houghton Mifflin, 1994.

Guillemin, Jeanne. *Hidden Atrocities: Japanese Germ Warfare and American Obstruction of Justice at the Tokyo Trial*. New York: Columbia University Press, 2017.

Halberstam, David. *The Fifties*. New York: Random House, 1993.

Hanhimaki, Jussi M., and Odd Arne Westad, eds. *The Cold War: A History in Documents and Eyewitness Accounts*. Oxford: Oxford University Press, 2004.

Harris, Robert, and Jeremy Paxman. *A Higher Form of Killing: The Secret Story of Chemical and Biological Warfare*. New York: Chatto & Windus, 1982.

Harris, Sheldon H. *Factories of Death: Japanese Biological Warfare, 1932–45, and the American Cover-up*. New York: Routledge, 1994.

Heidenrich, Chris. *Frederick: Local and National Crossroads*. Mount Pleasant, SC: Arcadia Publishing, 2003.

Helms, Richard. *A Look over My Shoulder: A Life in the Central Intelligence Agency*. New York: Random House, 2003.

Hersh, Seymour M. *Chemical and Biological Warfare: America's Hidden Arsenal*. New York: Anchor Books, 1969.

———. *The Dark Side of Camelot*. Boston: Back Bay, 1998.

Hixon, Walter L. *George F. Kennan: Cold War Iconoclast*. New York: Columbia University Press, 1991.

Hofmann, Albert. *LSD: My Problem Child*. London: McGraw-Hill, 1983.

Hollington, Ken. *Wolves, Jackals, and Foxes: The Assassins Who Changed History*. New York: Thomas Dunne Books, 2008.

Hunt, Linda. *Secret Agenda: The United States Government, Nazi Scientists, and Project Paperclip, 1944–1990*. New York: St. Martin's Press, 1991.

Hunter, Edward. *Brain-washing in Red China: The Calculated Destruction of Men's Minds*. New York: Pyramid, 1951.

Jacobsen, Annie. *Operation Paperclip: The Secret Intelligence Program That Brought Nazi Scientists to America*. New York: Back Bay, 2014.

Janney, Peter, *Mary's Mosaic: The CIA Conspiracy to Murder John F. Kennedy, Mary Pinchot Meyer, and Their Vision for World Peace*. New York: Skyhorse, 2016.

Jeffers, H. Paul. *Command of Honor: General Lucian Truscott's Path to Victory in World War II*. Open Library: NAL Hardcover, 2008.

Johnson, Loch K. *A Season of Inquiry: Congress and Intelligence*. Chicago: Dorsey, 1988.

———. *Spy Watching: Intelligence Accountability in the United States.* New York: Oxford University Press, 2018.

———, ed. *Strategic Intelligence: Covert Action: Behind the Veils of Secret Foreign Policy.* Westport, CT: Praeger, 2006.

———, ed. *Strategic Intelligence: Understanding the Hidden Side of Government.* Westport, CT: Praeger, 2007.

Jones, Howard. *Crucible of Power: A History of American Foreign Relations from 1945.* Lanham, MD: Rowman and Littlefield, 2008.

Kennan, George F. *Memoirs 1925–1950.* New York: Pantheon, 1967.

———. *Encounters with Kennan: The Great Debate.* New York: Routledge, 1979.

Kessler, Pamela. *Undercover Washington: Where Famous Spies Lived, Worked and Loved.* Sterling, VA: Capital Books, 2005.

Kessler, Ronald. *Inside the CIA: Revealing the Secrets of the World's Most Powerful Spy Agency.* New York: Pocket Books, 1992.

Kingsolver, Barbara. *The Poisonwood Bible.* New York: Harper Perennial Modern Classics, 2008.

Kleps, Art. *Millbrook: The True Story of the Early Years of the Psychedelic Revolution.* Oakland: Bench Press, 1977.

Koch, Egmont R., and Michael Wech. *Deckname Artischocke: Die Geheimen Menschenversuche der CIA.* Munich: Bertelsmann, 2002.

Kontou, Tatiana. *The Ashgate Research Companion to Nineteenth-Century Spiritualism and the Occult.* New York: Routledge, 2012.

Kouzminov, Alexander. *Biological Espionage: Special Operation of the Soviet and Russian Foreign Intelligence Services in the West.* London: Greenhill, 2005.

Krishnan, Armin. *Military Neuroscience and the Coming Age of Neurowarfare.* Abingdon, UK: Routledge, 2018.

Kross, Peter. *American Conspiracy Files: The Stories We Were Never Told.* Kempton, IL: Adventures Unlimited, 2016.

Lasby, Clarence G. *Project Paperclip: German Scientists and the Cold War.* New York: Atheneum, 1971.

Lattin, Don. *The Harvard Psychedelic Club: How Timothy Leary, Ram Dass, Huston Smith, and Andrew Weil Killed the Fifties and Ushered in a New Age for America.* New York: HarperOne, 2010.

le Carré, John. *The Secret Pilgrim.* New York: Ballantine, 2008.

Lee, Martin A., and Bruce Shlain. *Acid Dreams: The Complete Social History of LSD: The CIA, the Sixties, and Beyond.* New York: Grove Press, 1985.

Lehr, Dick, and Gerard O'Neill. *Whitey: The Life of America's Most Notorious Mob Boss.* New York: Broadway, 2013.

Lenzner, Terry. *The Investigator: Fifty Years of Uncovering the Truth.* New York: Penguin Random House / Blue Rider Press, 2013.

Lichtblau, Eric. *The Nazis Next Door: How America Became a Safe Haven for Hitler's Men.* New York: Houghton Mifflin Harcourt, 2014.

Lifton, Robert J. *The Nazi Doctors: Medical Killing and the Psychology of Genocide.* New York: Basic Books, 1986.

Lipschutz, Ronnie D. *Cold War Fantasies: Film, Fiction, and Foreign Policy*. London: Rowman and Littlefield, 2001.

Lockwood, Jeffrey A. *Six-Legged Soldiers: Using Insects as Weapons of War*. New York: Oxford University Press, 2009.

Lovell, Stanley. *Of Spies and Stratagems*. London: Prentice-Hall, 1963.

Mailer, Norman. *Harlot's Ghost*. New York: Random House, 1992.

Marchetti, Victor, and John Marks. *The CIA and the Cult of Intelligence*. New York: Alfred A. Knopf, 1974.

Marks, John. *The Search for the "Manchurian Candidate": The CIA and Mind Control*. New York: W. W. Norton, 1978.

Martin, David C. *Wilderness of Mirrors: Intrigue, Deception, and the Secrets That Destroyed Two of the Cold War's Most Important Agents*. New York: Harper and Row, 1980.

McCoy, Alfred W. *A Question of Torture: CIA Interrogation, from the Cold War to the War on Terror*. New York: Henry Holt / Owl Books, 2006.

———. *Torture and Impunity: The U.S. Doctrine of Coercive Interrogation*. Madison: University of Wisconsin Press, 2012.

McDermott, Jeanne. *The Killing Winds: The Menace of Biological Warfare*. New York: Arbor, 1987.

McNally, Dennis. *A Long Strange Trip: The Inside History of the Grateful Dead*. New York: Three Rivers Press, 2003.

Meerloo, Joost A. M. *Rape of the Mind: The Psychology of Thought Control, Menticide, and Brainwashing*. Cleveland: World Publishing, 1956.

Melley, Timothy. *The Covert Sphere: Secrecy, Fiction, and the National Security State*. Ithaca: Cornell University Press, 2012.

———. *Empire of Conspiracy: The Culture of Paranoia in Postwar America*. Ithaca: Cornell University Press, 2000.

Melton, Keith. *CIA Special Weapons and Equipment: Spy Devices of the Cold War*. New York: Sterling, 1994.

Miller, Nathan. *Spying for America: The Hidden History of U.S. Intelligence*. New York: Paragon, 1989.

Monje, Scott C. *The Central Intelligence Agency: A Documentary History*. Westport, CT: Greenwood, 2008.

Moran, Christopher. *Company Confessions: Secrets, Memoirs, and the CIA*. New York: St. Martin's Press, 2015.

Moreno, Jonathan D. *Undue Risk: Secret State Experiments on Humans*. New York: W. H. Freeman, 1999.

Mosley, Leonard. *Dulles*. New York: Dial Press, 1978.

Mulholland, John. *John Mulholland's Book of Magic*. New York: Charles Scribner's Sons, 1963.

Muller-Hill, Benno. *Murderous Science: Elimination by Scientific Selection of Jews, Gypsies and Others, Germany 1933–1945*. Oxford: Oxford University Press, 1988.

Nagib, Judith. *MK-ULTRA: A Tale of One Family, the CIA and the War on Drugs*. Bloomington, IN: XLibris, 2000.

Nisson, Lee. "Acknowledging Plunder: The Consequences of How the United States Acquired Japanese and German Technological Secrets after WWII." Senior thesis, Brandeis University, 2014.

Otterman, Michael. *American Torture: From the Cold War to Abu Ghraib and Beyond.* London: Pluto, 2007.

Pash, Boris T. *The Alsos Mission.* New York: Charter, 1969.

Pocock, Chris. *Dragon Lady: The History of the U2 Spyplane.* Shrewsbury, UK: Airlife, 1989.

Polmar, Norman. *Spyplane: The U-2 History Declassified.* Minneapolis: Zenith, 2001.

Potash, John L. *Drugs as Weapons Against Us: The CIA's Murderous Targeting of SDS, Panthers, Hendrix, Lennon, Cobain, Tupac, and Other Leftists.* Waterville, OR: Trine Day, 2015.

Powers, Francis Gary, and Curt Gentry. *Operation Overflight: A Memoir of the U-2 Incident.* Lincoln, NE: Potomac, 2003.

Powers, Thomas. *The Man Who Kept the Secrets: Richard Helms and the CIA.* New York: Pocket Books, 1979.

Prados, John. *Lost Crusader: The Secret Wars of CIA Director William Colby.* New York: Oxford University Press, 2003.

Preston, Richard. *The Hot Zone.* New York: Random House, 2004.

Proctor, Robert N. *The Nazi War on Cancer.* Princeton: Princeton University Press, 1999.

Ranelagh, John. *The Agency: The Rise and Decline of the CIA.* New York: Simon and Schuster, 1986.

———. *CIA: A History.* London: BBS, 1992.

Redfern, Nick. *Secret History: Conspiracies from Ancient Aliens to the New World Order.* Canton Township, MI: Visible Ink, 2005.

Regis, Ed. *The Biology of Doom: The History of America's Secret Germ Warfare Project.* New York: Henry Holt / Owl Books, 1999.

Richelson, Jeffrey T. *The Wizards of Langley: Inside the CIA's Directorate of Science and Technology.* Boulder, CO: Westview, 2001.

Robinson, Ben. *The Magician: John Mulholland's Secret Life.* Library.com, 2008.

Ronson, John. *The Men Who Stare at Goats.* London: Picador, 2004.

Ross, Colin. *The CIA Doctors: Human Rights Violations by American Psychiatrists.* Richardson, TX: Manitou, 2006.

———. *Bluebird: Deliberate Creation of Multiple Personality by Psychiatrists.* Richardson, TX: Manitou, 2000.

Rotter, Julian B. *Psychology.* Glenview, IL: Scott, Foresman, 1975.

Rush, John, ed. *Entheogens and the Development of Culture: The Anthropology and Neurobiology of Ecstatic Experience.* Berkeley: North Atlantic, 2013.

Sargant, William. *Battle for the Mind.* London: Heinemann, 1957.

———. *The Unquiet Mind: The Autobiography of a Physician in Psychological Medicine.* London: Heinemann, 1967.

Schaub, Thomas. *American Fiction in the Cold War.* Madison: University of Wisconsin Press, 1991.

Schnabel, Jim. *Remote Viewers: The Secret History of America's Psychic Spies*. New York: Dell, 1997.

Schwartz, Richard A. *The 1950s: An Eyewitness History*. New York: Facts on File, 2003.

Scott, Katherine A., ed. *Church Committee Members and Staff, 1975–1976, Oral History Interviews*. Washington, DC: U.S. Senate Historical Office, 2016.

Seed, David. *The Fictions of Mind Control: A Study of Novels and Films since World War II*. Kent, OH: Kent State University Press, 2004.

Simpson, Christopher. *Blowback: The First Full Account of America's Recruitment of Nazis and Its Disastrous Effects on Our Domestic and Foreign Policy*. New York: Weidenfeld and Nicolson, 1998.

Smith, Joseph B. *Portrait of a Cold Warrior: Second Thoughts of a Top CIA Agent*. New York: G. P. Putnam's Sons, 1976.

Snider, L. Britt. *The Agency and the Hill: CIA's Relationship with Congress, 1946–2004*. Washington, DC: Center for the Study of Intelligence, 2008.

Solomon, Philip, ed. *Sensory Deprivation: A Symposium at Harvard Medical School*. Cambridge, MA: Harvard University Press, 1961.

Spang, Christian W., and Rolf-Harald Wippich, eds. *Japanese-German Relations, 1895–1945: War, Diplomacy and Public Opinion*. New York: Routledge, 2008.

Spitz, Vivien. *Doctors from Hell: The Horrific Account of Nazi Human Experiments*. Boulder, CO: Sentient, 2005.

Starrs, James, and Katherine Ramsland. *A Voice for the Dead: A Forensic Investigator's Pursuit for Truth in the Grave*. New York: Putnam, 2005.

Stevens, Jay. *Storming Heaven: LSD and the American Dream*. New York: Harper and Row, 1987.

Streatfeild, Dominic. *Brainwash: The Secret History of Mind Control*. New York: Thomas Dunne Books, 2007.

Takafuji, Ernest T. *Biological Weapons and Modern Warfare*. Washington, DC: National Defense University Press, 1991.

Talbot, David. *The Devil's Chessboard: Allen Dulles, the CIA, and the Rise of America's Secret Government*. New York: HarperCollins, 2015.

Taylor, Kathleen. *Brainwashing: The Science of Thought Control*. Oxford: Oxford University Press, 2004.

Thomas, Evan. *The Very Best Men: The Daring Early Years of the CIA*. New York: Simon and Schuster, 2006.

Thomas, Gordon. *Journey into Madness: Medical Torture and the Mind Controllers*. New York: Bantam, 1988.

———. *Secrets and Lies: A History of CIA Mind Control and Germ Warfare*. Old Saybrook, CT: Konecky and Konecky, 2007.

Trento, Joseph J. *The Secret History of the CIA*. New York: MJF, 2001.

Tsuneishi, Keeichi. *The Germ Warfare Unit That Disappeared: The Kwangtung Army's 731st Unit*. Tokyo: Kai-mei-sha, 1982.

Tucker, Jonathan B. *War of Nerves: Chemical Warfare from World War I to al-Qaeda*. New York: Pantheon, 2006.

United Nations War Crimes Commission. *Law Reports of Trials of War Criminals,* vol 10: *The I. G. Farben and Krupp Trials.* London: His Majesty's Stationery Office, 1949.

United States House of Representatives. *Inquiry into the Alleged Involvement of the Central Intelligence Agency in the Watergate and Ellsberg Matters.* Washington, DC: Government Printing Office, 1974.

United States Senate. *Alleged Assassination Plots Involving Foreign Leaders.* Washington, DC: Government Printing Office, 1975.

———. *Biological Testing Involving Human Subjects by the Department of Defense.* Washington, DC: Government Printing Office, 1977.

———. *Biomedical and Behavioral Research.* Washington, DC: Government Printing Office, 1975.

———. *Project MK-ULTRA, the CIA's Program of Research on Behavioral Modification.* Washington, DC: Government Printing Office, 1977.

———. *Unauthorized Storage of Toxic Agents.* Washington, DC: Government Printing Office, 1975.

Volodarsky, Boris. *The KGB's Poison Factory: From Lenin to Litvinenko.* Minneapolis: Zenith, 2009.

Walker, J. Samuel. *Permissible Dose: A History of Radiation Protection in the Twentieth Century.* Berkeley: University of California Press, 2000.

Wallace, David Foster. *Infinite Jest.* New York: Back Bay, 2006.

Wallace, Robert, and Keith Melton, eds. *The Official CIA Manual of Trickery and Deception.* New York: William Morrow, 2010.

Wallace, Robert, and Keith Melton, with Henry Robert Schlesinger. *Spy Sites of Washington, DC: A Guide to the Capital Region's Secret History.* Washington, DC: Georgetown University Press, 2017.

———. *Spycraft: The Secret History of the CIA's Spytechs from Communism to Al-Qaeda.* New York: Dutton, 2008.

Walsh, Ryan H. *Astral Weeks: A Secret History of 1968.* New York: Penguin, 2018.

Wansell, Geoffrey. *Haunted Idol: The Story of the Real Cary Grant.* New York: William Morrow, 1984.

Wasson, Gordon, and Valentina Wasson. *Mushrooms, Russia and History.* New York: Pantheon, 1957.

Weber, Ralph E., ed. *Spymasters: Ten CIA Officers in Their Own Words.* Wilmington, DE: Scholarly Resources, 1999.

Weiner, Tim. *Legacy of Ashes: The History of the CIA.* New York: Anchor, 2008.

Weinstein, Harvey. *Father, Son and CIA: The Riveting Account of the Destruction of One Man's Life by Secret Mind Control Experiments Funded by the CIA.* Halifax: Goodread, 1990.

Welsome, Eileen. *The Plutonium Files: America's Secret Medical Experiments in the Cold War.* New York: Dial, 1999.

Wetmore, Karen. *Surviving Evil: CIA Mind Control Experiments in Vermont.* Richardson, TX: Manitou, 2014.

Whitmer, Peter. *Aquarius Revisited: Seven Who Created the Sixties Counterculture That Changed America.* New York: Citadel, 1987.

Whitney, Craig R. *Spy Trade: The Darkest Secrets of the Cold War*. New York: Times, 1994.

Williams, Peter, and David Wallace. *Unit 731: The Shattering Exposé of the Japanese Army's Secret of Secrets*. London: Grafton, 1989.

Wolfe, Tom. *The Electric Kool-Aid Acid Test*. New York: Farrar, Straus and Giroux, 1968.

Woods, Randall B. *Shadow Warrior: William Egan Colby and the CIA*. New York: Basic Books, 2013.

Worger, William H., et al. *Africa and the West: A Documentary History*, vol. 2, *From Colonialism to Independence, 1875 to the Present*. New York: Oxford University Press, 2010.

Documentary Films

"American Experience—The Living Weapon—PBS Documentary." Dailymotion video, 52:44. Posted by Shortfilms, 2016. https://www.dailymotion.com/video/x35q3xt.

Channel 4—Jon Ronson—*Crazy Rulers of the World: Episode 3, The Psychic Footsoldiers* (2004). YouTube video, 59:01. Posted by TheDocumentaryChannel103, May 6, 2014. https://www.youtube.com/watch?v=EQKTMjApnkI&t=1029s.

"CIA Documentary—Biological Weapons and Experimentation on Humans (Frank Olson)." YouTube video, 50:29. Posted by Proper Gander, September 18, 2016. https://www.youtube.com/watch?v=XHEis6616AM&t=5s.

"CIA Drug Conspiracy." Science Channel video, 42:00. April 8, 2018. https://www.sciencechannel.com/tv-shows/deadly-intelligence/full-episodes/cia-drug-conspiracy.

"Counterpoint: The U-2 Story." Villon video, 54:58. Posted by Peter Davis, November 12, 2012. http://www.villonfilms.ca/counterpoint-the-u-2-story/.

"Deckname Artischocke—Geheime Menschenversuche." YouTube video, 44:47. Posted by Taurus322, June 15, 2011. https://www.youtube.com/watch?v=O7xD7_IJIrk&t=145s.

"Folterexperten—Die geheimen Methoden der CIA—Doku." Dailymotion video, 43:52. Posted by Dokuhouse, 2013. https://www.dailymotion.com/video/xvzl7j.

"John Foster Dulles Interview: U.S. Secretary of State under Dwight D. Eisenhower (1952)." YouTube video, 12:16, posted by the Film Archives, May 23, 2012. https://www.youtube.com/watch?v=7EJZdikc6OA.

"Maria Sabina Documental." YouTube video, 1:20:47. Posted by Soy Eus, July 16, 2016. https://www.youtube.com/watch?v=30s3ZCF7E3A.

"Mind Control Murder." YouTube video, 45:12. Posted by Capitan Black, March 18, 2016. https://www.youtube.com/watch?v=e2ot9noqQUw.

"MK ULTRA (History Channel Documentary)." YouTube video, 41:20. Posted by Truth Talk News Channel 2, June 22, 2017. https://www.youtube.com/watch?v=64Z1hcn5UZE.

Morris, Errol, director. *Wormwood* (film). Netflix, 2017. https://www.netflix.com/title/80059446.

"Munich City 1945 in Colour—Old City," YouTube video, 3:22, posted by Timeline, February 24, 2014. https://www.youtube.com/watch?v=idiJegt7tFw.

"National Geographic—CIA Secret Experiments Documentary." YouTube video, 50:12. Posted by Somebody Smoking, December 26, 2016. https://www.youtube.com/watch?v=7Afjf2ZgGZE.

"Operation Harness, 1948–1949 [Allocated Title]." Video. Posted by the Imperial War Museum, catalog no. DED 85. https://www.iwm.org.uk/collections/item/object/1060017887.

"Tusko: The Elephant Who Died on LSD." YouTube video, 8:23. Posted by Audible484, October 25, 2017. https://www.youtube.com/watch?v=hy1fD-0ZwtU.

Acknowledgments

Everything in this book is true, but not everything that's true is in this book. The stories recounted on these pages tell only part—probably a small part—of what Sidney Gottlieb did during his twenty-two years at the CIA. Most of the rest is likely to remain unknown. Gottlieb did not manage to wipe his legacy off the face of history, as he hoped when he ordered the destruction of MK-ULTRA files. He did, however, succeed in preventing the world from learning the full story of his life and career.

Soon after Gottlieb died, the *Washington Post* looked back on his legacy and concluded, "The name Sidney Gottlieb is but an obscure footnote in the nation's history." Years later, I met a former director of the CIA and told him that I was writing Gottlieb's biography. He shook his head and said, "Never heard of him." Others who served at the CIA in the decades after Gottlieb retired told me the same thing. I believe them. Piecing together Gottlieb's story required deep dives into obscure history. I am grateful to the many who helped guide me.

Several authors have researched aspects of Gottlieb's life and career. The first was John Marks, who filed the Freedom of Information Act request that led to discovery of MK-ULTRA documents that Gottlieb had failed to destroy. Those documents shaped Marks's groundbreaking book *The Search for the "Manchurian Candidate,"* which won the 1979

Investigative Reporters and Editors prize for exemplifying "the best in investigative reporting." Other books followed, each peeling away layers of Gottlieb's mystery. *A Terrible Mistake*, by H. P. Albarelli, is a rich source. So are the works of Linda Hunt, Alfred McCoy, Egmont R. Koch and Michael Wech, Ed Regis, and Colin Ross.

I am also grateful to the people who agreed to sit for interviews to recall their connections with Gottlieb or his work. Manfred Kopp, the local historian in the German town of Oberursel, where Camp King was located, generously shared his insights and archive. The owner of nearby Villa Schuster, where CIA officers conducted harsh experiments during the 1950s, opened the house to me and allowed me to visit basement rooms that were once used as cells. Lanessa Hill, the public affairs supervisor at Fort Detrick in Maryland, arranged a tour of the base and conversations with scientists who work there. The retired Fort Detrick historian Norman Covert provided valuable background about the base's past activities. Sidney Bender, the New York lawyer who took Gottlieb's depositions in two long-running court cases, shared boxes of files that had lain untouched for years. Archivists at the Presbyterian Historical Society in Philadelphia helped me locate letters and essays written by Gottlieb's wife, Margaret. Eric Olson, son of the CIA chemist Frank Olson, spent hours responding to questions about his lifelong search for the truth behind his father's death. Lawyers and investigators who worked for congressional committees that questioned Gottlieb in the 1970s provided valuable insights. Several CIA officers who crossed paths with Gottlieb, all of whom asked to remain anonymous, shared their memories. The CIA public affairs office confirmed important details about Gottlieb's career. Although the office declined to provide some information I sought, it did release three photographs showing Gottlieb as he looked while at the Agency—the first such images that have ever been published.

Several other well-informed Americans shared their insights but do not want to be publicly acknowledged. They know who they are. I thank them.

As I was conceiving this book, several of my highly motivated students at Brown University wrote research memos that helped shape my work. Sarah Tucker discovered records that document Gottlieb's early life. June Gersh traced Operation Paperclip, under which Nazi scientists were brought to work for American government agencies. Hansol Hong dug into the history of Fort Detrick. Weng Lin Isaac Leong researched the origins of MK-ULTRA and investigated Gottlieb's role in making the suicide pin given to U-2 pilots. Drashti Brahmbatt traced MK-ULTRA subprojects and Gottlieb's work overseeing them. Oliver Hermann produced a survey of "black sites" where CIA officers conducted harsh interrogations during the 1950s. Fiona Bradley surveyed the literature of mind control. Benjamin Guggenheim compiled valuable information from primary sources. Daniel Steinfeld traced Gottlieb's involvement in assassination plots and his work as head of the CIA's Technical Services Staff. Isabel Paolini reviewed and analyzed published material, including Gottlieb's testimony before congressional committees. Sean Hyland assessed Gottlieb's role in bringing LSD to the American counterculture. Brandon Wen Long Chia examined cases of prominent Americans who came to LSD through Gottlieb's experiments and discovered material about Gottlieb's work after he left the CIA. Vladimir Borodin researched aspects of Gottlieb's life in retirement. Michelle Schein traced the path from Gottlieb's work to techniques of interrogation that the CIA brought to Latin America, Vietnam, Abu Ghraib, and Guantanamo. A student at Emory University, Ethan Jampel, helped assemble images for the photo section.

I greatly appreciate my colleagues at the Watson Institute for International and Public Affairs at Brown University. The director, Edward Steinfeld, and associate director Steven Bloomfield encouraged me to pursue unorthodox research. At Brown's international relations program, the director, Nina Tannenwald, associate director Claudia Elliott, and academic programs manager Anita Nester unfailingly supported my academic ambitions.

Astute readers reviewed this book's final manuscript and measurably improved it. James Stone identified a section that was too long and detailed. Michael Rezendes suggested a better way of organizing the book. Jonathan Sperber pointed out a flaw in one key section. My editor, Paul Golob, added clarity and elegance.

The name of the project Gottlieb directed is variously spelled with and without a hyphen. I have standardized it as MK-ULTRA to avoid confusion.

Discovering Sidney Gottlieb as I wrote this book was a fascinating but troubling experience. All who helped me have my gratitude. The conclusions and assessments on these pages, along with any errors of fact or judgment, are my own.

Index

ABOUT THE AUTHOR

STEPHEN KINZER is the author of nine books, including *The True Flag,*
The Brothers, Overthrow, and *All the Shah's Men.* An award-winning
foreign correspondent, he served as the *New York Times* bureau chief
in Nicaragua, Germany, and Turkey. He is a senior fellow at the Watson
Institute for International and Public Affairs at Brown University and
writes a world affairs column for *The Boston Globe.* He lives in Boston.